Chicago

"All you've got to do is decide to go
and the hardest part is over.

So go!"

TONY WHEELER, COFOUNDER – LONELY PLANET

Contents

Plan Your Trip 4

Explore Chicago 40

Understand Chicago 243

Survival Guide 271

Chicago Maps 296

(left) **City skyline** View of Chicago from Lincoln Park Zoo (p99).

(above) **Pritzker Pavilion p47** Designed by architect Frank Gehry.

(right) **Deep-dish pizza p262** A Chicago specialty.

Lincoln Square & Ravenswood p136

Andersonville & Uptown p124

Lake View & Wrigleyville p109

Logan Square & Humboldt Park p163

Wicker Park, Bucktown & Ukrainian Village p146

Lincoln Park & Old Town p95

Gold Coast p81

Near North & Navy Pier p67

West Loop & Near West Side p174

The Loop p44

Pilsen & Near South Side p189

Hyde Park & South Side p202

Welcome to Chicago

Steely skyscrapers, top chefs, rocking festivals — the Windy City will blow you away with its low-key cultured awesomeness.

Art & Architecture

It's hard to know what to gawk at first. High-flying architecture is everywhere, from the stratospheric, glass-floored Willis Tower to Frank Gehry's swooping silver Pritzker Pavilion to Frank Lloyd Wright's stained-glass Robie House. Whimsical public art studs the streets; you might be walking along and wham, there's an abstract Picasso statue that's not only cool to look at, but you're allowed to go right up and climb on it. For art museums, take your pick: impressionist masterpieces at the massive Art Institute, psychedelic paintings at the mid-sized Museum of Mexican Art or outsider drawings at the small Intuit gallery.

Chowhounds' Delight

Loosen your belt – you've got a lot of eating to do. On the menu: peanut-butter-and-banana-topped waffles for breakfast (at Stephanie Izard's Little Goat), pork-shoulder posole and garlicky yucca enchiladas for lunch (at Dove's Luncheonette) and fine dining on foraged foods for dinner (at Iliana Regan's Elizabeth). You can also chow down on a superb range of global eats from Vietnamese pho to Mexican carnitas, Polish pierogi and Macanese fat rice. Still hungry? Order a late-night deep-dish pizza or seek out a hot and spicy Italian beef sandwich at a local fast-food joint.

Sports Fanatics

Chicago is a maniacal sports town, with a pro team for every season (two teams, in baseball's case). Watching a game is a local rite of passage, whether you slather on the blue-and-orange body paint for a Bears football game, join the raucous baseball crowd in Wrigley Field's bleachers, or plop down on a bar stool at the neighborhood tavern for whatever match is on TV. Count on making lots of spirited new friends. Should the excitement rub off and inspire you to get active yourself, the city's 26 beaches and 580 parks offer a huge array of play options.

Rollicking Festivals

Chicago knows how to rock a festival. Between March and September it throws around 200 shindigs. The specialty is music. Blues Fest brings half a million people to Millennium Park to hear guitar notes slide and bass lines roll, all for free. During the four-day Lollapalooza megaparty, rock bands thrash while the audience dances in an arm-flailing frenzy. Smaller, barbecue-scented street fests take place in the neighborhoods each weekend – though some rival downtown for star power on their stages (oh, hey, Olivia Newton-John at Northalsted Market Days).

Why I Love Chicago

By Karla Zimmerman, Writer

I've lived in Chicago for almost 30 years, and the skyline still kills me. Every time I take the train toward downtown it's like the buildings suddenly pop up and expand storybook-style. I never get bored here; there's something groovy happening nightly. Like tonight: should I listen to an Afrobeat ensemble playing at SummerDance, see free improv at the neighborhood dive bar, or watch a musical about the bubonic plague at a storefront theater? Mostly I love how total strangers watching a Cubs or Hawks game in a bar become high-fiving pals by evening's end.

For more about our writers, see p336

Chicago's
Top 10

Art Institute of Chicago *(p49)*

1 The second-largest art museum in the country, the Art Institute houses a treasure trove from around the globe. The collection of impressionist and post-impressionist paintings is second only to those in France, and the number of surrealist works is tremendous. Wander the endless marble and glass corridors, and rooms stuffed with Japanese prints, Grecian urns, suits of armor, Grant Wood's *American Gothic*, Edward Hopper's *Nighthawks* and one very big, dotted Seurat. The Modern Wing dazzles with Picassos and Mirós.

Below Left: The Deering Family Galleries of Medieval & Renaissance Art, Arms & Armor

👁 *The Loop*

Global Eats *(p26)*

2 In recent years chefs such as Grant Achatz, Rick Bayless and Stephanie Izard put Chicago on the culinary map winning a heap of James Beard awards. Suddenly international critics were dubbing Chicago one of the globe's top eating destinations. The beauty is that even the buzziest restaurants are accessible: visionary yet traditional, pubby at the core and decently priced. Chow down on a range of global eats in Chicago's neighborhoods, from Puerto Rican *jibaritos* (steak covered in garlicky mayo and served between thick, crispy-fried plantain slices) to Indian samosas to Polish pierogi (pictured below right).

🍴 *Eating*

Millennium Park *(p46)*

3 The playful heart of the city, Millennium Park shines with whimsical public art. Go ahead, walk under Anish Kapoor's *Cloud Gate* – aka 'the Bean' – and touch its silvery smoothness. Let the human gargoyles of Jaume Plensa's *Crown Fountain* gush water on you to cool down in summer. Unfurl a blanket by Frank Gehry's swooping silver band shell (pictured top left) as the sun dips, wine corks pop and gorgeous music fills the twilight air. Or try to find the secret garden abloom with prairie flowers and a wee, gurgling river.

◉ *The Loop*

Architecture Cruises *(p66)*

4 Who cares if all the backward neck-bending causes a little ache? There's no better way to feel Chicago's steely power than from low on the water looking up while cloud-poking towers glide by and iron bridges arch open to lead the way. The skyline takes on a surreal majesty as you float through its shadows on a river tour, and landmark after eye-popping landmark flash by. Guides' architecture lessons carry on the breeze, so you'll know your beaux art from International style by day's end.

🚶 *The Loop*

Blues & Rock *(p31)*

5 In Chicago no genre is as iconic as the blues – the electric blues, to be exact. When Muddy Waters and friends plugged in their amps c 1950, guitar grooves reached new decibel levels. Hear it in clubs around town, such as Buddy Guy's Legends (p62), where the icon himself still takes the stage, or Rosa's Lounge (p173), where it's a bit more down and dirty. The blues paved the way for rock and roll, so no surprise cool little clubs hosting edgy indie bands slouch on many a street corner.

Above: James 'Blood' Ulmer

☆ *Entertainment*

Public Art *(p269)*

6 You can't walk two blocks downtown without bumping into an extraordinary sculpture. The granddaddy is Picasso's untitled sculpture (what the heck is it – an Afghan hound?), set smack in Daley Plaza. Jean Dubuffet's abstract creation is officially titled *Monument with Standing Beast* (pictured below; p55) but everyone calls it 'Snoopy in a Blender.' Marc Chagall's grand mosaic *Four Seasons* is more recognizable, depicting Chicago scenes. And Alexander Calder's hulking, red-pink *Flamingo* could indeed pass for its namesake, but only after you've had a few beers.

⊙ *Music & the Arts*

Sky-High Views *(p83)*

7 For superlative seekers, Willis Tower (p51) is it: the city's tallest building (and one of the world's loftiest). Breathe deeply during the ear-popping, 70-second elevator ride to the 103rd-floor Skydeck, then stride to one of the glass-enclosed ledges that jut out in midair. Look down some 1400ft. Crikey. The lakeside 875 N Michigan Ave building (formerly known as the Hancock Center; p83) also rises high in the sky. Ascend to the 96th-floor Signature Lounge, order a cocktail and watch the city sparkle around you (pictured top right). It's especially lovely at night.

⊙ *Gold Coast*

7

8

Comedy & Theater *(p269)*

8 A group of jokesters began performing intentionally unstructured skits in a Chicago bar a half century ago, and voilà – improv comedy was born. Second City (p107) still nurtures the best in the biz, though several other improv theaters also work from booze-fueled suggestions that the audience hollers up. Among the city's 200 theaters are powerhouse drama troupes such as Hollywood-star-laden Steppenwolf (p107) and Goodman Theatre (pictured left; p64), and heaps of fringey, provocative 'off-Loop' companies, such as the Neo-Futurist Theater (p134), which bases its admission cost on a dice roll.

☆ *Music & the Arts*

Wrigley Field *(p111)*

9 A tangible sense of history comes alive at this 100-plus-year-old baseball park, thanks to the hand-turned scoreboard (pictured right), iconic neon entrance sign, legendary curses and time-honored traditions that infuse games played here. Shoveling down hot dogs and drinking beer in the raucous bleachers makes for an unforgettable afternoon. The area around the stadium is like a big street festival on game days: young people party in alfresco bars, kids lick ice-cream cones, and die-hard fans occupy stools in age-old, sticky-floored taverns.

Lake View & Wrigleyville

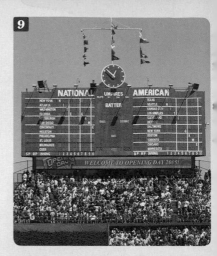

Navy Pier *(p69)*

10 Stretching away from the skyline and into the blue of Lake Michigan, half-mile-long Navy Pier is one of Chicago's most visited attractions. Its charms revolve around the cool breezes and sweet views, especially from the stomach-turning, 196ft Ferris wheel. High-tech rides, splash fountains, big boats and greasy snacks blow the minds of young ones. Live music, Shakespearean theater and whopping fireworks displays entertain everyone else. A smart renovation has added public plazas, performance spaces, art installations and free cultural programming.

Near North & Navy Pier

What's New

Chicago Architecture Center
The center has moved to new riverside digs and beefed up its galleries, which now include a dandy interactive 3-D model of Chicago's skyline, plus exhibits on skyscrapers around the world. (p52)

Wrigley Field
The area immediately around the ballpark has erupted with new cocktail bars, beer bars, foodie eateries and baseball-themed hotels, as well as a public plaza for free concerts, movies and kids' activities. (p111)

Art on theMart
Several nights a week, theMart, one of the world's largest buildings, becomes a trippy canvas for video art cast on its exterior. The two-hour light show is done with projectors set up along the Riverwalk. (p70)

Wrightwood 659
Pritzker Prize–winner Tadao Ando designed this soaring gallery dedicated to rotating exhibits of modern architecture and 'socially engaged' art. It hides in a former 1920s apartment building in Lincoln Park. (p98)

Lakefront Trail
The popular 18-mile path has received a multi-million-dollar upgrade that widened and split it into separate lanes for cyclists and runners, a game changer for relieving congestion and improving safety. (p35)

Arts Block
Artist-activist Theaster Gates and the University of Chicago have worked together to transform a stretch of E Garfield Blvd by launching the Arts Incubator (p208), Green Line Performing Arts Center (p215), Peach's cafe (p214) and more.

Chicago Magic Lounge
The city's only custom-built magic performance theater has opened in Andersonville, offering incredible sleights of hand in two theater spaces with a 1930s-style bar. Kids can get in on the action, too. (p134)

Malt Row
An industrial corridor of bygone factories in Ravenswood has turned into Malt Row, home to several modern breweries lined up in a 2-mile, walkable route. (p142)

Navy Pier
Renovations on the pier have been going on for a while, but the new stuff keeps coming: more free programming (yoga classes, concerts, films), more public spaces for hanging out and a refreshed children's museum. (p69)

Cycle Savvy
Chicago's Divvy bike-share program isn't new, but it's added handy new pass options that make it much more user friendly, including a $15 day pass that lets you keep a bike for up to three-hour increments. (p273)

For more recommendations and reviews, see **lonelyplanet. com/Chicago**

Need to Know

For more information, see Survival Guide (p271)

Currency
US dollar ($)

Language
English

Visas
Generally not required for stays of up to 90 days; check www.travel.state.gov for details.

Money
ATMs widely available. Credit cards accepted at most hotels, restaurants and shops.

Cell Phones
International travelers can use local SIM cards in a smartphone provided it is unlocked. Alternatively, you can buy a cheap US phone and load it up with prepaid minutes.

Time
Central Standard Time (GMT/UTC minus six hours)

Tourist Information
Choose Chicago (www.choosechicago.com) is the city's official tourism site, with loads of information online.

Daily Costs

Budget: Less than $125
➡ Dorm bed: $35–55
➡ Lunch specials: $10–15
➡ Transit day pass: $10
➡ Discount theater or blues club ticket: $10–25

Midrange: $125–325
➡ Hotel or B&B double room: $175–275
➡ Dinner in a casual restaurant: $25–35
➡ Architecture boat tour: $47
➡ Cubs bleacher seat: $45–65

Top end: More than $325
➡ Luxury hotel double room: $400
➡ Dinner at Alinea: $290
➡ Lyric Opera ticket: $200

Advance Planning
Two months before Book your hotel. Reserve at hot restaurants such as Alinea, Girl & the Goat, Smyth and Giant.

Two weeks before Reserve a table at your other must-eat restaurants, and book tickets for sports events and blockbuster museum exhibits.

One week before Check www.hottix.org for half-price theater tickets. Check www.chicagoreader.com to see entertainment options and make bookings.

Useful Websites
Lonely Planet (www.lonelyplanet.com/chicago) Destination information, hotel bookings, traveler forum and more.

Choose Chicago (www.choosechicago.com) Official tourism site with sightseeing and event info.

Chicago Reader (www.chicagoreader.com) Great listings for music, arts, restaurants and film, plus news and politics.

WHEN TO GO

Peak season is June to August when it's warm. Between November and March it's freezing; May, September and October bring back decent weather.

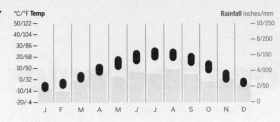

Arriving in Chicago

O'Hare International Airport
The Blue Line L train ($5) runs 24/7 and departs every 10 minutes or so. The journey to the city center takes 40 minutes. Shuttle vans cost $35, taxis around $50.

Midway International Airport
The Orange Line L train ($3) runs between 4am and 1am, departing every 10 minutes or so. The journey takes 30 minutes to downtown. Shuttle vans cost $28, taxis $35 to $40.

Union Station All trains arrive here. For transportation onward, the Blue Line Clinton stop is a few blocks south (thought it's not a great option at night). The Brown, Orange, Purple and Pink Line station at Quincy is about a half mile east. Taxis queue along Canal St outside the station entrance.

For much more on **arrival** see p272

Getting Around

The L (a system of elevated and subway trains) is the main way to get around. Buses are also useful. Buy a day pass for $10 at L stations. The Chicago Transit Authority (www.transit chicago.com) runs the transport system.

Bicycle Abundant rental shops and the Divvy bike-share program make cycling doable.

Boat Water taxis travel along the river and lakefront and offer a fun way to reach the Museum Campus or Chinatown.

Bus Buses cover areas that the L misses. Most run at least from early morning until 10pm; some go later. Some don't run on weekends.

Taxi Easy to find downtown, north to Andersonville and west to Wicker Park/Bucktown. Costly.

Train L trains are fast, frequent and ubiquitous. Red and Blue Lines operate 24/7, others between roughly 4am and 1am.

For much more on **getting around** see p273

Sleeping

Accommodations will likely be your biggest expense in Chicago. The best digs are groovy, wired-up boutique hotels, especially those set in architectural landmarks. Several independent hostels have popped up in fun, outlying neighborhoods such as Wicker Park and Wrigleyville. Enormous business hotels cater to conventioneers in the Loop and Near North. Low-key B&Bs are scattered in Wicker Park and Lake View and are often cheaper than hotels.

Useful Websites

Lonely Planet (www.lonely planet.com/hotels) Recommendations and bookings.

Chicago Bed & Breakfast Association (www.chicago-bed-breakfast.com) Represents around 11 properties.

Hotel Tonight (www.hotel tonight.com) National discounter with last-minute deals; book via the free app.

Choose Chicago (www.choose chicago.com) Options from the city's official website.

For much more on **sleeping** see p226

Top Itineraries

Day One

The Loop (p44)

 You might as well dive right into the main sights. Take a boat or walking tour with the **Chicago Architecture Center** and ogle the most skyscraping collection of buildings the US has to offer. Saunter over to **Millennium Park** to see 'the Bean' reflect the skyline and to splash under Crown Fountain's human gargoyles.

> ✖ **Lunch** The Gage (p60) dishes out pub grub with a fanciful twist.

The Loop (p44)

 Explore the **Art Institute of Chicago**, the nation's second-largest art museum. It holds masterpieces aplenty, especially impressionist and postimpressionist paintings (and paperweights). Next, head over to **Willis Tower**, zip up to the 103rd floor and step out onto the glass-floored ledge. Yes, it is a long way down.

> ✖ **Dinner** Taxi or L train to the West Loop for Little Goat (p181).

West Loop & Near West Side (p174)

☾ The West Loop parties in the evening. Sit on the glittery patio sipping a glass of bubbly at **RM Champagne Salon**. **Haymarket Pub & Brewery** pours great beers. Or down a cocktail made with the house vodka at **CH Distillery**.

Day Two

Near North & Navy Pier (p67)

 Take a stroll on Michigan Ave – aka the **Magnificent Mile** – where big-name department stores ka-ching in a sparkling row. Mosey over to **Navy Pier**. Wander the half-mile promenade and take a spin on the high-in-the-sky Ferris wheel.

> ✖ **Lunch** Heft a mighty slice of pizza at Giordano's (p75).

Pilsen & Near South Side (p189)

☼ Spend the afternoon at the **Museum Campus** (the water taxi from Navy Pier is a fine way to get there). Miles of aisles of dinosaurs and gemstones stuff the **Field Museum**. Sharks and other fish swim in the kiddie-mobbed **Shedd Aquarium**. Meteorites and supernovas are on view at the **Adler Planetarium**.

> ✖ **Dinner** Hop the Blue Line to Damen for Dove's Luncheonette (p151).

Wicker Park, Bucktown & Ukrainian Village (p146)

☾ Wander along Milwaukee Ave and take your pick of booming bars, indie-rock clubs and hipster shops. **Quimby's** shows the local spirit: the bookstore stocks zines and graphic novels, and is a linchpin of Chicago's underground culture. The **Hideout** and **Empty Bottle** are sweet spots to catch a bad-ass band.

Day Three

Lincoln Park & Old Town (p95)

 Dip your toes in Lake Michigan at **North Avenue Beach**. Amble northward through the sprawling greenery of **Lincoln Park**. Stop at **Lincoln Park Zoo** to see lions, zebras and bears (the polar kind). Pop into **Lincoln Park Conservatory** to smell exotic blooms.

> **Lunch** Munch sassy fried chicken or Korean veggies at Crisp (p114).

Lake View & Wrigleyville (p109)

 Make your way north to **Wrigley Field** for an afternoon baseball game. The atmospheric, century-old ballpark hosts the Cubs, and it's full of legendary traditions. Afterward practice your home-run swing at **Sluggers** and your beer drinking at **Murphy's Bleachers**, two of the many rip-roaring bars that circle the stadium.

> **Dinner** Mmmm, mussels and *frites* (fries) at Hopleaf (p131).

Andersonville & Uptown (p124)

Andersonville has several fine taverns to hang out at and sink a pint, like **Simon's**. Or see what's on at the **Neo-Futurist Theater**. Jazz hounds can venture to the **Green Mill**, a timeless venue to hear jazz, watch a poetry slam or swill a martini. Al Capone used to groove at it.

Day Four

Hyde Park & South Side (p202)

 The **Museum of Science & Industry** isn't kidding around with its acres of exhibits. There's a German U-boat, mock tornado and exquisite dollhouse for starters. Groovy university bookstores like **Seminary Co-op** and **Powell's** offer shelves of weighty tomes. Architecture buffs can tour **Robie House**, Frank Lloyd Wright's Prairie-style masterpiece.

> **Lunch** Eat like Barack Obama at Valois Restaurant (p212).

Gold Coast (p81)

See what's going on in the chichi district. There's boutique shopping, of course. The **Museum of Contemporary Art** always has something odd and provocative showing. And you can't leave the 'hood without getting high. For that, ascend to the 94th-floor observatory at **360° Chicago** or the 96th-floor Signature Lounge.

> **Dinner** Sip whiskey while waiting for a table at Longman & Eagle (p169).

Logan Square & Humboldt Park (p163)

 Nightlife options abound in Logan Square. Knock back slurpable beers at **Revolution Brewing**. See what arty band is playing for free at wee **Whistler**. Or imbibe at **Scofflaw**, a true gin joint where juniper is treated with reverence.

If You Like...

Famous Museums

Art Institute of Chicago Gawk at Monets, modern works, paperweights and much more at the nation's second-largest art museum. (p49)

Field Museum of Natural History Explore collections of dinosaurs, gems, mummies and enormous taxidermied lions. (p191)

Museum of Science & Industry Geek out at the largest science museum in the western hemisphere. (p205)

Adler Planetarium Journey to the nether regions of outer space at this lakeside gem, designed by architect Ernest A Grunsfeld Jr. (p193)

Contemporary Art.

Museum of Contemporary Art Consider it the Art Institute's brash, rebellious sibling: a collection that always pushes boundaries. (p84)

Millennium Park Jaume Plensa's video-screen *Crown Fountain* leads the pack of whimsical artworks throughout the park. (p280)

Museum of Contemporary Photography Tidy, engaging and free, it's a great stop in the South Loop. (p54)

Pilsen Public Art Tours Locals lead you through the neighborhood's trove of art-splashed buildings. (p201)

Intuit: The Center for Intuitive & Outsider Art Small museum featuring outsider artists and Henry Darger's re-created apartment. (p148)

Adler Planetarium (p193)

Stony Island Arts Bank African American cultural center and gallery that puts on thought-provoking exhibitions. (p206)

Parks & Gardens

Lincoln Park Chicago's largest green space is where the city comes out to play. (p97)

Lurie Garden Find Millennium Park's secret garden and you'll see a prairie's worth of wildflowers. (p280)

Garfield Park Conservatory Pretty plants under glass, plus Claude Monet's re-created garden. (p179)

Jackson Park Huge lakefront patch with bird-rich lagoons, Japanese gardens and sweet-smelling meadows. (p206)

Northerly Island Prairie-grassed nature park that offers a tranquil escape from the abutting Museum Campus. (p193)

Alfred Caldwell Lily Pool A home for dragonflies and native plants offers a sublime oasis within Lincoln Park. (p98)

Lincoln Park Conservatory The small but potent dose of tropical blooms is especially welcome during winter. (p102)

Skyscrapers

Willis Tower Ascend 103 floors, then peer straight down from a glass-floored ledge in Chicago's tallest building. (p51)

Aqua Tower Jeanne Gang's 86-story beauty has won numerous awards for its dramatic, wavy design. (p52)

360° Chicago Get high at the lakeside tower's 94th-floor observatory or 96th-floor lounge. (p83)

Tribune Tower This neo-Gothic cloud-poker is inlaid with stones from the Taj Mahal, Parthenon and more. (p70)

Marina City The groovy corn-cob towers look like something from a *Jetsons* cartoon. (p70)

Kluczynski Federal Building Ludwig Mies van der Rohe launched the modern skyscraper look with this boxy structure. (p53)

History

Chicago History Museum Tells the city's story with artifacts such as Prohibition-era booze stills. (p98)

DuSable Museum of African American History Smithsonian-affiliated pioneer teaching about African American art, history and culture. (p207)

Graceland Cemetery A who's who of famous Chicagoans, including Ludwig Mies van der Rohe and Marshall Field. (p126)

Haymarket Square Site where the world's labor movement began after a riot. (p178)

Pullman National Monument Learn about labor history and urban planning at a capitalist's fallen utopia. (p208)

Windy City Icons

Billy Goat Tavern Subterranean dive where newspaper reporters have long boozed; also spawned the Cubs' Curse. (p77)

Buddy Guy's Legends Top spot to hear the blues, especially when Mr Guy himself takes the stage. (p64)

Wrigley Field Old-time ballpark that's still going strong with its hand-turned scoreboard and raucous bleacher seats. (p111)

Pizzeria Uno Deep-dish pizza was invented here, although the claim to fame is hotly debated. (p76)

Second City Launched the improv comedy genre and the

For more top Chicago spots, see the following:

➡ Eating (p26)

➡ Drinking & Nightlife (p29)

➡ Entertainment (p31)

➡ Shopping (p33)

➡ Sports & Activities (p35)

careers of Bill Murray, Tina Fey and many more. (p107)

Multicultural Neighborhoods

Pilsen Chicago's Mexican community clusters here, primed for tamales, salsas, *paletas* (popsicles) and fresh tortillas. (p196)

Chinatown Small but bustling, with charms that include nibbling chestnut cakes, sipping tea and slurping noodles. (p196)

Argyle Street The heart of 'Little Saigon,' good for bubble tea, pho and exotic Asian wares. (p126)

Paseo Boricua The 'Puerto Rican Promenade' is a colorful, half-mile stretch of Division St in Humboldt Park. (p168)

Devon Avenue A mash-up of Indian and Pakistani businesses, with Russian and Orthodox Jewish shops mixed in. (p130)

Greektown Greek culture is still going strong in baklava-wafting bakeries and wine-pouring tavernas on Halsted St. (p179)

Ukrainian Village Slavic culture thrives in churches, museums and bars. Down a frosty *piwo* (beer) with locals. (p43)

Free Stuff

Millennium Park Chicago's showpiece features a trove of free and arty sights. (p280)

Chicago Cultural Center Gorgeous building where you'll find gratis art exhibitions, lunchtime concerts and downtown tours on offer. (p278)

National Museum of Mexican Art One of the city's best, filled with paintings, altars, folk art and politically charged pieces. (p192)

SummerDance Rollicking mash-up of world beats and dance lessons in the park. (p64)

Whistler Great live-music venue that never charges a cover – so buy a drink or three! (p173)

Chicago Greeter Local volunteers take visitors on personalized walking tours around town, by neighborhood or theme. (p276)

Lagunitas Brewing Company Cheery tour of the city's largest brewery, with copious samples on weekdays. (p200)

Newberry Library Free tours and fascinating exhibits from the library's huge collection. (p85)

Kid-Friendly Activities

Navy Pier The whirling swing, sky-high Ferris wheel, musical carousel – all here, plus boats. (p69)

Maggie Daley Park Imaginative playgrounds where kids can swing and climb for hours, plus rock climbing and mini-golf. (p280)

Lincoln Park Zoo Swinging chimps, roaring lions and a barnyard full of farm animals to feed. (p99)

Peggy Notebaert Nature Museum The butterfly haven, bird garden and marsh full of frogs provide gentle thrills. (p102)

Chicago Children's Museum The slew of building, climbing and inventing exhibits keep young ones busy. (p70)

Photo Ops

Chicago Theatre Sign What's more perfect than a six-story-high neon sign spelling out the city's name? (p64)

Cloud Gate The awesomely mirrored sculpture (aka 'the Bean') lets you take a self-portrait with a skyline background. (p46)

Art Institute Lions The iconic beasts guard the entrance and wear special gear for holidays and big events. (p49)

Wrigley Field Entrance The red, art-deco-style marquee makes an especially fine backdrop when neon-lit at night. (p111)

Mr Beef Sign Snap a photo under the sign before indulging in the city's famed Italian beef sammie. (p75)

Greetings from Chicago Mural It's like a giant postcard that shows the world exactly where you are. (p165)

Frank Lloyd Wright

Robie House The graceful lines of Wright's Hyde Park masterpiece were emulated around the world. (p204)

Rookery Wright gave the atrium a light-filled, Prairie-style renovation that features 'floating' staircases. (p53)

Frank Lloyd Wright Home & Studio See where the master lived and worked for the first 20 years of his career. (p218)

Charnley-Persky House Only 19 years old when he designed it, Wright declared the 11-room abode the first modern building. (p90)

Offbeat Museums

International Museum of Surgical Science Antique equipment and fascinating exhibits on the history of medical science fill a lakefront mansion. (p86)

Money Museum Emerge with a take-home bag of shredded currency and photo with the million-dollar briefcase. (p53)

Leather Archives & Museum Displays about leather, fetish and S&M subcultures, including relics like the Red Spanking Bench. (p37)

Chicago Sports Museum The Cubs' infamous Bartman ball and Sammy Sosa's corked bat fill displays beside Harry Caray's tavern. (p85)

American Writers Museum Engrossing interactive displays on American literature will keep book lovers absorbed for hours. (p54)

Pop Culture

Daley Plaza Site of the *Blues Brothers* epic car-crashing chase scene. (p52)

Marina City The corncob-shaped towers show up everywhere from Wilco album covers to Steve McQueen films. (p70)

Original Playboy Mansion Hugh Hefner launched the magazine and began wearing his all-day pajamas here. (p90)

Route 66 Sign The famous Mother Road starts downtown by the Art Institute. (p54)

Buckingham Fountain The water spout features in the opening credits of the TV classic *Married...with Children*. (p53)

Month By Month

January

It's the coldest month, with temperatures hovering around 22°F (-6°C), and the snowiest month, with around 10in total. Everyone stays inside and eats and drinks.

☀ Chinese New Year Parade

Crowds amass on Wentworth Ave in Chinatown to watch dragons dance, firecrackers burst and marching bands bang their gongs during this parade (www.chicagochinatown. org). The exact date varies according to the lunar calendar, but it's typically in late January or early to mid-February.

March

Will the sun ever shine again? Windy City-zens fret during the grayest and windiest month, when temperatures linger at 37°F (3°C). Some fun events take the edge off.

☀ Chiditarod

The Chiditarod (www. chiditarod.org) is a Burning Man–esque version of the Iditarod (the famed Alaskan sled-dog race) that swaps humans for huskies and shopping carts for sleds. Teams haul canned food for local pantries along the Wicker Park route. Held on the first Saturday in March.

⊙ St Patrick's Day Parade

It's a city institution: the local plumbers' union dyes the Chicago River shamrock green (pouring in the secret, biodegradable coloring near the N Columbus Dr bridge), and then a big parade follows along S Columbus Dr. Held the Saturday before March 17.

May

Finally, the weather warms and everyone dashes for the parks, lakefront trails, baseball stadiums and beer gardens. Beaches open over Memorial Day weekend. Hotels get busy.

✗ Mole de Mayo

The food's the star at this weekend-long Pilsen street festival (www.facebook. com/MoleDeMayo), especially the mole sauce. Chef judges award top honors to their favorite recipe. Traditional Mexican dancers and acrobatic *lucha libre* wrestlers add to the atmosphere. It takes place on 18th St.

🏃 Bike the Drive

The last Sunday in May, cars are banned from Lake Shore Dr, and 20,000 cyclists take to the road during Bike the Drive (www.bikethedrive.org). Riding 30 miles along the lakefront as the sun bursts out is a thrill. Pancakes and live music follow in Grant Park.

June

Schools let out. Beaches get busy. Festival season ramps up. The temperature hangs at an ideal 69°F (21°C). Alas, it rains a third of the days.

🎊 Printers Row Lit Fest

This popular free event (www.printersrowlitfest. org), sponsored by the *Chicago Tribune,* features thousands of rare and not-so-rare books for sale, plus author readings. The browsable booths line the 500 to 700 blocks of S Dearborn St in early June.

☆ Chicago Blues Festival

It's the globe's biggest free blues fest (www.chicago bluesfestival.us), with three days of the electrified music that made Chicago famous. Thousands unfurl blankets by the multiple stages that take over Millennium Park in mid-June.

☆ Grant Park Music Festival

The Grant Park Orchestra, composed of top musicians from symphonies around the globe, plays free concerts in Millennium Park's Pritzker Pavilion on Wednesday, Friday and Saturday evenings from mid-June through mid-August (www. grantparkmusicfestival. com). It's a summer ritual to bring wine and a picnic.

🎊 Pride Parade

On the last Sunday in June, colorful floats and risqué revelers pack Halsted St in Boystown. It's the LGBT+ community's main event (http://chicagopride.go pride.com), and more than 800,000 people come to the party.

July

The month Chicagoans wait for all year. Festivals rock the neighborhoods every weekend. Millennium

Park has concerts downtown nightly. Fireflies glow everywhere. It can be hot and humid, but who cares?

🍴 Taste of Chicago

The midmonth, five-day food festival (www.tasteof chicago.us) in Grant Park draws hordes for a smorgasbord of ethnic, meaty, sweet and other local edibles – much of it served on a stick. Several stages host free live music, including big-name bands.

☆ Pitchfork Music Festival

It's sort of Lollapalooza Jr for bespectacled alternative-music fans. They come to see taste-making acts shake up Union Park for three days in mid-July. A day pass costs $75 (www.pitchfork musicfestival.com).

August

Ah, more awesome summer: warm weather, concerts, festivals, baseball games, beach frolicking. Tourists are still here en masse, so lodging prices are high and lines can be long.

☆ Lollapalooza

This mega rock festival (www.lollapalooza.com) once traveled city to city; now its permanent home is in Chicago. It's a raucous event, with 170 bands – including many A-listers – spilling off eight stages in Grant Park the first Thursday to Sunday in August.

☆ Chicago Jazz Festival

Chicago's longest-running free music fest (www. chicagojazzfestival.us), well into its fourth decade,

attracts top names on the national jazz scene. The brassy notes bebop over Labor Day weekend on multiple stages in Millennium Park and the Chicago Cultural Center.

September

Kids go back to school and beaches close after Labor Day weekend. Peak season begins to wind down.

◉ EXPO Chicago

Top galleries from around the globe show off their contemporary and modern art on Navy Pier during EXPO Chicago (www.expo chicago.com), held over a long weekend in mid-September. Local galleries get in on the action by offering special tours and programs concurrently.

October

Temperatures drop, to an average of 53°F (12°C). Baseball is over, but basketball and hockey begin at month's end. The Bears and tailgate parties are in full swing.

🏃 Chicago Marathon

More than 45,000 runners compete on this 26-mile course (www.chicago marathon.com) through the city's heart, cheered on by a million spectators. Held on a Sunday in October (when the weather can be pleasant or freezing), it's considered one of the world's top five marathons.

◉ Chicago Architecture Biennial

The three-and-a-half-month biennial (www.chicago-architecturebiennial.org)

(Top) Competitors in the Chicago Marathon
(Bottom) Pride Parade

FERNANDA PARADIZO / SHUTTERSTOCK ©

CAFEBEANZ COMPANY / SHUTTERSTOCK ©

brings together designers from around the world for free exhibitions, tours and public programs about groovy architecture. It takes place from mid-September through early January every two years. The next biennials are in 2021 and 2023.

☆ Chicago International Film Festival

Showing a few big-name flicks among myriad not-so-big-name flicks, this festival (www.chicagofilm-festival.com) brings some big-name Hollywood stars to town to add a glamorous sheen to the proceedings. It unspools over two weeks, starting in mid-October, at varying venues.

December

'Tis the holiday season, and the city twinkles with good cheer, Michigan Ave bustles with shoppers and shines with a million lights. The ice rinks open. Hotel bargains abound.

🛍 Christkindlmarket

A traditional German holiday market (www.christkindlmarket.com) takes over Daley Plaza all month, selling sausages, roasted nuts and spiced wine along with Old World handicrafts. It starts around Thanksgiving and goes until Christmas Eve.

◉ ZooLights

Lincoln Park Zoo (p99) gets gussied up for the holidays with sparkling trees, Santa-spotting, ice-skating and seasonal displays from late November to early January.

With Kids

Ferocious dinosaurs at the Field Museum, an ark's worth of beasts at Lincoln Park Zoo, lakefront boat rides and sandy beaches are among the top choices for toddlin' times. Add in magical playgrounds, family cycling tours and lots of pizza, and it's clear Chicago is a kid's kind of town.

CONCH MARTINEZ / SHUTTERSTOCK ©

Museum of Science & Industry (p205)

Outdoor Activities

Parks

Millennium Park (p46) is a hot favorite. Kids love to run underneath and touch 'the Bean' sculpture, while Crown Fountain (p46) serves as a de facto water park to splash in. Nearby Maggie Daley Park (p52) offers imaginative playgrounds where kids can swing and climb for hours. Lincoln Park has a free zoo (p99) where lions roar and apes swing. At the southern end of the zoo, kids can get up close to goats, ponies, cows and chickens at the Farm-in-the-Zoo, and they can also see ducks along the Nature Boardwalk. The train ride and the carousel (each $3 per ride) – with its wood-carved pandas, cheetahs and tigers – bring squeals of delight.

Beaches

Sand and swimming! Lifeguards patrol the city's 26 lakefront beaches throughout the summer. Waves are typically pint-sized – perfect for pint-sized swimmers. North Avenue Beach (p98) is the most crowded (and you do have to share it with skimpy-suited 20-somethings), but the selling point is the location near both downtown and Lincoln Park Zoo. The steamboat-shaped beach house is totally kid friendly, serving ice cream and burgers, and it has bath-rooms and lockers. Montrose Beach (p135) is further flung, but it also has bathrooms and a snack bar. It's less crowded and more dune-packed and nature-filled. Re-member to check the beach website (www.chicagoparkdistrict.com/parks-facilities/beaches) before you head out to make sure the water isn't off-limits due to high winds or bacteria levels.

Navy Pier

Amusements abound on the half-mile-long wharf (p69). A giant whirling swing, the sky-high Ferris wheel, a musical, hand-painted carousel, remote-control boats, fountains to splash in are all here, and then some. Popcorn, ice cream, burgers and oth-er treats add to the carnival atmosphere.

Cycling

Bobby's Bike Hike (p80) and Bike & Roll (p66) rent children's bikes and bikes with child seats. Both also offer child-friendly tours. Try Bobby's 'Tike Hike,' which rolls by Lincoln Park Zoo and a statue of Abe Lincoln. Kids aged 10 and under are welcome on the 4.5-mile route. Bike & Roll's 'Lincoln Park Adventure' is also suitable for kids.

Boat Rides

The schooner *Windy* (p80) departs from Navy Pier and offers a pirate-themed cruise on most days, plus kids can help sail the boat. Water taxis offer another wind-in-your-hair experience. The boats that toddle along the lakefront between Navy Pier and the Museum Campus are popular with families.

Kid-Friendly Museums

Chicago Children's Museum

It is the reigning favorite, geared to kids aged 10 and under, with a slew of hands-on building, climbing and inventing exhibits. Bonus: It's located on Navy Pier (p70).

Field Museum of Natural History

Bring on the dinosaurs! The Crown Family PlayLab (p191), on the ground floor, lets kids excavate bones and make loads of other discoveries. It's open Thursday to Monday from 10am to 3:30pm.

Museum of Science & Industry

Families could spend a week here (p205) and not see it all. Staff conduct 'experiments' in various galleries throughout the day, like dropping things off the balcony and creating mini explosions. The Idea Factory lets scientists aged 10 and under 'research' properties of light, balance and water pressure.

Peggy Notebaert Nature Museum

This museum (p102) is somewhat overlooked, but its butterfly haven and marsh full of frogs provide gentle thrills. Bonus: it's located in Lincoln Park by the zoo.

Theater Fun

Chicago Children's Theatre

This theater (p187) puts on terrific shows. The stories are often familiar, as they're frequently adapted from kids' books. Many use puppets or music. Performances take place in the group's spiffy new West Loop facility.

Emerald City Theatre Company

The Emerald City Theatre Company (p121) is another kid-focused troupe. It presents well-known shows such as *School House Rock Live,* as well as original, lesser-known works like *Three Little Kittens.* Performances are at the group's on-site theater and at other venues around town.

Festivals

Chicago Kids & Kites Festival

On a Saturday in early May, hundreds of colorful kites soar and dip around Montrose Beach (p135). The city supplies free kite-making kits, and professional flyers demonstrate how to harness the wind. Face painting and balloon artists round out the fun.

Kidzapalooza

Lollapalooza (p22) isn't just for arm-flailing, mosh-pit-thrashing adults. Kidzapalooza is a festival within the giant rock festival. In addition to the stellar lineup of kid-favorite bands, budding rock stars can bang sticks in the Drum Zone and get a Mohawk in the kids' area.

Magnificent Mile Lights Festival

During the free **Magnificent Mile Lights Festival** (www.themagnificentmile.com/lights-festival; Streeterville; ⊙late Nov), held the Saturday before Thanksgiving, Mickey Mouse and a slew of family-friendly musicians march in a parade and flip on Michigan Ave's one million twinkling lights.

NEED TO KNOW

➡ For kid-friendly happenings, see Chicago Parent (www.chicagoparent.com) and Chicago Kids (www.chicago kids.com).

➡ Children under age seven ride free on the L train and public buses; those aged seven to 11 pay a reduced fare.

Chicago-style hot dog (p263)

Eating

Chicago has become a chowhound's hot spot. For the most part, restaurants here are reasonably priced and pretension-free, serving masterful food in come-as-you-are environs. You can also tuck into a superb range of international eats, especially if you break out of downtown and head for neighborhoods such as Pilsen or Uptown.

A Foodie's Perfect Day

Start the morning at a farmers market; Green City Market (p98), the city's largest, has cooking demos by top chefs. Next go on a graze with **Chicago Food Planet Tours** (☏312-932-0800; www.chicagofoodplanet.com; 2-3hr tours $45-60). For dinner, go upscale in the West Loop, where Girl & the Goat (p182) gets creative with the namesake animal. Or opt for laid-back in Logan Square, where Longman & Eagle (p169) serves comfort food alongside fine whiskey.

Food Trucks

Strict local regulations keep Chicago's food-truck scene limited compared to other big cities. Still, there are several good ones, and they generally prowl office-worker-rich hot spots, such as the Loop and Near North around lunchtime, and then Wicker Park and Lake View toward evening. Chicago Food Truck Finder (www.chicagofoodtruckfinder.com) amalgamates many truck locations on one map. Daley Plaza hosts several trucks on Fridays at lunchtime.

Eat Streets

Randolph Street, West Loop Chicago's best and brightest chefs cook at downtown's edge.

Clark Street, Andersonville Nouveau Korean, traditional Belgian and Lowcountry crawfish.

Division Street, Wicker Park Copious sidewalk seating spills out of hip bistros and cafes.

Argyle Street, Uptown Thai and Vietnamese noodle houses steam up this little corridor.

18th Street, Pilsen Mexican bakeries and taquerias mix with hipster cafes and barbecue joints.

Milwaukee Avenue, Logan Square Wood-fired pizzas, ramen parlors, classy vegetarian spots: if it's on trend it's here.

Eating by Neighborhood

➡ **The Loop** (p58) Lunch spots for office workers, not much late at night.

➡ **Near North & Navy Pier** (p74) Huge variety, from deep-dish pizza to ritzy seafood.

➡ **Gold Coast** (p90) Epicenter of sceney steakhouses and swanky eateries.

➡ **Lincoln Park & Old Town** (p102) A smorgasbord, from elite Alinea to cute French bakeries and student bites.

➡ **Lake View & Wrigleyville** (p113) Good-time midrange places for vegetarians and global food lovers.

➡ **Andersonville & Uptown** (p126) Cozy, international array in Andersonville; noodle houses in Uptown's Little Saigon.

➡ **Lincoln Square & Ravenswood** (p140) Modest, Michelin-starred little restaurants have staked a claim.

➡ **Wicker Park, Bucktown & Ukrainian Village** (p149) Dense with nouveau comfort food and cafes.

➡ **Logan Square & Humboldt Park** (p168) Inventive foodie mecca, sans reservations.

➡ **West Loop & Near West Side** (p178) West Loop for Chicago's hottest chefs; Greektown and Little Italy for international fare.

➡ **Pilsen & Near South Side** (p196) Authentic Mexican food in Pilsen gives way to Chinatown flavors.

➡ **Hyde Park & South Side** (p212) Hipster chow in Bridgeport, earthy cafes in Hyde Park, soul-food cafeterias in neighborhoods beyond.

NEED TO KNOW

Opening Hours

Breakfast 7am or 8am to 11am

Lunch 11am or 11:30am to 2:30pm

Dinner 5pm or 6pm to 10pm Sunday to Thursday, to 11pm or midnight Friday and Saturday

Price Ranges

The following price ranges refer to the cost of a main dish at dinner.

$ less than $15

$$ $15 to $25

$$$ more than $25

Reservations

➡ Make reservations for eateries in the midrange and top-end price bracket, especially on weekends.

➡ Apps like OpenTable and Resy can get you a last-minute table.

➡ For no-reservations hot spots, arrive at opening time or a bit before to get in line. Make sure your cell phone is charged; once the host takes your name, many restaurants will let you wait elsewhere (ie a nearby bar) and will text when your table is ready.

Tipping

Most people tip between 18% and 20% of the final price of the meal. For takeout, it's polite to drop a few dollars in the tip jar.

PLAN YOUR TRIP EATING

Lonely Planet's Top Choices

Giant (p169) Small storefront with big flavors and well-matched cocktails.

Passerotto (p127) Anderson-ville's hot spot features an exuberant Korean-Italian fusion menu.

Hopleaf (p131) Locals pile in for the mussels, *frites* (fries) and 200-strong beer list.

Pleasant House Pub (p196) Savory pies and fish fries in a friendly neighborhood space.

Dove's Luncheonette (p151) Sit at the retro counter for Tex-Mex dishes, pie and whiskey.

Best by Budget

$

Lou Mitchell's (p181) Route 66 diner where waitstaff call you 'honey' without irony.

Irazu (p149) Chicago's lone Costa Rican eatery whips up distinctive, peppery fare.

Publican Quality Meats (p181) Beefy sandwiches straight from the butcher's block.

Revival Food Hall (p58) A slew of all-local, hipster eats to choose from.

Taste of Lebanon (p130) Locals have voted this cheap-and-cheerful Middle Eastern joint Chicago's best.

$$

Monteverde (p181) Housemade pastas that draw legions of fans.

Luella's Southern Kitchen (p140) Rich recipes from the chef's Mississippi-born great-grandmother.

Gorée Cuisine (p214) Friendly cafe for *yassa* chicken and other real-deal Senegalese dishes.

Longman & Eagle (p169) Shabby-chic tavern for break-fast, lunch or dinner with a side of whiskey.

Little Goat (p181) Iron Chef Stephanie Izard's delicious comfort-food diner.

$$$

Goosefoot (p141) Unpredict-able, Michelin-starred tasting menu that pays attention to detail.

Girl & the Goat (p182) Rockin' ambience and dishes starring the titular animal.

Alinea (p104) Molecular gas-tronomy at one of the world's best restaurants.

Boka (p104) Michelin-starred Mod American that's perfect for a pretheater meal.

Elizabeth (p141) Foraged ingre-dients spun into whimsical bites inspired by pop-culture themes.

Best by Cuisine

Pizza

Giordano's (p75) It's like deep-dish pizza on steroids, with awesomely bulked-up crusts.

Pequod's Pizza (p103) Sweet sauce and caramelized cheese.

Pizano's (p60) Makes a great thin crust to supplement the deep dish.

Dimo's Pizza (p150) Creatively topped meat and vegan pizzas at a late-night Wicker Park standby.

Asian

Crisp (p114) Cheerful cafe for Korean fried chicken and mixed vegetable bowls.

Le Colonial (p91) Banana-leaf-wrapped fish that will transport you to Saigon.

Qing Xiang Yuan Dumplings (p197) Popular dough pockets with dozens of fillings to choose from.

Parachute (p172) Michelin-starred spin on Korean street food in a far-flung neighborhood.

Fat Rice (p169) A wild Chinese-Portuguese-Indian mash-up by a Beard Award–winning chef.

Latin

Topolobampo/Frontera Grill (p76) Rick Bayless' flavor-packed signature restaurants.

Don Pedro Carnitas (p196) Authentic Pilsen haunt for the city's best tacos.

5 Rabanitos (p197) Complex, standout food in a storefront taqueria.

Cafecito (p58) Fat Cuban sandwiches.

Vegetarian & Vegan

Ground Control (p168) Super delicious, all-vegetarian dishes with global flair and a side of pinball.

Handlebar (p150) Bike-messenger hangout with many meat-free dishes on the menu.

Chicago Diner (p113) Chicago's long-standing all-veg linchpin.

Veggie Grill (p59) Entirely plant-based with a mock-meat menu that even omnivores love.

Sweets

Hoosier Mama Pie Company (p152) Supreme flaky goodness.

Jennivee's (p114) LGBT+-friendly cafe for creamy-frosted cakes.

Pretty Cool Ice Cream (p170) Wildly flavored frozen novelties on a stick.

Stan's Donuts (p149) Sink your teeth into a cookie-butter-filled pocket.

Drinking & Nightlife

Chicagoans love to hang out in drinking establishments. Blame it on the long winter, when folks need to huddle together somewhere warm. Blame it on summer, when sunny days make beer gardens and sidewalk patios so splendid. Whatever the reason, drinking in the city is a widely cherished pastime.

Beer Tours & Festivals

Walking tours led by companies like **Chicago Beer Experience** (☎312-818-2172; www.chicagobeerexperience.com; 3hr tours $67) visit a neighborhood – Lincoln Park/Lake View, Bucktown/Wicker Park or Loop/South Loop – to uncover its beer history along with a little Chicago history. Jaunts typically hit about four bars, include a snack to soak up the suds, and cover about a mile.

True beer lovers should mark their calendars for **Illinois Craft Beer Week** (www.illinoisbeer.org/icbw; ⊙May) in late May, which attracts hundreds of breweries for tastings and pairing dinners.

Local Spirit

Chicago has its own unique liquor. It's called Malört, and a Swedish immigrant introduced it to the city in the 1930s. It's famous for tasting awful.

Drinkers have described it variously as the flavor of pencil shavings, canal water, cleaning fluid and sweaty socks. Wormwood is what gives it its bitter taste. People typically drink it as a shot, and there are entire Instagram hashtags devoted to #malortface, which is the grimace you make upon swallowing. Practically every bar in town stocks it, and downing a shot is a weird Chicago right of passage. Malört is also occasionally used in cocktails. CH Distillery makes the brand.

Drinking & Nightlife by Neighborhood

➧ **The Loop** (p60) Rooftop hotel bars, Riverwalk cafes, not much after 10pm.

➧ **Near North & Navy Pier** (p77) Scores of options from dives to champagne bars; also a club hub.

➧ **Gold Coast** (p92) Martini lounges for folks on the prowl.

➧ **Lincoln Park & Old Town** (p105) Student saloons around Lincoln and Halsted Sts; quirky gems in Old Town.

➧ **Lake View & Wrigleyville** (p116) Sports and cocktail bars around Wrigley Field; dance clubs in Boystown.

➧ **Andersonville & Uptown** (p131) Awesome beer bars and low-key LGBT drinkeries.

➧ **Lincoln Square & Ravenswood** (p141) Breweries galore, many grouped together along 'Malt Row.'

➧ **Wicker Park, Bucktown & Ukrainian Village** (p155) Cocktail lounges and wine bars, peppered with mom-and-pop joints.

➧ **Logan Square & Humboldt Park** (p172) Hipster dive bars, microbreweries, gin lounges and tiki bars.

➧ **West Loop & Near West Side** (p183) Fancy cocktail bars and distilleries, less fancy breweries.

➧ **Pilsen & Near South Side** (p198) Neighborhood pubs, patios and taprooms, plus artist hangouts in Pilsen.

➧ **Hyde Park & South Side** (p215) Sip alongside locals in Bridgeport and Hyde Park.

PLAN YOUR TRIP DRINKING & NIGHTLIFE

NEED TO KNOW

Opening Hours

Bars 5pm to 2am (3am on Saturday); some licensed until 4am (5am on Saturday)

Nightclubs 10pm to 4am; often closed Monday through Wednesday

Tipping

Tip 15% to 20% per round, or a minimum per drink of $1 for standard drinks, $2 for specialty cocktails.

Lonely Planet's Top Choices

Old Town Ale House (p105) Trendy tipplers and grizzled regulars sip under bawdy paintings.

Matchbox (p158) Teensy cocktail lounge with big gimlets.

Signature Lounge (p92) Ascend to the skyscraper's 96th floor and gawk at the view.

Lagunitas Brewing Company (p200) Rollicking beer-hall-esque taproom for hoppy suds and free tours.

RM Champagne Salon (p185) Twinkling West Loop spot that feels like a Parisian cafe.

Best Clubs

Smart Bar (p120) Intimate club that's serious about its DJs.

Late Bar (p173) Groovy, new-wave club that draws an ubermixed crowd.

Berlin (p117) Welcome-one, welcome-all space to dance your ass off.

Disco (p78) Spin on the LED floor like it's 1977.

Best Beer

Marz Community Brewing (p215) Wild creations sipped alongside home brewers and artists.

Delilah's (p105) Spirited punk bar with all kinds of odd ales (and whiskeys too).

Metropolitan Brewing (p173) German-style lagers at the river's edge.

Centennial Crafted Beer & Eatery (p78) Warm beer bar with 50 taps.

Revolution Brewing (p172) Industrial-chic brewpub pouring righteous ales.

Best Cocktails

Violet Hour (p155) Beard Award–winning cocktails in a hidden bar.

Lost Lake (p172) Cool, refreshing tiki concoctions.

Sparrow (p92) Bespoke rum-based cocktails in a cozy retro bar.

Arbella (p78) Daring drinks from around the globe served in snuggly environs.

Aviary (p186) Molecular gastronomy applied to booze.

Best Wine

Bar Ramone (p78) Sparkling nightcap in a European-style salon.

Press Room (p186) Reds and whites in a candle-lit basement.

Bar Pastoral (p117) Sample widely via half glasses and supplement with cheese.

Lush Wine & Spirits (p159) Buy a bottle in the shop, drink it in the hip bar.

Best Like a Local

Simon's Tavern (p131) Neighborhood stalwart with a ballsy jukebox and Swedish spiced wine in winter.

Skylark (p198) Where Pilsen's underground goes for cheap drinks and tater tots.

Ten Cat Tavern (p116) Shoot pool, check out the art and swill beers by the fireplace.

Innertown Pub (p158) Authentic kitsch and cheap drinks tucked away in Ukrainian Village.

Archie's Iowa Rockwell Tavern (p173) Corner bar chock full of neon, dartboards and regulars downing shots.

Best Coffee

Big Shoulders Coffee (p93) Housemade latte flavors feature at this local roaster chain.

Sawada Coffee (p186) Fanciful coffee and punk-skateboard decor.

Intelligentsia Coffee (p62) Local roaster known for strong java.

Dollop (p79) Baristas create caffeinated wonders in this sunny space.

Best Distilleries

CH Distillery (p185) Where the West Loop crowd goes for organic vodka and gin drinks.

Maplewood Brewery & Distillery (p172) Alluring tasting room for beer, whiskey, gin and beer cocktails.

Rhine Hall Distillery (p183) Family-run little spot for fruit brandies.

Entertainment

From the evening-wear elegance of the Lyric Opera to pay-what-you-can storefront theaters and quirky magic lounges, Chicago puts on an impressive slate of performances. Improv laughs and live music spill out of muggy clubs and DIY dive bars nightly. Chicago's spectator sports might just have the most rabid fans of all.

Live Music

Blues and jazz have deep roots in Chicago, and indie rock clubs slouch on almost every corner. Besides megabashes such as Blues Fest, Lollapalooza and Pitchfork, the following are a must for any music fan's calendar:

Riot Fest (www.riotfest.org; North Lawndale) Big-name punk and rock bands scream in Douglas Park for three days in mid-September.

World Music Festival (www.worldmusicfestival chicago.org) Musicians from around the globe descend for two weeks of performances, anchored by the Chicago Cultural Center. Held in mid-September.

West Fest (www.westfestchicago.com; W Chicago Ave, East Village; suggested donation $5) Ubercool indie bands rock this three-day Ukrainian Village street fair, often considered a Pitchfork warm-up. Held in July.

Free Summer Movies

Movies in the Parks is a summer tradition. The Chicago Park District (www.chicagopark district.com) has the nightly schedule.

The Chicago International Film Festival (p23) is the city's star event; it rolls in October.

Entertainment by Neighborhood

➡ **The Loop** (p62) The neon-lit Theater District, everything classical and free concerts in Millennium Park.

➡ **Near North & Navy Pier** (p79) Shakespeare, jazz and blues.

➡ **Gold Coast** (p93) Smattering of theater, jazz.

➡ **Lincoln Park & Old Town** (p107) Second City, iO Theater improv, blues, outdoor and indoor theaters.

➡ **Lake View & Wrigleyville** (p120) Heaps of rock, improv and little jazzy clubs, but mostly the Cubs at Wrigley Field.

➡ **Andersonville & Uptown** (p133) Historic venues like the Green Mill cluster in Uptown, and there's magic in Andersonville.

➡ **Lincoln Square & Ravenswood** (p144) Folk music and a vintage cinema.

➡ **Wicker Park, Bucktown & Ukrainian Village** (p159) Best area for cool-cat rock clubs.

➡ **Logan Square & Humboldt Park** (p175) Artsy, far-reaching music and theater venues.

➡ **West Loop & Near West Side** (p187) Pro basketball and hockey at United Center.

➡ **Pilsen & Near South Side** (p200) Great live-music halls and the Bears at Soldier Field.

➡ **Hyde Park & South Side** (p215) Performing arts, the White Sox, and soul and funk nights.

NEED TO KNOW

Discount Tickets

Hot Tix (www.hottix.org) Sells same-week drama, comedy and performing-arts tickets for half price (plus a $5 to $10 service charge). Book online or at the two Hot Tix outlets: E Randolph St (p64) and in Block 37 (p54).

Goldstar (www.goldstar. com) Half-price offers from national ticket broker.

Lonely Planet's Top Choices

Green Mill (p133) Listen to jazz or a poetry slam while sipping martinis with Al Capone's ghost.

Wrigley Field (p111) It's hard to beat a day in the sun-splashed bleachers.

Second City (p107) The group that invented improv is still the best in the biz.

Buddy Guy's Legends (p64) The iconic bluesman's club puts the best bands on stage.

Chicago Magic Lounge (p134) You won't believe your eyes at this custom-built magic theater.

Best Blues

Buddy Guy's Legends (p64) Sick licks fill the air day and night.

Rosa's Lounge (p173) Un-varnished joint where dedicated fans feel the blues.

BLUES (p107) Small, crackling club with seasoned local players.

Blue Chicago (p79) Handy Near North spot with good local acts.

Kingston Mines (p107) Hot and sweaty late-night venue with two stages jamming daily.

Best Jazz

Green Mill (p133) Big names in jazz bebop at this timeless tavern.

Whistler (p173) Artsy little club where indie bands and jazz trios brood.

Constellation (p120) Intimate spot for progressive jazz and improvised music.

Jazz Showcase (p64) Elegant room where national acts blow their horns.

Winter's Jazz Club (p79) Straight-ahead jazz for an audience of dedicated fans.

Best Theater

Steppenwolf Theatre (p107) Drama club of Malkovich, Sinise and other Hollywood stars.

Neo-Futurist Theater (p134) Original works make you laugh and ponder.

Goodman Theatre (p64) Excellent new and classic American plays.

House Theatre (p159) Magic, music and storytelling by playwrights on the rise.

Prop Thtr (p173) Stellar fringe group that's always thought-provoking and original.

Best Comedy

Second City (p107) The improv bastion that's launched many a jokester's career.

iO Theater (p107) This good-time, four-theater improv house has sent many on to stardom.

Annoyance Theatre (p121) Naughty and absurd shows for late-night chuckles.

CSz Theater (p122) Two teams compete for your laughs.

Best Rock

Hideout (p159) Feels like your grandma's basement but with alt-country bands and literary readings.

Metro (p120) Bands on the way up thrash here first.

Empty Bottle (p159) Go-to club for edgy indie rock.

Lincoln Hall (p107) Indie bands love to play this intimate room with pristine acoustics.

Best Dance

SummerDance (p64) Locals young and old come out for free world-music concerts and dance lessons.

Hubbard Street Dance Chicago (p64) Foremost modern troupe in town.

Joffrey Ballet (p65) Famed dancers leap through the classical repertoire.

Best Spectator Sports

Wrigley Field (p111) The Cubs' iconic ballpark is rife with traditions and curses.

Guaranteed Rate Field (p216) Cheap tickets and fun giveaways rule at the White Sox' ballpark.

Soldier Field (p200) Die-hard Bears fans flock to games no matter how cold it is.

United Center (p187) Legendary house of Michael Jordan, where the Bulls shoot hoops and the Blackhawks play hockey.

 # Shopping

From the glossy stores of the Magnificent Mile to the indie designers of Wicker Park to the brainy booksellers of Hyde Park, Chicago is a shopper's destination. It has been that way from the get-go. After all, this is the city that birthed the department store and traditions such as the money-back guarantee, bridal registry and bargain basement.

Chicago Specialties

Music is big. Independent record stores flood Chicago's neighborhoods, supported by the thriving live-music scene in town. Vinyl geeks will find heaps of stacks to flip through.

Vintage and thrift fashions are another claim to fame. Folks here don't throw out their old bowling shirts, pillbox hats, faux-fur coats and costume jewelry. Instead, they deposit used duds at vintage or second-hand stores, of which there are heaps.

Art- and architecture-related items are another Chicago specialty.

Locally Made Goods

Several stores proffer handbags, pendants, dresses and journals that city artisans have stitched, sewed and glue-gunned themselves. You're pretty much guaranteed a one-of-a-kind item to take home.

The Indie Designer Market, inside the massive Randolph Street Market (p188), is the epicenter of such craftiness.

Shopping by Neighborhood

➡ **The Loop** (p65) National chains, plus souvenir and arts-and-crafts winners.

➡ **Near North & Navy Pier** (p79) Home to the Magnificent Mile, lined with sleek big-name retailers.

➡ **Gold Coast** (p93) Oak St offers luxury brand boutiques, while malls rise on Michigan Ave.

➡ **Lincoln Park & Old Town** (p108) Urban living chains throng Halsted and Clybourn Sts; posh shops around Armitage Ave.

➡ **Lake View & Wrigleyville** (p122) Naughty stuff in Boystown, sports souvenirs around Wrigley, cool comics and vintage sprinkled in between.

➡ **Andersonville & Uptown** (p134) Fashion, quality antiques and locally made wares along Clark St.

➡ **Lincoln Square & Ravenswood** (p145) Cute boutiques and European-goods emporiums.

➡ **Wicker Park, Bucktown & Ukrainian Village** (p160) Vintage, hip fashion, book and record shops on Milwaukee Ave; crafters on Division St.

➡ **Logan Square & Humboldt Park** (p173) Far-flung indie shops with stylish goods for hipsters.

➡ **West Loop & Near West Side** (p187) Where the markets are.

➡ **Pilsen & Near South Side** (p200) Inexpensive homewares and trinkets in Chinatown; funky vintage shops in Pilsen.

➡ **Hyde Park & South Side** (p216) Bookstores galore, plus markets.

NEED TO KNOW

Opening Hours

Shops 11am to 7pm Monday to Saturday, noon to 6pm Sunday

Malls 10am to 8pm or 9pm Monday to Saturday, 11am to 6pm Sunday

Taxes

Sales tax on goods (excluding food) is 10.25%.

Lonely Planet's Top Choices

Chicago Architecture Center Shop (p65) Pick up a mini Willis Tower model or skyline poster.

Quimby's (p160) Ground zero for comics, zines and underground culture.

Transit Tees (p160) Creative Chicago logo designs found on anything you can imagine.

Katherine Anne Confections (p173) Truffles, salted caramels and crazy-good hot chocolate.

Pilsen Community Books (p201) Charming shop with floor-to-ceiling books.

Best Music

Reckless Records (p160) Great place to get the scoop on local indie rock bands.

Dusty Groove (p160) Killer stacks of vinyl hold rare soul and funk beats.

Dave's Records (p108) *Rolling Stone* magazine dubbed it one of the nation's best stores.

Gramaphone Records (p123) Favorite haunt of DJs and electronic-music fans.

Best Food & Drink

Gene's Sausage Shop (p145) European meats and cheeses inside, rooftop beer garden outside.

Provisions (p134) Pick up some gourmet bitters or a small-batch whiskey for that perfect cocktail.

Spice House (p108) Its rich, pungent air comes from the dizzying number of international herbs and spices.

Koval Distillery (p145) Grab a take-home bottle of organic whiskey, gin or jasmine liqueur.

TeaGschwender (p94) Choose from 200 varieties at this loose-leaf tea specialist.

Vosges Haut-Chocolat (p108) Gourmet chocolate mixed with unconventional ingredients.

Best Souvenirs

Art Institute of Chicago (p49) Posters and note cards of the collection's masterpieces.

Garrett Popcorn (p79) The sweet and salty mix will haunt your dreams.

Cubs Store (p122) Two-story shop packed with Cubs-logoed hats, jerseys, shot glasses and more.

Strange Cargo (p135) Huge array of iconic T-shirt iron-ons, from Coach Ditka to a Chicago-style hot-dog diagram.

Best Fashion & Vintage

Una Mae's (p161) Emerge looking all Jackie O in your new old hat.

Knee Deep Vintage (p201) Groovy garb from the 1920s to the 1970s.

Wolfbait & B-girls (p173) Local designers sew wares on-site.

Buffalo Exchange (p161) Browse through curated trendy threads at this popular resale shop.

Best Books

Seminary Co-op Bookstore (p216) Brainy shop beloved by Nobel Prize winners.

Open Books (p187) Welcoming used bookstore with a whopping selection.

Chicago Comics (p122) Beloved emporium for comics, zines and graphic novels.

57th Street Books (p216) Lose yourself in the labyrinth.

Women & Children First (p135) Find history's untold stories at this long-standing feminist bookstore.

Best Arts & Crafts

ShopColumbia (p65) Goods from Columbia College's arty students.

Andersonville Galleria (p134) Three floors of craftiness from local indie vendors.

Virtu (p161) Bucktown gem featuring jewelry, textiles and other crafts from regional artisans.

Pilsen Outpost (p201) Artist-run gallery with unique T-shirts, posters and paintings for sale.

Sports & Activities

Chicago offers plenty of places to get active via its city-spanning shoreline, 26 beaches and 580 parks. After a long, cold winter, everyone dashes outside to play. Top marks go to the 18-mile Lakefront Trail, prime for cycling and running. Meanwhile, Lake Michigan and the Chicago River provide loads of paddling possibilities.

Water Sports

Visitors often don't realize Chicago is a beach town, thanks to mammoth Lake Michigan lapping its side. There are 26 official strands of sand patrolled by lifeguards in summer. Swimming is popular, though the water is pretty freaking cold. Beaches at Montrose and North Ave have rental places offering kayaks and stand-up paddleboards. Other kayak companies have set up shop along the Chicago River.

Cycling

The flat, 18-mile **Lakefront Trail** is a beautiful ride along the water, though on nice days it's jam-packed. It starts at Ardmore Ave and rolls all the way south to 71st St. The path is split so cyclists and runners have separate lanes; look for signposts and markers painted on the ground to tell you what's what. The trail is most congested between Lincoln Park and the Museum Campus; it's least congested heading south from the museums. The Active Transportation Alliance (www.activetrans.org) publishes a bike trail map. Check @active transLFT on Twitter for updates on trail conditions; some parts close in bad weather.

Health & Fitness

For a fun and free exercise session, try **Millennium Park Workouts** (www.millennium park.org; 201 E Randolph St; ⏰7-11am Sat Jun-Aug; ⓜBrown, Orange, Green, Purple, Pink Line to Randolph) **FREE**. Every Saturday morning between 7am and 11am, from June through August, the park hosts a workout on the Great Lawn. It starts with 45 minutes of Pilates, followed by yoga (8am), strength training (9am) and Zumba dance (10am). There are additional single classes on Tuesday and Thursday mornings at 7:30am.

Activities by Neighborhood

➡ **The Loop** (p66) Cycling, ice-skating and kayaking options; free workouts in Millennium Park.

➡ **Near North & Navy Pier** (p80) Bike rentals near Navy Pier; kayaking at the neighborhood's western edge.

➡ **Gold Coast** Busy Oak Street Beach (p85) fringes the skyscrapers.

➡ **Lincoln Park & Old Town** (p108) The masses play in Lincoln Park and at North Avenue Beach.

➡ **Lake View & Wrigleyville** (p123) Can't beat it for bowling, golfing and canoeing.

➡ **Andersonville & Uptown** (p135) Montrose Beach is the surfing and skateboarding hot spot.

➡ **Wicker Park, Bucktown & Ukrainian Village** (p162) The 606 trail rambles along a repurposed train track, perfect for walking or cycling.

➡ **Logan Square & Humboldt Park** The 606 trail (p153) continues here, plus walking paths in Humboldt Park (p165).

➡ **Pilsen & Near South Side** (p201) Sledding at Soldier Field, paddling in Chinatown, walking and cycling paths on Northerly Island.

➡ **Hyde Park & South Side** (p216) Beaches, meadows and lagoon-filled Jackson and Washington Parks.

NEED TO KNOW

Opening Hours

Parks 6am to 11pm

Beaches 11am to 7pm late May to early September for swimming; same hours as parks otherwise

Online Resources

Chicago Beaches (www. chicagoparkdistrict.com/ parks-facilities/beaches) Info on swim advisories due to currents or water pollution.

Chicago Park District (www.chicagoparkdistrict. com) Lowdown on all the parks and their facilities and events.

Chicago Park District Golf (www.cpdgolf.com) Book tee times.

Lonely Planet's Top Choices

Lakefront Trail (p35) Eighteen miles to cycle, run or walk along the green-glinting waterfront.

The 606 (p153) Elevated trail rambles along a repurposed train track through Wicker Park and Logan Square.

McCormick Tribune Ice Rink (p66) Sublime skating set between 'the Bean' and Michigan Ave.

Bobby's Bike Hike (p80) Friendly guides lead the way on South Side and hot-dog-eating rides.

Montrose Beach (p135) Lovely stretch of sand, surf, dunes and a beach bar.

Best Bike Rides

Lakefront Trail (p35) Head south of the Loop and you can really pick up speed.

Bobby's Bike Hike (p80) Groovy tours for children, and pizza and beer lovers.

Bike & Roll (p66) Excellent tours from Lincoln Park to far-flung breweries.

Divvy (p273) Stations around the city rent bicycles for trips of up to three hours.

Best Paddling

Wateriders (p80) Slither past downtown's skyscrapers on a river kayaking tour.

Kayak Chicago (p135) Learn to paddleboard at Montrose Beach.

Urban Kayaks (p66) Rentals and fireworks tours launch downtown from the Riverwalk.

Chicago River Canoe & Kayak (p123) Design-savvy boathouse and relaxed paddling from a northside perch.

Boathouse at Ping Tom Park (p201) Dramatic city-railroad-bridge views while kayaking in Chinatown.

Best Beaches

Montrose Beach (p135) Bird-watching and kitesurfing add to the usual beachy sports.

North Avenue Beach (p98) Party time at the boathouse and on the volleyball courts.

Margaret T Burroughs Beach (p216) Amenity-laden strand with great skyline views, fishing dock and waterside cafe.

Oak Street Beach (p85) Sandbox in the shadow of skyscrapers.

Best Winter Activities

McCormick Tribune Ice Rink (p66) The city's most popular and atmospheric rink.

Maggie Daley Park (p52) The ice ribbon makes for fine skating.

Sledding Hill (p201) Big slope by Soldier Field with snowmaking machine.

Best Golf

Diversey Driving Range (p108) Hit buckets of balls in Lincoln Park.

Sydney R Marovitz Golf Course (p123) Nine-hole course with killer skyline views.

Jackson Park Golf Course (p216) The only city-run course with 18 holes.

Float at the Pride Parade (p22)

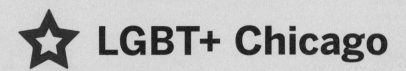

☆ LGBT+ Chicago

Exploring kinky artifacts in the Leather Archives & Museum, or playing a game of naughty Twister at a rollicking street fair? Shopping for gay literature, or clubbing alongside male go-go dancers? Chicago's flourishing gay and lesbian scene in party-hearty Boystown and easygoing Andersonville offers plenty of choices.

Festivals

The main event on the calendar is the Pride Parade (p22), held the last Sunday in June. It winds through Boystown and attracts more than 800,000 risqué revelers. **Northalsted Market Days** (www.northalsted.com; Ⓜ Red Line to Addison), held in Boystown, is a steamy two-day street fair in mid-August. Crafty, incense-wafting vendors line Halsted St, but most folks come for the drag queens in feather boas, Twister games played in the street and disco divas (Gloria Gaynor!) on the main stage. The International Mr Leather (www.imrl.com) contest brings out lots of

men in, well, leather in late May. Workshops and parties take place around town, with the main event happening at a downtown hotel or theater.

Museums & Tours

The **Leather Archives & Museum** (Off Map p316; ☎ 773-761-9200; www.leatherarchives.org; 6418 N Greenview Ave, Rogers Park; $10; ⊙ 11am-7pm Thu & Fri, to 5pm Sat & Sun; ☐ 36 or 151) holds all sorts of fetish and S&M artifacts, from the Red Spanking Bench to the painting *Last Supper in a Leather Bar with Judas Giving Christ the Finger*. It's inside a repurposed

NEED TO KNOW

Opening Hours

Bars 5pm to 2am (3am on Saturday); some licensed until 4am (5am on Saturday)

Nightclubs 10pm to 4am; often closed Monday through Wednesday

Websites

Windy City Times (www.windycitymedia group.com) LGBT newspaper, published weekly. The website is the main source for events and entertainment.

Purple Roofs (www.purpleroofs.com) Listings for queer accommodations, travel agencies and tours.

Chicago Pride (www.chicagopride.org) Events and happenings in the community.

synagogue north of Andersonville. Chicago Greeter (p276) offers free, guided sightseeing trips through the city's gay neighborhoods. You must reserve at least 10 days in advance.

Theater

Keep an eye out for **About Face Theatre** (☏773-784-8565; www.aboutfacetheatre.com), an itinerant ensemble that stages plays dealing with gay and lesbian themes at theaters around Chicago. Comedies, dramas and musicals all get their due. It's well regarded and has won Jeff Awards (sort of like the local Tony Award) for its work.

Community Centers

The mod, glassy Center on Halsted (p113) is the Midwest's largest LGBT+ community center. It's mostly a social service organization for locals, but visitors can use the free wi-fi and reading library, plus there's a Whole Foods grocery store attached to it.

LGBT+ by Neighborhood

➡ **Lake View & Wrigleyville** Home to Boystown, dense with bars and clubs on N Halsted St between Belmont Ave and Grace St.

➡ **Andersonville & Uptown** Chicago's other main area of LGBT+ bars, but in a more relaxed, less party-oriented scene.

Hamburger Mary's (p131)

Best Restaurants

Home Bistro (p113) Bring your own wine and settle in for nouveau comfort food in Boystown's center.

Tweet (p131) Decadent organic breakfasts next door to Big Chicks bar.

Vincent (p127) Join the guys for mussels and fries.

Jennivee's (p114) Cute bakery open late at night catering to the party crowd.

Best Bars

Big Chicks (p133) It's often called the friendliest gay bar in Chicago.

Hamburger Mary's (p131) Swill the housemade brews and watch the action from the patio.

Wang's (p116) Sip a pear martini under red-lit paper lanterns.

Second Story (p79) Cash-only, disco-ball-spinning bar that hides downtown.

Roscoe's Tavern (p116) Boystown stalwart with a casual bar in front and dance club in back.

Best Shopping

Unabridged Bookstore (p122) Well-curated stacks on hard-to-find LGBT+ topics; good sci-fi, too.

Women & Children First (p135) Feminist-focused tomes, children's books and big-name author readings.

Men's Room (p123) Boystown stop for fetish gear, handcuffs and harnesses.

Best Dance Clubs

Sidetrack (p116) It's massive and packed with frisky boys in tight jeans.

Berlin (p117) For more than three decades it's been where party people dance until the wee hours.

Hydrate (p116) Guys, just take off your shirt and boogie.

Best Sleeping

Best Western Hawthorne Terrace (p239) Reasonably priced hotel steps from Boystown's main vein.

Villa Toscana (p239) Silky B&B on Halsted St, smack in Boystown's midst.

City Suites Hotel (p240) Art deco-style boutique property that buzzes near Boystown.

Explore Chicago

CHICAGO'S TOP SIGHTS

Neighborhoods at a Glance

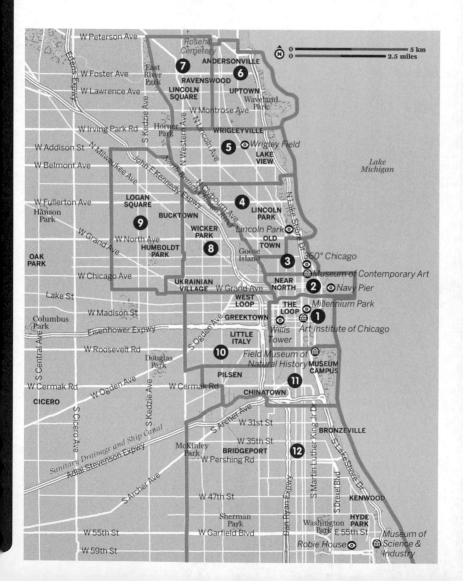

W Peterson Ave

Rosehill Cemetery

7

ANDERSONVILLE

6

East River Park

W Foster Ave

RAVENSWOOD

W Lawrence Ave

LINCOLN SQUARE

UPTOWN

Waveland Park

W Montrose Ave

Horner Park

W Irving Park Rd

WRIGLEYVILLE

5 ⊙ Wrigley Field

LAKE VIEW

W Addison St

W Belmont Ave

Lake Michigan

4

W Fullerton Ave

LOGAN SQUARE

LINCOLN PARK

Hanson Park

BUCKTOWN

9

Lincoln Park ⊙

W North Ave

WICKER PARK

OLD TOWN

OAK PARK

HUMBOLDT PARK

8

Goose Island

W Grand Ave

3 ⊙ 360° Chicago

W Chicago Ave

🏛 Museum of Contemporary Art

UKRAINIAN VILLAGE

NEAR NORTH

2 ⊙ Navy Pier

W Grand Ave

Lake St

WEST LOOP

THE LOOP

⊙ Millennium Park

Columbus Park

W Madison St

GREEKTOWN

🏛 **1**

Eisenhower Expwy

Willis Tower

Art Institute of Chicago

W Roosevelt Rd

LITTLE ITALY

Douglas Park

10

Field Museum of Natural History 🏛

MUSEUM CAMPUS

W Cermak Rd

PILSEN

CICERO

W Cermak Rd

CHINATOWN

11

S Archer Ave

W 31st St

BRONZEVILLE

McKinley Park

W 35th St

BRIDGEPORT

12

Sanitary Drainage and Ship Canal

W Pershing Rd

Adlai Stevenson Expwy

S Archer Ave

W 47th St

KENWOOD

W 55th St

Sherman Park

W Garfield Blvd

Washington Park

HYDE PARK

E 55th St

W 59th St

Robie House ⊙

🏛 Museum of Science & Industry

0 5 km
0 2.5 miles

❶ The Loop p44

Chicago's cente, named for the elevated train tracks that encircle its busy streets. The Art Institute, Willis Tower, the Theater District and Millennium Park are the top draws.

❷ Near North & Navy Pier p67

The Near North packs in pizza parlors, bistros, art galleries and so many upscale stores that Michigan Ave has been dubbed the 'Magnificent Mile.' Bulging to the east is Navy Pier, a half-mile-long wharf of boats, carnival rides and a flashy Ferris wheel.

❸ Gold Coast p81

Home to the wealthiest Chicagoans for over a century. Sights-wise, the 360° Chicago observatory and Museum of Contemporary Art are the top attention-grabbers.

❹ Lincoln Park & Old Town p95

Lincoln Park is the city's premier playground, filled with lagoons, walking paths, beaches and zoo animals. To the south, Old Town hangs on to its free-spirited, bohemian past with artsy bars and improv-comedy.

❺ Lake View & Wrigleyville p109

Lake View is known for its nonstop lineup of bars, theaters, rock halls and global eateries. Wrigleyville is the pocket that surrounds star attraction, Wrigley Field, where cocktail bars, fancy doughnut shops and trendy eateries have joined the game.

❻ Andersonville & Uptown p124

Andersonville's Swedish past remain, but today the area is more about foodie taverns, boutiques and gay and lesbian bars. To the south, the historic entertainment enclave of Uptown offers vintage jazz houses along with the thriving eateries of 'Little Saigon', and a picturesque cemetery.

❼ Lincoln Square & Ravenswood p136

Lincoln Square has blossomed into a stylish eating, drinking and shopping destination. As trendy places emerge they mix in with the neighborhood's traditional beer-and-bratwurst bars. Next-door Ravenswood is mostly residential, except for an industrial corridor of bygone factories that have morphed into modern breweries known as Malt Row.

❽ Wicker Park, Bucktown & Ukrainian Village p146

These three neighborhoods in the larger area of West Town are trendy hot property. Wicker Park is the more commercial heart; it's flanked by Bucktown (a bit posher), Ukrainian Village and East Village (a bit shabbier), and smaller Noble Square.

❾ Logan Square & Humboldt Park p163

Logan Square is the city's hipster haven, the place to go for the buzziest tiki lounge or all-the-rage fried-chicken cafe. Puerto Rican stronghold Humboldt Park is the place to sample a *jibarito*, the local sandwich specialty, and to seek out retro coffeehouses.

❿ West Loop & Near West Side p174

The neighborhood is edgy and flashy and has the largest percentage of millennial residents of any community in the USA. Eating and drinking here is an essential. Greektown and Little Italy serve their respective fare nearby and are also fun for a night out.

⓫ Pilsen & Near South Side p189

The Field Museum, Shedd Aquarium and Adler Planetarium cluster at lakefront Museum Campus. Peaceful 12th Street Beach and hilly Northerly Island offer refuges to ditch the crowds and Chinatown bustles with noodle shops and exotic wares. West is Pilsen, where Mexican culture mixes with Chicago's bohemian underground.

⓬ Hyde Park & South Side p202

Brainy Hyde Park holds bookstores galore and sights like Frank Lloyd Wright's Robie House and the Museum of Science & Industry. Irish enclave Bridgeport has with bars and galleries, while Bronzeville has jazzy architecture and important (if often overlooked) shrines to African American history.

The Loop

Neighborhood Top Five

❶ Millennium Park (p46) Exploring the freebies of this art-dotted park all day long, from morning yoga classes to afternoon splashes in *Crown Fountain* and evening concerts at Frank Gehry's swooping silver bandshell.

❷ Art Institute of Chicago (p49) Admiring color-swirled Monets, Renoirs and one very large Seurat, plus unexpected delights such as the miniature rooms and glass paperweight collection.

❸ Chicago Architecture Center (p52) Gaping at the sky-high ingenuity on display through an architecture tour by boat or on foot.

❹ Willis Tower (p51) Stepping onto the glass-floored ledge and peering a *loonnngggg* way down.

❺ Chicago Cultural Center (p52) Popping in to see free art exhibitions, concerts and the world's largest Tiffany glass dome.

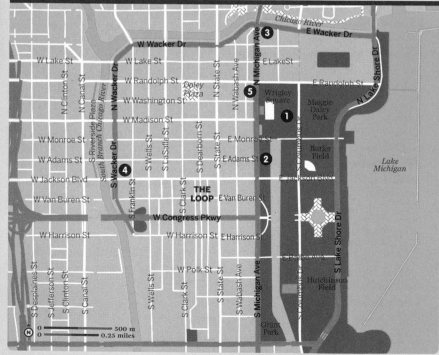

For more detail of this area see Map p298 and p302 ➡

Explore The Loop

The Loop is Chicago's financial and historic heart and it pulses with energy. Tumultuous tides of pinstriped businessfolk rush the sidewalks, while rackety L trains roar overhead. Above the melee, a towering forest of steel and stone soaks in the sun (or snow, as the case may be).

But it's not all work, work, work here. The Loop also contains Chicago's favorite playground: Grant Park, which unfurls as a sprawling green buffer between the skyscrapers and Lake Michigan. Millennium Park is Grant's crown jewel, sparkling in the northwest corner. Both host celebrations galore, especially in summer, when everything from Blues Fest and Lollapalooza to the Grant Park Orchestra make music for the masses.

Most of Chicago's big-ticket attractions are here, such as the Art Institute, the neon-lit Theater District and the city's world-famous architecture and public art, so count on devoting some significant time to the neighborhood. Take in the parks, art and cloud-scraping towers by day, then see a theatrical production or free Millennium Park concert at night. Despite the evening entertainment on offer, the Loop clears out by 9pm or so.

Local Life

→ **Amish doughnuts** Office workers throng the farmers market at Daley Plaza (p52) every Thursday. Keep an eye out for the Amish women who tempt passersby with free doughnuts.

→ **German fests** It's tradition to pay a visit to the Berghoff (p60) in December, when it's festooned with old-world Christmas decorations, and during Berghoff's Oktoberfest, which takes over the plaza at Adams and Dearborn Sts in mid-September.

→ **Global dance party** Learn to salsa, rumba or tango with Chicagoans from all over the city at SummerDance (p64).

Getting There & Away

→ **The L** All lines converge in the Loop. Clark/Lake is a useful transfer station between them. Washington/Wabash is handy for the parks, Quincy station for Willis Tower.

→ **Metra** Trains going south to Hyde Park and on into Indiana depart from Millennium Station (p275); most other regional trains depart from Ogilvie (p275) or Union (p273) Station.

→ **Car** City meters cost $6.50 per hour. Parking lots cost around $40 per day; Millennium Park Garage is one of the cheapest. Try SpotHero (www.spothero.com) to reserve a spot in advance.

Lonely Planet's Top Tip

Gather the makings of a picnic meal and meander over to Millennium Park to hear a free concert. Indie rock, jazz or classical performers take the stage nightly in summer, including many big-name musicians. Pastoral (p58) and Toni Patisserie (p61) can set you up with deli goods and wine.

✗ Best Places to Eat

→ Gage (p60)
→ Mercat a la Planxa (p60)
→ Cafecito (p58)
→ Revival Food Hall (p58)
→ Pizano's (p60)
→ Oasis (p58)

For reviews, see p58.➡

🍷 Best Places to Drink

→ Berghoff (p60)
→ Monk's Pub (p60)
→ Cindy's (p60)
→ Toni Patisserie & Cafe (p61)

For reviews, see p60.➡

🔒 Best Places to Shop

→ Chicago Architecture Center Shop (p65)
→ ShopColumbia (p65)
→ Optimo Hats (p66)
→ Dial Bookshop (p66)

For reviews, see p65.➡

◉ TOP SIGHT
MILLENNIUM PARK

Chicago's showpiece shines with whimsical public art. Where to start amid the mod designs? Perhaps Pritzker Pavilion, Frank Gehry's swooping silver band shell. Jaume Plensa's *Crown Fountain*, with its human gargoyles. Anish Kapoor's silvery sculpture *Cloud Gate* (aka 'the Bean'). Or maybe someplace away from the crowds, like the veiled Lurie Garden, abloom with prairie flowers.

The Magic Bean

The park's biggest draw is 'the Bean' – officially titled *Cloud Gate* – Anish Kapoor's 110-ton, silver-drop **sculpture** (Map p298). It reflects both the sky and the skyline, and everyone clamors around to take a picture and to touch its silvery smoothness. Good vantage points for photos are at the sculpture's northern and southern ends. For great people-watching, go up the stairs on Washington St, on the Park Grill's northern side, where there are shaded benches.

The Bean wasn't always so well loved. Kapoor was still polishing and grinding the 168 stainless-steel plates that comprise the sculpture when the city first showed it to the public in 2004. The surface was supposed to be seamless – and it is now. But it wasn't then, and soon after its debut it went back under wraps. It didn't re-emerge until 2006.

Crown Fountain

Jaume Plensa's **Crown Fountain** (Map p298) is another crowd-pleaser. Its two 50ft-high glass-block towers contain video displays that flash a thousand different faces. The people shown are all native Chicagoans and they all agreed to strap into Plensa's special dental chair, where he immobilized their heads for filming. Each mug puckers up and spurts

DON'T MISS
→ Skyline photo with the Bean
→ Getting wet in *Crown Fountain*
→ Concert and picnic at Pritzker Pavilion
→ Lurie Garden tour
→ Winter ice-skating

PRACTICALITIES
→ Map p298, G4
→ ☏312-742-1168
→ www.millenniumpark.org
→ 201 E Randolph St
→ ⊘6am-11pm
→ 🚻
→ ⓜBrown, Orange, Green, Purple, Pink Line to Washington/Wabash

water, just like the gargoyles atop Notre Dame Cathedral. A fresh set of nonpuckering faces appears in winter, when the fountain is dry.

On hot days the fountain crowds with locals splashing in the streams to cool off. Kids especially love it. Bring a towel to dry off.

Pritzker Pavilion

Millennium Park's acoustically awesome band shell, **Pritzker Pavilion** (Map p298) was designed by architect Frank Gehry, who gave it his trademark swooping silver exterior. Supposedly it's inspired by gefilte fish, a classic Jewish dish that as a child Gehry watched his grandma make every week; he was struck by the fish's shape and movement before she hacked it to death. The pipes that crisscross over the lawn are threaded with speakers, so that's where the sound comes from.

The pavilion hosts free concerts at 6:30pm several nights weekly from June to August, ranging from indie rock and world music to jazz and classical. On Tuesday there's usually a movie beamed onto the huge screen on stage. Seats are available up close in the pavilion, or you can sit on the grassy Great Lawn that unfurls behind.

For all shows – but especially the classical ones, which the top-notch Grant Park Orchestra performs – folks bring blankets, picnics, wine and beer. There is nothing quite like sitting on the lawn, looking up through Gehry's wild grid and seeing the grandeur of the skyscrapers forming the backdrop to the soaring music. If you want a seat up close, arrive early. Find more information at www.grantparkmusic festival.com.

The pavilion also hosts daytime action. Concert rehearsals take place Tuesday to Friday, usually from 11am to 1pm, offering a taste of music if you can't catch the evening show. Tuesday, Thursday and Saturday mornings (from 7am) see free exercise classes turn the Great Lawn into a groovy fitness center. Instructors backed by live music-makers lead classes in Pilates, yoga, strength training and Zumba dance.

Lurie Garden

If the crowds at the Bean, *Crown Fountain* and Pritzker Pavilion are too much, seek out the peaceful **Lurie Garden** (Map p298; www.luriegarden.org; ⊙6am-11pm; Ⓜ Brown, Orange, Green, Purple, Pink Line to Randolph), which uses native plants to form a botanical tribute to Illinois' tallgrass prairie. Visitors often miss the area as it's hidden behind a big hedge. Yellow coneflowers, poet's daffodils, bluebells and other gorgeous blooms carpet the 5-acre oasis;

TOURS

Volunteers provide free walking tours of the park at 11:30am and 1pm daily from late May to mid-October. Departure is from the Chicago Cultural Center's Randolph St lobby, across the road at 77 E Randolph St. Space is limited to 10 people on a first-come, first-served basis.

The **Harris Theater for Music and Dance** (Map p298; ☑312-334-7777; www.harristheaterchicago. org; 205 E Randolph St) anchors the park's northern side on Randolph St. More than 35 cutting-edge troupes, from the Chicago Opera Theater to Hubbard Street Dance Chicago, call it home. This is ground zero for the city's dance scene.

FAMILY FUN

The Family Fun Tent in the park's northwest corner offers free arts, crafts and games for kids between 10am and 2pm daily in summer.

Concessions, bathrooms and a gift shop are available at McCormick Tribune Plaza (by the outdoor cafe/ice rink) on Michigan Ave.

everything is raised sustainably and without chemicals. A little river runs through it, where folks kick off their shoes and dangle their feet.

From mid-May to mid-September, volunteers lead free **tours** through the garden on Thursday and Friday between 11am and 1:15pm, and on Sunday between 11am and 2:15pm. They last around 20 minutes and depart every 15 to 20 minutes. No reservations are required; just show up at the southern end of the boardwalk. Staff also offer free workshops on topics such as how to make lip balm using herbs from the garden. These require advance registration; sign up on the website. The garden is at the park's southeastern end.

BP Bridge & Nichols Bridgeway

In addition to Pritzker Pavilion, architect Frank Gehry also designed the snaking **BP Bridge** (Map p298) that spans Columbus Dr. The luminous sheet-metal walkway connects Millennium Park (from the back of the Great Lawn) to the new Maggie Daley Park (p52), which has ice-skating and rock climbing among its activity arsenal. The bridge offers great skyline views too.

The **Nichols Bridgeway** (Map p298) is another pedestrian-only span. Renzo Piano designed this silver beauty. It arches from the park over Monroe St to the Art Institute's 3rd-floor contemporary sculpture terrace (which is free to view). Piano, incidentally, also designed the museum's Modern Wing, which is where the sculpture terrace is located.

Cycling & Ice-Skating

The McDonald's Cycle Center, in the park's northeastern corner near the intersection of Randolph St and Columbus Dr, is the city's main facility for bike commuters, with 300 bike-storage spaces plus showers. It's also a convenient place to pick up rental bikes from Bike & Roll (p66), including road, hybrid, tandem and children's bikes.

Tucked between the Bean sculpture and the twinkling lights of Michigan Ave, the McCormick Tribune Ice Rink (p66) fills with skaters in winter. It operates from late November to late February and it is hands down the city's most scenic rink. Admission is free; skate rental costs $13 to $15 (more on weekends). Free lessons start an hour before the rink opens. In summer the rink morphs into the alfresco cafe of the Park Grill (p62).

Wrigley Square & Boeing Galleries

The big plaza at the corner of Michigan Ave and Randolph St is Wrigley Square. The Greek-looking structure rising up from it is the Millennium Monument, a replica of the original peristyle that stood here between 1917 and 1953. The semi-circular row of Doric columns shoots up nearly 40ft. It juxtaposes oddly with the modern art throughout the rest of the park, but it's meant to tie past and present together. The lawn in front is dandy for lazing about.

The two Boeing Galleries flank the park on the northern and southern sides. The outdoor spaces display changing exhibits of contemporary sculpture and photo-murals.

Park History

Millennium Park was originally slated to open in 2000 to coincide with the millennium (hence the name), but construction delays and escalating costs pushed it back. The whole thing seemed headed for disaster, since the original budget was $150 million but costs were rising far in excess of that. The final bill came to $475 million. Private donors – families such as the Pritzkers and Crowns, and corporate donors such as Boeing – ended up paying $200 million to complete the project.

TOP SIGHT
ART INSTITUTE OF CHICAGO

The USA's second-largest art museum, the Art Institute houses a treasure trove from around the globe. The collection of impressionist and postimpressionist paintings is second only to those in France, and the number of surrealist works is tremendous. The Modern Wing dazzles with Picassos and Mirós, while Japanese prints, Grecian urns and suits of armor stuff endless rooms beyond.

Must-See Works: Floor 2

This floor is where the majority of the museum's celebrated highlights hang.

Get close enough to Georges Seurat's *A Sunday Afternoon on the Island of La Grande Jatte* (Gallery 240) for the painting to break down into its component dots and you'll see why it took the artist two long years to complete his pointillist masterpiece. It sometimes resides in Gallery 201.

The Bedroom (Gallery 241) by Vincent van Gogh depicts the sleeping quarters of the artist's house in Arles. It's the second of three versions of the painting, executed during Van Gogh's 1889 stay at an asylum.

Claude Monet's *Stacks of Wheat* (Gallery 243) – paintings of the 15ft-tall stacks by the artist's farmhouse in Giverny – were part of a series that effectively launched his career when they sold like hotcakes at a show he organized in 1891.

Nighthawks (Gallery 262), Edward Hopper's lonely, poignant snapshot of four solitary souls at a neon-lit diner, was inspired by a Greenwich Ave restaurant in Manhattan.

Grant Wood, a lifelong resident of Iowa, used his sister and his dentist as models for the two stern-faced farmers in his iconic painting *American Gothic* (Gallery 263).

DON'T MISS

→ *American Gothic*
→ *Nighthawks*
→ *A Sunday Afternoon on the Island of La Grande Jatte*
→ *The Bedroom*
→ Lions guarding the entrance

PRACTICALITIES

→ Map p298, F5
→ ☎312-443-3600
→ www.artic.edu
→ 111 S Michigan Ave
→ adult/child $25/free
→ ⏲10:30am-5pm Fri-Wed, to 8pm Thu
→ ♿
→ Ⓜ Brown, Orange, Green, Purple, Pink Line to Adams

LION SCULPTURES

·······························

The beloved lions guarding the entrance may seem identical at first glance, but they actually have different stances, expressions and measurements. Their creator, Edward Kemeys, described the south lion as closely watching something in the distance, while the north lion has his back up and is ready to spring. They remain regal and dignified, even when the museum plops fiberglass Blackhawks helmets on their heads when the team is in the Stanley Cup (or Cubs caps when the team is in the World Series etc).

·······························

The museum puts on a full array of children's programming. Stop by the Ryan Learning Center (on Level 1 in the Modern Wing) to see what hands-on activities are on offer.

Must-See Works: Floors 1 & 3

The *America Windows* (Gallery 144) – huge, blue stained-glass pieces – were created by Marc Chagall to celebrate the USA's bicentennial.

The elongated figure of *The Old Guitarist* (Gallery 391) by Pablo Picasso is from the artist's Blue Period, reflecting not only Picasso's color scheme but also his experience as a poor, lonely artist in Paris in the early years.

Salvador Dalí's *Inventions of the Monsters* (Gallery 396) was painted in Austria immediately before the Nazi annexation. The title refers to a Nostradamus prediction that the apparition of monsters presages the outbreak of war. The artist's profile is visible in the lower left corner, along with that of his wife, Gala.

Other Intriguing Galleries

The Thorne Miniature Rooms (Lower Level, Gallery 11) and Paperweight Collection (Lower Level, Gallery 15) are awesome, overlooked galleries. In the light-drenched Modern Wing, the ongoing exhibition 'The New Contemporary' (Galleries 288 and 290–99) bursts with iconic works by Andy Warhol, Roy Lichtenstein and Jasper Johns.

Outdoor Freebies

You can see a fair bit of art without even entering the museum. The north garden (enter from Michigan Ave; closed in winter) has Alexander Calder's *Flying Dragon*, a little buddy to his Flamingo (p55) in the Loop. The Stock Exchange Arch, a revered architectural relic, rises up on the museum's northeast side. The 3rd-floor contemporary sculpture terrace provides cool city views and connects to Millennium Park via the modern, pedestrian-only Nichols Bridgeway.

Top Tips

➡ Allow two hours to browse the museum's highlights; art buffs should allocate much longer.

➡ Advance tickets are available online (surcharge $2), but unless there's a blockbuster exhibit on they're usually not necessary. The entrance queue moves fast.

➡ Ask at the information desk about free talks and tours once you're inside.

➡ Download the museum's free app, either at home or using the on-site wi-fi. It offers several audio tours through the collection. Highlights, architecture and pop art are among the themes.

➡ The museum's main entrance is on Michigan Ave, but you can also enter via the Modern Wing on Monroe St.

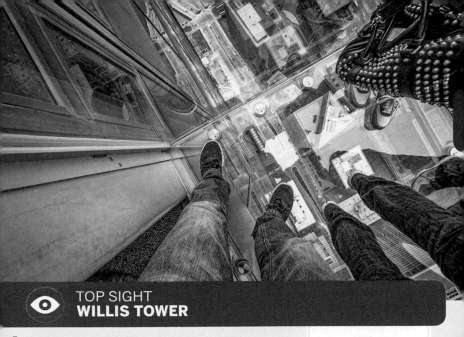

TOP SIGHT
WILLIS TOWER

For superlative-seekers, Willis Tower is it: Chicago's tallest skyscraper, rising 1450ft into the heavens. Built in 1973 as the Sears Tower, the black-tubed behemoth reigned as the world's tallest building for almost 25 years. It still wins the prize for views from its 103rd-floor Skydeck, where glass-floored ledges jut out in midair and give a knee-buckling perspective straight down.

Before ascending, there are factoid-filled murals to ponder and an informational movie to watch. You'll learn about the 43,000 miles of phone cable used, the 2232 steps to the roof, and how the tower height is the equivalent of 313 Oprahs (or 262 Michael Jordans). Then it's time for the ear-popping, 70-second elevator ride to the top. From here, the entire city stretches below and you can see exactly how Chicago is laid out. On good days you can see for 40 to 50 miles, as far as Indiana, Michigan and Wisconsin. (On hazy or stormy days you won't see much at all, so don't bother.)

The four ledges are on the deck's western side. They're like glass-encased boxes hanging out from the building's frame. If crowds are light, you can sprawl out on one for the ultimate photo op. If the ledges crack – which they did in 2014 when some folks stepped on them – fear not: that's not the glass cracking, but the protective coating covering the 1.5-inch-thick glass. You won't fall. Really. So don't even worry about it.

A new company recently bought the Willis Tower and announced plans to expand the Skydeck's features, though these have still yet to be solidified. Keep an eye on the sky here for more on the unnerving possibilities to come.

Avoid peak times in summer, between 11am and 4pm Friday to Sunday, when queues can surpass an hour.

DON'T MISS

➡ The ledges
➡ Sunset views
➡ Skyscraper trivia during the elevator ride
➡ Feeling the tower sway

PRACTICALITIES

➡ Map p298, C5
➡ ☎312-875-9696
➡ www.theskydeck.com
➡ 233 S Wacker Dr
➡ adult/child $24/16
➡ ⏰9am-10pm Mar-Sep, 10am-8pm Oct-Feb, last entry 30 min prior
➡ Ⓜ Brown, Orange, Purple, Pink Line to Quincy

⊙ SIGHTS

MILLENNIUM PARK PARK
See p46.

ART INSTITUTE OF CHICAGO MUSEUM
See p49.

WILLIS TOWER TOWER
See p51.

**CHICAGO
ARCHITECTURE CENTER** GALLERY
Map p298 (CAC; ☑312-922-3432; www.
architecture.org; 111 E Wacker Dr; adult/student/
child $12/8/free; ☺9:30am-5pm; ☐151, ⓂBrown,
Orange, Green, Purple, Pink Line to Clark/Lake) The
CAC is the premier keeper of Chicago's architectural flame. Pop in to explore its excellent
galleries, which feature an interactive 3-D
model of Chicago and displays on the city's
architectural history, as well as giant models
of and exhibits on skyscrapers around the
world and the amazing technologies needed
to build them, from construction to security
to sustainability. You can also check out the
CAC's extensive roster of boat and walking
tours (p66) and make bookings here. The
foundation's shop (p65) sells stacks of books
about local buildings and architects, as well
as architecture- and design-themed apparel
and gifts. Formerly known as the Chicago
Architecture Foundation, the organization
rebranded when it moved from Michigan
Ave to its new digs on Wacker Dr.

**CHICAGO
CULTURAL CENTER** NOTABLE BUILDING
Map p298 (☑312-744-6630; www.chicago
culturalcenter.org; 78 E Washington St; ☺10am-
7pm Mon-Fri, to 5pm Sat & Sun; ⓂBrown, Orange,
Green, Purple, Pink Line to Washington/Wabash)
FREE This exquisite, beaux-arts building
began its life as the Chicago Public Library
in 1897. Today the block-long structure
houses terrific art exhibitions (especially
the 4th-floor Yates Gallery), as well as classical concerts at lunchtime every Wednesday
(12:15pm). It also contains the world's largest Tiffany stained-glass dome, on the 3rd
floor where the library circulation desk used
to be. InstaGreeter (p276) tours of the Loop
depart from the Randolph St lobby, as do
Millennium Park tours. And it's all free!

Oh, and there's more. Free foreign films
screen on Wednesday at 6:30pm from June
through September. StoryCorps' recording
studio (where folks tell their their tale, get a CD
of it and have it preserved in the Library of
Congress) operates on Thursday (noon to
6pm) and Saturday (10am to 4pm). Check
the daily schedule online or posted at the
entrances (at both Randolph and Washington Sts) to see what else is going on.

The Gilded Age interior mixes white Carrara and green Connemara marble throughout. The building's splendor was meant to
inspire the rabble toward loftier goals. You
can explore on your own, or take a free
building tour (1:15pm Wednesday through
Saturday), which departs from the Randolph St lobby. There's also free wi-fi and
seating areas throughout the building.

DALEY PLAZA PLAZA
Map p298 (50 W Washington St; ⓂBlue Line to
Washington) Picasso's eye-popping untitled
sculpture (p55) marks the heart of Daley
Plaza, which is the place to be come lunchtime, particularly when the weather warms
up. You never know what will be going on
– dance performances, bands, ethnic festivals, holiday celebrations – but you do know
it'll be free. A summertime farmers market
sets up on Thursday (7am to 3pm, May to
October) and food trucks add to the action
once a week (11am to 3pm, often on Friday)
from March through October.

AQUA TOWER ARCHITECTURE
Map p298 (225 N Columbus Dr; ⓂBrown, Orange,
Green, Purple, Pink Line to State/Lake) Aqua
made waves when it appeared in 2009.
Local architect Jeanne Gang designed the
86-story tower (set to be surpassed in 2020,
when her 93-story Vista Tower will open
nearby). Dramatic undulating balconies
curve out from the core, interspersed with
reflective glass that forms 'pools' shimmering from the white rippled tiers. The Radisson Blu Aqua Hotel takes up floors 1 to 18;
the remaining floors hold multi-million-
dollar apartments and offices.

MAGGIE DALEY PARK PARK
Map p298 (www.maggiedaleypark.com; 337 E
Randolph St; ☺6am-11pm; ⊞; ⓂBrown, Orange,
Green, Purple, Pink Line to Washington/Wabash)
Families love this park's fanciful, free playgrounds in all their enchanted-forest and
pirate-themed glory. There's also a rock-
climbing wall, an 18-hole mini-golf course,
a winding, in-line skating track called the
Skating Ribbon (used for ice-skating in winter) and tennis courts; these features have
various fees. Multiple picnic tables make the

FAMOUS LOOP ARCHITECTURE
••

Ever since Chicago presented the world with the first skyscraper in 1885, its motto has been 'think big' – over the decades its architecture has pushed the envelope of modern design. Be careful not to strain your neck from all the craning.

Monadnock Building (Map p298; www.monadnockbuilding.com; 53 W Jackson Blvd; M Blue Line to Jackson) Architecture buffs go gaga at the Monadnock, two buildings in one that delineate a critical turning point in skyscraper-development history. The older north half dates to 1891 and has a traditional design with thick brick walls and a plain façade, while the steel frame of the newer, more modern south half allows for fancier walls and larger windows.

Rookery (Map p298; ☎312-994-4000; www.flwright.org; 209 S LaSalle St; ⏰9am-5pm Mon-Fri; M Brown, Orange, Purple, Pink Line to Quincy) The 1888 Rookery looks hulking and fortress-like outside, but it's light and airy inside thanks to Frank Lloyd Wright's atrium overhaul. Step inside and have a look. Tours ($10 to $15) are available at 11am, noon and 1pm on weekdays. It's named for the flocks of pigeons that once roosted here.

Marshall Field Building (Map p298; 111 N State St; ⏰10am-9pm Mon-Thu, 9am-10pm Fri & Sat, 11am-7pm Sun; M Brown, Orange, Green, Purple, Pink Line to Washington/Wabash) Die-hard locals may weep over the old Marshall Field's becoming Macy's, but the building remains a classic. Busy Loop workers have told the time by its iconic bronze corner clocks for more than a century. Inside, the north-side atrium is capped by a 6000-sq-ft dome; Louis Comfort Tiffany designed it, and 50 artists toiled for 18 months to make it.

Sullivan Center (Map p298; 1 S State St; M Red Line to Monroe) Designed by Louis Sullivan in 1899, this ornate building long housed the Carson Pirie Scott & Co department store. The metalwork around the main entrance (at State and Madison Sts) is superb. Try to find Sullivan's initials amid the flowing botanical and geometric forms. A Target store now occupies the building's main space.

Marquette Building (Map p298; http://marquette.macfound.org; 140 S Dearborn St; ⏰7am-6pm; M Blue Line to Monroe) Sculptured panels and mosaics inside the Marquette Building recall the exploits of French explorer Jacques Marquette; you'll find them above the entrance and in the lobby. The whole building is characterized by its natural light and ventilation.

Reliance Building (Map p298; 1 W Washington St; M Blue Line to Washington) A breath of fresh air, the Reliance Building's 16 stories of shimmering glass are framed by brilliant white terra-cotta details. A lightweight internal metal frame supports the building; this innovative style didn't become universal until after WWII. Today it houses a chic hotel. What's now Room 809 was once the office of Al Capone's dentist.

Santa Fe Building (Map p298; 224 S Michigan Ave; M Brown, Orange, Green, Purple, Pink Line to Adams) Architect Daniel Burnham kept his offices in this 1904 terra-cotta beauty, and placed a vast light well in the center of its lobby (a feature he also gave to the Rookery).

Kluczynski Federal Building (Map p298; 230 S Dearborn St; M Blue Line to Jackson) Last, but certainly not least: no tour of Loop architecture is complete without a gander at Ludwig Mies van der Rohe's 1974 Kluczynski Building, part of the Chicago Federal Center. It's a prime example of his mod, boxy, metal-and-glass style. He designed many more buildings at the Illinois Institute of Technology on the South Side.

park an excellent spot to relax. It connects to Millennium Park via the pedestrian BP Bridge (p48).

BUCKINGHAM FOUNTAIN   FOUNTAIN
Map p298 (301 S Columbus Dr; M Red Line to Harrison) Grant Park's centerpiece is one of the world's largest fountains, with a 1.5-million-gallon capacity and a 15-story-high spray.

It lets loose on the hour from 9am to 11pm early May to mid-October, accompanied at night by multicolored lights and music.

MONEY MUSEUM   MUSEUM
Map p298 (☎312-322-2400; www.chicagofed. org; 230 S LaSalle St; ⏰8:30am-5pm Mon-Fri; M Brown, Orange, Purple, Pink Line to Quincy) **FREE** This small museum in the Federal

Reserve Bank of Chicago is fun for a quick browse. The best exhibits include a giant glass cube stuffed with one million $1 bills (they weigh 2000lb) and a counterfeit display differentiating real bills from fakes. Learn why we call $1000 a 'grand'; learn more about Alexander Hamilton and his creation of a new nation's financial infrastructure; and snap a sweet photo clutching the million-dollar-stuffed briefcase.

ROUTE 66 SIGN HISTORIC SITE

Map p298 (E Adams St, btwn S Michigan & Wabash Aves; M Brown, Orange, Green, Purple, Pink Line to Adams) Attention Route 66 buffs: the Mother Road begins in downtown Chicago. Look for the 'Historic 66 Begin' sign at the northwestern corner of Adams St and Michigan Ave, across from the Art Institute. (There's another sign at the end of the block, but this one is a replica of the original.) From Chicago the route traverses 2400 miles to Los Angeles, past neon signs, mom-and-pop motels and pie-and-coffee diners...but it all starts here.

MUSEUM OF CONTEMPORARY PHOTOGRAPHY MUSEUM

Map p302 (☑312-663-5554; www.mocp.org; 600 S Michigan Ave, Columbia College; ☺10am-5pm Mon-Wed, Fri & Sat, to 8pm Thu, noon-5pm Sun; M Red Line to Harrison) FREE This small museum focuses on American and international photography from the early 20th century onward, and is the only institution of its kind between the coasts. The permanent collection includes the works of Henri Cartier-Bresson, Harry Callahan, Sally Mann, Victor Skrebneski, Catherine Wagner and 500 more of the best photographers working today. Special exhibitions (also free) augment the rotating permanent collection.

AMERICAN WRITERS MUSEUM MUSEUM

Map p298 (www.americanwritersmuseum.org; 180 N Michigan Ave, 2nd fl; adult/child $12/free; ☺10am-5pm; ♣; M Brown, Orange, Green, Purple, Pink Line to Randolph or State/Lake) Bibliophiles will have a grand time in this museum, where American writers spanning the ages – from Edgar Allen Poe to Elie Wiesel, James Baldwin to Edith Wharton – get their due. Interactive exhibits trace the history of the American voice in nonfiction and literature, while rotating displays celebrate individual wordsmiths. Another exhibit provides exercises and tips for your own writing (along with a table of old typewriters). The colorful Children's Literature gallery features story times and books to read.

FINE ARTS BUILDING ARTS CENTER

Map p298 (☑312-566-9800; www.finearts building.com; 410 S Michigan Ave; ☺7am-10pm Mon-Fri, to 9pm Sat, 9am-9pm Sun; M Brown, Orange, Purple, Pink Line to HW Library) This building has been an artists' haven for more than a century. You'll still hear opera voices and trumpet music drift out of the music studios, which sit alongside workshops for violin makers, an old sheet-music store, an excellent bookstore (p66) and even an escape room and an axe-throwing club. Take the vintage elevator – the last one in the city operated manually by an attendant – up to the 10th floor for a quirky exploration on your way back down.

DESIGN MUSEUM OF CHICAGO MUSEUM

Map p298 (☑312-894-6263; https://design chicago.org; 108 N State St, 3rd fl, Block 37; ☺noon-7pm Tue-Sat; M Blue Line to Washington) FREE This small industrial space in the **Block 37** (Map p298; ☑312-261-4700; http://blockthirtyseven.com; ☺10am-8pm Mon-Sat, 11am-6pm Sun) mall puts on nifty free exhibitions about contemporary and historical design. The shows change every four months, so you'll see something new each time you visit. It shuts down when new exhibitions are being installed, so call ahead first.

GRANT PARK PARK

Map p298 (Michigan Ave, btwn E Roosevelt Rd & Randolph St; ☺6am-11pm; M Brown, Orange, Green, Purple, Pink Line to Adams) Grant Park hosts the city's mega-events, such as Taste of Chicago, Blues Fest and Lollapalooza. Buckingham Fountain (p53) is the park's centerpiece. The skateboard park in the southwest corner draws a cool-cat crowd. Other features include a rose garden and loads of baseball diamonds.

RIVERWALK WATERFRONT

Map p298 (www.chicagoriverwalk.us; Chicago River waterfront, btwn N Lake Shore Dr & W Lake St; ☺6am-11pm; M Brown, Orange, Green, Purple, Pink, Blue Line to State/Lake) Winding along the Chicago River's southern side next to Wacker Dr, this 1.25-mile-long promenade is a fine spot to escape the crowds and watch boats glide by. Access it from the stairs at any bridge. Outdoor cafes, umbrella-shaded bars, a kayak-rental shop and a fountain you

THE LOOP'S BEST PUBLIC ART

Several mind-blowing public artworks have been placed in the Loop over the decades.

Picasso's untitled (Map p298; 50 W Washington St; MBlue Line to Washington) The grand-daddy of Chicago's public art, this abstract work is widely known simply as 'the Picasso.' It was commissioned when the artist was 82 and made to his specifications by the US Steel Works in Gary, IN. Picasso refused payment for the work, saying the sculpture was meant as a gift to the city. Little-loved by many locals when it was erected in Daley Plaza in 1967, it's an icon today.

Miró's *Chicago* (Map p298; 69 W Washington St; MBlue Line to Washington) Originally called *The Sun, The Moon and One Star*, Joan Miró's 40ft monument sits across the street from Daley Plaza. The artist hoped the sculpture, made of various metals, cement and tile in 1981, would evoke the 'mystical force of a great earth mother.'

Monument with Standing Beast (Map p298; 100 W Randolph St; MBrown, Orange, Green, Purple, Pink, Blue Line to Clark/Lake) Dubbed by some as 'Snoopy in a Blender,' the 1984 white fiberglass work by French sculptor Jean Dubuffet looks a little like inflated puzzle pieces and has a definite Keith Haring–esque feel to it. It's a hands-on piece of art: feel free to let the kids crawl around inside.

Four Seasons (Map p298; 10 S Dearborn St; MBlue Line to Monroe) This grand mosaic by Russian-born artist Marc Chagall, made up of thousands of bits of glass and stone, portrays six scenes of Chicago in hues reminiscent of the Mediterranean coast of France, where Chagall kept his studio. The artist loved Chicago and donated the work to the city in 1974; he continued to make adjustments, such as updating the skyline, after it arrived here.

Flamingo (Map p298; 50 W Adams St, at S Dearborn Ave; MBlue Line to Jackson) Surrounded by the stark facades of federal buildings, Alexander Calder's soaring red-pink sculpture provides some much-needed visual relief. The dedication of the sculpture in October 1974 saw a circus parade accompany the artist as he rode into the Loop on a bandwagon pulled by 40 horses.

For the locations of more public artworks stashed around the city, check the website www.cityofchicago.org/publicart. And don't forget to visit *Cloud Gate*, aka the Bean (p46), the reigning Loop fave.

---

can splash in dot the way. The broad steps between Clark and LaSalle Sts offer a good refuge to sit and relax.

HAROLD WASHINGTON LIBRARY CENTER
LIBRARY

Map p298 (312-747-4300; www.chipublib.org; 400 S State St; 9am-9pm Mon-Thu, to 5pm Fri & Sat, 1-5pm Sun; MBrown, Orange, Purple, Pink Line to Library) This grand, art-filled building with free internet terminals and wi-fi is Chicago's whopping main library. Major authors give readings, and impressive performances take place in the auditorium (Chance the Rapper often shows up for the OpenMike for teens on Wednesday evenings). The light-drenched, 9th-floor Winter Garden is a sweet spot for reading, writing or just taking a load off; the floor also has good exhibitions in its galleries. The 3rd-floor Maker Lab features 3-D printers and drop-in demonstrations.

UNION STATION
FILM LOCATION

Map p298 (312-655-2385; www.chicagounion station.com; 225 S Canal St; MBlue Line to Clinton) This wonderfully restored 1925 train station looks like it stepped right out of a gangster movie. In fact, it has been used to great effect in exactly this way. Remember director Brian De Palma's classic *The Untouchables,* when Eliot Ness loses his grip on the baby carriage during the shoot-out with Al Capone's henchmen? And the carriage bounces down the stairs in slow motion? Those steps are here.

CHICAGO BOARD OF TRADE
ARCHITECTURE

Map p298 (141 W Jackson Blvd; MBrown, Orange, Purple, Pink Line to LaSalle) The Board of Trade is a 1930 art deco gem. Inside, manic traders swap futures and options – or, at least, they used to. Most trading is done these days by computer, not people yelling on a trading-pit

(Continued on page 58)

The Loop Architecture

When the Great Fire of 1871 burned down the city, it created the blank canvas that allowed Chicago's mighty architecture to flourish. The city presented the world with the first skyscraper soon after, and it has been home to big ideas in modern design ever since. The Loop is ground zero for gawking.

1. **Chicago Board of Trade (p55)**
A 1930's art deco gem.

2. **Pritzker Pavilion (p47)**
The Frank Gehry–designed pavilion in Millennium Park.

3. **Chicago Cultural Center (p52)**
The world's largest Tiffany glass dome in the Preston Bradley Hall.

4. **Staircase, Rookery (p53)**
Completed in 1888 the Rookery was one of the tallest buildings in the world when built.

PRINTER'S ROW ARCHITECTURE

Chicago was a center for the printing trade at the turn of the 20th century, and the rows of buildings on S Dearborn St from W Congress Pkwy south to W Polk St housed the heart of the city's publishing industry. By the 1970s the print shops had been moved to more economical quarters elsewhere, and the buildings had been largely emptied out.

In the late 1970s savvy developers saw the potential in these derelicts, and one of the most successful gentrification projects in Chicago began. The following describes some of the notable buildings in the area as you travel from north to south.

Mergenthaler Lofts (Map p302; 531 S Plymouth Ct; Ⓜ Red Line to Harrison) A snazzy renovation has turned this building, the 1886 headquarters for the legendary Linotype company, into upscale condo apartments.

Pontiac Building (Map p302; 542 S Dearborn St; Ⓜ Red Line to Harrison) This classic 1891 design by Holabird & Roche features the same flowing masonry surfaces as the firm's famed Monadnock Building in the Loop.

Second Franklin Building (Map p302; 720 S Dearborn St; Ⓜ Red Line to Harrison) A 1912 factory, it shows the history of printing on its tiled facade. The sloping roof allows for a huge skylight over the top floor where books were hand-bound – the building existed long before fluorescent lights or high-intensity lamps. The large windows on many of the other buildings in the area served the same purpose.

Dearborn Station (Map p302; 47 W Polk St; Ⓜ Red Line to Harrison) This 1885 building was the Chicago terminal of the Santa Fe Railroad, the main station for trains to and from California. Today it's mostly an office building.

(Continued from page 55)

floor. Outside, crane your neck to see the giant aluminum statue of Ceres, Roman goddess of agriculture, that tops the building. In the small plaza just east are two allegorical statues, *Industry* and *Agriculture,* which adorned the building's 1885 predecessor.

EATING

Most Loop eateries are geared to lunch crowds of office workers. There's not much open after 9pm.

★ REVIVAL FOOD HALL   AMERICAN $

Map p298 (✆773-999-9411; www.revivalfoodhall. com; 125 S Clark St; mains $7-12; ◎7am-7pm Mon-Fri; 🖗; Ⓜ Blue Line to Monroe) The Loop needed a forward-thinking food court, and Revival Food Hall delivered. Come lunchtime, hip office workers pack the blond-wood tables of this ground-floor modern marketplace in the historic National building. The all-local dining concept brings 15 of Chicago's best fast-casual food outlets to the masses, from Antique Taco and Smoque BBQ to Furious Spoon ramen and HotChocolate Bakery. A bar at the front serves beer and cocktails (open to 9pm). There's even a small book and record store curated by the award-winning local indie book publisher Curbside Splendor.

CAFECITO   CUBAN $

Map p302 (✆312-922-2233; www.cafecitochicago. com; 26 E Congress Pkwy; mains $6-13; ◎7am-9pm Mon-Fri, 10am-6pm Sat & Sun; 🖗; Ⓜ Brown, Orange, Purple, Pink Line to Library) Attached to the HI-Chicago (p230) hostel and perfect for the hungry, thrifty traveler, Cafecito serves killer Cuban sandwiches layered with citrus-garlic-marinated roasted pork and ham. Strong coffee and hearty egg sandwiches make a fine breakfast. It's popular enough to have lines out the door at lunchtime.

OASIS   MIDDLE EASTERN $

Map p298 (✆312-443-9534; www.oasiscafe chicago.com; 21 N Wabash Ave; mains $6-10.50; ◎10am-5:30pm Mon-Fri, 11am-4pm Sat; Ⓜ Brown, Orange, Purple, Pink, Green Line to Washington/ Wabash) Walk past diamonds, gold and other bling in a small jewelers mall before striking it rich in this cafe at the back. Creamy hummus, crisp falafel and other Middle Eastern favorites fill plates at bargain prices. Eat in or carry out to nearby Millennium Park.

PASTORAL   DELI $

Map p298 (✆312-658-1250; www.pastoralartisan. com; 53 E Lake St; sandwiches $8-11; ◎10:30am-8pm Mon-Fri, 11am-6pm Sat & Sun; 🖉; Ⓜ Brown, Orange, Green, Purple, Pink Line to Randolph or State/Lake) Pastoral makes a mean sandwich. Fresh-shaved serrano ham, Calabrese salami and other carnivorous fixings meet smoky mozzarella, Gruyère and piquant spreads slathered on crusty baguettes. Vegetarians also have options. There's limited seating; most folks take away for picnics in Millennium Park (call in your order a few hours in advance to avoid a queue). The shop sells bottles of beer and wine too. Pastoral has another branch in the Loop's French Market, plus one in Lakeview.

YOLK   BREAKFAST $
Map p302 (☑312-789-9655; www.eatyolk.com; 1120 S Michigan Ave; mains $10-14; ⊗6am-3pm Mon-Fri, from 7am Sat & Sun; ☝; MᴿRed, Orange, Green Line to Roosevelt) This cheerful diner is worth the long wait – you'll dig into the best traditional breakfast in the South Loop. The five-egg omelets include healthy options (the Iron Man is made from egg whites and comes loaded with veggies and avocado), while sweets lovers have stacks of cinnamon-roll French toast and Nutella crepes to drench in syrup.

VEGGIE GRILL   VEGAN $
Map p298 (☑312-658-1338; www.veggiegrill.com; 204 N Wells St; mains $10-13; ⊗10:30am-8pm Mon-Fri, 11am-6pm Sat; ☑) Vegheads don't have to miss out on the Chicago food experience – this 100%-plant-based fast-casual restaurant rocks the mock meat with a wide-ranging menu of classics like burgers, brats, fried chicken – even mac 'n' 'cheese.' Or opt for lighter fare such as salads, sandwiches and rice bowls. Tastes so much like the real thing even many of the customers can't tell.

ELEVEN CITY DINER   DELI, JEWISH $
Map p302 (☑312-212-1112; www.elevencitydiner. com; 1112 S Wabash Ave; mains $9-16; ⊗8am-9pm Mon-Thu, to 10pm Fri, 8:30am-10pm Sat, 8:30am-9pm Sun; ☑; MᴳGreen, Orange, Red Lines to Roosevelt) Plates groan under massive portions of Jewish-diner meals while subway tiles and giant menu signs evoke the spirit of a classic New York deli. There's all your *bubbe*'s favorites – brisket, smoked fish, Reuben sandwiches, matzo-ball soup, even egg creams and Junior's cheesecake from Brooklyn – plus an all-day breakfast menu, meatless options and a full bar. So go nosh!

DO-RITE DONUTS   BAKERY $
Map p298 (www.doritedonuts.com; 50 W Randolph St; doughnuts $2-4; ⊗6:30am-2pm Mon-Fri, from 7am Sat & Sun; MBlue Line to Washington) At Do-Rite's shoebox-size shop, office workers clamor for peanut-butter banana, coffee cream and chocolate-ganache-dripping Boston cream doughnuts to jump-start their day. They're typically served warm (small fryers mean frequent, hot-off-the press batches). Several vegan and gluten-free options are always available.

NATIVE FOODS CAFE   VEGAN $
Map p298 (☑312-332-6332; www.nativefoods. com; 218 S Clark St; mains $9-12; ⊗10:30am-9pm Mon-Sat, 11am-7pm Sun; ☑; MᴮBrown, Orange, Purple, Pink Line to Quincy) For tasty, vegan fast-casual fare, Native Foods is your spot. The big ol' BBQ burger features seitan bacon and melted mock American cheese on a plant-based patty; try it with the signature nacho fries. Local beers and organic wines accompany the wide-ranging, internationally inspired menu, which features changing seasonal dishes. Soy-free, gluten-free and nut-free allergy menus are available.

EPIC BURGER   BURGERS $
Map p302 (☑312-913-1373; www.epicburger.com; 517 S State St; mains $4-8; ⊗10:30am-10pm Mon-Thu, to 11pm Fri & Sat, to 9pm Sun; ☑; MᴮBrown, Orange, Purple, Pink Line to Library) ✔ This sprawling, sunny-orange restaurant beloved by South Loop college students brings eco-conscious fast-food eaters the goods they crave: burgers made with all-natural beef, no hormones or antibiotics, topped with cage-free organic eggs and nitrate-free bacon; preservative-free buns; vanilla-bean-speckled milkshakes; and no petroleum-based packaging. Some vegan options, too. No cash accepted – credit cards only.

FRENCH MARKET   FOOD HALL $
Map p298 (www.frenchmarketchicago.com; 131 N Clinton St; mains $6-13; ⊗7am-7:30pm Mon-Fri, 8:30am-5:30pm Sat; ☎; MᴳGreen, Pink Line to Clinton) Located in the Ogilvie train station just west of the Loop, this sprawling Euro-style food hall has stalls offering Belgian fries, Montreal-style smoked-meat sandwiches, Peruvian-style ceviches, lobster rolls, Hawaiian poke bowls, vegan soul food, pastries and organic produce. Tables at back make it great for a quick meal, even if the French accordion music is a bit much.

PIZANO'S   PIZZA $$
Map p298 (☑312-236-1777; www.pizanos chicago.com; 61 E Madison St; small pizzas from $16; ⊗11am-2am Sun-Fri, to 3am Sat; ☎; MᴿRed, Blue Line to Monroe) Pizano's is a good

recommendation for deep-dish newbies, since it's not jaw-breakingly thick. The thin-crust pies that hit the checker-clothed tables are good too, winning rave reviews for crispness. Some of the wait staff are characters who've been around forever, which adds to the convivial ambience. It's open late-night (with a full bar), which is a Loop rarity.

LOU MALNATI'S
PIZZA $$

Map p302 (☑312-786-1000; www.loumalnatis. com; 805 S State St; small pizzas from $13; ☉11am-11pm Sun-Thu, to midnight Fri & Sat; ⓂRed Line to Harrison) One of the city's premier deep-dish pizza makers, Lou Malnati's claims to have invented the gooey behemoth (though that's a matter of never-ending dispute). Not in dispute: the deliciousness of Malnati's famed butter crust. Gluten-free diners can opt for either a wheat-free thin crust or the 'sausage crust' (it's literally just meat, no dough). The restaurant has outlets citywide.

★MERCAT A LA PLANXA
SPANISH $$$

Map p302 (☑312-765-0524; www.mercatchicago. com; 638 S Michigan Ave; tapas $10-18, tasting menus from $65; ☉dinner 5-10pm Sun-Thu, to 11pm Fri & Sat, brunch 7am-3pm Sat & Sun; ⓂRed Line to Harrison) This Barcelona-style tapas and seafood restaurant buzzes in an enormous, convivial room where light streams in through the floor-to-ceiling windows. It cooks all the specialties of Catalonia and stokes a festive atmosphere, enhanced by copious quantities of *cava* (sparkling wine) and sangria. It's located in the beaux-arts Blackstone Hotel (p231).

★GAGE
GASTROPUB $$$

Map p298 (☑312-372-4243; www.thegagechicago. com; 24 S Michigan Ave; mains $15-36, steaks $47-65; ☉11am-11pm Mon-Thu, to midnight Fri, 10am-midnight Sat, 10am-10pm Sun; ⓂBrown, Orange, Green, Purple, Pink Line to Washington/Wabash) This always-hopping gastropub dishes up fanciful grub, from Gouda-topped venison burgers to mussels vindaloo or Guinness-battered fish and chips; a steak menu offers massive cuts. The booze rocks too, including a solid whiskey list and small-batch beers that pair with the food.

TRATTORIA NO 10
ITALIAN $$$

Map p290 (☑312-984-1718; www.trattoriaten.com; 10 N Dearborn St; mains $22-41; ☉5-9pm Mon-Thu, to 10pm Fri & Sat; ⓂBlue Line to Washington) This clubby bistro is just steps from the Loop theater district and fills up fast with ticket-holders. The seasonal menu provides exceptionally flavorful takes on familiar items such as ravioli (try the smoked eggplant, ricotta and kale) and whole roasted branzino with *maitake* mushrooms. Gluten-free pasta is available. Reservations are a good idea.

🍷 DRINKING & NIGHTLIFE

Rooftop hotel bars, outdoor Riverwalk cafes and a couple of trusty old-time taverns are on tap in the Loop. Only a handful of places stay open much later than 10pm, though.

★BERGHOFF
BAR

Map p298 (☑312-427-3170; www.theberghoff.com; 17 W Adams St; ☉11am-9pm Mon-Fri, from 11:30am Sat; ⓂBlue, Red Line to Jackson) The Berghoff dates from 1898 and was the first Chicago bar to serve a legal drink after Prohibition (ask to see the liquor license stamped '#1'). Little has changed around the antique wood bar since. Belly up for mugs of local and imported beers and order sauerbraten, schnitzel and pretzels the size of your head from the adjoining German restaurant.

CINDY'S
BAR

Map p298 (☑312-792-3502; www.cindysrooftop. com; 12 S Michigan Ave; ☉11am-1am Mon-Fri, 10am-2am Sat, 10am-midnight Sun; ⓂBrown, Orange, Green, Purple, Pink Line to Washington/Wabash) Cindy's unfurls awesome views of Millennium Park and the lake from atop the Chicago Athletic Association Hotel. Sit at one of the long wood tables under twinkling lights and sip snazzy cocktails with ingredients such as orange saffron bitters. Alas, everyone wants in on the action, so come early to avoid having to wait for a seat.

MONK'S PUB
PUB

Map p298 (☑312-357-6665; www.monkspub chicago.com; 205 W Lake St; ☉9am-11pm Mon-Wed, to 2am Thu & Fri, 11am-5pm Sat; 🛜; ⓂBlue, Brown, Orange, Green, Purple, Pink Line to Clark/Lake) Pull open the huge wooden doors and enter this dimly lit Belgian beer cave. Old barrels, vintage taps and faux antiquarian books set the mood, accompanied by a whopping international brew selection (almost 200!) and free peanuts. Office workers and the occasional TV weather presenter are the main folks hanging out at Monk's, which also set you good, burger-y pub grub.

TRAILBLAZING ARCHITECT MARION MAHONY GRIFFIN
....

Chicago is internationally known for its architecture, and many of the profession's biggest names have worked here. One name you may not have heard, however, is Marion Mahony Griffin (1871–1961), the first woman licensed to practice architecture in Illinois and a founding member of the Prairie School made famous by Frank Lloyd Wright.

Marion Mahony was born in Chicago and raised in nearby Winnetka, where her parents moved after the family escaped the Great Fire. After graduating from MIT with an architecture degree in 1894 – one of the first few women to do so – she returned to Chicago and began working for her first cousin, noted architect Dwight Perkins. He shared office space with other architects, including Frank Lloyd Wright, who soon started his own practice and hired Mahony as his first employee. She executed most of the beautiful watercolor designs associated with his works, though he never publicly acknowledged this – typical for Wright, who generally claimed sole credit for much of the collaborative work done in his firm. Mahony had considerable influence in developing the Prairie Style that Wright became known for, and is today considered one of its earliest practitioners.

Her greatest work was still to come. In 1911 she married another architect, Walter Burley Griffin; that same year the Australian government announced a competition to design the country's new capital city, Canberra. The Griffins' entry was picked out of 137 competitors, in no small part due to Marion's masterful, artistic delineations of the gracefully geometric city layout. The Griffins moved to Sydney in 1914 to oversee Canberra's construction; over the next two decades they also designed numerous buildings in Sydney and Melbourne. In 1935 Walter received a commission in Lucknow, India, where they both practiced until Walter died suddenly in 1937 from peritonitis. Marion closed up their India office, sold their Sydney office to a partner and moved back to Chicago, where she retired from architecture and settled in Rogers Park. She died in 1961 and is buried in Graceland Cemetery (p126) along with other famed Chicago architects, such as Louis Sullivan, Daniel Burnham and Ludwig Mies van der Rohe.

During her life, Marion Mahony Griffin's considerable talents were seen mainly as an extension of the work done by male architects, but in modern times she has been given her due and is considered one of the greatest artistic renderers of the field, and a pioneering woman in a male-dominated field who blazed the way for architects such as Jeanne Gang, designer of the Aqua Tower (p52). Though sadly only a fraction of Mahony Griffin's work survives – other than Canberra itself, there's Melbourne's Capitol Theatre and a handful of private residences in Australia, Illinois and Michigan – she is remembered in Chicago by a small beach park at Jarvis Ave in Rogers Park and in Australia by the Marion Mahony Griffin Prize, which is awarded annually to a notable female architect.

TONI PATISSERIE & CAFE   CAFE
Map p298 (⌂312-726-2020; www.tonipatisserie.com; 65 E Washington St; ⊗7am-7pm Mon-Fri, from 8am Sat, 9am-5pm Sun; Ⓜ Brown, Orange, Green, Purple, Pink Line to Washington/Wabash) Toni's provides a cute refuge for a glass of wine. The Parisian-style cafe has a small list of French red, white and sparkling wines to sip at close-set tables while you try to resist the éclairs, macaroons and tiered cakes tempting you from the glass case. It also sells bottles for takeout – handy for park picnics.

ARGO TEA   TEAHOUSE
Map p298 (⌂312-324-3899; www.argotea.com; 16 W Randolph St; ⊗6:30am-10pm Mon-Fri, from 8am Sat, 8am-9pm Sun; ⓦ; Ⓜ Brown, Orange, Green, Purple, Pink Line to State/Lake) This whimsical, Bavarian-looking tea shop is a great place to get some work done over an exotic beverage. Grab a maté latte (South American–style tea with milk) or ginger-root-infused Japanese green tea, then head to the quieter 2nd floor and settle in to some comfy chairs to use the free wi-fi. Coffee drinks and healthy sandwiches are available, too.

MILLER'S PUB   PUB
Map p298 (⌂312-263-4988; www.millerspub.com; 134 S Wabash Ave; ⊗11am-4am; Ⓜ Brown, Orange, Green, Purple, Pink Line to Adams) The beauty of Miller's isn't to be found in the dark-wood furnishings, stained glass or nostalgic sports photos adorning the walls, but from its late-night hours in an area where most places close by 10pm. Even better is a whopping

selection of craft and Belgian brews and a big, meaty menu (to 2am Monday through Saturday, to midnight Sunday).

INTELLIGENTSIA COFFEE COFFEE
Map p298 (☎312-920-9332; www.intelligentsia coffee.com; 53 E Randolph St; ☺6:30am-8pm Mon-Fri, from 7am Sat, 7am-7pm Sun; ⓜBrown, Orange, Green, Purple, Pink Line to Randolph) Intelligentsia is a local chain that roasts its own beans and percolates good, strong stuff. The modern, industrial coffee bar makes a good fuel stop before or after visiting nearby Millennium Park. There's another Loop **outlet** in the Monadnock Building (Map p298; ☎312-253-0594; 55 W Jackson Blvd; ☺6am-6pm Mon-Fri, 8am-4pm Saturday; ⓜBlue Line to Jackson).

PLAZA AT PARK GRILL CAFE
Map p298 (☎312-521-7275; www.parkgrillchicago. com/the-plaza; 11 N Michigan Ave; ☺11am-10pm mid-May–early Oct; ⓜBrown, Orange, Green, Purple, Pink Line to Madison) If you want lively people-watching in the thick of it, hit the Plaza. Set in Millennium Park between the Bean sculpture and Michigan Ave, the summer-only bar sprawls where the ice-skating rink is during colder months. It can be pricey and cheesy (cover bands!), but it's the neighborhood's hot spot for alfresco boozing.

☆ ENTERTAINMENT

★ GRANT PARK ORCHESTRA CLASSICAL MUSIC
Map p298 (☎312-742-7638; www.grantparkmusic festival.com; Pritzker Pavilion, Millennium Park; ☺6:30pm Wed & Fri, 7:30pm Sat mid-Jun–mid-Aug; ⓜBrown, Orange, Green, Purple, Pink Line to Washington/Wabash) It's a summertime must-do. The Grant Park Orchestra – composed of top-notch musicians from symphonies worldwide – puts on free classical concerts at Millennium Park's Pritzker Pavilion (p47). Patrons bring lawn chairs, blankets, wine and picnic fixings to set the scene as the sun dips, the skyscraper lights flicker on and glorious music fills the night air.

★ BUDDY GUY'S LEGENDS BLUES
Map p302 (☎312-427-1190; www.buddyguy.com; 700 S Wabash Ave; cover charge Sun-Thu $10, Fri & Sat $20; ☺5pm-2am Mon & Tue, from 11am Wed-Fri, noon-3am Sat, noon-2am Sun; ⓜRed Line to Harrison) Top local and national acts wail on the stage of local icon Buddy Guy. The man himself usually plays a series of shows in

🏃 Neighborhood Walk
A Postcard Perspective

START PICASSO SCULPTURE
END WILLIS TOWER
LENGTH 2.25 MILES; FOUR HOURS

Why buy postcards when you can make your own? All you need is a camera, comfortable shoes and a free day to spend shooting Loop sights and you'll have your own picture-postcard perspective of this charmingly photogenic city.

Begin at Daley Plaza, where Picasso's ❶ **untitled sculpture** (p55) may have you scratching your head. The artist never did say what the 1967 iron work represents; most people believe it's the head of a woman – but Picasso also drew similar-looking pictures of his dog. (And then there's the baboon theory...). Whatever is, it's become a well-known Chicago symbol. The most intriguing perspective may just be lying faceup, camera angled, looking at the nose of the beast(?).

For more landmark public art, cross the street to ❷ **Miró's Chicago** (p55). Spaniard Joan Miró unveiled his robot/pagan-fertility-goddess-like sculpture in 1981, on his 88th birthday, originally calling it *The Sun, the Moon and One Star*. The star is the fork projecting off the top. The moon is the sphere at the center. The sun is... Oh, never mind. Just take a photo.

What could be more postcard-perfect than a six-story-high sign spelling out the city's name? Any time is fine to capture the brilliantly illuminated 1920s marquee for the ❸ **Chicago Theatre** (p64), but if you stop by on a cloudy day, that may eliminate harsh shadows.

'Meeting under the clock' has been a Chicago tradition since 1897, when retailer Marshall Field installed the ❹ **Old Marshall Field's Clock** at Washington and State streets outside his department store (now Macy's). The elaborate timepiece weighs more than 7.5 tons. A photo beneath the clock is a must.

The 38ft-diameter Tiffany dome, the world's largest, at the ❺ **Chicago Cultural Center** (p52) is well worth photographing (as is the 1897 building's hodgepodge of Greek, Roman and European architectural styles). But you're really

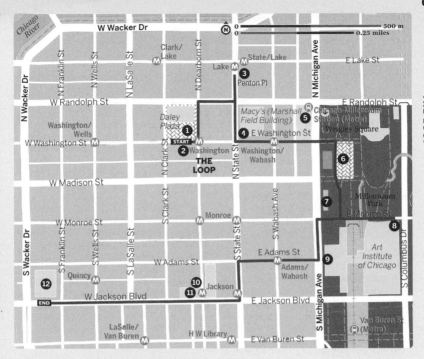

here to get inspiration from the architectural photos in the Landmark Chicago Gallery. The ongoing exhibition shows 72 black-and-white images of prominent structures by well-known local shutterbugs such as Richard Nickel. Plenty of Kodak moments happen at 24-acre Millennium Park. Your first stop is ❻ *Cloud Gate* (p46). Stand on the west side of the giant mirrored blob, hold your camera at waist level and you can take a self-portrait with a skyline background.

Mosey onward to the human gargoyles puckering up at the ❼ *Crown Fountain* (p46). Geysers spout from the ground in front of two 50ft-tall LED screens projecting images of peoples' faces. When an open-mouthed guy or gal appears, the fountain spews water so it looks like they're spitting. Use a fast shutter speed and stick to a side view unless you've got a waterproof camera.

Many of renowned architect Louis Sullivan's buildings have been demolished, but you can get up close to his exquisite terra-cotta ornamentation at the ❽ **Chicago Stock Exchange Arch**, which was rescued and placed outside the Art Institute. A telephoto lens can isolate the detail. Your arch pictures will be considerably less risky than those Richard Nickel took. While the Stock

Exchange was abandoned and awaiting demolition in 1972, the famed photographer entered to document the architecture. Tragically, the building collapsed, killing him.

Around the front of the Art Institute stand two 1894 ❾ **bronze lions** – city mascots of sorts. They wore Blackhawks helmets when the team won the 2010, 2013 and 2015 Stanley Cup, White Sox caps during their 2005 World Series win and Cubs caps for theirs in 2016. They wear wreathes around their necks at Christmastime. Zoom in for a striking profile shot silhouetted against city buildings.

Alexander Calder's ❿ *Flamingo* (p55) is another easily recognized piece of monumental public art in Chicago. That bright-red paint job should photograph well, especially if you frame it against Ludwig Mies van der Rohe's groundbreaking 1974 glass-and-steel ⓫ **Kluczynski Building** (p53) in the Chicago Federal Center.

Aligning the building's edge on a slight diagonal will add dynamism to a shot of the 1450ft-tall ⓬ **Willis Tower** (p51), one of the world's tallest buildings. A final photo from the 103rd-floor Skydeck makes the perfect capper for your album: high-rises galore, lake beyond – that's Chicago in a snapshot.

January; tickets go on sale in October. Free, all-ages acoustic shows are staged at lunch and dinner (the place doubles as a Cajun restaurant); note that you must pay to stay on for late-evening shows.

CHICAGO THEATRE
THEATER

Map p298 (📞312-462-6300; www.thechicago theatre.com; 175 N State St; Ⓜ Brown, Orange, Green, Purple, Pink Line to State/Lake) Take a gander at the illuminated six-story sign – it's an official landmark and an excellent photo op. Everyone from Duke Ellington to Dolly Parton to Prince has played here over the years (and left their signature on the famous backstage walls). The real show-stopper, though, is the opulent French baroque architecture, including a lobby modeled on the Palace of Versailles.

CHICAGO SYMPHONY ORCHESTRA
CLASSICAL MUSIC

Map p298 (CSO; 📞312-294-3000; www.cso.org; 220 S Michigan Ave; Ⓜ Brown, Orange, Green, Purple, Pink Line to Adams) Riccardo Muti leads the CSO, one of America's best symphonies, known for its fervent subscribers and an untouchable brass section. Cellist Yo-Yo Ma is the creative consultant and a frequent soloist. The season runs from September to June at Symphony Center; Daniel Burnham designed the Orchestra Hall.

HUBBARD STREET DANCE CHICAGO
DANCE

Map p298 (📞312-635-3799; www.hubbardstreet dance.com; 205 E Randolph St; Ⓜ Brown, Orange, Green, Purple, Pink Line to Washington/Wabash) Hubbard Street is the preeminent dance company in the city, with a well-deserved international reputation to match. The group is known for energetic and technically virtuosic performances under the direc-

---

ⓘ DISCOUNT TICKETS
....

Swing by the **Hot Tix** (Map p298; www. hottix.org; 72 E Randolph St; ⊘10am-6pm Tue-Sat, 11am-4pm Sun; Ⓜ Brown, Orange, Green, Purple, Pink Line to Washington/ Wabash) office, which sells same-week theater tickets for half-price (plus a service charge of $5 to $10). Drama, comedy and performing-arts venues citywide have seats on offer. You can also look and book online. The earlier in the week you visit, the better the selection.

---

tion of some of the best choreographers in the world. It performs at the Harris Theater (p47) in Millennium Park.

JAZZ SHOWCASE
JAZZ

Map p302 (📞312-360-0234; www.jazzshowcase. com; 806 S Plymouth Ct; tickets $20-45; Ⓜ Red Line to Harrison) The Jazz Showcase, set in a gorgeous room on the eastern side of the historic Dearborn Station (p58), is Chicago's top club for national names. In general, local musicians take the stage Monday through Wednesday, with visiting jazz-cats blowing their horns Thursday through Sunday.

SUMMERDANCE
WORLD MUSIC

Map p302 (www.chicagosummerdance.org; 601 S Michigan Ave; ⊘6-9pm Wed, to 9:30pm Thu-Sat, 4-7pm Sun late Jun-Aug; Ⓜ Red Line to Harrison) To boogie with a multiethnic mash-up of locals, head to the Spirit of Music Garden in Grant Park for SummerDance. Bands play a wide range of toe-stepping music: swing, house, rumba, samba, Afrobeat and other styles, preceded by an hour of fun dance lessons – all free. Ballroom-quality moves are absolutely not required.

GOODMAN THEATRE
THEATER

Map p298 (📞312-443-3800; www.goodman theatre.org; 170 N Dearborn St; Ⓜ Brown, Orange, Green, Purple, Pink, Blue Line to Clark/Lake) One of Chicago's premier drama houses, with a gorgeous Theater District facility. It specializes in new and classic American productions and has been cited several times as one of the USA's best regional theaters. Unsold tickets for the current day's performance go on sale at 10am for half-price online; they're also available at the box office from noon.

LYRIC OPERA OF CHICAGO
OPERA

Map p298 (📞312-827-5600; www.lyricopera.org; 20 N Wacker Dr; Ⓜ Brown, Orange, Purple, Pink Line to Washington/Wells) Tickets are hard to come by for this bold modern opera company, which fills the chandeliered Civic Opera House with a shrewd mix of common classics and daring premieres from September to May. If your Italian isn't up to snuff, don't worry – the company projects English 'supertitles' above the proscenium.

GENE SISKEL FILM CENTER
CINEMA

Map p298 (📞312-846-2800; www.siskelfilmcenter. org; 164 N State St; Ⓜ Brown, Orange, Green, Pur-

CHICAGO'S THEATER PALACES
....

Chicago boasts several dreamboat old theaters that have been renovated and re-opened in recent years as part of the Loop's Theater District. Signs are posted in front of each palatial property, detailing whatever zaniness went on during its 1920s heyday. The theaters now host touring shows – everything from Cuban ballet companies to Disney musicals. Broadway in Chicago (www.broadwayinchicago.com) handles tickets for most of them. The venues cluster around State and Randolph Sts; try to walk by at night when they're at their festive, neon-lit best.

Auditorium Theatre (Map p302; ✆312-341-2300; www.auditoriumtheatre.org; 50 E Congress Pkwy; MBrown, Orange, Purple, Pink Line to Library)

CIBC Theatre (Map p298; ✆312-977-1700; www.broadwayinchicago.com; 18 W Monroe St; MBlue, Red Line to Monroe)

Cadillac Palace Theatre (Map p298; ✆312-977-1700; www.broadwayinchicago.com; 151 W Randolph St; MBrown, Orange, Purple, Pink Line to Washington/Wells)

Chicago Theatre (p64)

Nederlander Theatre (Map p298; ✆312-977-1700; www.broadwayinchicago.com; 24 W Randolph St; MBrown, Orange, Green, Purple, Pink Line to State/Lake)

ple, Pink Line to State/Lake) The former Film Center of the School of the Art Institute was renamed for the late *Chicago Tribune* film critic Gene Siskel. It shows everything from amateurish stuff by students to wonderful but unsung gems by European directors. The monthly schedule includes theme nights of forgotten American classics.

JOFFREY BALLET   DANCE
Map p298 (✆312-386-8905; www.joffrey.com; 10 E Randolph St; MBrown, Orange, Green, Purple, Pink Line to Randolph) The famed Joffrey has flourished since it relocated from New York in 1995. Noted for its energetic work, the company frequently travels the world and boasts an impressive storehouse of regularly performed repertoire. Joffrey practices and instructs in the swanky Joffrey Tower on Randolph St in the Theater District, though it typically performs at the Auditorium Theatre.

CIVIC ORCHESTRA OF CHICAGO   CLASSICAL MUSIC
Map p298 (✆312-294-3420; www.cso.org/civic; 220 S Michigan Ave; MBrown, Orange, Green, Purple, Pink Line to Adams) Founded in 1919, this orchestra is a kid sibling to the Chicago Symphony Orchestra – made up of young players who often graduate to the big-time professional symphonic institutions around the world. It's the only training orchestra of its kind in the world. Tickets to performances at Symphony Center are free (with a $5 ticket fee to reserve in advance).

 SHOPPING

★CHICAGO ARCHITECTURE CENTER SHOP   GIFTS & SOUVENIRS
Map p298 (✆312-922-3432; http://shop.architecture.org; 111 E Wacker Dr; ◎9am-5pm Mon, Wed & Fri-Sun, to 8pm Tue & Thu; ▣151; MBrown, Orange, Green, Purple, Pink Line to State/Lake) Browse through skyline T-shirts and posters, Frank Lloyd Wright note cards, skyscraper models and heaps of books that celebrate local architecture at this haven for anyone with an edifice complex; a children's section has books to pique the interest of budding builders. The items make excellent 'only in Chicago' souvenirs.

★SHOPCOLUMBIA   ART
Map p302 (✆312-369-8616; http://shop.colum.edu; 619 S Wabash Ave; ◎11am-5pm Mon-Fri; MRed Line to Harrison) This is Columbia College's student store, where student artists and designers sell their wares. The shop carries original, handcrafted pieces spanning all media and disciplines: clothes, jewelry, prints, mugs, paintings, stationery and more. Students earn 75% of the price, and part of the proceeds also goes toward student scholarships.

OPTIMO HATS   FASHION & ACCESSORIES
Map p298 (✆312-922-2999; www.optimo.com; 51 W Jackson Blvd; ◎10am-5pm Mon-Sat; MBlue Line to Jackson) Optimo is a Chicago institution, the last custom hat-maker for men in town. Want a lid like Al Capone's? Get one

here, made with serious, old-school craftsmanship. Clients include actor Johnny Depp, musician Jack White and a slew of local bluesmen. The shop is located in the landmark Monadnock Building (p53).

DIAL BOOKSHOP   BOOKS
Map p298 (www.dialbookshop.com; 410 S Michigan Ave, Ste 210; ⊙11am-7pm Mon-Fri, to 5pm Sat; Ⓜ Brown, Orange, Purple, Pink Line to Library) As bookstores go, it's hard to beat Dial's literary pedigree: it's housed in the Fine Arts Building (p54), once headquarters to groundbreaking modernist magazines *The Little Review, Poetry* and the eponymous *Dial*. Honey-colored hardwood floors and massive windows overlooking Grant Park set a handsome stage for browsing new and used fiction, art tomes and local literary mags.

AFTER SCHOOL
MATTERS STORE   ART
Map p298 (☑312-702-8975; 66 E Randolph St; ⊙10am-6pm Mon-Fri, 11am-4pm Sat; Ⓜ Brown, Orange, Green, Purple, Pink Line to Randolph) Painters, sculptors and other visual artists and craftspeople get paid for creating their wares while teaching inner-city teens – who serve as apprentices – to do the same at this nonprofit entity. Artworks made by the teens, including paintings, illustrative prints, jewelry, mosaic tables, puppets and carved-wood walking sticks, are sold in the gallery here. Profits return to the organization.

🏃 SPORTS & ACTIVITIES

★ CHICAGO ARCHITECTURE
CENTER TOURS   TOURS
(CAC; ☑312-922-3432; www.architecture.org; 111 E Wacker Dr; tours $20-55) Gold-standard boat tours ($47) sail from the **river dock** (Map p298; Ⓜ Brown, Orange, Green, Purple, Pink Line to State/Lake) on the southeast side of the Michigan Ave Bridge. Also popular are the Historic Skyscrapers walking tours ($26) and tours exploring individual landmark buildings ($20). CAC sponsors bus, bike and L train tours, too. Buy tickets online or at the CAC's front desk; boat tickets can also be purchased at the dock.

CHICAGO GREETER   WALKING
(www.chicagogreeter.com) 🆓 A volunteer Chicagoan will take you on a free, personal two- to four-hour tour customized by theme (architecture, history, gay and lesbian, and more) or neighborhood. Travel is by foot and/or public transportation; departure locations vary. Reserve at least 10 business days in advance online – or you can just show up to one of the regularly held one-hour InstaGreeter (p276) walks.

BIKE & ROLL   CYCLING
Map p298 (☑312-729-1000; www.bikechicago. com; 239 E Randolph St; tours adult/child from $45/35; ⊙9am-7pm; Ⓜ Brown, Orange, Green, Purple, Pink Line to Washington/Wabash) Summer guided tours (adult/child from $45/35) cover themes such as lakefront parks, breweries and historic neighborhoods, or downtown's sights and fireworks at night (highly recommended). Prices include lock, helmet and map. Operates out of the McDonald's Cycle Center in Millennium Park; there's another branch on Navy Pier. It also rents out bikes for DIY explorations (per hour/day from $12.50/35).

MCCORMICK
TRIBUNE ICE RINK   ICE SKATING
Map p298 (www.millenniumpark.org; 55 N Michigan Ave; ⊙noon-8pm Mon-Thu, to 10pm Fri, 10am-9pm Sat & Sun mid-Nov–mid-Mar; Ⓜ Brown, Orange, Green, Purple, Pink Line to Washington/Wabash) Millennium Park's busy rink is the city's most scenic, tucked between the reflecting Bean sculpture and the twinkling lights of Michigan Ave. Admission to the ice is free; skate rental costs $13 (Monday through Thursday) or $15 (Friday through Sunday). Free ice-skating lessons are offered an hour before the rink opens.

URBAN KAYAKS   KAYAKING
Map p298 (☑312-965-0035; www.urbankayaks. com; 435 E Riverwalk S; rental per hour per person $30, tours $55; ⊙9am-6pm Mon-Fri, to 7pm Sat & Sun May-early Oct; Ⓜ Brown, Orange, Green, Purple, Pink Line to State/Lake) On the Riverwalk (p54), this outfitter rents out kayaks for DIY explorations and offers guided tours that glide past downtown's skyscrapers and historic sites; beginners are welcome, with a 20-minute training session starting off each tour. For extra help, try the hour-long 'intro to paddling' class ($35). Night-time tours on Wednesdays and Saturdays take in the Navy Pier summer fireworks show.

Near North & Navy Pier

RIVER NORTH | STREETERVILLE | NAVY PIER | NEAR NORTH

Neighborhood Top Five

❶ Navy Pier (p69) Walking on the boat-bedecked wharf and taking in the views – especially from the stomach-churning 196ft Ferris wheel.

❷ Giordano's (p75) Hefting a gooey slice of pizza that's even mightier than deep-dish.

❸ Magnificent Mile (p70) Shopping with the frenzied masses along this busy stretch of Michigan Ave jampacked with retailers from Burberry to Nike to a very spiffy Apple.

❹ Driehaus Museum (p70) Ogling the gilded mansion's marble stairwells, French

porcelain vases, bronze candelabras and Tiffany stained glass.

❺ Billy Goat Tavern (p77) Submerging beneath Michigan Ave to eat burgers and knock back Schlitz beer with local journalists while getting the lowdown on famed local stories.

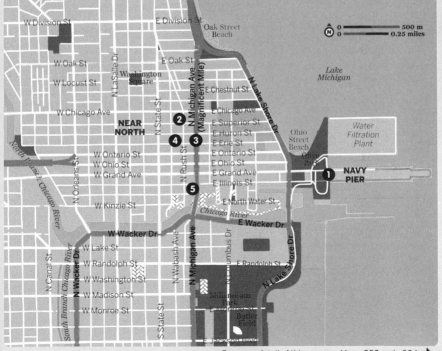

For more detail of this area see Map p303 and p304 ➡

Lonely Planet's Top Tip

Navy Pier is about a mile from the closest L station, and the pier itself is a half-mile long. Prepare for lots of walking. The free trolley can help in summer and during special events the rest of the year. It picks up at the Red Line Grand station, makes several stops along Illinois St heading east toward the pier, and then loops back along Grand Ave to the L station.

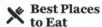

✕ Best Places to Eat

➡ Giordano's (p75)

➡ Billy Goat Tavern (p77)

➡ GT Fish & Oyster (p75)

➡ Topolobampo/Frontera Grill (p76)

➡ Doughnut Vault (p74)

For reviews, see p74.➡

🍷 Best Places to Drink

➡ Centennial Crafted Beer & Eatery (p78)

➡ Arbella (p78)

➡ Clark Street Ale House (p78)

➡ Bar Ramone (p78)

For reviews, see p77.➡

🔒 Best Places to Shop

➡ Garrett Popcorn (p79)

➡ P.O.S.H. (p79)

➡ Apple Michigan Avenue (p80)

➡ After-Words Books (p79)

For reviews, see p79.➡

Explore Near North & Navy Pier

The Near North is unapologetically commercial. The epicenter is upscale shopping along N Michigan Ave, aka the Magnificent Mile. Stretching north from the Chicago River to Oak St are multistory malls, high-end department stores and big-name national chains.

The River North area is west of Michigan Ave. A formerly grimy assortment of warehouses is now Chicago's high-end art gallery district, with a bazillion restaurants and several huge dance clubs. Streeterville lies to the east of Michigan Ave, home to heaps of eateries, plus universities and medical facilities.

Jutting off the neighborhood's eastern edge is Navy Pier, with kid-oriented shops and carnival rides, though adults will appreciate the jumbo Ferris wheel and opportunity for viewtastic strolling. Several boat tours depart from here, and free concerts and art installations add to the scene.

Allocate a full day to take in the neighborhood. Eat breakfast at Xoco or Doughnut Vault, then shop the Mag Mile. Move on to Navy Pier in the afternoon. Art fans can check out the Driehaus Museum or Arts Club of Chicago. At night get deep-dish pizza and settle in at a blues or jazz club. Expect tourist crowds wherever you go.

Local Life

➡ **Speakeasy entertainment** After munching a burger alongside locals at Green Door Tavern (p75), head down to the basement bar for jugglers, tarot-card readings and burlesque shows.

➡ **Happy hour** Clark Street Ale House (p78) and Centennial Crafted Beer & Eatery (p78) are neighborhood favorites for kicking back after work with a Midwest microbrew.

➡ **Peace and quiet** Olive Park, next to Ohio Street Beach, is a rare patch of solitude in the 'hood, where locals in the know go to take a breather.

Getting There & Away

➡ **L Train** Red Line to Grand for the Magnificent Mile's southern end (to Chicago for its northern end); Brown, Purple Line to Chicago or Merchandise Mart for River North.

➡ **Trolley** A free trolley runs from the Red Line Grand stop to Navy Pier from late May to early September.

➡ **Bus** Bus151 runs along N Michigan Ave; 65 heads to Navy Pier.

➡ **Car** Parking garages (around $35 per day) dominate near the Mag Mile. Metered parking ($4 per hour) becomes more common as you move west from there. Navy Pier's garage costs around $30 per day.

TOP SIGHT
NAVY PIER

Navy Pier was once the city's municipal wharf. Today it's Chicago's most visited attraction, with eight million people per year flooding its half-mile length. Locals may groan about its commercialization, but even they can't refute the brilliant lakefront views, cool breezes and fireworks displays in summer. Kids love the rides, fast-food restaurants and trinket vendors.

No visit to the pier is complete without a stomach-curdling turn on the gigantic, 196ft-tall **Centennial Wheel** (adult/child $18/15), which unfurls great views. The **carousel** (per ride $9; ☉May-Oct) is a beloved kiddie classic, with carved horses bobbing to organ music. There's also a giant swing that spins you out over the pier. Each attraction costs $9 to $18. The Chicago Children's Museum (p70) is on the pier near the main entrance.

An **IMAX Theater** (☏312-595-5629; www.amctheatres.com; 700 E Grand Ave; tickets $15-22) and the Chicago Shakespeare Theater (p79) also call the pier home. The white-canopied 'tent' holds the Shakespeare Theater's kicky new venue called the Yard, one of three performance spaces that show its populist takes on the Bard. Competing tour boats depart from the pier's southern side, where you can set sail in everything from a tall-masted schooner (p80) to thrill-ride speedboat (p276).

Polk Bros Park, by the pier's entrance, entertains with a splashy fountain with lights and dancing spouts. Feel free to jump in with all the kids doing the same. The park also has performance lawns for free concerts and movies. Other spots to relax include the Wave Wall stairs overlooking the lake; the Crystal Gardens, with palm trees and tables under a soaring glass roof; and the big wood lounge chairs that dot the pier.

DON'T MISS

➡ Fireworks
➡ Centennial Wheel
➡ Lakefront views
➡ Boat rides
➡ Shakespeare Theater

PRACTICALITIES

➡ Map p303, B3
➡ ☏312-595-7437
➡ www.navypier.com
➡ 600 E Grand Ave
➡ admission free
➡ ☉10am-10pm Sun-Thu, to midnight Fri & Sat Jun-Aug, 10am-8pm Sun-Thu, to 10pm Fri & Sat Sep-May
➡ ♿
➡ ☐65

⊙ SIGHTS

Navy Pier (p69) is the top sight, located by its lonesome at the neighborhood's eastern edge. Its Ferris wheel, boat tours and kid-friendly amusements draw swarms of visitors. Architecture is a neighborhood highlight, thanks to iconic buildings such as the Tribune Tower and Marina City. Art is another strong suit, especially underrated sights such as the Driehaus Museum and Arts Club of Chicago, as well as River North's many galleries.

NAVY PIER   WATERFRONT
See p69.

★ DRIEHAUS MUSEUM   MUSEUM
Map p304 (✆312-482-8933; www.driehaus museum.org; 40 E Erie St, River North; adult/child $20/free; ◷10am-5pm Tue-Sun; ⓂRed Line to Chicago) Set in the exquisite Nickerson Mansion, the Driehaus immerses visitors in Gilded Age decorative arts and architecture. You'll feel like a *Great Gatsby* character as you wander three floors stuffed with sumptuous objets d'art and heaps of Tiffany stained glass. Recommended guided tours ($5 extra) are available four times daily. The price seems steep, but the museum is a prize for those intrigued by opulent interiors.

MAGNIFICENT MILE   AREA
Map p304 (www.themagnificentmile.com; N Michigan Ave, Streeterville; ⓂRed Line to Grand) Spanning N Michigan Ave between the river and Oak St, the 'Mag Mile' is Chicago's much-touted upscale shopping strip, where Bloomingdale's, Apple, Burberry and many more will lighten your wallet. The retailers are mostly high-end chains that have stores nationwide.

TRIBUNE TOWER   ARCHITECTURE
Map p304 (435 N Michigan Ave, Streeterville; ⓂRed Line to Grand) Take a close look when passing by this 1925 neo-Gothic edifice. Colonel Robert McCormick, eccentric owner of the *Chicago Tribune* in the early 1900s, collected – and asked his reporters to send – rocks from famous buildings and monuments around the world. He stockpiled pieces of the Taj Mahal, Westminster Abbey, the Great Pyramid and more than 140 others, which are now embedded around the tower's base.

The unusual 'bricks' are all marked and viewable from street level. And the tradition continues: a twisted piece from the World Trade Center wreckage is one of the more recent additions. Alas, the *Tribune* offices are no longer here; they moved out in 2018, and the building is being converted into condominiums.

CHICAGO CHILDREN'S MUSEUM   MUSEUM
Map p303 (✆312-527-1000; www.chicagochildrens museum.org; 700 E Grand Ave, Navy Pier; $15; ◷10am-5pm, to 8pm Thu; ♿; 🚌65) Designed to challenge the imaginations of toddlers to 10-year-olds, this colorful museum near Navy Pier's main entrance gives young visitors enough hands-on exhibits to keep them climbing and creating for hours. Among the favorites, Dinosaur Expedition explores the world of paleontology and lets kids excavate 'bones.' They can also climb a ropey schooner; get wet in Waterways (and learn about hydroelectric power); and use real tools to build things in the Tinkering Lab.

MARINA CITY   ARCHITECTURE
Map p304 (300 N State St, River North; ⓂBrown, Orange, Green, Purple, Pink Line to State/Lake) The twin corncob towers of Marina City are an Instagram favorite for their futuristic, cartoony look. Bertrand Goldberg designed the 1964 high-rise, and it has become an iconic part of the Chicago skyline (check out the cover of the Wilco CD *Yankee Hotel Foxtrot*). And yes, there is a marina at the towers' base.

ARTS CLUB OF CHICAGO   GALLERY
Map p304 (✆312-787-3997; www.artsclubchicago. org; 201 E Ontario St, Streeterville; ◷11am-6pm Tue-Fri, to 3pm Sat; ⓂRed Line to Grand) 𝗙𝗥𝗘𝗘 It sounds stuffy: a club for patrons of the arts, and it looks the part as men in fancy suits and women in furs drop by for lunch in the members-only dining room. Ignore all that. You're here for the 1st-floor galleries that are free and open to the public. They host four exhibitions per year, often by well-known artists. Definitely worth checking out.

THEMART   NOTABLE BUILDING
Map p304 (✆800-677-6278; www.themart. com; 222 W Merchandise Mart Plaza, River North; ◷9am-6pm Mon-Fri, 10am-3pm Sat; ⓂBrown, Purple Line to Merchandise Mart) TheMart, as the Merchandise Mart is now called, is the world's largest commercial building. Spanning two city blocks, the 1931 behemoth has

its own zip code and gives most of its copious space to wholesale showrooms for home furnishing and design professionals. Many are on floors 6, 14, 15 and 16, if you want to browse. The first two floors are mall-like with eateries and clothing shops. At night, theMart becomes a psychedelic canvas for video art projected on the exterior.

The eye candy is called Art on theMart (www.artonthemart.com), and it's a very cool public light show done with 34 projectors set up along the Riverwalk (p54). Times vary, but it happens for two hours sometime between 5pm and 9pm Wednesday through Sunday (except no show during January and February). The website has the schedule. The best views are from the Riverwalk.

Also outdoors on theMart's river side is a collection of heads on poles that rise up like giant Pez dispensers. This is the Merchant's Hall of Fame, and the creepy busts depict famous local retailers such as Marshall Field and Frank Woolworth.

HOLY NAME CATHEDRAL CHURCH
Map p304 (☑312-787-8040; www.holyname cathedral.org; 735 N State St, River North; Ⓜ Red Line to Chicago) Holy Name Cathedral is the seat of Chicago's Catholic Church and where its powerful cardinals do their preaching. It provides a quiet place for contemplation, unless the excellent choirs are practicing, in which case it's an entertaining respite. Check out the sanctuary's ceiling while you're inside. The hanging red hats are for Holy Name's deceased cardinals; the hats remain until they turn to dust.

Built in 1875 to a design by the unheralded Patrick Keely, the neo-Gothic cathedral has been remodeled several times. Look closely and you can still see bullet holes from a Capone-era hit in the building's exterior. Actually, a couple of gangland killings took place near here. In 1924 North Side boss Dion O'Banion was gunned down in his florist shop (738 N State St) after he crossed Al Capone. In 1926 his successor, Hymie Weiss, died en route to the cathedral in a hail of bullets that came from the window at 740 N State St. Both buildings have since been razed; they stood in what's now a parking lot across from the State St main entrance. Meanwhile, the bullet holes appear just south of this entrance, in the cornerstone at the edge of the steps, where four very faded pockmarks surround the dedication year.

The cathedral is open most of the day and holds frequent services. If the State St entrance is closed, try the door around the corner on Superior St.

WRIGLEY BUILDING ARCHITECTURE
Map p304 (400 N Michigan Ave, Streeterville; Ⓜ Red Line to Grand) The Wrigley Building glows as white as the Doublemint Twins' teeth, day or night. Chewing-gum guy William Wrigley built it that way on

(Continued on page 74)

(side text) **NEAR NORTH & NAVY PIER** SIGHTS

NEAR NORTH ART GALLERIES
....

The River North district is the most established of Chicago's five gallery-rich zones (West Loop, Pilsen, Bridgeport and Wicker Park/Bucktown are the others), with art from top international names. Several venues hover within a few-block radius. Franklin and Superior Sts are the bull's-eye. Most galleries have a map you can take covering the scene. Local favorites:

Richard Norton Gallery (Map p304; ☑312-644-8855; www.richardnortongallery.com; 222 W Merchandise Mart Plaza, Suite 612; ◷9am-5pm Mon-Fri; Ⓜ Brown, Purple Line to Merchandise Mart) Specializes in colorful impressionist, modernist and historical Chicago-focused works. Check out the early beach and street scenes of the city.

Carl Hammer Gallery (Map p304; ☑312-266-8512; www.carlhammergallery.com; 740 N Wells St; ◷11am-5:30pm Tue-Fri, to 5pm Sat; Ⓜ Brown, Purple Line to Chicago) Focuses on eye-popping folk and outsider art from the US and abroad, and is known for its excellent exhibitions.

Art Works Projects (Off Map p304; ☑312-649-0025; www.artworksprojects.org; 625 N Kingsbury St; ◷noon-5pm Mon-Fri; Ⓜ Brown, Purple Line to Chicago) A nonprofit organization that uses the arts to educate about human rights issues. The group's small office does double duty as a makeshift photography gallery where you might see an exhibition focused on families facing deportation or a photo series of women in rural Togo. It's an intriguing browse if you're in the area.

On the Waterfront at Near North & Navy Pier

Chicago has a nautical side, and Navy Pier is the place to experience it. Boats galore still tie up at the old municipal wharf, from powerboats to tall-masted schooners to water taxis that ply green-glinting Lake Michigan. The Chicago River slices through the neighborhood, too, adding more tour boats to the mix.

1

ELESI / SHUTTERSTOCK ©

MOAB REPUBLIC / SHUTTERSTOCK ©

1. Centennial Wheel & Carousal (p69)
No visit to Navy Pier is complete without a turn on one of the amusement rides.

2. Navy Pier (p69)
Once the city's municipal wharf, Navy Pier is now Chicago's most visited tourist attraction.

3. Chicago Skyline
Looking across Lake Michigan towards Navy Pier.

4. Tall Ship *Windy* (p80)
Sailing in Lake Michigan provides beautiful views of Chicago's famous skyline.

HISHAM IBRAHIM / GETTY IMAGES ©

(Continued from page 71)

purpose, because he wanted it to be attention-grabbing like a billboard. More than 250,000 glazed terra-cotta tiles make up the facade; a computer database tracks each one and indicates when it needs to be cleaned and polished.

CENTENNIAL FOUNTAIN
FOUNTAIN

Map p304 (N McClurg Ct, Streeterville) Centennial Fountain shoots a massive arc of water across the Chicago River. It spurts for five minutes straight every hour on the hour, from 10am to midnight from May through September. The exercise is meant to commemorate the labor-intensive reversal of the Chicago River in 1900, which tidily began sending all of the city's waste downriver rather than into the lake. (Chicago's neighbors downstate, as you can imagine, do not go out of their way to celebrate this feat of civil engineering.)

MUSEUM OF BROADCAST COMMUNICATIONS
MUSEUM

Map p304 (☑312-245-8200; www.museum.tv; 360 N State St, River North; adult/child $6/free, special exhibitions from $20; ☺10am-6pm Tue-Thu, to 5pm Fri & Sat, noon-5pm Sun; ⓂRed Line to Grand) This museum of radio and TV nostalgia is pretty sparsely populated. But if you have a hankering to see old Bozo the Clown clips, or the camera that taped the famous Nixon-Kennedy debate, or the salvaged door from Oprah's studio, it might be for you.

POETRY FOUNDATION
LIBRARY

Map p304 (☑312-787-7070; www.poetry foundation.org; 61 W Superior St, River North; ☺11am-4pm Mon-Fri; ⓂRed Line to Chicago) **FREE** This odd, mod building is where *Poetry* magazine is published. The reading room makes a nice refuge from inclement weather. Pop in and grab a book or journal to read on the low-slung couches. Well-known poets do readings here. The website offers a free downloadable audio tour of iconic city sites matched with the poetry they inspired.

✖️ EATING

This is where you'll find Chicago's mother lode of restaurants. It's a touristy area, so prices can be high. Most streets are loaded with options. Clark St is particularly bountiful.

✖️ River North

DOUGHNUT VAULT
BAKERY $

Map p304 (☑312-285-2830; www.doughnutvault. com; 401 N Franklin St; doughnuts $2.25-3.50; ☺8am-2:30pm Mon-Fri, from 9:30am Sat & Sun; ⓂBrown, Purple Line to Merchandise Mart) This teensy, chandelier-clad shop is indeed in a vault – an old bank vault – with room for only a handful of people. The glazed doughnuts (vanilla or chestnut) are the beauties here, giant and fluffy as a pillow. These usually sell out before closing time, so check Twitter (@doughnutvault) before embarking. Don't be put off by the queue: it moves fast.

LOU MALNATI'S
PIZZA $

Map p304 (☑312-828-9800; www.loumalnatis. com; 439 N Wells St; small pizzas from $13; ☺11am-11pm Sun-Thu, to midnight Fri & Sat; ⓂBrown, Purple Line to Merchandise Mart) It's a matter of dispute, but some say Malnati is the innovator of Chicago's deep-dish pizza (Lou's father Rudy was a cook at Pizzeria Uno, which also lays claim to the title). Malnati's certainly concocted the unique 'buttercrust' and the 'sausage crust' (it's literally just meat, no dough) to cradle its tangy toppings.

3 GREENS MARKET
AMERICAN $

Map p304 (☑312-888-9195; www.3greensmarket. com; 354 W Hubbard St; burgers $9-10, food bar per pound $12; ☺7am-8pm Mon-Fri, 8am-3pm Sat & Sun; ⓂBrown, Purple Line to Merchandise Mart) Neighborbood professionals swarm this place to refuel while typing away on their laptops. The big tables and comfy chairs are part of the appeal. So are the food options at different stations: there's a coffee and pastry bar, salad and hot foods bar, and a burger bar that's a branch of Small Cheval (p149).

XOCO
MEXICAN $

Map p304 (☑312-661-1434; www.rickbayless. com; 449 N Clark St; mains $9-15; ☺8am-9pm Tue-Thu, to 10pm Fri & Sat; ⓂRed Line to Grand) ⚑ At celeb-chef Rick Bayless' Mexican street-food restaurant (pronounced '*show*-co') everything's sourced from local farms. Crunch into warm churros with bean-to-cup hot chocolate for breakfast, and crusty *tortas* (sandwiches, such as the fab mushroom and goat's cheese) and *caldos* (meal-in-a-bowl soups) for lunch and dinner. It's a fast-casual, order-at-the-counter type ambience, where Latin music blares and the metallic decor gleams.

MR BEEF
SANDWICHES $

Map p304 (312-337-8500; 666 N Orleans St; sandwiches $6-13; 10am-6pm Mon-Thu, to 4am Fri, to 5am Sat; Brown, Purple Line to Chicago) The signature Italian beef sandwich, a Chicago specialty, arrives on a long white bun loaded with thin-cut roast beef that's been simmered and ladled with its own cooking juices. Ask for it 'dipped' (bun and all dunked into the juices) and 'hot' (with *giardiniera*, aka spicy pickled vegetables, added). It's soggy but delicious. Cash only. Don't fear the dumpy decor.

GREEN DOOR TAVERN
PUB FOOD $

Map p304 (312-664-5496; www.greendoor chicago.com; 678 N Orleans St; mains $10-15; 11:30am-2am Mon-Fri, 10am-3am Sat, 10am-midnight Sun; ; Brown, Purple Line to Chicago) The Green Door, tucked in an 1872 building, is your place to mingle with locals over a beer and well-made burger amid old photos and memorabilia. During Prohibition, a door painted green meant there was a speakeasy in the basement. It's still there and now holds a small cocktail bar with jazz singers, burlesque shows, jugglers and other quirky entertainment.

PORTILLO'S
AMERICAN $

Map p304 (312-587-8910; www.portillos.com; 100 W Ontario St; mains $4-7; 10am-1am Mon-Sat, to midnight Sun; Red Line to Grand) Hotdog purists might bemoan the lack of true Chicago wieners available in the downtown area, but this outpost of the local Portillo's chain – gussied up with a *nearly* corny 1930s gangster theme – is the place to get one. Try one of its famous dogs and a slice of the heavenly chocolate cake.

★GT FISH & OYSTER
SEAFOOD $$

Map p304 (312-929-3501; www.gtoyster.com; 531 N Wells St; mains $17-30; 5-10pm Mon-Thu, to 11pm Fri, 10am-2:30pm & 5-11pm Sat, 10: 2:30pm & 5-10pm Sun; Red Line to Grand) Seafood restaurants can be fusty. Not so G. Fish & Oyster. The clean-lined room bustles with date-night couples and groups of friends drinking fizzy wines and slurping mollusks. Many of the dishes are shareable, which adds to the convivial, plate-clattering ambience. The sublime clam chowder arrives in a glass jar with housemade oyster crackers and bacon.

★GIORDANO'S
PIZZA $$

Map p304 (312-951-0747; www.giordanos.com; 730 N Rush St; small pizzas from $18; 11am-11pm Sun-Thu, to midnight Fri & Sat; Red Line to Chicago) Giordano's makes 'stuffed' pizza, a bigger, doughier version of deep dish. It's awesome. If you want a slice of heaven, order the 'special,' a stuffed pie containing sausage, mushroom, green pepper and onions. Each pizza takes 45 minutes to bake, so don't arrive starving. Giordano's has loads of **branches** around town, including one at Navy Pier (Map p303; 312-288-8783700 E Grand Ave; 10am-9pm Sun-Thu, to 10pm Fri & Sat; 65), but this huge, open, industrial-vibed one is particularly festive.

BEATRIX
AMERICAN $$

Map p304 (312-284-1377; www.beatrix restaurants.com; 519 N Clark St; mains $17-28; 7am-10pm Mon-Thu, to 11pm Fri, 8am-11pm Sat, to 9pm Sun; ; Red Line to Grand) Beatrix buzzes with business types, ladies who lunch and tourists staying at the attached hotel. Light-wood tables and mason jars full of seeds form the rustic decor. The all-encompassing menu spans *shakshuka* (poached eggs in tomato sauce) to pot-roast sandwiches to chili-and-chocolate-glazed salmon. With lots of gluten-free and vegetarian options to boot, Beatrix is a crowd-pleaser.

THE DEEP-DISH DEBATE

Everyone agrees the Near North neighborhood is where deep-dish pizza originated. But as to who invented it? That's where the consensus ends.

What we do know is that pizza first bulked up in 1943. That's when a chef who thought big arrived. He rolled out the mighty dough that cradled the first deep-dish pie – with a full inch of red sauce, chopped plum tomatoes and shredded American-style mozzarella cheese – and the city went gaga.

So who is this genius? The nod usually goes to Ike Sewell, who owned a restaurant called Pizzeria Uno (p76). But Ike's cook Rudy Malnati – father of Lou – claimed he created the gooey-cheesed behemoth. The war over who's first, and best, continues today.

ALY FOOD HALL **$$**

p p304 (☑312-521-8700; www.eataly.com; 43 Ohio St; cafe items $4-14, restaurant mains $15-26; ⏱10am-11pm Mon-Sat, to 10pm Sun; Ⓜ Red Line to Grand) This two-story Italian food emporium overwhelms when you step inside. The winners among the many restaurants and cafe stations strewn throughout include La Focaccia (warm, bread-y goodness; 2nd floor), Ravioli & Co (housemade pasta bar; 1st floor) and the Cannoli and Rosé Bar (sweet ricotta and vino; 1st floor).

PIZZERIA UNO PIZZA **$$**

Map p304 (☑312-321-1000; www.unos.com; 29 E Ohio St; small pizzas from $13; ⏱11am-1am Mon-Fri, to 2am Sat, to 11pm Sun; Ⓜ Red Line to Grand) Ike Sewell supposedly invented Chicago-style pizza here in 1943, although his claim to fame is hotly contested. A light, flaky crust holds piles of cheese and a herb-laced tomato sauce. The pizzas take a while, but kill time with the pitchers of beer and red wine and avoid the salad and other distractions to save room for the main event.

TOPOLOBAMPO/ FRONTERA GRILL MEXICAN **$$$**

Map p304 (☑312-661-1434; www.rickbayless. com; 445 N Clark St; Topolo set menus $95-140, Frontera mains $22-35; ⏱11:30am-10pm Tue-Thu, to 11pm Fri, 10:30am-11pm Sat; Ⓜ Red Line to Grand) 🍴 You've seen chef-owner Rick Bayless on TV, stirring pepper sauces and other jump-off-the-tongue Mexican creations. His isn't your typical taco menu: Bayless uses seasonal ingredients for his wood-grilled meats, flavor-packed mole sauces, chili-thickened braises and signature margaritas. Though they share space, Topolobampo and Frontera Grill are two separate restaurants: Michelin-starred Topolo is sleeker and pricier, while Frontera is more informal.

Both places are always packed. Frontera takes some reservations but mostly seats on a first-come, first-served basis. Reserve in advance for Topolobampo (eight to 10 weeks beforehand is recommended). Its menu is based around DIY tasting menus with five to seven courses. Note the restaurants close between 2pm and 5:30pm, in which case you might want to try Bayless' lower-priced Xoco (p74) eatery next door.

If you're in the mood for an unusual Mexican-inspired cocktail, say the mezcal-and-avocado 'Guacamole,' head to Bayless' new, small, trendy Bar Sótano in the building's basement. It pours from 4pm to midnight Tuesday through Thursday, to 2am Friday and Saturday. Enter via the alley behind Frontera and take the freight elevator down.

SHAW'S CRAB HOUSE SEAFOOD **$$$**

Map p304 (☑312-527-2722; www.shawscrab house.com; 21 E Hubbard St; mains $24-46; ⏱11:30am-10pm Mon-Thu, 11:30am-11pm Fri, 10am-11pm Sat, 10am-10pm Sun; Ⓜ Red Line to Grand) Shaw's beautiful old dining room and adjoining lounge have an elegant, historic feel, complemented by dark woods and sea-worn nautical decor. The efficient servers know what selections are freshest; they can also provide a sustainable seafood menu. A crab-cake appetizer and key-lime-pie dessert make faultless bookends to any meal. Free blues bands play in the lounge Sunday, Tuesday and Thursday.

NOMI KITCHEN AMERICAN **$$$**

Map p304 (☑312-239-4030; www.nomi chicago.com; 800 N Michigan Ave; mains $37-48; ⏱6:30am-10pm Mon-Fri, 7am-10pm Sat, 9am-2pm Sun; Ⓜ Red Line to Chicago) NoMi is perched on the Park Hyatt hotel's 7th floor, providing a sleek, art-filled interior and spectacular Magnificent Mile views. The seasonally driven menu changes regularly. There's an open kitchen, so you can watch your lamb stew with turnip puree or Maine lobster with fava beans being cooked. Reserve a window table around sunset for a truly romantic experience.

KITCHEN CHICAGO AMERICAN **$$$**

Map p304 (☑312-836-1300; www.thekitchen bistros.com; 316 N Clark St; mains $22-34; ⏱11am-10pm Mon-Fri, from 10am Sat & Sun; Ⓜ Blue, Brown, Orange, Green, Purple, Pink Line to Clark/Lake) 🍴 This space right on the river is a knockout: an airy room of exposed concrete, glittery chandeliers and chunky wood tables with water views. The motto is 'community through food,' which translates into an upscale hippie-type ambience where you can watch the chefs create your sustainably sourced pan-seared salmon, mustard-glazed chicken and minty lamb meatballs in the open kitchen.

CHICAGO CHOP HOUSE STEAK **$$$**

Map p304 (☑312-552-7729; www.chicagochop house.com; 60 W Ontario St; mains $45-75; ⏱4-10:30pm Mon-Fri, to 11pm Sat, to 10pm Sun; Ⓜ Red Line to Grand) This comfortable, upscale steakhouse does Chicago proud. Expect perfectly cured meats hand-cut on-site and an atmosphere befitting the city's famous politicos and mob bosses – many of whom look down from framed portraits lining the walls. If you're not up for a slab of meat, you can always pop in to the piano bar and sample the 600-strong wine list.

✕ Streeterville

★ BILLY GOAT TAVERN

BURGERS $

Map p304 (☎312-222-1525; www.billygoattavern. com; 430 N Michigan Ave, lower level; burgers $4-8; ⏰6am-1am Mon-Thu, to 2am Fri, to 3am Sat, 9am-2am Sun; Ⓜ Red Line to Grand) *Tribune* and *Sun Times* reporters have guzzled in the subterranean Billy Goat for decades. Order a 'cheezborger' and Schlitz beer, then look around at the newspapered walls to get the scoop on infamous local stories, such as the Cubs' Curse. This is a tourist magnet, but a deserving one. Follow the tavern signs leading below Michigan Ave to get here.

If the cantankerous Greeks manning the grill sound familiar, it's because they enjoyed the fame of John Belushi's *Saturday Night Live* skit ('Cheezborger! Cheezborger! No fries! Cheeps!'). The Billy Goat is also a fine spot for cheap, late-night boozing. And ignore the other outlets around town; this is the original and the one with the most personality.

PURPLE PIG

MEDITERRANEAN $$

Map p304 (☎312-464-1744; www.thepurple pigchicago.com; 500 N Michigan Ave; $10-20; ⏰11:30am-11pm; 🍴; Ⓜ Red Line to Grand) The Pig's Magnificent Mile location, lively ambience and wide-ranging meat, cheese and veggie menu make it a crowd-pleaser. Milk-braised pork shoulder is the hamtastic specialty. Dishes are meant to be shared, and the long list of affordable vinos gets the good times rolling at communal tables both indoors and out. Alas, there are no reservations to help beat the crowds.

GINO'S EAST

PIZZA $$

Map p304 (☎312-266-3337; www.ginoseast.com; 162 E Superior St; small pizzas from $18; ⏰11am-9pm Sun-Thu, to 10pm Fri & Sat; Ⓜ Red Line to Chicago) In the great deep-dish pizza wars, Gino's is easily one of the top-five heavies. And it encourages customers to do something wacky: cover every available surface – walls, chairs, staircases – with graffiti. The classic cheese-and-sausage pie oozes countless pounds of gooey goodness over a crispy golden crust. Prepare to wait for the pleasure as reservations are not accepted.

BANDERA

AMERICAN $$$

Map p304 (☎312-644-3524; www.bandera restaurants.com; 535 N Michigan Ave; mains $20-30; ⏰11:30am-10pm Sun-Thu, to 11pm Fri & Sat; Ⓜ Red Line to Grand) Looking up at the entry to this 2nd-story restaurant on Michigan Ave, you'd have no idea of the gem that waits inside. The restaurant has the comfortable retro feel of an expensive supper club, without the snooty waiters. American classics – grilled fish, rotisserie chicken and ice-cream sandwiches – predominate here.

🍷 DRINKING & NIGHTLIFE

You definitely will not go thirsty in the neighborhood. Top marks go to the cozy cocktail and wine bars. Good beer bars pour here, too. It's also a club hub. Pick any street and you'll have options.

🍷 Navy Pier

HARRY CARAY'S TAVERN

BAR

Map p303 (☎312-527-9700; www.harrycarays tavern.com; 700 E Grand Ave; ⏰11am-8pm Mon-Thu, to 10pm Fri & Sat, to 7pm Sun; 🚌65) Order a brewski at this bar named after the Cubs' famed announcer and then sip while perusing the photos and memorabilia of local sports heroes that are strewn throughout. The tavern is located on Navy Pier, near the entrance. The water-facing patio is dog friendly.

🍷 River North & Near North

★ CENTENNIAL CRAFTED BEER & EATERY

CRAFT BEER

Map p304 (☎312-284-5353; www.centennial chicago.com; 733 N LaSalle Dr, Near North; ⏰4pm-midnight Mon-Wed, 11:30am-midnight Thu, to 2am Fri, 10:30am-3am Sat, 10:30am-midnight Sun; Ⓜ Brown, Purple Line to Chicago) Centennial hides in plain sight. It's rarely mobbed, like many of its neighborhood competitors, yet its 50 taps of carefully chosen craft beer and its cozy, candelabra-and-weathered-wood vibe are exactly what you vant in a bar. Beer lovers will never want to leave. Four-beer flights are available that let you expand your hops horizon.

★ARBELLA
COCKTAIL BAR

Map p304 (☑312-846-6654; www.arbellachicago.com; 112 W Grand Ave, River North; ⏱5pm-midnight Mon, to 2am Tue-Fri, to 3am Sat; ⓂRed Line to Grand) Named for a 17th-century ship full of wine-guzzling passengers, Arbella is an adventurous cocktail bar. Booze from around the globe makes its way into the drinks, from rye to rum, pisco to mezcal. Park yourself at a dark leather banquette, under sparkly globe lights, and taste-trip the night away in one of the city's warmest, coziest rooms.

CLARK STREET ALE HOUSE
BAR

Map p304 (☑312-642-9253; www.clarkstreetalehouse.com; 742 N Clark St, River North; ⏱4pm-4am Mon-Fri, from 11am Sat & Sun; ⓡ; ⓂRed Line to Chicago) Do as the retro sign advises and 'Stop & Drink.' Midwestern microbrews are the main draw. Work up a thirst on the free pretzels, order a three-beer sampler for $7 and cool off in the beer garden out back. In a neighborhood where many bars lean toward pretentious, this is a great unassuming spot with an old-school vibe.

BAR RAMONE
WINE BAR

Map p304 (☑312-985-6909; www.barramone.com; 441 N Clark St, River North; ⏱4-10pm Sun & Mon, to 11pm Tue-Thu, to midnight Fri & Sat; ⓂRed Line to Grand) A hodgepodge of funky light fixtures dangles from the ceiling, and paintings hang on the exposed-brick walls so the room resembles a salon. Settle in to a romantic table and choose from more than 25 wines available by the glass, including Txakolina, the sparkler from Spain's Basque region. Bar Ramone is perfect for a date night or after-dinner nightcap.

DISCO
CLUB

Map p304 (☑312-828-9000; www.discochicago.com; 111 W Hubbard St, River North; ⏱10pm-4am Thu & Fri, to 5am Sat; ⓂBrown, Purple Line to Merchandise Mart) The 1970s are back, complete with furry couches, a trippy LED dance floor and glittery mirrored balls spinning from the ceiling. Disco pays homage to its namesake era in a fun way. Expect authentic tunes (ABBA, Bee Gees) and a youthful crowd dancing like mad. It's located above the cocktail bar Celeste.

HENRY'S
BAR

Map p304 (☑312-955-8018; www.henrys-chicago.com; 18 W Hubbard St, River North; ⏱5pm-midnight Sun-Thu, 4pm-2am Fri, 5pm-3am Sat; ⓂRed Line to Grand) Many bars in this neighborhood are annoyingly trendy and uppity. Henry's is refreshing because it's not: it's welcoming, laid-back and relatively cheap. Hang out on one of the couches, play pool or cards, and swill a craft cocktail or small-batch beer (seven good ones on tap). It gets more lounge-like on weekends, when DJs spin.

WATERSHED
BAR

Map p304 (☑312-266-4932; www.watershedbar.com; 601 N State St, River North; ⏱5pm-1am Tue-Sun; ⓂRed Line to Grand) This snug basement bar has a speakeasy-meets-ski-lodge vibe. All of the beer and spirits hail from the Great Lakes region (hence the name) and staff procure several hard-to-find gems. Watershed sits beneath Pop's for Champagne, the long-standing wine bar where a mature crowd sips from an impressive list of sparkling vintages. Enter via Pop's to reach the staircase to Watershed.

SOUND-BAR
CLUB

Map p304 (☑312-787-4480; www.sound-bar.com; 226 W Ontario St, River North; ⏱10pm-4am Fri, to 5am Sat; ⓂBrown, Purple Line to Chicago) This enormous nightspot rises above the city's other megaclubs by way of big-name touring trance and house DJs, as well as a sturdy lineup of resident DJs. There's an excellent sound system and a dramatic setting of futuristic neon and steely, minimalist decor. No cover charge if you arrive before 11pm; otherwise expect to pay at least $20.

🍸 Streeterville

SECOND STORY
GAY

Map p304 (☑312-923-9536; 157 E Ohio St, 2nd fl; ⏱noon-2am; ⓂRed Line to Grand) Climb the stairs that lead above Sayat Nova Armenian restaurant, and voilà, you've arrived at a friendly gay dive bar that most people don't even know is there. The wood-paneled walls, rainbow flags, disco ball and cheap drinks lend it a scruffy charm. Cash only.

DOLLOP
COFFEE

Map p304 (☑312-929-4007; www.dollopcoffee.com; 345 E Ohio St; ⏱7am-7pm; ⓡ; ⓂRed Line to Grand) Modern, sunny coffee-slinger Dollop fires up a mean espresso among its caffeinated arsenal. Local baked treats such as Hoosier Mama pies provide the sugar. Branches all over the city.

⭐ ENTERTAINMENT

★BLUE CHICAGO
BLUES

Map p304 (☑312-661-0100; www.bluechicago. com; 536 N Clark St, River North; tickets $10-12; ☺8pm-1:30am Sun-Fri, to 2:30am Sat; Ⓜ Red Line to Grand) Commanding local acts wither the mikes nightly at this mainstream blues club. It's a pretty spartan setup, with a small, narrow room that gets packed. Arrive early to get a seat. The crowd and River North environs are touristy, the bands are the real deal.

WINTER'S JAZZ CLUB
JAZZ

Map p304 (☑312-344-1270; www.wintersjazzclub. com; 465 N McClurg Ct, Streeterville; tickets $15-20; ☺5:30-11:30pm Tue-Sun; Ⓜ Red Line to Grand) One of the city's newer clubs, Winter's provides an elegant little room for straight-ahead jazz. National and local performers let loose for an audience of true appreciators. The 75-minute sets start at 7:30pm and 9:30pm. Note there is a $10 minimum drink purchase. The club's entrance is on the promenade, behind the Target Express shop.

CHICAGO SHAKESPEARE THEATER
THEATER

Map p303 (☑312-595-5600; www.chicagoshakes. com; 800 E Grand Ave, Navy Pier; 🚌65) Snuggled into a beautiful glass home on Navy Pier, this company is at the top of its game, presenting works from the Bard that are fresh, inventive and timeless. In summer the group puts on Shakespeare in the Parks – free performances of one of Will's classics that travel to more than a dozen neighborhoods.

HOUSE OF BLUES
LIVE MUSIC

Map p304 (☑312-923-2000; www.houseofblues. com/chicago; 329 N Dearborn St, River North; ☺restaurant 11:30am-midnight Mon-Wed, to 1:30am Thu-Sat, 4pm-midnight Sun; Ⓜ Brown, Orange, Green, Purple, Pink Line to State/Lake) Bands of all genres play in the eye-popping Music Hall, a wildly colored space decorated with far-out art. Some pretty big names take the stage. In addition, blues bands play nightly in the restaurant, and while they may not be famous, they're always high quality; for these shows there's usually no cover charge until after 9pm, when it costs $10.

🛍 SHOPPING

Near North is home to the Magnific⸱ Mile (p70), lined with sleek name retaile⸱ along Michigan Ave. It dominate⸱ the scene, though occasionally an independent bookstore or vintage shop crops up on a quieter street.

★GARRETT POPCORN
FOOD

Map p304 (www.garrettpopcorn.com; 625 N Michigan Ave, Streeterville; ☺10am-8pm Mon-Thu, to 9pm Fri & Sat, to 7pm Sun; Ⓜ Red Line to Grand) People form long lines outside this store on the Mag Mile. Granted, the caramel corn is heavenly and the cheese popcorn decadent, but is it worth waiting in the whipping snow for a chance to buy some? Actually, it is. Try the Garrett Mix, which combines the two flavors. The entrance is on Ontario St.

★P.O.S.H.
HOMEWARES

Map p304 (☑312-280-1602; www.poshchicago. com; 613 N State St, River North; ☺10am-7pm Mon-Sat, 11am-5pm Sun; Ⓜ Red Line to Grand) Travel fiends and design junkies alike will delight in this charmingly curated shop, which deals in quirky finds such as tableware from steamships and vintage French match strikers. It's situated in River North's Tree Studios, a former artists colony distinguished by a striking Queen Anne–style cast-iron facade.

AFTER-WORDS BOOKS
BOOKS

Map p304 (☑312-464-1110; www.after-words chicago.com; 23 E Illinois St, River North; ☺10:30am-10pm Mon-Thu, to 11pm Fri, 10am-11pm Sat, noon-7pm Sun; Ⓜ Red Line to Grand) After-Words is one of the few bookstores in this area. The new and used tomes spread over two floors. Upstairs holds children's, architecture and Chicago-focused titles, while the jam-packed downstairs has everything else, from *The Guide to Knots* to *French Home Cooking* to Jean-Paul Sartre's *The Age of Reason*.

APPLE MICHIGAN AVENUE
ELECTRONICS

Map p304 (☑312-529-9500; www.apple.com/retail/michiganavenue; 401 N Michigan Ave, Streeterville; ☺9am-9pm Mon-Sat, 10am-7pm Sun; 🛜; Ⓜ Red Line to Grand) Even jaded consumers have to admit this is an amazing-looking Apple store. The all-glass facade looks over the Chicago River flowing directly outside. The wide, tiered steps inside are designed as a community gathering place where locals sit, gape and use the free wi-fi. Free

...tional sessions take place daily on ...cs such as photography, music creation ...d coding.

NIKE CHICAGO
SPORTS & OUTDOORS

Map p304 (☑312-642-6363; www.nike.com/chicago; 669 N Michigan Ave, Streeterville; ◎10am-9pm Mon-Sat, noon-6pm Sun; Ⓜ Red Line to Chicago) This flashy, four-story Nike brand store is fun to meander. It has loads of Cubs, White Sox and other local team gear, and pays homage to Chicago Bulls legend Michael Jordan by carrying more Jordan-brand merchandise than any other store worldwide. The 4th floor has an area to design your own swooshed kicks.

🤸 SPORTS & ACTIVITIES

★BOBBY'S BIKE HIKE
CYCLING

Map p304 (☑312-245-9300; www.bobbysbikehike.com; 540 N Lake Shore Dr, Streeterville; per hr/day from $8/27, tours $38-70; ◎8:30am-8pm Mon-Fri, 8am-8pm Sat & Sun Jun-Aug, 9am-7pm Mar-May & Sep-Nov; Ⓜ Red Line to Grand) Bobby's earns rave reviews from riders. It rents bikes and has easy access to the Lakefront Trail (p35). It also offers tours of gangster sites, the lakefront, nighttime vistas and pizza and beer venues. The Tike Hike caters to kids. Enter through the covered driveway to reach the shop. Call for winter hours.

OHIO STREET BEACH
BEACH

Map p303 (www.cpdbeaches.com; 600 N Lake Shore Dr, Streeterville; ☐65) Just a few minutes' walk from Navy Pier, this small beach is convenient for those who want a quick dip. The water's shallowness makes it the preferred spot for triathletes practicing open-water swims. A cafe pours beer and wine and serves sandwiches.

SHORELINE SIGHTSEEING
BOATING

(☑312-222-9328; www.shorelinesightseeing.com; 75min tours adult/child from $37/19; ◎Mar-Oct) Provides architecture, lake and fireworks cruises. Tours depart from three docks: the Navy Pier lake dock, Polk Bros Park river dock (just west of Navy Pier's entrance) and Michigan Ave dock (under the bridge, northeast corner). It also operates the Shoreline Water Taxi with lake service to the Museum Campus, as well as service to various docks along the river.

CHOPPING BLOCK
COOKING

Map p304 (☑312-644-6360; www.thechoppingblock.com; 222 Merchandise Mart Plaza, Suite 107, River North; 2½hr class $55-95) Master knife skills or learn to make deep-dish pizza at Chopping Block, which provides cooking classes at the four kitchens here. The shop in front sells groovy cookware.

UNTOUCHABLE GANGSTER TOURS
BUS

Map p304 (☑773-881-1195; www.gangstertour.com; 600 N Clark St, River North; 2hr tours $35; Ⓜ Red Line to Grand) Comic, costumed actors take you by bus to some of Chicago's famous gangster sights. It's corny-good fun. There's usually a daily tour at 11am, plus 1pm in summer, with additional offerings Friday to Sunday. Reservations are wise. Departs from outside McDonald's.

WINDY
BOATING

Map p303 (☑312-451-2700; www.tallshipwindy.com; 600 E Grand Ave, Navy Pier; 60-75min tours adult/child $30/10; ◎May-Oct; ☐65) The four-masted schooner sets sail from Navy Pier. Trips have different themes (pirates, architecture, sailing skills etc). With only the sound of the wind in your ears, these tours are the most relaxing way to see the skyline from offshore.

WEIRD CHICAGO TOURS
BUS

Map p304 (☑217-791-7859; www.weirdchicago.com; 600 N Clark St, River North; 3hr tours $40; Ⓜ Red Line to Grand) Hop on a bus to swing by ghost, gangster and grisly crime sites. In summer the company also puts on two-hour haunted walking tours (per person $25). Check the website for the schedule. All jaunts depart from outside McDonald's.

WATERIDERS
KAYAKING

Map p304 (☑312-953-9287; www.wateriders.com; 500 N Kingsbury St, East Bank Club Riverwalk, River North; per person 1st hour weekday/weekend $25/30; ◎May-Sep; Ⓜ Brown, Purple Line to Merchandise Mart) Wateriders rents kayaks for paddles on the Chicago River; after the first hour, it's $5 for each 15-minute block. It also has excellent tours for both daytime and evenings, including the 2½-hour 'Ghosts and Gangsters' ($65), which glides by notorious downtown sites. Its dock is on the Riverwalk behind the East Bank Club, just north of Kinzie St.

Gold Coast

Neighborhood Top Five

❶ Signature Lounge (p92) Getting high by soaring up in the 20mph elevator to this 96th-floor lounge for some tall drinks and sparkling views.

❷ Museum of Contemporary Art (p84) Perusing the avant-garde paintings, sculptures and videos by day, then sticking around for an experimental performance in the museum's theater at night.

❸ Astor Street (p90) Ogling the genteel mansions where Chicago's rich and powerful have lived since the 1880s.

❹ International Museum of Surgical Science (p86) Examining the eerie surgical instruments and fascinating medical-science exhibits at this esoteric museum set in an old mansion.

❺ Rush Street Wandering between flashy bars and restaurants during the see-and-be-seen weekend nights.

For more detail of this area see Map p308

Lonely Planet's Top Tip

The Gold Coast may be one of Chicago's most moneyed neighborhoods, but it offers several freebies to take advantage of: the Charnley-Persky House (p90) has free tours on Wednesdays (though donations are appreciated), while the Newberry Library (p85) and City Gallery (p85) at the Water Tower are always free.

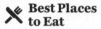

✖ Best Places to Eat

➡ Le Colonial (p91)
➡ Gibson's (p91)
➡ Hendrickx Belgian Bread Crafter (p91)
➡ Pizano's (p91)
➡ Velvet Taco (p90)

For reviews, see p90.➡

☕ Best Places to Drink

➡ Signature Lounge (p92)
➡ Coq d'Or (p92)
➡ 3 Arts Club Cafe (p93)
➡ Sparrow (p92)
➡ Booth One (p93)

For reviews, see p92.➡

🔒 Best Places to Shop

➡ American Girl Place (p94)
➡ Lego Store (p94)
➡ Uniqlo (p94)
➡ Barneys New York (p94)

For reviews, see p93.➡

Explore Gold Coast

The Gold Coast has been the address of Chicago's crème de la crème for more than 125 years. A stroll through the neighborhood, especially the Astor St area, will let you take in some of the most beautiful old mansions in town.

Beyond the sky-high 360° Chicago observatory and the underappreciated Museum of Contemporary Art, the Gold Coast offers several small, quirky sights, such as the arcane International Museum of Surgical Science and memorabilia-filled Chicago Sports Museum. The best way to get a feel for the neighborhood's moneyed milieu is to spend an afternoon browsing luxuriant designer goods around Oak and Rush Sts, or an evening among the glittering high heels and expensive suits on display in the neighborhood's nightlife. On Friday evening, the glamorous set glides through bars and restaurants at Rush and State Sts, where wealthy men of industry carve up porterhouses while downing martinis and ogling the action – no wonder locals call the area the 'Viagra Triangle.'

East along Michigan Ave the shopping gives way to high-rise malls offering family-friendly options like American Girl Place and the Lego Store. Oak Street Beach is a stone's throw away, offering a bit of breathing room from the high-rise jungle and a fine place to dip your toes in the lake.

Local Life

➡ **Hidden treats** Only neighborhood folks know that Hendrickx Belgian Bread Crafter (p91), purveyor of top-notch chocolate croissants, hides inside a bland apartment building on Walton St.

➡ **Low-key drinks** Locals looking for a well-made cocktail without the usual Gold Coast vibe head upstairs to the relaxed bar at Le Colonial (p91).

➡ **Late-night munchies** When the bars and clubs close, everyone heads to Tempo Cafe (p91), open 24/7 for skillet-fried replenishment.

Getting There & Away

➡ **The L** Red Line to Clark/Division for the neighborhood's northern reaches; Red Line to Chicago for the southern areas.

➡ **Bus** Bus 151 runs along Michigan Ave, handy for further-flung sights.

➡ **Car** Resident-only streets stymie street parking. Try LaSalle St, much of which is unmetered.

TOP SIGHT
360° CHICAGO

Located atop the city's fourth-tallest skyscraper, 875 N Michigan Ave, 360° Chicago is a dandy place to get high in Chicago. In many ways the view here surpasses the one at Willis Tower, as the building is closer to the lake and provides unfettered panoramic vistas. If that's not enough, the observatory offers a couple of thrill features as well.

The 94th-floor observatory offers informative displays that tell you the names of the surrounding buildings. It has the Skywalk, a sort of screened-in porch that lets you feel the wind and hear the city sounds. The biggest draw is Tilt, a set of floor-to-ceiling windows that you stand in as they move and tip out over the ground; it costs $7.20 extra and is actually less spine-tingling than it sounds. The observatory is probably your best bet if you have kids or if you're a newbie and want to beef up your Chicago knowledge, but there are other options.

Not interested in frivolities? Head straight for the building's 96th-floor Signature Lounge (p92), where the view is free if you buy a drink ($10 to $18). That's right, here you'll get a glass of wine and a comfy seat while staring out at almost identical views from a few floors higher than the observatory. The elevators for the lounge (and its companion restaurant on the 95th floor) are separate from those for the observatory. Look for signs that say 'Signature 95th/96th' one floor up from the observatory entrance.

The John Hancock Center, as the building was then known, was completed in 1969. Fazlur Khan and Bruce Graham were the chief architects, and they designed the structure to sway as much as 5in to 8in in Chicago's windy conditions. They went on to build the Willis Tower four years later.

DON'T MISS

- ➡ Skywalk
- ➡ Signature Lounge
- ➡ Nighttime views, including summer fireworks

PRACTICALITIES

- ➡ Map p308, F6
- ➡ ☏888-875-8439
- ➡ www.360chicago.com
- ➡ 875 N Michigan Ave, 94th fl
- ➡ adult/child $22/15
- ➡ ⊙9am-11pm, last tickets 10:30pm
- ➡ Ⓜ Red Line to Chicago

Welcome to
the Commons

TOP SIGHT
MUSEUM OF CONTEMPORARY ART (MCA)

In contrast to the classical collection of the Art Institute, the MCA exhibits contemporary, avant-garde works from the past century that often straddle the worlds of visual art and mixed media. Its modern photography collections are especially strong. With regularly changing displays, you're sure to see something unconventional, and maybe even controversial.

The museum mounts themed exhibitions that typically focus on underappreciated or up-and-coming artists that curators are introducing to American audiences. Shows last three months or so before the galleries morph into something new.

The terraced sculpture garden at the back of the museum makes for a nifty browse. In summer (June through September) a jazz band plays amid the greenery every Tuesday at 5:30pm. Patrons bring blankets and sip drinks from the bar. The museum's front plaza also sees lots of action, especially on Tuesday mornings in June through October when a farmers market with veggies, cheeses and baked goods sets up from 7am to 2pm. Both events are big local to-dos.

The Museum of Contemporary Art's theater regularly hosts dance, music and film events by contemporary A-listers. Much of it is pretty far out, eg an Inuit throat singer performing to a silent-film backdrop, a play about ventriloquists performed by a European puppet troupe, or nude male dancers leaping in a piece about how technology affects life. Bonus: a theater ticket stub provides free museum admission any time during the week after the show.

Docents lead free, 45-minute tours of the exhibitions every day at 1pm, as well as 2pm on Saturdays and Sundays. Enquire at the 2nd-floor visitor service desk. Also worth a visit is the museum's fantastic, two-level shop. Besides extensive book offerings in all kinds of art and designand a well-stocked children's book section, it features a whole floor of housewares, gifts, accessories and jewelry.

DON'T MISS

➡ Free docent-led tours
➡ Funky museum shop
➡ Sculpture garden
➡ Terrace with lake views

PRACTICALITIES

➡ MCA
➡ Map p308, F7
➡ ☎312-280-2660
➡ www.mcachicago.org
➡ 220 E Chicago Ave
➡ adult/child $15/free
➡ ⊙10am-9pm Tue & Fri, to 5pm Wed, Thu, Sat & Sun
➡ Ⓜ Red Line to Chicago

 SIGHTS

360° CHICAGO　　　　　OBSERVATORY
See p83.

**MUSEUM OF
CONTEMPORARY ART**　　　MUSEUM
See opposite.

NEWBERRY LIBRARY　　　LIBRARY
Map p308 (☑312-943-9090; www.newberry.org;
60 W Walton St; ⊙galleries 8:15am-5pm Mon, Fri
& Sat, to 7:30pm Tue-Thu; Ⓜ Red Line to Chicago)
FREE The Newberry's public galleries are a
treat for bibliophiles: those who swoon over
original Thomas Paine pamphlets about the
French Revolution, or get weak-kneed seeing Thomas Jefferson's copy of the *History
of the Expedition under Captains Lewis
and Clark* (with margin notes!). Intriguing exhibits rotate yellowed manuscripts
and tattered 1st editions from the library's
extensive collection. The on-site bookstore
is tops for Chicago-themed titles. Free tours
of the impressive building take place at 3pm
Thursday and 10:30am Saturday.

The building's upper floors house the library itself (open 9am to 5pm Tuesday to
Friday, and to 1pm Saturday), stacked with
books, maps, photographs and other hu-
manities-related materials. Those trying to
research far-flung branches of their family
tree will have a field day with the extensive
genealogy section.

Entry requires a library card, but one-
day passes are available for curious brows-
ers. Once inside, you can pester the patient
librarians with requests for help in tracking
down all manner of historical ephemera.

**CHICAGO
SPORTS MUSEUM**　　　MUSEUM
Map p308 (☑312-202-0500; www.chicagos-
portsmuseum.com; 835 N Michigan Ave, 7th fl,
Water Tower Place; ⊙11:30am-
8:30pm Mon-Thu, to 9pm Fri, 11am-9pm Sat,
11am-6pm Sun; Ⓜ Red Line to Chicago) To understand Chicago's sports psyche, peruse
the memorabilia-filled cases at this gallery
attached to Harry Caray's 7th Inning Stretch
restaurant. See the cleats Cubs infielder Kris
Bryant wore on the winning final play of the
2016 World Series, which ended the team's
108-year championship drought. Examine
Sammy Sosa's corked bat and the infamous
'Bartman ball.' The museum also enshrines
relics for Da Bears, Bulls, Blackhawks and

White Sox. (Admission is free if you eat or
drink at the restaurant.)

Don't miss getting a picture with the restaurant's newest acquisition – a gigantic,
hyperrealistic (down to the ear hairs!) bust
of legendary sports announcer Harry Caray
himself. Just head up to the 7th floor of the
Water Tower Place (p94) mall.

OAK STREET BEACH　　　BEACH
Map p308 (www.cpdbeaches.com; 1000 N Lake
Shore Dr; ⊙6am-11pm; Ⓜ Red Line to Chicago)
This beach at the edge of downtown packs
in bodies beautiful to play volleyball or
sunbathe in the shadow of skyscrapers.
Swimming is permitted in summer when
lifeguards are on duty (11am to 7pm). You
can rent umbrellas and lounge chairs. The
island-themed, yellow-umbrella-dotted cafe
provides drinks and DJs.

CITY GALLERY　　　GALLERY
Map p308 (☑312-742-0808; 806 N Michigan Ave;
⊙10am-7pm Mon-Fri, to 5pm Sat & Sun; Ⓜ Red
Line to Chicago) **FREE** Set inside the historic
Water Tower (p86), this small gallery showcases Chicago-themed works by local photographers and artists.

WASHINGTON SQUARE　　　PARK
Map p308 (901 N Clark St; Ⓜ Red Line to Chicago)
This plain-looking park across from the
Newberry Library (p85) has quite a history.
In the 1920s it was known as 'Bughouse
Square,' where communists, socialists, anarchists (and other -ists) congregated and
gave impassioned soapbox orations. ('Bughouse' was the term for an insane asylum,
or an adjective for someone in one.) Lawyer
Clarence Darrow and poet Carl Sandburg
are among the respected speakers who
climbed up and shouted.

In the 1970s, when Washington Square
was a gathering place for young male pros-
titutes, it gained tragic infamy as the preferred pick-up spot of mass murderer John
Wayne Gacy. Gacy took his victims back to
his suburban home, where he killed them
and buried their bodies in the basement.
Convicted on 33 counts of murder (although the actual tally may be higher), he
was executed in 1994.

Today the square bears little trace of its
past lives – except for one weekend a year
in late July. That's when the Bughouse De-
bates occur and orators return to holler at
each other (more info is available on the
Newberry Library website).

WATER TOWER
LANDMARK

Map p308 (108 N Michigan Ave; MRed Line to Chicago) This 154ft-tall, turreted tower is a defining city icon: it was the sole downtown survivor of the 1871 Great Chicago Fire, thanks to its yellow limestone bricks, which withstood the flames. Today the tower houses the free City Gallery (p85), which is well worth a peek for its Chicago-themed works by local artists.

Built in 1869, the tower and its companion Water Works Pumping Station were constructed in a Gothic style popular at the time. They were the great hope of Chicago when they first opened, part of a technological breakthrough that was going to provide fresh, clean water for the city. Alas, the plan was ultimately a failure. By 1906 the Water Tower was obsolete and only public outcry saved it from demolition three times. Restoration in 1962 ensured its survival.

INTERNATIONAL MUSEUM OF SURGICAL SCIENCE
MUSEUM

Map p308 (☏312-642-6502; www.imss.org; 1524 N Lake Shore Dr; adult/child $17/9; ☺9:30am-5pm Mon-Fri, from 10am Sat & Sun; ☒151) This small but fascinating museum, set inside a former residential mansion facing the lake, is dedicated to the world of surgery and medicine. Exhibits demonstrate the amazing strides made in medical science throughout history, on subjects as diverse as eyeglasses, wound healing, anesthesia and X-rays, as well as the history of nursing. Artifacts range from creaky old limb prosthetics and rather intimidating antique surgical instruments to an actual iron lung.

WATER WORKS PUMPING STATION
NOTABLE BUILDING

Map p308 (163 E Pearson St; ☺9am-7pm Mon-Sat, 10am-7pm Sun; MRed Line to Chicago) Built in 1869, the Pumping Station and Water Tower, its companion building across the street, were constructed in Gothic style with yellow limestone. It's this stone that saved them when the Great Fire roared through town in 1871. Today the building holds the Lookingglass Theatre Company (p93) and a small branch of the Chicago Public Library.

🏃 Local Life
Gold Coast Saunter

The name might clue you in: Chicago's wealthiest residents have called the Gold Coast home since the late 1800s. Bentleys sit parked outside elegant city mansions; fur-wearing women hobnob in stylish cafes. But hints of this posh neighborhood's quietly seamier side can also be found in between the wallet-busting boutiques and well-heeled restaurants.

❶ Newberry Library
Whether it's a map of Lewis and Clark's westward trek or a Shakespeare First Folio, the historic Newberry Library (p85) has it. Stop by for a free tour, check out the public galleries and browse the on-site bookstore, one of your best bets for Chicago-themed books.

❷ Washington Square
Across from Newberry Library is Washington Square (p85), a park famed for its history of soapbox orators (often considered religious or political nuts, hence its nickname, 'Bughouse Square'). Local residents walk their dogs, workers eat lunch alfresco and crusty old-timers argue by the central fountain. It was added to the National Register of Historic Places in 1991.

❸ Oak Street
Moneyed locals stroll Oak Street to find a sleek Prada bag, a Harry Winston diamond or the perfect pair of Jimmy Choo pumps. (Everyone else comes to window-shop and sigh.) The designer boutiques line up in a pretty row between Michigan Ave and Rush St.

❹ 3 Arts Club Cafe
Pop into this sophisticated cafe (p93) for a light lunch, sitting on stylish couches in a sunny glass atrium replete with chandeliers, trees and a fountain. The original Three Arts Club, founded in 1912, was a home for women in the 'three arts' of music, painting and drama.

1400 N Astor St

⑤ Astor Street

Home to some of Chicago's richest denizens past and present, Astor Street was named for the USA's first multimillionaire, John Jacob Astor (he never lived there, but the area's builders thought his name added dazzle). Several turn-of-the-century mansions rise up between the 1300 and 1500 blocks.

⑥ Original Playboy Mansion

This 1899 mansion (p90) was bought by Hugh Hefner at the start of the sexual revolution of the 1960s. It's all private condos now, so you can't go inside – but you can let your imagination run wild about the debauched carousing that once took place here in Hef's basement 'grotto' pool.

⑦ Lodge Tavern

The woodsy Lodge Tavern (p93) has been catering to the Gold Coast's more downmarket crowd since 1957. Pick out an oldie on the Wurlitzer, grab a draft beer and share a free bowl of peanuts with the hard-drinking locals who hang out here until late.

GOLD COAST

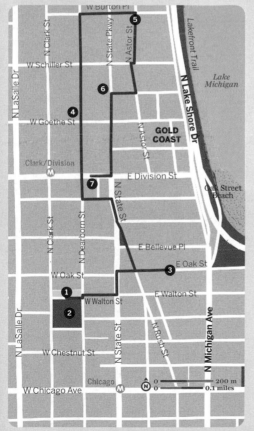

Magnificent Mansions of the Gold Coast

Astor St has been the address of Chicago's elite for more than 125 years. Several spectacular pieces of real estate went up back then, with well-heeled families trying to outdo each other in grandeur. Everyone from Frank Lloyd Wright to Hugh Hefner has passed through the neighborhood's distinguished doors.

1. Archbishop's Residence (p90)
Former guests at the Archbishop's Residence include Franklin D Roosevelt and Pope John Paul II.

2. Patterson-McCormick Mansion (p90)
This 1893 neoclassical home is now luxury apartments.

3. Astor Street (p87)
Several turn-of-the-century mansions rise up between the 1300 and 1500 blocks along Astor St.

4. Charnley-Persky House (p90)
Designed by Louis Sullivan and his then assistant draftsperson Frank Lloyd Wright, the building was completed in 1892.

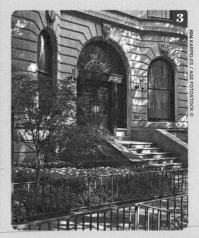

ORIGINAL PLAYBOY MANSION
NOTABLE BUILDING

Map p308 (1340 N State Pkwy; MRed Line to Clark/Division) The sexual revolution partied hearty for 15 years in the basement 'grotto' of this 1899 mansion. *Playboy* founder Hugh Hefner bought it in 1959 and hung a brass plate over the door warning *Si Non Oscillas, Noli Tintinnare* (Latin for 'If You Don't Swing, Don't Ring'). In the mid-1970s, Hef decamped to LA, and the building now comprises ultraluxury condos – but stopping by for a selfie still allows you to boast 'I've been to the Playboy Mansion.'

Playboy Enterprises stayed headquartered in Chicago until 2012, and then it too moved west. The last vestige is 'Honorary Hugh M Hefner Way,' which is what the city renamed Walton St (at Michigan Ave) in an official tip of the hat to Hef.

✖ EATING

The Gold Coast is the epicenter of hot-spot steakhouses and swanky eateries. Rush St is the main vein.

★ VELVET TACO
TACOS $

Map p308 (☎312-763-2654; www.velvettaco.com; 1110 N State St; tacos $3.50-7; ☉11am-midnight Mon, to 2am Tue & Wed, to 3am Thu, to 5am Fri, 10am-5am Sat, 10am-midnight Sun; 🍴; ☒36, MRed Line to Clark/Division) An excellent late-night option for this area, Velvet Taco features hip new takes on the eminently adaptable taco: spicy chicken tikka; Nashville hot tofu with Napa slaw; shredded pork with avocado crema and grilled pineapple; Kobe bacon-burger with smoked cheddar; even shrimp and grits. Down a few accompanied by a margarita or a beer.

ASTOR STREET RICHES
....

In 1882 Bertha and Potter Palmer were the power couple of Chicago. Potter's web of businesses included the city's best hotel, the Palmer House (p232), and a huge general-merchandise store that he later sold to a clerk named Marshall Field. When the Palmers decided to move north from Prairie Ave to a manor at what is now 1350 N Lake Shore Dr, they set off a trendsetting rush of Chicago's wealthy to the neighborhood around them. The mansions sitting along Astor St, especially the 1300 to 1500 blocks, reflect the grandeur of that heady period. Here are the highlights, from south to north:

Charnley-Persky House (Map p308; ☎312-573-1365; www.charnleyhouse.org; 1365 N Astor St; tours Wed/Sat free/$10; ☉noon Wed & Sat year-round, plus 10am Sat Apr-Oct; MRed Line to Clark/Division) As a 19-year-old employee of famed architect Louis Sullivan, Frank Lloyd Wright designed the 11-room Charnley-Persky House, leaving behind the baroque decorations of Victorian design and kicking off a new style of simple, abstract forms that would lay the foundation for modern architecture. Completed in 1892, the house now holds the offices of the Society of Architectural Historians. Free guided tours (first-come, first-served) are offered on Wednesdays, or you can reserve a spot for the paid guided tours on Saturdays.

Patterson-McCormick Mansion (Map p308; 1500 N Astor St; ☒151) This 1893 neo-classical home, originally designed by New York architect Stanford White for newspaper scion Elinor Patterson, is one of the neighborhood standouts. Industrialist Cyrus McCormick bought it in 1914 and lived in it with his family, but today it's divided up into condos. This is still the high-rent district – a 3700-sq-ft two-bedroom unit goes for about $2.8 million.

Archbishop's Residence (Map p308; 1555 N State Pkwy; ☒72, 151) The 19 chimneys of this 1885 mansion, still owned by the Catholic Church, speak to its past life of hospitality: not only have seven Chicago archbishops lived here over the years, but their guest list would fill a *Who's Who*. World figures from Franklin D Roosevelt to Pope John Paul II have all rested their head beneath this roof. (The current archbishop lives in the rectory at Holy Name Cathedral.)

HENDRICKX BELGIAN
BREAD CRAFTER
BAKERY $

Map p308 (☑312-649-6717; www.hendrickx bakery.com; 100 E Walton St; mains $7-13; ☺8am-7pm Tue-Sat, 9am-3pm Sun, 8am-3:30pm Mon; Ⓜ Red Line to Chicago) Hiding in a nondescript apartment building, Hendrickx is a local secret. Push open the bright orange door and behold the waffles, brioche and croissants (in 12 flavors!), among other flaky, buttery, Belgian treats. The place is tiny, with just a few indoor seats, but in warm weather it sets up tables on the sidewalk. Soups and sandwiches are also available.

SPRINKLES CUPCAKES
BAKERY $

Map p308 (www.sprinkles.com; 50 E Walton St; cupcakes $4; ☺9am-9pm Mon-Sat, 10am-8pm Sun; Ⓜ Red Line to Chicago) Sink your teeth into chocolate marshmallow, chai latte, salty caramel and other creamy-frosted mini cakes. The cupcake ATM out front dispenses the goods 24/7. One vegan and two gluten-free options are usually available.

TEMPO CAFE
DINER $

Map p308 (☑312-943-4373; www.tempochicago. com; 6 E Chestnut St; mains $9-15; ☺24hr; Ⓜ Red Line to Chicago) Bright and cheery, this diner serves up most of its meals in a skillet. The omelet-centric menu includes all manner of fresh veggies and meat, as well as pancakes, waffles and sandwiches. It's nothing fancy, but it's open round the clock and is relatively cheap for the pricey Gold Coast. Has gluten-free options.

FOODLIFE
INTERNATIONAL $

Map p308 (☑312-787-7100; www.foodlife chicago.com; 835 N Michigan Ave, Water Tower Place; mains $8-14; ☺11:30am-8pm Mon-Thu, to 8:30pm Fri & Sat, noon-7pm Sun; Ⓜ Red Line to Chicago) It bills itself as an 'urban food hall,' which translates to a midrange food court with more than a dozen different globally themed kitchens featuring gourmet à la carte options in a sleek atmosphere. Sushi, stir-fries, pizza, pasta, burritos and barbecue are among the offerings. It's situated inside Water Tower Place (p94) mall on the mezzanine level.

PIZANO'S
PIZZA $$

Map p308 (☑312-751-1766; www.pizanos chicago.com; 864 N State St; 10in pizzas from $16; ☺11am-2am Sun-Fri, to 3am Sat; Ⓜ Red Line to Chicago) Congenial Pizano's gets lost amid Chicago's pizza places, which is a shame since it's one of the best and has an illustrious pedigree (founded by Rudy Malnati Jr, whose dad created the deep-dish pizza, so the legend goes). The buttery crust impresses, even more so in its thin-crust incarnation. (Gluten-free crust is also available.) There's another Pizano's in the Loop (p60).

FRANCESCA'S
ON CHESTNUT
ITALIAN $$

Map p308 (☑312-482-8800; www.miafrancesca. com; 200 E Chestnut St; mains $16-35; ☺11am-10pm Mon-Thu, to 11pm Fri & Sat, 10am-9pm Sun; Ⓜ Red Line to Chicago) Part of a well-loved local chain, Francesca's buzzes with regulars who come for the trattoria's rustic standards, such as linguine with salmon and wild mushrooms, housemade gnocchi and roast chicken, all prepared with simple flair. It's a sweet, unpretentious spot for the neighborhood. It's located in the Seneca building.

★LE COLONIAL
FRENCH, VIETNAMESE $$$

Map p308 (☑312-255-0088; www.lecolonial chicago.com; 937 N Rush St; mains $20-34; ☺11:30am-3pm & 5-10pm Sun-Thu, to 11pm Fri & Sat; ☑; Ⓜ Red Line to Chicago) Step into the dark-wood, candlelit room, where ceiling fans swirl lazily and big-leafed palms sway in the breeze, and you'd swear you were in 1920s Saigon. Staff can arrange vegetarian and gluten-free substitutions among the curries and banana-leaf-wrapped fish dishes. If you want spicy, be specific; everything typically comes out mild.

Le Colonial is perfect for a romantic date. You'll need reservations for a table, though walk-ins can head upstairs to the bar and eat there.

GIBSON'S
STEAK $$$

Map p308 (☑312-266-8999; www.gibsons-steakhouse.com; 1028 N Rush St; mains $24-63; ☺11am-midnight; Ⓜ Red Line to Clark/Division) There's a scene every night at this local original. Politicians, movers, shakers and the shaken-down swirl the famed martinis and compete for prime table space in the buzzing dining room. The rich and beautiful mingle at the bar, often to live piano music. The steaks here are as good as they come, and ditto for the ginormous lobsters.

SIGNATURE ROOM
AT THE 95TH
AMERICAN $$$

Map p308 (☑312-787-9596; www.signatureroom. com; 875 N Michigan Ave, 95th fl; mains $34-51;

lunch 11am-2:30pm Mon-Fri, from 10am Sat & Sun, dinner 5-10pm Sun-Thu, to 11pm Fri & Sat; ✈; M Red Line to Chicago) Given that diners spend most of the meal view-gaping, you'd think the kitchen atop 875 N Michigan wouldn't trouble itself over the food, but the chef does a fine job with the fish, steak and pasta dishes. Vegetarians will find a fair number of options available. Dress for dinner is business casual; no ripped jeans or tennis shoes allowed.

Weekend brunch features an all-you-can-eat buffet (adult/child $60/25). Cheapskates should note they can get the same vista for the price of a (costly) beer, one floor up in the Signature Lounge.

MORTON'S
STEAK $$$

Map p308 (✆312-266-4820; www.mortons. com/statestreet; 1050 N State St; mains $35-114; ⏰5:30-11pm Mon-Sat, 5-10pm Sun; M Red Line to Clark/Division) Morton's is a chain now, but Chicago is where it all began, with meat aged to perfection and displayed table-side before cooking. See that half a cow? It's the 42oz double porterhouse ($114). Smaller – but still dangerous if dropped on your toe – are the fillets, strip steaks and other cuts. The immense baked potatoes could prop up church foundations.

MIKE DITKA'S RESTAURANT
AMERICAN $$$

Map p308 (✆312-587-8989; www.ditkas restaurants.com; 100 E Chestnut St; mains $22-60; ⏰11am-10pm Mon-Thu, to 11pm Fri, 10am-11pm Sat, 10am-10pm Sun; M Red Line to Chicago) When it's too cold for a tailgate party, come to this spot in the **Tremont Hotel** (✆312-751-1900; www.tremonthotelchicago.com) owned by the famously cantankerous former coach of the Chicago Bears (who often pops in).

CUPCAKES 24/7

The cupcake craze may be losing its pizzazz, but the novelty of getting a fondant-iced chocolate marshmallow or triple cinnamon confection at 2am from an automated vending machine is hard to resist. The 'Cupcake ATM' dispenses 24 hours a day in front of Sprinkles Cupcakes (p91). The machine even stocks one for dogs (sugar-free, of course).

The menu is as meaty as you'd expect, with steaks galore and heaps of oysters, crab legs and other seafood. Fans will love the memorabilia-filled display cases.

🍷 DRINKING & NIGHTLIFE

Martini lounges for pretty people on the prowl are the specialty in the zone formed by Chicago, State and Rush Sts. Glamorous old-time lounges and skyscraper bars with spectacular views are also found here.

⭐SIGNATURE LOUNGE
LOUNGE

Map p308 (www.signatureroom.com; 875 N Michigan Ave, 96th fl; ⏰11am-12:30am Sun-Thu, to 1:30am Fri & Sat; M Red Line to Chicago) Take the elevator to the 96th floor of the building formerly called the John Hancock Center and order a (pricey) beverage while looking out over the city from some 1000ft up in the sky. It's especially gape-worthy at night. There's a particularly good southern view from the women's bathroom (sorry, guys).

The place is deservedly popular so be prepared for a crowd. The lounge and restaurant (p91) have a separate elevator from the observatory (p83); look for signs that say 'Signature 95th/96th.' Children aren't allowed in the lounge after 7pm.

COQ D'OR
LOUNGE

Map p308 (✆312-932-4623; 140 E Walton St; ⏰11am-1am Sun-Thu, to 2am Fri & Sat; M Red Line to Chicago) This classy joint in the Drake Hotel (p237) opened the day after Prohibition was repealed. It offers a taste of old Chicago: burgundy-colored leather booths, old-school bartenders and bejeweled women in furs sipping Manhattans. There's live music in the evenings on Thursday, Friday and Saturday.

⭐SPARROW
COCKTAIL BAR

Map p308 (✆312-725-0732; www.sparrow chicago.com; 12 W Elm St; ⏰4pm-2am Mon-Fri, to 3am Sat, to midnight Sun; M Red Line to Clark/Division) This refined lounge, inspired by hotel lobby bars of the 1930 and '40s, is a Gold Coast hidden gem. Tucked behind an unassuming storefront in an art deco apartment building, Sparrow emphasizes rum-focused cocktails, but there's also an extensive wine list and 10 rotating beers on tap. It's a great place to duck into after a nice dinner downtown.

3 ARTS CLUB CAFE   CAFE

Map p308 (☑312-475-9116; www.3artscafe. com; 1300 N Dearborn St; ☺10am-9pm Mon-Sat, 11am-7pm Sun; 🛜; Ⓜ Red Line to Clark/Division) Chandeliers dangle from the high ceiling, fountains gurgle, and sleek couches offer respite under leafy trees in a light-bathed glass atrium. This elegant cafe sits inside a five-floor Restoration Hardware home-decor store. See the host for seats in the gorgeous main room, or grab an espresso or glass of wine that you can take up to the serene roof garden.

The cafe serves casual comfort food (mains $18 to $29) by the chef behind Doughnut Vault and Small Cheval. The Three Arts Club, which long occupied the century-old building, was a home for women in the 'three arts' of music, painting and drama.

BOOTH ONE   COCKTAIL BAR

Map p308 (☑312-601-2970; http://boothone. com; 1301 N State Pkwy; ☺5-10pm Sun-Thu, to midnight Fri & Sat; Ⓜ Red Line to Clark/Division) Frank Sinatra and Bette Davis were among the celebs who used to swirl martinis in the old Pump Room, which recently got a modern rebranding as Booth One. Sip cocktails from a menu of historic drinks from past decades, underneath chandeliers reminiscent of champagne bubbles. Be sure to check the walls for photos of all the famous past patrons.

BIG SHOULDERS COFFEE   COFFEE

Map p308 (☑312-631-3970; www.bigshoulders coffee.com; 858 N State St; ☺6am-6pm Mon-Fri, from 7am Sat & Sun; 🛜; Ⓜ Red Line to Chicago) A local chain, Big Shoulders offers high-quality, no-nonsense coffee, with specialty flavored lattes like vanilla, cardamom, caramel, marshmallow and the housemade horchata. The Gold Coast location is a comfy little cafe with Scandinavian midcentury styling and plenty of well-placed power outlets and wi-fi.

LODGE TAVERN   BAR

Map p308 (☑312-642-4406; http://lodgetavern. com; 21 W Division St; ☺10am-4am Sun-Fri, to 5am Sat; Ⓜ Red Line to Clark/Division) Dressed up like a misplaced hunting cabin, the Lodge hasn't changed a mote since 1957. It has a bit more polish than most of its neighbors on Division St; a Wurlitzer jukebox spins oldies and bowls of salty peanuts complement the abundance of draft beers. The crowd of mostly 40-somethings drinks like they mean it, sometimes until dawn.

☆ ENTERTAINMENT

LOOKINGGLASS
THEATRE COMPANY   THEATER

Map p308 (☑312-337-0665; www.looking glasstheatre.org; 821 N Michigan Ave; Ⓜ Red Line to Chicago) This well-regarded troupe works in a nifty theater hewn from the old Water Works Pumping Station (p86) building. The ensemble cast – which sometimes includes cofounder David Schwimmer of TV's *Friends* – often uses physical stunts and acrobatics to enhance its dreamy, magical, literary productions.

ZEBRA LOUNGE   LIVE MUSIC

Map p308 (☑312-642-5140; www.the zebralounge.net; 1220 N State St; ☺6pm-2am Mon-Fri, 7:30pm-3am Sat, 7:30pm-2am Sun; Ⓜ Red Line to Clark/Division) The piano in this tiny, dark and mirrored room – originally opened as a speakeasy during Prohibition – can get as scratchy as the voices of the crowd, which consists mainly of older folks who like to sing along. The ivory ticklers here are veterans who know their stuff. Live music starts at 9pm nightly. You'll find it in a residential building.

🛍 SHOPPING

Oak St offers luxury-brand boutiques (Harry Winston, Tory Burch, Prada, Armani et al); Walton St, one block south, has a selection appealing to a younger and more athletic set (Burton, Patagonia, Lululemon et al). Malls rise high in the air on Michigan Ave.

★ AMERICAN GIRL PLACE   TOYS

Map p308 (☑877-247-5223; www.americangirl. com; 835 N Michigan Ave, Water Tower Place; ☺10am-8pm Mon-Thu, to 9pm Fri, 9am-9pm Sat, 9am-6pm Sun; 🚼; Ⓜ Red Line to Chicago) This is not just a doll shop – it's an *experience*. Kids can create a completely customized doll that looks just like them, and even buy matching outfits. The cafe seats the dolls as part of the family during tea service. While there are American Girl stores in many cities, this flagship remains the largest and busiest.

LEGO STORE   TOYS

Map p308 (☑312-202-0946; www.lego.com; 835 N Michigan Ave, 2nd fl, Water Tower Place; ☺10am-9pm Mon-Sat, 11am-6pm Sun; ⊞; Ⓜ Red Line to Chicago) After *ooohhing* and *aaahhing* at the cool models of rockets, castles and dinosaurs scattered throughout the store, kids can build their own designs at pint-sized tables equipped with bins of the signature little bricks.

UNIQLO   CLOTHING

Map p308 (☑877-486-4756; www.uniqlo.com; 830 N Michigan Ave; ☺10am-9pm Mon-Sat, 11am-8pm Sun; ☏; Ⓜ Red Line to Chicago) Japanese fashion retailer Uniqlo puts on a spread that draws men and women of all ages. Take the escalators up from street level to the rainbow array of affordable, clean-lined jeans, T-shirts, jackets and other clothing staples.

If you tire of flipping through racks, hit the 6th-floor Starbucks for a drink and great views out over Michigan Ave.

BARNEYS NEW YORK   CLOTHING

Map p308 (☑312-587-1700; www.barneys.com; 15 E Oak St; ☺10am-7pm Mon-Sat, 11am-6pm Sun; Ⓜ Red Line to Chicago) Barneys provides the quintessential Gold Coast shopping experience, with six floors sparkling with mega-high-end designer goods. Up in the penthouse is **Fred's** (mains $20-36), a posh restaurant with a toasty fireplace.

TEAGSCHWENDER   TEA

Map p308 (☑312-932-0639; www.tgtea.com; 1160 N State St; ☺10am-7pm Mon-Sat, to 6pm Sun; Ⓜ Red Line to Clark/Division) A wall of drawers contains 200 different kinds of top-notch loose-leaf tea – Indian black teas, Japanese *sencha,* Chinese gunpowder, South African rooibos and more – which knowledgable staff will happily brew up for you to try. Fill a decorative tin with one of the seasonal flavors or pick up a teapot and accessory set as a thoughtful gift.

WATER TOWER PLACE   MALL

Map p308 (www.shopwatertower.com; 835 N Michigan Ave; ☺10am-9pm Mon-Sat, 11am-6pm Sun; Ⓜ Red Line to Chicago) Water Tower Place launched the city's love affair with vertical shopping centers. Many locals swear this first one remains the best. The mall houses 100 stores on seven levels, including Abercrombie & Fitch, Macy's, Aritzia (the mod Canadian chain), Akira (the hip local clothing vendor), the Lego Store and American Girl Place (p93).

TOPSHOP   CLOTHING

Map p308 (☑312-280-6834; www.topshop.com; 830 N Michigan Ave; ☺10am-9pm Mon-Sat, 11am-8pm Sun; Ⓜ Red Line to Chicago) The popular British purveyor of youthful, urban-cool style has a large store on the Magnificent Mile.

900 N MICHIGAN   MALL

Map p308 (☑312-915-3916; www.shop900.com; 900 N Michigan Ave; ☺10am-7pm Mon-Sat, noon-6pm Sun; Ⓜ Red Line to Chicago) This huge mall is home to an upscale collection of stores including Kate Spade, Max Mara, Gucci and J Crew, among many others. Water Tower Place is under the same management; they simply placed all the really expensive stores over here.

JIL SANDER   CLOTHING

Map p308 (☑312-335-0006; www.jilsander.com; 48 E Oak St; ☺10am-6pm Mon-Sat; Ⓜ Red Line to Chicago) Jil Sander's minimalist colors and simple designs somehow manage to remain fashionable long after other trendsetters have disappeared from the scene.

Lincoln Park & Old Town

Neighborhood Top Five

1 Lincoln Park (p97) Meandering along the park's byways and hearing lions roar in the zoo, then smelling exotic flowers in the conservatory and discovering the calm of the hidden lily pool.

2 Second City (p107) Laughing, drinking and shouting out plot sugges-

tions at this legendary comedy improv venue.

3 Alinea (p104) Digging into space-age modern cuisine at one of the world's best restaurants.

4 North Avenue Beach (p98) Enjoying fun in the sun with a jaunt on a kayak or stand-up paddleboard, joining a beach yoga class or

volleyball game, or just sipping on a frosty margarita.

5 Steppenwolf Theatre (p107) Seeing a provocative play from the Pulitzer Prize–winning, star-filled ensemble.

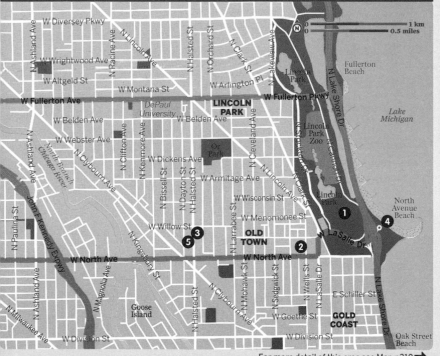

For more detail of this area see Map p310 ➡

Lonely Planet's Top Tip

While you have to pay admission to see a show at Second City (p107), there's free improv afterward. You heard right: show up at the Mainstage or ETC stage after the last show of the evening (Friday excluded) and you can watch the performers riff through a half hour of improv. The freebie begins around 10pm Monday through Thursday, 1am on Saturday and 9pm on Sunday. Arrive 15 minutes prior.

Best Places to Eat

➡ Alinea (p104)

➡ La Fournette (p104)

➡ Small Cheval (p104)

➡ Pequod's Pizza (p103)

➡ Boka (p104)

➡ Twin Anchors (p104)

For reviews, see p102. ➡

Best Places to Drink

➡ Old Town Ale House (p105)

➡ Delilah's (p105)

➡ Eva's Cafe (p107)

➡ J Parker (p105)

➡ Kibbitznest Books, Brews & Blarney (p105)

For reviews, see p105. ➡

☆ Best Entertainment

➡ Steppenwolf Theatre (p107)

➡ Second City (p107)

➡ BLUES (p107)

➡ Kingston Mines (p107)

➡ Lincoln Hall (p107)

➡ iO Theater (p107)

For reviews, see p107. ➡

Explore Lincoln Park & Old Town

Almost 50% larger than Central Park in New York, Lincoln Park is where Chicagoans flock when the weather warms up to savor the lakefront oasis of ponds, walking paths and exotic creatures in the free zoo.

Lincoln Park is also the name for the surrounding neighborhood, which is home to the city's young professional population mixed with DePaul University's large student body. The area is alive day and night with people walking dogs, riding bikes, pushing strollers, shopping in swanky boutiques and eating in excellent restaurants. Add in several top-caliber theaters – led by the world-renowned Steppenwolf – and boisterous live-music clubs, and you've got a whole lot of action here.

Old Town was the epicenter of Chicago's hippie culture in the 1960s. A few trippy holdovers from the old days remain, but now stylish stores and eateries dot the neighborhood, which joins Lincoln Park to the south. Wells St is the main artery and most visitors make a pilgrimage here at some point – it's the home of the comedy club and improv stronghold Second City.

Local Life

➡**Funny bar** Performers from Second City often duck into the Old Town Ale House (p105) for a beverage after the show.

➡**Blues jam** Musicians aged 17 to 70 tune up for the free blues jam at Kingston Mines (p107) every Sunday.

➡**Farmers market** Chicagoans flock to the park to stock up on farm fare at Green City Market (p98) on Wednesday and Saturday mornings from May to October.

➡**Smartass sausage** Join the late-night weekend crowd at the Wieners Circle (p103) for a side dish of sass with your hot dog.

Getting There & Away

➡**The L** Brown, Purple, Red Line to Fullerton for Lincoln Park; Brown, Purple Line to Sedgwick for Old Town.

➡**Bus** Bus 151 from downtown (along Michigan Ave) for zoo and park sites.

➡**Car** Parking is difficult. In Lincoln Park, try the meters along Diversey Harbor. In Old Town, try the pay garage at Piper's Alley, at North Ave and Wells St.

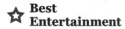
LINCOLN PARK & OLD TOWN

 TOP SIGHT
LINCOLN PARK

Chicago's largest park (1200 acres) runs for 6 miles through the neighborhood that bears its name, from North Ave up to Diversey Pkwy (after which a sliver of it continues to the end of Lake Shore Dr). It's a favorite playground of locals, who flock here to stroll, picnic, sunbathe and play sports, as well as visit the eponymous zoo.

Opened in 1868, the free Lincoln Park Zoo (p99) has entertained generations of Chicagoans. Families swarm the grounds, which are smack in the park's midst. The Regenstein African exhibit lets you get close to pygmy hippos and dwarf crocodiles, while swingin' gorillas and chimps populate the Ape House and snow monkeys chill in the Macaque Forest. The leafy conservatory (p102; pictured) and hidden lily garden (p98) are also nearby – and free.

At the park's southern edge, sculptor Augustus Saint-Gaudens' ***Standing Lincoln*** (off W LaSalle Dr; 🚌22) shows the 16th US president deep in contemplation before giving a speech. Saint-Gaudens based the work on casts of Lincoln's face and hands made while Lincoln was alive. It stands behind the Chicago History Museum (p98).

Nearby, at the corner of LaSalle Dr and Clark St, take a gander at the **Couch Tomb** (www.chicagoparkdistrict.com; off W LaSalle Dr; 🚌22). It's the sole remainder of the land's pre-1864 use as a municipal cemetery – which included burials of Confederate soldiers who died as prisoners of war at Camp Douglas, a Union stockade on the South Side of town. The city eventually relocated the bodies when Lincoln Park was created.

Head north to find sailboat harbors, golf courses, bird sanctuaries and rowing clubs out gliding on the lagoons. Walk east from anywhere in the park and you'll come to the Lakefront Trail (p35), which connects several beaches along the way.

DON'T MISS

➡ Zoo
➡ Conservatory
➡ *Standing Lincoln* statue
➡ Couch Tomb
➡ Alfred Caldwell Lily Pool

PRACTICALITIES

➡ Map p310, G5
➡ www.chicagopark district.com
➡ Lincoln Park
➡ ⊘6am-11pm
➡ ♿
➡ 🚌22, 151, 156

⊙ SIGHTS

With a zoo, beaches and gardens, leafy Lincoln Park is where Chicago comes to relax and play. Several overlooked museums are in the neighborhood, including the Chicago History Museum, Peggy Notebaert Nature Museum and DePaul Art Museum, as is the newest gallery on the Chicago scene, Wrightwood 659.

LINCOLN PARK
PARK

See p97.

NORTH AVENUE BEACH
BEACH

Map p310 (www.cpdbeaches.com; 1600 N Lake Shore Dr, Lincoln Park; ☺6am-11pm; ♿; ☐151) Chicago's most popular strand of sand gives off a bit of a Southern California vibe in summer. Buff teams spike volleyballs, kids build sandcastles and everyone jumps in for a swim when the weather heats up. Bands and DJs rock the steamboat-shaped beach house, which serves ice cream and margaritas in equal measure. Kayaks, Jet Skis, stand-up paddleboards, bicycles and lounge chairs are available to rent, and there are daily beach yoga classes.

A short walk on the curving breakwater yields postcard-perfect skyline views. Swimming is permitted when lifeguards are on duty, which is every day (11am to 7pm) throughout the summer.

GREEN CITY MARKET
MARKET

Map p310 (☎773-880-1266; www.greencitymarket.org; 1790 N Clark St, Lincoln Park; ☺7am-1pm Wed & Sat May-Oct; ☐22) Stands of purple cabbages, red radishes, green asparagus and other bright-hued produce sprawl through Lincoln Park at Chicago's biggest farmers market. Follow your nose to the demonstration tent, where local cooks such as *Top Chef* winner Stephanie Izard prepare dishes – say rice crepes with a mushroom *gastrique* (reduction) – using market ingredients.

WRIGHTWOOD 659
GALLERY

Map p310 (☎773-437-6601; www.wrightwood659.org; 659 W Wrightwood Ave, Lincoln Park; $20; ☺2-8:30pm Wed, from 10am Thu & Fri, 10am-5pm Sat; ☐22) Fans of modern architecture shouldn't miss Chicago's newest gallery, designed by Pritzker Prize–winner Tadao Ando. Walk past the facade of the former 1920s apartment building on a residential street and into a soaring four-story atrium of concrete and reclaimed brick; interior galleries on each floor are dedicated to rotating exhibits of architecture and 'socially engaged' art. (The inaugural exhibit covered previous works of Ando's and modern master Le Corbusier.) Reservations must be made online in advance; no walk-ins allowed.

Tickets are $20, but a limited number of free tickets are available weekly; search the website's ticketing page to find them. Don't miss a visit to the open-air balconies on the top floor, which offer some lovely views.

DEPAUL ART MUSEUM
MUSEUM

Map p310 (☎773-325-7506; http://museums.depaul.edu; 935 W Fullerton Ave, Lincoln Park; ☺11am-7pm Wed & Thu, to 5pm Fri-Sun; ⓂBrown, Purple, Red Line to Fullerton) FREE DePaul University's compact art museum hosts changing exhibits of 20th-century works by Chicago-based artists. Pieces from the permanent collection – by sculptor Claes Oldenburg, cartoonist Chris Ware, architect Daniel Burnham and more – are sometimes on display but share the two floors of gallery space with temporary new exhibits. It's definitely worth swinging by if you're in the neighborhood; you can see everything in less than 30 minutes.

ALFRED CALDWELL LILY POOL
GARDENS

Map p310 (www.lincolnparkconservancy.org; 2391 N Stockton Dr, Lincoln Park; ☺7:30am-dusk mid-Apr–mid-Nov; ☐151) FREE The enchanting Lily Pool hides in a plot northeast of the Lincoln Park Conservatory, at the corner of Fullerton and Cannon Drs. Built in 1938 by landscape architect Jens Jenson, the garden is designated a National Historic Landmark for its Prairie School style, native-plant use and stonework that resembles the stratified canyons of the Wisconsin Dells.

The pool has become an important stopover for migrating birds and also welcomes turtles and dragonflies. It's a lovely escape from the Lincoln Park crowds. Docents lead free, half-hour tours on various weekends.

CHICAGO HISTORY MUSEUM
MUSEUM

Map p310 (☎312-642-4600; www.chicagohistory.org; 1601 N Clark St, Lincoln Park; adult/child $19/free; ☺9:30am-4:30pm Mon & Wed-Sat, to 9pm Tue, noon-5pm Sun; ♿; ☐22) Curious about Chicago's storied past? Multimedia displays at this museum cover it all, from the Great Fire to the 1968 Democratic Convention. President Lincoln's deathbed is here, as is the bell worn by Mrs O'Leary's cow. So is the chance to 'become' a Chicago hot dog covered in condiments (in the kids' area, but adults are welcome for the photo op).

The Diorama Hall is nifty, especially the model that shows the 1893 World's Fair setup. The on-site bookstore stocks a good assortment of local history books, postcards and other Chicago-themed gifts.

LINCOLN PARK ZOO ZOO

Map p310 (☑312-742-2000; www.lpzoo.org; 2200 N Cannon Dr, Lincoln Park; ⊙10am-5pm Mon-Fri, to 6:30pm Sat & Sun Jun-Aug, 10am-5pm Apr, May, Sep & Oct, 10am-4:30pm Nov-Mar; ☑; ☐22, 151, 156) FREE The zoo has been around since 1868 and is a local freebie favorite, filled with lions, zebras, snow monkeys and other exotic creatures in the shadow of downtown. Check out the Regenstein African Journey, polar-bear-stocked Arctic Tundra and dragonfly-dappled Nature Boardwalk for the cream of the crop. The Gateway Pavilion (on Cannon

(Continued on page 102)

HENRY DARGER IN THE REALMS OF THE UNREAL

Chicago is famously associated with international artists like Picasso, Seurat and Miró, but there's also some homegrown talent with far-reaching influence: Chicago native Henry Darger (1892–1973), one of the world's most famous 'outsider' (ie self-taught) artists. His early life was traumatic: his mother died when he was four; at eight he was sent to an orphanage 175 miles downstate when his penniless and ailing father entered a nursing facility (where he died several years later). Darger lived in juvenile institutions until he was 16, when he escaped back to Chicago and found work as a janitor in a Catholic hospital. Intensely religious, he became an impoverished recluse, attending Mass several times daily, scavenging for discarded items from the streets and living most of his life in a single-room apartment at 851 W Webster Avenue in Lincoln Park. It was only shortly before his death, when Darger entered the same nursing home where his father had died, that his landlords discovered the immense body of work he had left behind in his room.

And immense it was. Over six decades, Darger had created a 15,145-page, single-spaced illustrated novel in fifteen volumes called *The Story of the Vivian Girls, in What is Known as the Realms of the Unreal, of the Glandeco-Angelinian War Storm Caused by the Child Slave Rebellion,* using a combination of watercolors, freehand drawing and traced pictures cut out from magazines and catalogues, sometimes on scroll-like pages up to 30 feet wide. The surreal story tells of seven young princesses from the Christian land of Abbieannia who take up arms to lead a rebellion of child slaves against their captors, the Glandelinians. Many of the images are intensely disturbing, including scenes of the vicious torture and murder of enslaved children, with the heroic Vivian Girls rushing into daring battle with their adult foes. Darger apparently never intended to show his efforts to anyone, telling his landlords just before he died that they could throw all of his possessions out, but as they sorted through the piles they recognized the artistic merit of Darger's creations, including his talent for composition and vibrant use of color, not to mention his prodigious imagination. He also left behind dozens of journals and two other sprawling written works spanning thousands of pages.

Since then Darger's art has been shown in international galleries and fetched hundreds of thousands of dollars at auction. His work has been collected by a dozen museums worldwide, and is on display at Intuit: The Center for Intuitive & Outsider Art (p148), which has also physically re-created Darger's cramped room, including his ancient typewriter and hoarded treasures such as balls of twine, broken eyeglasses, boxes of old paint and pencils, and stacks of magazines and newspapers. In a twist Darger could never have imagined, his life and art have become a posthumous pop-culture inspiration, influencing not only other visual artists and graphic novelists, but poets, writers and musicians – even video-game creators. Watch Jessica Yu's 2004 documentary *In the Realms of the Unreal* for more on the tragic and fascinating life of this unconventional artist.

Park Life at Lincoln Park

Chicago's largest park is where locals come out to play, whether it's swimming and spiking volleyballs at North Ave Beach or ogling the lions, gorillas and other creatures in the zoo. Other options include browsing for fresh regional produce and homemade pies at the Green City farmers market, or just hanging out, kicking a soccer ball or jogging the leafy pathways.

THERESE FLANAGAN / GETTY IMAGES ©

CONCH MARTINEZ / SHUTTERSTOCK ©

1. Lincoln Park Zoo (p99)
The historic 1912 Kovler Lion House is a highlight of Lincoln Park Zoo.

2. Walter Family Arctic Tundra
Polar bear swimming at an exhibit built specifically for them at Lincoln Park Zoo.

3. Nature Boardwalk (p102)
The half-mile-long boardwalk snakes through the South Ponds wetlands ecosystem.

4. Alfred Caldwell Lily Pool (p98)
A designated National Historic Landmark, noted for its stonework resembling the Wisconsin Dells.

CHENLU / EYEEM / GETTY IMAGES ©

(Continued from page 99)

Dr) is the main entrance; pick up a map and schedule of feedings and training sessions.

Families swarm the grounds. Kids beeline for the African exhibit, which puts them close to pygmy hippos and dwarf crocodiles. The Ape House pleases with its swingin' gorillas and chimps while snow monkeys chill in the Macaque Forest. **Farm-in-the-Zoo** (Map p310; www.lpzoo.org/exhibit/farm-zoo; 1911 North Stockton Dr, Lincoln Park; ☺10am-5pm Mon-Fri, to 6:30pm Sat & Sun Jun-Aug, 10am-5pm Apr, May, Sep & Oct, 10am-4:30pm Nov-Mar) FREE features a full range of barnyard animals and offers frequent demonstrations of cow milking, horse grooming and other farm work, along with kid-centric play events.

The half-mile-long **Nature Boardwalk** circles the adjacent South Pond and teaches about wetlands ecology; keep an eye out for endangered birds such as the black-crowned night heron. Kids can also climb aboard the vintage train and carousel ($3 per ride). A completely revamped exhibit house for the zoo's pride of lions and a state-of-the-art new visitor center should have been completed by 2020.

As well as the Gateway Pavilion, the zoo has multiple entrances around its perimeter. Drivers be warned: parking here is among the city's worst. If you do find a spot in the Cannon Dr lot, it can cost up to $35 for four hours.

PEGGY NOTEBAERT NATURE MUSEUM
MUSEUM

Map p310 (☏773-755-5100; www.naturemuseum.org; 2430 N Cannon Dr, Lincoln Park; adult/child $9/6; ☺9am-5pm Mon-Fri, from 10am Sat & Sun; ⏸; ☐76, 151) This hands-on museum has turtles and croaking frogs in its 1st-floor marsh, fluttering insects in its 2nd-floor butterfly haven and a bird boardwalk meandering through its rooftop garden. It's geared mostly to kids. Check the schedule for daily creature feedings. In winter the Green City Market (p98) sets up inside on Saturday morning.

LINCOLN PARK CONSERVATORY
GARDENS

Map p310 (☏312-742-7736; www.lincolnparkconservancy.org; 2391 N Stockton Dr, Lincoln Park; ☺9am-5pm; ☐151) FREE Walking through the conservatory's 3 acres of desert palms, jungle ferns and tropical orchids is like taking a trip around the world in 30 minutes. The glass-bedecked hothouse remains a sultry 75°F (24°C) escape even in winter.

BIOGRAPH THEATER
HISTORIC SITE

Map p310 (2433 N Lincoln Ave, Lincoln Park; ⓜBrown, Purple, Red Line to Fullerton) In 1934 the 'lady in red' betrayed notorious bank robber John Dillinger (aka Public Enemy Number One) at this theater, which used to show movies. FBI agents shot him in the alley beside the building.

The whole thing started out as a date: Dillinger took new girlfriend Polly Hamilton to a show and Polly's roommate Anna Sage tagged along, wearing a red dress (her signal to the feds). Sage had her own troubles with the law and was about to be deported; to save herself she had agreed to set up Dillinger (but unfortunately for her ended up getting deported later anyway). The venue now hosts plays by the **Victory Gardens Theater** (Map p310; ☏773-871-3000; www.victorygardens.org).

ST VALENTINE'S DAY MASSACRE SITE
HISTORIC SITE

Map p310 (2122 N Clark St, Lincoln Park; ☐22) At this infamous spot on February 14, 1929, Al Capone's henchmen, dressed as cops, lined up seven members of Bugs Moran's gang against the garage wall that used to stand here and sprayed them with bullets. After that, Moran cut his losses and Al Capone gained control of Chicago's North Side vice. The garage was torn down in 1967 to make way for a retirement home and its parking lot (which is all you'll see at the site now).

A house (2119 N Clark St) used as a lookout by the killers stands across the street.

✖️ EATING

Mega-high-end restaurants such as Alinea and Boka hold court here, but Lincoln Park caters to budget tastes, too, thanks to the DePaul University student population. You'll find some cheap 'n' cheerful options along both Clark and Wells Sts, among others. Halsted St, Lincoln Ave and Fullerton Ave are good bets for trendy eateries. Old Town's options are quieter and quainter.

✖ Lincoln Park

★ SULTAN'S MARKET
MIDDLE EASTERN **$**
Map p310 (☑872-253-1489; 2521 N Clark St; mains $4-10; ⊙10am-10pm Mon-Sat, to 9pm Sun; ☑; M Brown, Purple, Red Line to Fullerton) Neighborhood folks dig into plates heaped with falafel sandwiches, creamy hummus, lamb shawarma, spinach pies and other quality Middle Eastern fare at family-run Sultan's Market. There's a large salad bar, too. The small, homey space doesn't have many tables, but Lincoln Park is nearby for picnicking.

PEQUOD'S PIZZA
• PIZZA **$**
Map p310 (☑773-327-1512; www.pequodspizza. com; 2207 N Clybourn Ave; small pizzas from $12; ⊙11am-2am Mon-Sat, to midnight Sun; ☑9 to Webster) Like the ship in *Moby Dick* from which this neighborhood restaurant takes its name, Pequod's pan-style (akin to deep-dish) pizza is a thing of legend – head and shoulders above chain competitors for its caramelized cheese, generous toppings and sweetly flavored sauce. Neon beer signs glow from the walls, and Blackhawks jerseys hang from the ceiling in the affably rugged interior.

Wait times can be long (45 minutes isn't unheard of), but you can pass the time drinking (from 4pm) at the WhaleTale bar one door down; Pequod's will page you when your table is ready.

ALOHA EATS
HAWAIIAN **$**
Map p310 (☑773-935-6828; www.alohaeats.com; 2534 N Clark St; mains $3-14; ⊙11am-10pm Tue-Sun; M Brown, Purple, Red Line to Fullerton) It's all about whopping portions of Hawaiian food here, from *musubis* (rice rolls wrapped in seaweed) to *saimin* (egg noodle soup) to *katsus* (breaded cutlets). Spam, aka 'the Hawaiian steak,' is the main ingredient in many dishes, including the popular Loco Moco (meat, fried eggs and brown gravy atop rice). Macaroni salad or fries always arrive on the side.

FLORIOLE CAFE
BAKERY **$**
Map p310 (☑773-883-1313; www.floriole.com; 1220 W Webster Ave; dishes $5-12; ⊙7am-5:30pm Tue-Fri, from 8:30am Sat-Mon; ☎☑☑; M Brown, Purple, Red Line to Fullerton) Floriole's chef started out selling lemon tarts, twice-baked croissants and rum-tinged *caneles* (a pastry with a custard center and caramelized crust) at the Green City Market (p98). She now sells French-influenced baked goods and sandwiches, salads and quiches (using Midwest-sourced meats, cheeses and produce) in an airy, loft-like space punctuated by a big wooden farm table. There's a kids menu, too.

RJ GRUNTS
BURGERS **$**
Map p310 (☑773-929-5363; www.rjgrunts chicago.com; 2056 N Lincoln Park W; mains $11.50-22; ⊙11:30am-11pm Mon-Fri, from 10am Sat, 10am-9pm Sun; ☑; ☑22) The very first of the now-ubiquitous Lettuce Entertain You stable of restaurants, RJ Grunts came on to the scene in the 1970s, when Lincoln Park emerged as the young singles' neighborhood of choice. Now, as then, the huge salad bar, burgers and beer are the mainstays.

WIENERS CIRCLE
AMERICAN **$**
Map p310 (☑773-477-7444; 2622 N Clark St; hot dogs $3.50-5.50; ⊙11am-4am Sun-Thu, to 5am Fri & Sat; M Brown, Purple Line to Diversey) As famous for its unruly, foul-mouthed ambience as for its charred hot dogs and cheddar fries, the Wieners Circle is a normal hot-dog stand – with damn good food – daytimes and weeknights. The wild show comes weekend nights around 2am, when the nearby bars close and everyone starts yelling. The F-bombs fly and it can get raucous between staff and customers.

BOURGEOIS PIG
CAFE **$**
Map p310 (☑773-883-5282; www.facebook.com/ BourgeoisPigCafe; 738 W Fullerton Pkwy; mains $6-14.50; ⊙7am-10pm Mon-Sat, from 8am Sun; ☎☑; M Brown, Purple, Red Line to Fullerton) An old-style cafe, with creaking wooden tables and chairs set throughout several rambling rooms of a large old house; antique cameras and kitchen implements decorate the shelves. The menu features strong java and massive sandwiches, with numerous vegetarian options. It's a convivial place to grab a bite while reading through the newspaper or chatting with friends.

SWEET MANDY B'S
BAKERY **$**
Map p310 (☑773-244-1174; www.sweetmandybs. com; 1208 W Webster Ave; baked goods $2.50-5; ⊙8am-9pm Sun-Thu, to 10pm Fri & Sat; ☑74, M Brown, Purple Line to Armitage) Have a pillow ready for the inevitable sugar crash after you gorge yourself on the down-home, old-fashioned desserts made at this Lincoln Park bakery-cafe: peanut butter Rice

Krispies treats, chocolate-chip-cookie sandwiches stuffed with buttercream frosting and mint-frosted brownies, as well as cupcakes, fruit and cream pies and cakes. There are a couple of vegan and gluten-free options, too.

TWIN ANCHORS
BARBECUE $$

Map p310 (☎312-266-1616; www.twinanchors ribs.com; 1655 N Sedgwick St; mains $12-30; ⊗5-11pm Mon-Thu, to midnight Fri, noon-midnight Sat, noon-10pm Sun; 🚊37, Ⓜ Brown, Purple Line to Sedgwick) Twin Anchors is synonymous with ribs – smoky, tangy-sauced baby backs in this case. The meat drops from the ribs as soon as you lift them. The restaurant doesn't take reservations, so you'll have to wait outside or around the neon-lit 1950s bar, which sets the tone for the place. An almost-all-Sinatra jukebox completes the supper-club ambience.

PATIO AT CAFE BRAUER
CAFE $$

Map p310 (☎312-507-9053; www.lpzoo.org/dining/patio-cafe-brauer; 2021 N Stockton Dr; mains $13-19; ⊗11am-9pm Mon-Fri, from 8:30am Sat & Sun Apr-Aug, shorter hours Sep & Oct; 🚼; 🚊22, 151, 156) Take a break from zoo explorations at pretty Cafe Brauer. It's perfect for some ice cream, a Caesar salad, hamburger or glass of wine refresher while sitting by the pond, with beautiful skyline views. There's live acoustic music Tuesday, Wednesday and Thursday evenings (5:30pm to 7:30pm) from June through September.

CAFE BA-BA-REEBA!
TAPAS $$

Map p310 (☎773-935-5000; www.cafebaba reeba.com; 2024 N Halsted St; tapas $5-14; ⊗4-10pm Mon-Thu, 11:30am-midnight Fri, 9am-midnight Sat, 9am-10pm Sun; Ⓜ Brown, Purple Line to Armitage) At this long-standing, delightfully ersatz tapas joint, the garlic-laced menu changes often but always includes hot or cold small plates of vegetables and cheese, spicy meats and seafood or marinated fish. For a main event, order one of the paellas ($13 to $17 per person, minimum two people) as soon as you get seated – they take a while to prepare.

★ALINEA
GASTRONOMY $$$

Map p310 (☎312-867-0110; www.alinea restaurant.com; 1723 N Halsted St; 10-/16-course menus from $205/290; ⊗5-10pm; Ⓜ Red Line to North/Clybourn) One of the world's best restaurants, the triple-Michelin-starred Alinea purveys multiple courses of molecular gastronomy. Dishes may emanate from a centrifuge or be pressed into a capsule, à la duck served with a 'pillow of lavender air.' There are no reservations; instead Alinea sells tickets two to three months in advance via its website. Check Twitter (@ Alinea) for last-minute seats.

Chef Grant Achatz gutted and renovated the restaurant in early 2016, so it feels less mod and more classic. Three dining options are available: the salon menu (10 to 14 courses), the gallery menu (16 to 18 courses) and, most exclusive of all, the private kitchen table experience ($390 per person; parties of six only).

Vegetarians and vegans should call in advance to request accommodation. Note that there's no sign on the restaurant's door, so look for the house number.

★BOKA
MODERN AMERICAN $$$

Map p310 (☎312-337-6070; www.bokachicago. com; 1729 N Halsted St; mains $21-42, 8-course menus $125; ⊗5-10pm Sun-Thu, to 11pm Fri & Sat; Ⓜ Red Line to North/Clybourn) A Michelin-starred restaurant-lounge hybrid, Boka is a pre- and post-theater stomping ground for younger Steppenwolf patrons. Order a cocktail at the bar or slip into one of the booths for small-plate dishes such striped-jack crudo or veal sweetbreads with charred cabbage.

✖ Old Town

SMALL CHEVAL
BURGERS $

Map p310 (www.smallcheval.com; 1345 N Wells St; burgers $9-10; ⊗11am-11pm Mon-Thu, to 1am Fri & Sat, to 10pm Sun; Ⓜ Red Line to Clark/Division) Upscale burger shack Small Cheval does one thing and it does it well – serve up delicious all-beef patties, with or without cheese, and a side of golden fries, accompanied by shakes, shots or beer (or if it's that kinda night, maybe all three). Enjoy your food on the picnic tables of the long front patio. There's another in Wicker Park (p149).

LA FOURNETTE
BAKERY $

Map p310 (☎312-624-9430; www.lafournette. com; 1547 N Wells St; baked goods $2-10; ⊗7am-6:30pm Mon-Sat, to 5:30pm Sun; Ⓜ Brown, Purple Line to Sedgwick) The chef hails from France's Alsace region and he fills his narrow, rustic-wood bakery with bright-hued macarons (purple passionfruit, green pistachio, red raspberry-chocolate), cheese-infused breads, crust-crackling baguettes and buttery croissants. They all beg to be devoured on the spot with a cup of locally roasted Intelligentsia coffee. Staff make delicious soups, crepes, quiches and sandwiches with equal French love.

OLD JERUSALEM
MIDDLE EASTERN $

Map p310 (📞312-944-0459; www.oldjerusalem il.com; 1411 N Wells St; mains $9-15; ⏱11am-11pm; 📶; Ⓜ Brown, Purple Line to Sedgwick) A humble, hidden gem in Old Town, this mom-and-pop Middle Eastern spot has been serving falafel and pita sandwiches, kabobs and baked *kefta* (spiced lamb) for more than 40 years. Vegetarians will find lots of options. If the weather's good, get your food to go and feast in nearby Lincoln Park.

🍸 DRINKING & NIGHTLIFE

Student-favored saloons dot the area around Lincoln Ave and Halsted St, while quirky gems can be found in Old Town.

🍷 Lincoln Park

★ DELILAH'S
BAR

Map p310 (📞773-472-2771; www.delilahs chicago.com; 2771 N Lincoln Ave; ⏱4pm-2am Sun-Fri, to 3am Sat; Ⓜ Brown Line to Diversey) A bartender rightfully referred to this hard-edged black sheep of the neighborhood as the 'pride of Lincoln Ave': a title earned for the heavy pours and the best whiskey selection in the city – over 860 different labels! The no-nonsense staff know their way around a beer list, too, tapping unusual domestic and international suds. Cheap Pabst longnecks are always available.

KIBBITZNEST BOOKS, BREWS & BLARNEY
CAFE

Map p310 (📞773-360-7591; www.kibbitznest. com; 2212 N Clybourn Ave; ⏱3-11pm Wed & Thu, to midnight Fri, noon-midnight Sat, noon-6pm Sun; 🚌9, 74, Ⓜ Brown, Purple Line to Armitage) This warm, eclectic cafe rambling over several rooms is devoted to creating a 'third space' for face-to-face communication and intellectual discourse (there's purposely no wifi). Play the piano or some board games or sink into a comfy armchair and read one of the used books on display. Cocktails, beer, wine, coffee and a small nosh menu keep you going.

J PARKER
LOUNGE

Map p310 (📞312-254-4747; www.jparkerchicago. com; 1816 N Clark St, 13th fl; ⏱5pm-1am Mon-Thu, from 3pm Fri, from 11:30am Sat & Sun; 🚌22) It's all about the view from the 13th-floor rooftop bar of the Hotel Lincoln (p238). And it delivers, sweeping over the park, the lake and downtown skyline. Prepare to jostle with a young and preppy crowd, especially if it's a warm night.

COLECTIVO COFFEE
COFFEE

Map p310 (📞773-687-8078; http://colectivo coffee.com; 2530 N Clark St; ⏱6:30am-9:30pm; 📶; 🚌22, 36) This award-winning Wisconsin roaster has branched out to Chicago, bringing its fair-trade, single-origin coffees to three locations across the city. This flagship has a huge outdoor patio with a welcoming fire pit, an indoor seating section and a variety of hot and iced coffee and tea drinks. Sandwiches, pastries and all-day breakfast burritos are also on the menu.

ROSE'S LOUNGE
BAR

Map p310 (📞773-327-4000; 2656 N Lincoln Ave; ⏱6pm-2am Sun-Fri, to 3am Sat; Ⓜ Brown, Purple Line to Diversey) Once your eyes adjust to the dark of Rose's, the eclectic bric-a-brac, drop ceiling and groovy jukebox make it an odd duck among Lincoln Park's cocktail and sports bars. The ultracheap beers and free pretzels are the big draw, bringing in a motley set of spendthrift regulars. Late nights the young and drunk flock in.

🍷 Old Town

★ OLD TOWN ALE HOUSE
BAR

Map p310 (📞312-944-7020; www.theold townalehouse.com; 219 W North Ave; ⏱3pm-4am Mon-Fri, noon-5am Sat, noon-4am Sun; Ⓜ Brown, Purple Line to Sedgwick) Located near the Second City (p107) comedy club and the scene of late-night musings since the 1960s, this unpretentious neighborhood favorite lets you mingle with beautiful people and grizzled regulars, seated pint by pint under the paintings of nude politicians (just

🏃 Neighborhood Tour
Lincoln Park
for Families

START FARM-IN-THE-ZOO
END FULLERTON BEACH
LENGTH 2 MILES; FOUR TO FIVE HOURS

Traveling with little ones? A day in Lincoln Park will keep the whole family busy without breaking the bank. Generations of Chicagoans have been coming here to enjoy the greenery, the lakefront and the Lincoln Park Zoo, now one of the last free zoos in the country.

Start off at the big ol' barn at ❶**Farm-in-the-Zoo** (p102), where kids can pet sheep, watch chicks hatch and learn how to milk a cow. Just north of there is the ❷**Nature Boardwalk**, a half-mile path around the South Pond's wetlands ecosystem. Informational placards explain the marshy environment and its creatures. The mod-looking arch on the east side is the Education Pavilion. Local starchitect Jeanne Gang (of Aqua Tower fame) designed it; it's meant to resemble a turtle shell.

All that walking will no doubt lead to rumbling bellies, so head out of the park and over to ❸**RJ Grunts** (p103) for lunch. The staff can store your stroller while you chow down on chocolate-peanut-butter-banana milkshakes and burgers. The menu is entirely kid friendly.

After lunch explore re-created geographical regions in the Regenstein African Journey and watch Ape House monkeys play at the two best exhibits at the ❹**Lincoln Park Zoo** (p99). After strolling through the exhibits, continue north through the park and into the hidden oasis of the ❺**Alfred Caldwell Lily Pool** (p98), where you can sit and enjoy the serenity while your kids explore for turtles and dragonflies.

By now you've spent more than four hours in the park. If you have enough energy to continue, head east along Fullerton Pkwy to ❻**Fullerton Beach** (Map p310, G2; W Fullerton Pkwy), a quiet patch of sand perfect for lazing in the sun and building castles. Plus, the curving headland offers one of the city's best skyline views – the ideal background for a keepsake family photo of your day.

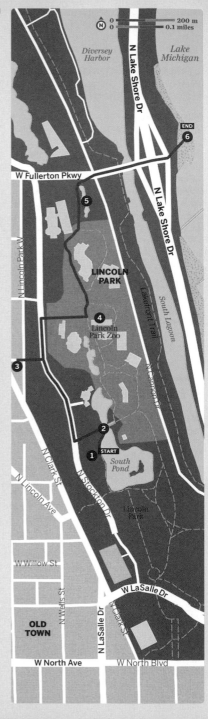

go with it). Classic jazz on the jukebox provides the soundtrack for the jovial goings-on. Cash only.

EVA'S CAFE
CAFE

Map p310 (🕿312-280-8900; www.evascafe oldtown.com; 1447 N Sedgwick St; ⏰7am-7pm Mon-Fri, 8am-8pm Sat & Sun; 🛜; Ⓜ Brown, Purple Line to Sedgwick) The long room at Eva's charms, with a fireplace, brick floor and antique wood tables and chairs. Coffee and tea steam out of mismatched ceramic cups. The young and bookish crowd tap-tap-taps on laptops, while the occasional philosophy group convenes to discuss big ideas. It's about as writerly as a cafe can be.

REAL GOOD JUICE CO
JUICE BAR

Map p310 (www.realgoodjuiceco.com; 1647 N Wells St; ⏰7am-8pm Mon-Fri, 8am-7pm Sat & Sun; 🚌9, 72) This small Old Town establishment features cold-pressed juices with punny names (Juicy Liu, Juicille Ball etc) and various smoothies made from nondairy milks. Fruits and vegetables are sourced locally. You'll shell out $10.50 for the Juice Springsteen – a blend packed with healthy greens – but, hey, that's still cheaper than the average craft cocktail.

☆ ENTERTAINMENT

★ STEPPENWOLF THEATRE
THEATER

Map p310 (🕿312-335-1650; www.steppenwolf. org; 1650 N Halsted St, Lincoln Park; ⏰box office 11am-6:30pm Tue-Sat, from 1pm Sun; Ⓜ Red Line to North/Clybourn) Steppenwolf is Chicago's top stage for quality, provocative theater productions. The Hollywood-heavy ensemble includes Gary Sinise, John Malkovich, Martha Plimpton, Gary Cole, Joan Allen and Tracy Letts. A money-saving tip: the box office releases 20 tickets for $20 for each day's shows; they go on sale at 11am Tuesday to Saturday and at 1pm Sunday, and are available by phone.

★ SECOND CITY
COMEDY

Map p310 (🕿312-337-3992; www.secondcity. com; 1616 N Wells St, Lincoln Park; tickets $35-55; Ⓜ Brown, Purple Line to Sedgwick) Bill Murray, Stephen Colbert, Tina Fey and more honed their wit at this slick venue with nightly shows. The Mainstage and ETC stage host sketch revues (with an improv scene thrown

in); they're similar in price and quality. If you turn up around 10pm Monday through Thursday (or 1am Saturday or 9pm Sunday) you can watch a free improv set.

The lounge-y, light-bulb-dotted bar-restaurant on-site provides pre- and post-show nourishment. Weekend shows sell out fast; buy tickets a few weeks in advance.

★ IO THEATER
COMEDY

Map p310 (🕿312-929-2401; www.ioimprov.com; 1501 N Kingsbury St, Old Town; tickets $5-16; Ⓜ Red Line to North/Clybourn) One of Chicago's top-tier (and original) improv houses, iO is a bit edgier (and cheaper) than its competition, with four stages hosting bawdy shows of regular and musical improv nightly. Two bars and a beer garden add to the fun. The Improvised Shakespeare Company is awesome; catch them if you can.

LINCOLN HALL
LIVE MUSIC

Map p310 (🕿773-525-2501; www.lh-st.com; 2424 N Lincoln Ave, Lincoln Park; 🛜; Ⓜ Brown, Purple, Red Line to Fullerton) Hyped national indie bands are the main players at this ubercool, midsize venue with excellent sound. The front room has a kitchen that offers small plates and sandwiches until 10pm (or 11pm on weekends).

BLUES
BLUES

Map p310 (🕿773-528-1012; www.chicagoblues bar.com; 2519 N Halsted St, Lincoln Park; cover charge $5-10; ⏰8pm-2am Wed-Sun; Ⓜ Brown, Purple, Red Line to Fullerton) Long, narrow and high volume, this veteran blues club draws a slightly older crowd that soaks up every crackling, electrified moment. As one local musician put it, 'The audience here comes out to *understand* the blues.' Big local names grace the small stage.

KINGSTON MINES
BLUES

Map p310 (🕿773-477-4646; www.kingston mines.com; 2548 N Halsted St, Lincoln Park; cover charge $12-15; ⏰7:30pm-4am Mon-Thu, from 7pm Fri, 7pm-5am Sat, 6pm-4am Sun; Ⓜ Brown, Purple, Red Line to Fullerton) Popular enough to draw big names on the blues circuit, Kingston Mines is so noisy, hot and sweaty that blues neophytes will feel as though they're having a genuine experience – sort of like a gritty Delta theme park. Two stages, seven nights a week, ensure somebody's always on. The blues jam session from 6pm to 8pm on Sunday is free.

ROYAL GEORGE THEATRE THEATER

Map p310 (☑312-988-9000; www.theroyal georgetheatre.com; 1641 N Halsted St, Lincoln Park; Ⓜ Red Line to North/Clybourn) The Royal George is actually four theaters in one building. The cabaret venue stages long-running mainstream productions such as *Late Nite Catechism,* a nun-centered comedy. The main stage presents works with big-name stars, and the galleries host various improv and small-troupe works.

FACETS CINEMA

Map p310 (☑773-281-4114; www.facets.org; 1517 W Fullerton Ave, Lincoln Park; tickets $10; Ⓜ Brown, Purple, Red Line to Fullerton) Facets' main business is as the country's largest distributor of foreign and cult films, so it follows that its 'cinematheque' movie house shows interesting, obscure art-house films that would never get booked on the big screens.

🛍 SHOPPING

If you want to hit upscale national chains such as Pottery Barn, CB2, Forever 21, Williams-Sonoma or an Apple store, head to the area around Clybourn and North Aves. Posh clothing shops and gift boutiques are dotted along Armitage Ave near the L.

ROTOFUGI TOYS

Map p310 (☑773-868-3308; www.rotofugi.com; 2780 N Lincoln Ave, Lincoln Park; ⊙11am-7pm Mon-Fri, 10am-6pm Sat & Sun; Ⓜ Brown, Purple Line to Diversey) Rotofugi has an unusual niche: urban designer toys. The spacey, robot-y, odd vinyl and plush items will certainly distinguish you from the other kids on the block. It's also a gallery showcasing artists in the fields of modern pop and illustration art. You can usually find locally designed Shawnimals here – cute critters from the mind of Chicago artist Shawn Smith.

SPICE HOUSE FOOD

Map p310 (☑312-274-0378; www.thespice house.com; 1512 N Wells St, Old Town; ⊙10am-7pm Mon-Sat, to 5pm Sun; Ⓜ Brown, Purple Line to Sedgwick) A bombardment of fragrance socks you in the nose upon entering this Old Town spice house, which offers delicacies such as black and red volcanic salt from Hawaii and pomegranate molasses. Best, though, are the housemade herb blends

themed after Chicago neighborhoods – such as the 'Bronzeville rib rub' – allowing you to take home a taste of the city.

CROSSROADS TRADING CO CLOTHING

Map p310 (☑773-296-1000; www.crossroads trading.com; 2711 N Clark St, Lincoln Park; ⊙10am-8pm Mon-Sat, 11am-7pm Sun; Ⓜ Brown, Purple Line to Diversey) Crossroads sells funky, name-brand used clothing for men and women that you can count on being in good condition. Lots of jeans usually hang on the racks, including labels such as Seven for all Mankind, Citizens of Humanity and Miss Sixty. Shoes, coats and handbags are also abundant. You can sell or trade items, too.

VOSGES HAUT-CHOCOLAT FOOD & DRINKS

Map p310 (☑773-296-9866; www.vosges chocolate.com; 951 W Armitage Ave, Lincoln Park; ⊙10am-8pm Mon-Sat, 11am-6pm Sun; Ⓜ Brown, Purple Line to Armitage) Owner-chocolatier Katrina Markoff has earned a national reputation for her brand by blending exotic ingredients such as curry powder, chilies and wasabi into her truffles, ice cream and candy bars. They sound weird but taste great, as the samples lurking around prove.

DAVE'S RECORDS MUSIC

Map p310 (☑773-929-6325; www.davesrecords chicago.com; 2604 N Clark St, Lincoln Park; ⊙11am-8pm Mon-Sat, noon-7pm Sun; Ⓜ Brown, Purple Line to Diversey) *Rolling Stone* magazine picked Dave's as one of the nation's best record stores. It has an 'all vinyl, all the time' mantra, meaning crate diggers will be in their element flipping through the stacks of rock, jazz, blues, folk and house. Dave himself usually mans the counter, where you'll find a slew of 25¢ cheapie records for sale.

🏃 SPORTS & ACTIVITIES

DIVERSEY DRIVING RANGE GOLF

Map p310 (☑866-223-5564; http://diversey. cpdgolf.com; 141 W Diversey Pkwy; ⊙7am-11pm; 🚍77) If you want to knock some balls around, this driving range in Lincoln Park will let you whack away to your heart's content. Rental clubs are available and a bucket of balls costs $10 to $16. You can also play an 18-hole round of mini-golf (adult/child $10/8); the scenic course is adjacent to the driving range.

Lake View & Wrigleyville

BOYSTOWN | LAKE VIEW | ROSCOE VILLAGE | WRIGLEYVILLE

Neighborhood Top Five

1 Wrigley Field (p111) Spending an afternoon in the bleachers, hot dog and beer in hand, hoping for a win at the ivy-clad home of the Cubs.

2 Metro (p120) Hearing a soon-to-be-famous band at Chicago's premier loud-rock venue, a tastemaker for more than three decades.

3 Boystown (p113) Joining the thumping nightlife amid the rainbow flags in the city's main gay neighborhood.

4 Global eats (p114) Chowing on Korean fried chicken, Filipino cakes, Thai noodles and more in the array of reasonably priced international restaurants,

such as Gundis Kurdish Kitchen.

5 Sluggers (p120) Practicing your home-run swing in the batting cages at this bar and grill a stone's throw from Wrigley Field.

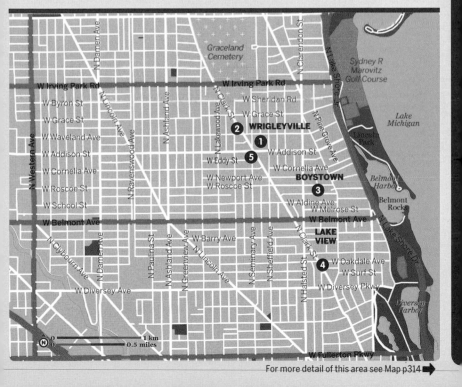

For more detail of this area see Map p314

Lonely Planet's Top Tip

If there's a Cubs game at Wrigley Field, plan on around 30,000 extra people joining you for a visit to the neighborhood. The trains and buses will be stuffed to capacity, traffic will be snarled, and bars and restaurants will be packed to the rafters. It can be fun... if that's your scene. If not, you might want to visit on a nongame day for a bit more elbow room.

✖ Best Places to Eat

➡ Jennivee's (p114)

➡ Gundis Kurdish Kitchen (p114)

➡ Crisp (p114)

➡ mfk (p114)

➡ Lucy's Cafe (p115)

For reviews, see p113.➡

🍷 Best Places to Drink

➡ Hungry Brain (p117)

➡ Ten Cat Tavern (p116)

➡ Nisei Lounge (p117)

➡ Mordecai (p117)

➡ Smart Bar (p120)

For reviews, see p116.➡

☆ Best Live Music

➡ Metro (p120)

➡ Constellation (p120)

➡ Schubas (p120)

➡ Martyrs' (p121)

➡ Beat Kitchen (p122)

For reviews, see p120.➡

LAKE VIEW & WRIGLEYVILLE

Explore Lake View & Wrigleyville

Most visitors start at Wrigley Field. The area around the ballpark is like a big street festival on game days, with people milling around outside and drinking on patios. Even nongame days see action, as the park next door to Wrigley hosts free concerts, alfresco fitness classes and farmers markets. Walk along Clark St to get the full effect of the lively scene.

Either the rainbow flags or the abundance of bars and dance clubs will let you know you've arrived in Boystown, just east of the ballpark. The well-heeled hub of Chicago's gay community, Boystown bustles on Broadway St during the day and gets hedonistic on Halsted St at night. Head west and you'll run into a funky shopping district centered on Belmont Ave and Clark St. The stores here cater to the lifestyle whims of local rockers and kitsch-loving hipsters.

The neighborhood is busiest at night, given all the bars, theaters, improv clubs and rock venues. Afternoons are relatively quiet and great for exploring the Kurdish, Korean, Spanish and other global eateries that speckle the streets. Of course, an afternoon Cubs game changes everything, and then the place becomes jam-packed.

Plan on an afternoon and/or evening to do justice to this energetic 'hood.

Local Life

➡ **Hometown bands** Beat Kitchen (p122) is a popular venue for local bands to play.

➡ **Hangouts** In a tourist-heavy neighborhood, the Hungry Brain (p117) and Ten Cat Tavern (p116) stand out as off-the-beaten-path bars where locals go for a relaxing beverage.

➡ **Brunch time** Even carnivores line up for the French toast and other vegetarian dishes at Lucy's Cafe (p115), a 'hood hot spot on weekend mornings.

➡ **Storefront theater** Otherworld Theatre (p121) and Strawdog Theatre Company (p121) stage works for a hometown audience.

Getting There & Away

➡ **L Train** Red Line to Addison for Wrigleyville and around; Red, Brown, Purple Line to Belmont for much of Boystown.

➡ **Bus** Bus 77 plies Belmont Ave.

➡ **Car** Parking is a nightmare, especially in Wrigleyville, where side streets are resident-only. Take the train!

TOP SIGHT
WRIGLEY FIELD

Built in 1914, Wrigley Field – aka the Friendly Confines – is the second-oldest baseball park in the major leagues. It's filled with legendary traditions and curses, including a team that didn't win a championship for 108 years. But a World Series victory coupled with heaps of new family-friendly and foodie hot spots around the stadium have given it new life.

Environs

The ballpark provides an old-school slice of Americana, with a hand-turned scoreboard, ivy-covered outfield walls and an iconic neon sign over the front entrance. The field is uniquely situated smack in the middle of a neighborhood, surrounded on all sides by houses, bars and restaurants. The grassy plaza just north of the main entrance – aka Gallagher Way (p113) – has tables, chairs, a coffee shop and a huge video screen. On nongame days it's open to the public and hosts free movie nights, concerts and alfresco fitness classes; on game days it's a beer garden for ticket holders. Kids love the grassy expanse, where they can run around, play catch or cool off in the splash pad. A slew of new cocktail bars, beer bars and hip taco, barbecue and fried-chicken eateries beckon across the way on Clark and Addison Sts.

The Curse & Its Reverse

It started with Billy Sianis, owner of the Billy Goat Tavern. The year was 1945 and the Cubs were in the World Series against the Detroit Tigers. When Sianis tried to enter Wrigley Field with his pet goat to see the game, ballpark staff refused, saying the goat stank. Sianis threw up his arms and called down a mighty hex, saying that the Cubs would never win another World Series. Years rolled by, and they didn't.

DON'T MISS

➡ Taking a photo under the neon entrance sign

➡ Harry Caray statue

➡ Hanging out on the grass at Gallagher Way

➡ Having a drink at a local bar

➡ Stadium tour

PRACTICALITIES

➡ Map p314, F3

➡ ☎800-843-2827

➡ www.cubs.com

➡ 1060 W Addison St, Wrigleyville

➡ Ⓜ Red Line to Addison

BABE'S CALLED SHOT

Babe Ruth's famous 'called shot' happened at Wrigley. During the 1932 World Series, Ruth pointed to center field to show where he was going to homer the next ball. And he did. It's still debated as to whether he called it or was just pointing at the pitcher.

If a ball gets lost in the ivy, it's considered a ground-rule double as long as the outfielder raises his hands to indicate that the ball is lost. If he doesn't, it's considered fair play.

WINDY CITY BASEBALL

Wrigley Field is known for its havoc-wreaking wind patterns caused by nearby Lake Michigan. If the wind is blowing in, it's a pitcher's paradise. If it's blowing out, expect a big day for home runs.

The Bears played at Wrigley from 1921 to 1970. They were called the Staleys for the first season but then renamed themselves to be in sync with the Cubs.

Then in 2016 it happened: the Cubs won the Series in a wild, come-from-behind set of games. The young team scrapped, slugged and pitched its way to victory, exorcising the curse. The city went insane. Streets filled with revelers. Neighbors high-fived neighbors. Grandparents cheered with grandkids. At the victory parade a few days later, an estimated five million fans partied with the team.

The Traditions

When the middle of the seventh inning arrives, it's time for the seventh inning stretch. You then stand up for the group sing-along of 'Take Me Out to the Ballgame,' often led by a guest celebrity along the lines of Mr T, Ozzy Osbourne or the local weather reporter. Here's another tradition: if you catch a home run slugged by the competition, you're honor-bound to throw it back onto the field. After every game the ballpark hoists a flag atop the scoreboard. A white flag with a blue 'W' indicates a victory; a blue flag with a white 'L' means a loss.

The Statues

Statues of Cubs heroes ring the stadium. Ernie Banks, aka 'Mr Cub,' stands near the main entrance on Clark St; the shortstop/first baseman was the team's first African American player. Billy 'Sweet-Swinging' Williams wields his mighty bat by the right field gate on Addison St at Sheffield Ave. Adored third baseman Ron Santo makes a smooth catch beside him. And mythic TV sportscaster Harry Caray dons his barrel-sized eyeglasses in front of the bleacher entrance on Waveland Ave. Caray was known for broadcasting among the raucous bleacher fans while downing a few Budweisers himself. It's said the sculptors mixed a dash of his favorite beer in with the white bronze used for the statue.

⊙ SIGHTS

Lake View is known more for its nightlife than its sights, but it does hold one top draw: historic Wrigley Field (p111). Even on nongame days events and activities take place at the plaza in front of the ballpark.

WRIGLEY FIELD STADIUM

See p111.

BOYSTOWN AREA

Map p314 (btwn Halsted St & Broadway, Belmont Ave & Addison St; M Red Line to Addison) What the Castro is to San Francisco, Boystown is to the Windy City. The mecca of queer Chicago (especially for men), the streets of Boystown are full of rainbow flags and packed with bars, shops and restaurants catering to residents of the gay neighborhood.

Halsted St is the main vein. Rainbow-colored pylons rise up along the road marking the district. Look closely and you'll see each pillar has placards on it telling the stories of different LGBTQ history makers or events. They span about a half-mile stretch between Melrose and Grace Sts and are known collectively as the Legacy Walk.

GALLAGHER WAY PARK

Map p314 (www.gallagherway.com; 3637 N Clark St, Wrigleyville; M Red Line to Addison) It's impossible to get any closer to Wrigley Field (p111) without actually crossing the stadium's threshold, making this newly developed plaza (formerly a parking lot) a hot gathering spot. On nongame days it's open to the public and hosts free events including concerts, alfresco fitness classes and movie nights on the jumbo video screen. On game days it's a beer garden for Cubs ticket holders.

CENTER ON HALSTED CENTER

Map p314 (☏773-472-6469; www.centeron halsted.org; 3656 N Halsted St, Boystown; ☺8am-9pm; M Red Line to Addison) The mod, glassy Center on Halsted is the Midwest's largest LGBT community center. It's mostly a social service organization for locals, but visitors can use the free wi-fi and reading library, plus there's a Whole Foods grocery store attached to it.

ALTA VISTA TERRACE AREA

Map p314 (btwn Byron & Grace Sts, Lake View; M Red Line to Sheridan) Chicago's first designated historic district is worthy of the honor. Developer Samuel Eberly Gross recreated a block of London row houses on Alta Vista Terrace in 1904. The 20 exquisitely detailed homes on either side of the street mirror each other diagonally and the owners have worked hard at maintaining the spirit of the block.

EATING

Good-time midrange places for vegetarians and global food lovers fill the neighborhood. Everything from Kurdish to Korean, Mexican and Italian hits the tables. Clark, Halsted, Broadway and Southport are fertile grazing streets. Hip new taco, doughnut, barbecue and fried-chicken eateries have opened directly around Wrigley Field.

✕ Boystown

CHICAGO DINER VEGETARIAN $

Map p314 (☏773-935-6696; www.veggiediner. com; 3411 N Halsted St; mains $10-14; ☺11am-10pm Mon-Thu, to 11pm Fri, 10am-11pm Sat, 10am-10pm Sun; ☞; M Red Line to Addison) It's the gold standard for Chicago vegetarians and a longtime favorite, as the 'meat-free since '83' tagline indicates. Top marks go to the mushroom lentil loaf (a truffle-sauced take on meatloaf), Radical Reuben (using corned beef seitan) and milkshakes (made with vegan ice cream and soy milk). Bright-red tables, hard-back booths and counter stools provide a vintage diner ambience.

There's another, sleeker branch (p168) in Logan Square.

YOSHI'S CAFE FUSION $$$

Map p314 (☏773-248-6160; www.yoshiscafe. com; 3257 N Halsted St; mains $22-35; ☺5-10pm Wed & Thu, 5-11pm Fri & Sat, 11am-2:30pm & 5-9:30pm Sun; M Red, Brown, Purple Line to Belmont) Yoshi's is one of the most innovative casual places in town, known for its changing Japanese- and French-flared menu and gracious standards during the past three decades. The chefs treat all ingredients with the utmost respect, from the salmon to the tofu to the Kobe beef. Service in the low-lit, well-spaced room is every bit as snappy as the food.

✖ Lake View

★ JENNIVEE'S
BAKERY $

Map p314 (☑773-697-3341; www.facebook.com/
jennivees; 3301 N Sheffield Ave; items $3.25-7.50;
◷noon-midnight Tue-Thu, to 2am Fri, 10am-2am
Sat, 10am-midnight Sun; Ⓜ Red, Brown, Purple
Line to Belmont) This LGBT-friendly bakery
mixes Filipino and American flavors. The
teeny room couldn't be any cuter. Chandeliers dangle from the ceiling, and a handful
of French-inspired tables and chairs let you
sit in dainty comfort as you fork into Jennivee's moist, creamy-frosted layer cakes
and cupcakes. Specialties include purple
velvet (made with purple yam) and mango
cream cakes.

CRISP
KOREAN $

Map p314 (☑773-697-7610; www.crisponline.com;
2940 N Broadway; mains $8-14; ◷11:30am-9pm;
Ⓜ Brown, Purple Line to Wellington) Music blasts
from the stereo while delicious Korean fu-
sions arrive from the kitchen at this cheerful little spot. The 'Bad Boy Buddha' bowl,
a variation on *bibimbap* (mixed vegetables
with rice), is one of the best healthy lunches
in town. Crisp's fried chicken (especially
the 'Seoul Sassy' with its savory soy-ginger
sauce) also wows the casual crowd.

WHEAT'S END
BREAKFAST $

Map p314 (☑773-770-3527; www.wheatsend
cafe.com; 2873 N Broadway; mains $9-13;
◷10am-3pm Tue-Fri, 9am-3pm Sat & Sun;
Ⓜ Brown, Purple Line to Wellington) The entire
menu at this sunny, modern space is 100%
gluten-free. Breakfast dishes are the specialty, including thick stacks of pancakes,
honey-butter-smeared cheddar chive biscuits and light, crispy popovers. The chefs
prepare it all with beyond-the-norm care. If
you're not hungry for a full meal, you can
always drop in for a cinnamon roll, espresso
and/or mimosa.

ANDY'S THAI KITCHEN
THAI $

Map p314 (☑773-897-0031; www.andysthai
kitchen.com; 946 W Wellington Ave; mains $11-15;
◷11am-9:30pm Mon-Fri, noon-9:30pm Sat & Sun;
Ⓜ Brown, Purple Line to Wellington) Little Andy's
earns big praise from foodies who swoon
over the authentic Thai menu. Andy's not
afraid to use organ parts in his dishes, or
to atomically spice them. Standouts include
the fish maw salad, basil preserved egg, and
boat noodles swimming with beef brisket

and pork skin. BYOB; cash only. Note: the
restaurant closes between 4pm and 5pm
daily.

CLARK STREET DOG
AMERICAN $

Map p314 (☑773-281-6690; www.clarkstdog.
com; 3040 N Clark St; mains $3.50-8; ◷9am-
3am Sun-Thu, to 4am Fri & Sat; Ⓜ Brown, Purple
Line to Wellington) Apart from signature hot
dogs, carnivorous delights include the Italian sausage combo – which marries Italian
beef *and* Italian sausage on a single soggy
bun – and the chili cheese fries. If all the
salty meats make you thirsty, head to the
adjoining divey Clark Street Bar for some
cheap cold ones.

★ GUNDIS
KURDISH KITCHEN
KURDISH $$

Map p314 (☑773-904-8120; www.thegundis.
com; 2909 N Clark St; mains $17-26; ◷9am-9pm
Mon, Wed & Thu, to 10pm Fri & Sat, to 8pm Sun;
Ⓜ Brown, Purple Line to Wellington) The owners,
who hail from southern Turkey, prepare
meals from their Kurdish homeland. Dish-
es include *sac tawa,* a traditional stir-fry of
meat, peppers and tomatoes on a sizzling
plate, and *tirsik,* a stew of eggplant, carrots
and other veggies in a spicy sauce. Sunshine
streams into the airy, exposed-brick room
by day, while pendant lights create a ro-
mantic vibe at night.

MFK
SPANISH $$

Off Map p314 (☑773-857-2540; www.mfk
restaurant.com; 432 W Diversey Pkwy; small
plates $10-20; ◷5-10pm Tue, noon-10pm Wed,
Thu & Sun, noon-midnight Fri & Sat; ☲22) In
mfk's teeny space it feels like you're having
a romantic meal at the seaside in Spain. Dig
into crunchy prawn heads, garlicky octopus
and veal meatballs amid the whitewashed
walls and decorative tiles. Sunny cocktails
and a wine list dominated by whites and
rosés add to the goodness.

CHILAM BALAM
MEXICAN $$

Map p314 (☑773-296-6901; www.chilambalam
chicago.com; 3023 N Broadway; small plates
$10-18; ◷5-10pm Tue-Thu, to 11pm Fri & Sat;
Ⓜ Brown, Purple Line to Wellington) The chef is
only in her 20s, but she has already appren-
ticed under Rick Bayless and brought his
'farm to table' philosophy to this vibrant
brick-and-Spanish-tile restaurant, which
sits below street level. The close-set tables
pulse with a young crowd ripping into fiery
ceviche, mushroom empanadas, chocolate-

chili mousse and other imaginative fare. It's BYOB. Cash only.

TANGO SUR
STEAK $$

Map p314 (📞773-477-5466; https://tango surgrill.com; 3763 N Southport Ave; mains $18-25; ⏱5-10:30pm Mon-Thu, to 11:30pm Fri, 3-11:30pm Sat, noon-10:30pm Sun; Ⓜ Brown Line to Southport) This candlelit BYOB Argentine steakhouse makes an idyllic date location, serving classic skirt steaks and other tender grass-fed options. In addition to the traditional cuts, the chef's special is 'Bife Vesuvio,' a prime strip stuffed with garlic, spinach and cheese – it's a triumph. In summer tables outside expand the seating from the small and spare interior.

✖ Roscoe Village

LUCY'S CAFE
VEGETARIAN $

Map p314 (📞733-665-0227; https://lucyscaferv. com; 2100 W Roscoe St; mains $9-12; ⏱8am-3pm, closed Tue; 🖉; Ⓜ Brown Line to Paulina) The tough decision at this revered breakfast house is between the free-range-egg omelets and the legendary French toast, cooked in rich cream batter and served with peach butter. New Age tunes and pastel colors give the room a soothing vibe, even when the place is mobbed on weekend mornings. Vegan and gluten-free patrons will find plenty to choose from.

VILLAGE TAP
PUB FOOD $

Map p314 (📞773-883-0817; www.villagetap.com; 2055 W Roscoe St; mains $10-14; ⏱5pm-2am Mon-Thu, 3pm-2am Fri, noon-3am Sat, noon-2am Sun; Ⓜ Brown Line to Paulina) Even though it can get packed on weekends, this neighborhood tavern does everything well: food, drink and atmosphere. The kitchen turns out great sandwiches and burgers (including a black-bean veggie burger) to go with the ever-changing and carefully chosen Midwestern microbrews. The picnic-table-dotted beer garden buzzes in warm weather. Inside, tables enjoy good views of the TVs for ball games.

✖ Wrigleyville

JENI'S
ICE CREAM $

Map p314 (📞773-666-5490; www.jenis.com; 3657 N Clark St; cones $5; ⏱11am-11pm; Ⓜ Red Line to Addison) With an Instagrammable vibe and supercreative flavors such as gooey butter cake and goat's cheese with red cherries, the Wrigleyville location of beloved Midwestern scoop shop Jeni's is making the neighborhood a little cooler. Owner and one-time aspiring perfumer Jeni Britton Bauer takes her recipe inspiration in part from her passion for aromatic essential oils.

BIG STAR
MEXICAN $

Map p314 (📞773-857-7120; www.bigstar chicago.com; 3640 N Clark St; tacos $2.50-4; ⏱11:30am-midnight Mon-Thu, to 2am Fri, 10am-2am Sat, 10am-midnight Sun; Ⓜ Red Line to Addison) Wicker Park favorite Big Star (p150) branched out into the Wrigleyville madness with this two-story restaurant across from the ballpark. While it's not quite on par with the original, it's fine and dandy for those seeking single-barrel whiskey, honky tonk tunes and tacos plumped with roasted pork shoulder, spicy tofu skins or sesame-crema-topped chicken thighs.

WEST TOWN
BAKERY & TAP
BAKERY $

Map p314 (📞773-269-5415; www.westtown bakery.com; 3626 N Clark St; cakeballs $1.75; ⏱7am-10pm Sun-Thu, to midnight Fri & Sat; Ⓜ Red Line to Addison) The Wrigleyville location of Chicago's West Town Bakery bucks the familiar bakeshop formula, offering quirky treats like French toast 'cakeballs' as well as a stocked bar. With both local coffee and beer on tap, the shop caters to the early morning laptop brigade as well as the post-ball-game crowd.

DUTCH & DOC'S
AMERICAN $$

Map p314 (📞773-360-0207; www.dutch anddocs.com; 3600 N Clark St; mains $18-24; ⏱11am-11pm Mon-Fri, 9am-11pm Sat & Sun; Ⓜ Red Line to Addison) Upmarket American dishes such as glazed short ribs, steaks and fried chicken are a hit at Dutch & Doc's, one of a new crop of restaurants gussying up Wrigleyville's dining scene. The most delicious item on the menu may be the eye-level views of Wrigley Field's iconic red marquee from the upstairs dining room.

SMOKE DADDY
BARBECUE $$

Map p314 (📞773-227-2583; www.thesmoke daddy.com; 3636 N Clark St; mains $14-29; ⏱11:30am-late Mon-Fri, 10am-late Sat & Sun; Ⓜ Red Line to Addison) The Wrigleyville location of long-running local favorite Smoke Daddy treats Cubs baseball fans to slow-cooked porcine delights and an easy-breezy vibe well suited to a pre-game meal. On balmy summer afternoons, thirsty patrons can sip frozen old-fashioneds and frosty local brews on the 2nd-story patio. Closing time is based on the night's crowd.

🍷 DRINKING & NIGHTLIFE

Nightlife is the specialty of Lake View and Wrigleyville, and there are heaps of options: traditional sports bars and new cocktail bars around Wrigley Field, dance clubs in Boystown, and cozy wine bars, English pubs and jazz-wafting little taverns scattered elsewhere throughout the neighborhood. Clark, Halsted and Broadway are all bountiful streets.

🍸 Boystown

ROSCOE'S TAVERN   GAY
Map p314 (☑773-281-3355; www.roscoes.com; 3356 N Halsted St; ⊗5pm-2am Mon-Thu, noon-2am Fri & Sun, noon-3am Sat; Ⓜ Red, Brown, Purple Line to Belmont) Roscoe's has been bringing in the Boystown crowd for more than three decades. Different parts of the venue have different vibes: a casual bar in front, a dance club in back and a sun-splashed patio outdoors. Drag-race viewing parties, karaoke and dueling piano events are sprinkled throughout the week.

WANG'S   GAY & LESBIAN
Map p314 (☑773-296-6800; 3317 N Broadway; ⊗4-11pm Sun-Tue, 5pm-midnight Wed & Thu, 6pm-2am Fri & Sat; Ⓜ Red, Brown, Purple Line to Belmont) The low red light, paper lanterns, floral wallpaper and carved peacock mirror give Wang's a Chinese-opium-den vibe. It's mostly guys sitting around the intimate, gay-friendly bar, hoisting cocktails such as the signature pear martini. It's attached to Japanese restaurant Wakamono.

SIDETRACK   CLUB
Map p314 (☑773-477-9189; www.sidetrack chicago.com; 3349 N Halsted St; ⊗3pm-2am Mon-Fri, 1pm-3am Sat, 1pm-2am Sun; Ⓜ Red, Brown, Purple Line to Belmont) Massive Sidetrack thumps dance music for gay and straight crowds alike. Events take place throughout the week: drag-queen nights, movie-viewing parties, Beyoncé dance parties. If the indoor action gets to be too much, the huge outdoor courtyard beckons.

CLOSET   GAY & LESBIAN
Map p314 (☑773-477-8533; www.thecloset chicago.com; 3325 N Broadway; ⊗4pm-4am Mon-Fri, noon-5am Sat, noon-4am Sun; 🛜; Ⓜ Red, Brown, Purple Line to Belmont) One of the few lesbian-centric bars in Chicago, the Closet changes mood and tempo at 2am, when the crowd becomes more mixed (male and female), the music gets louder and things get a little rowdier. Cash only.

HYDRATE   CLUB
Map p314 (☑773-975-9244; www.hydrate chicago.com; 3458 N Halsted St; ⊗8pm-4am Mon-Fri, to 5am Sat, 2pm-4am Sun; Ⓜ Red Line to Addison) A wild night on the Boystown club circuit requires a visit to this frenzied spot, which boasts an open-air feel (thanks to retractable windows) and a chatty pickup scene (thanks to cheap mixed drinks). It's not all roses: the service gets rude and the crowds unruly. The dance floor grooves hard in the wee hours.

🍸 Lake View

⭐TEN CAT TAVERN   PUB
Map p314 (☑773-935-5377; 3931 N Ashland Ave; ⊗3pm-2am; Ⓜ Brown Line to Irving Park) Pool is serious business on the two vintage tables that the pub refelts regularly with Belgian material. The ever-changing, eye-catching art comes courtesy of neighborhood artists and the furniture is a garage saler's dream. Regulars (most in their 30s) down leisurely drinks at the bar or, in warm weather, in the beer garden. The back room has a toasty fireplace.

LOBA PASTRY + COFFEE   CAFE
Map p314 (☑773-456-9266; www.lobapastry. com; 3422 N Lincoln Ave; ⊗7am-3pm Mon-Thu, to 4pm Fri, 8am-4pm Sat & Sun; Ⓜ Brown Line to Paulina) Featuring adventurous pastries and artisanal coffee, this diminutive cafe just east of Roscoe Village doesn't offer much in the way of space, but it makes up for that via innovative baked goods with bold flavor. Try the lemon-poppy-seed-coriander muffins, black-sesame buns or the pepita crunch bar inspired by *palanqueta* (a Mexican candy reminiscent of peanut brittle).

BAR PASTORAL
WINE BAR

Map p314 (☏773-472-4781; www.barpastoral.com; 2947 N Broadway; ☺5-10pm Mon-Wed, to 11pm Thu, to midnight Fri, 10am-midnight Sat, to 10pm Sun; Ⓜ Brown, Purple Line to Wellington) Popular deli minichain Pastoral has a wine bar at its Lake View shop. Half-glasses are available for $5, meaning you can sample widely. The deli's awesome breads and cheeses help soak it up (better to stick to these rather than the dishes listed on the menu).

SOUTHPORT LANES
BAR

Map p314 (☏773-472-6600; www.southport lanes.com; 3325 N Southport Ave; ☺4pm-2am Mon-Thu, from noon Fri-Sun; Ⓜ Brown Line to Southport) An old-fashioned, four-lane bowling alley with hand-set pins hides inside this busy neighborhood bar and grill. Those who prefer to shoot stick can chalk up at the six regulation pool tables. The main bar features an inspirational mural of cavorting nymphs, and tables sprawl onto the sidewalk in summer. A fine selection of regional beers flows from the taps.

BERLIN
CLUB

Map p314 (☏773-348-4975; www.berlinchicago.com; 954 W Belmont Ave; ☺10pm-2am Mon, to 4am Tue-Thu & Sun, 8pm-4am Fri, 8pm-5am Sat; Ⓜ Red, Brown, Purple Line to Belmont) Looking for a packed, sweaty dance floor that's loads of fun? Berlin caters to a mostly gay crowd midweek, though partiers of all stripes jam the place on weekends. Monitors flicker through the latest video dispatches from cult pop and electronic acts, while DJs take the dance floor on trancey detours. There's a $10 cover charge on Friday and Saturday.

GUTHRIE'S
PUB

Map p314 (☏773-477-2900; www.guthries tavern.com; 1300 W Addison St; ☺5pm-2am Mon-Fri, 2pm-3am Sat, 2pm-midnight Sun; Ⓜ Red Line to Addison) A local institution and the perfect neighborhood hangout, Guthrie's remains true to its mellow roots even as the Cubs-fueled neighborhood goes manic around it. The glassed-in back porch is fittingly furnished with patio chairs and filled with 30- and 40-somethings, and board games abound.

DUKE OF PERTH
PUB

Map p314 (☏773-477-1741; www.dukeofperth.com; 2913 N Clark St; ☺5pm-2am Mon, from noon Tue-Sun; Ⓜ Brown, Purple Line to Wellington) The UK beers and more than 80 bottles of single-malt scotch are nearly overwhelming at this cozy, laid-back pub.

After enough of them, try the fish and chips, which is all-you-can-eat for lunch and dinner for $14 on Wednesday and Friday.

🍷 Roscoe Village

★ HUNGRY BRAIN
BAR

Off Map p314 (☏773-935-2118; www.hungry brainchicago.com; 2319 W Belmont Ave; ☺7pm-2am, closed Tue; 🚌77) The owner of nearby music club Constellation (p120) also owns this off-the-beaten-path little bar. It charms with its kind bartenders and well-worn, thrift-store decor. It's a hub of the underground jazz scene; Sunday nights are the mainstay (suggested donation $10), though there are shows and literary readings other nights of the week, too. Cash only.

🍷 Wrigleyville

★ NISEI LOUNGE
BAR

Map p314 (☏773-525-0557; www.niseilounge chicago.com; 3439 N Sheffield Ave; ☺5pm-2am Mon-Fri, noon-3am Sat, noon-2am Sun; Ⓜ Red Line to Addison) Sometimes the new, cocktail-laden Wrigleyville weighs on your soul and you yearn for the cheap-beer-splashed days of yore. Enter the Nisei, a neighborhood dive bar since 1951. It's a bit gussied up from its original incarnation, but for those craving a pool table, dartboards, regretful shots of liquor and a raucous post-Cubs-game scene, this is your place.

MORDECAI
COCKTAIL BAR

Map p314 (☏773-269-5410; www.mordecai chicago.com; 3632 N Clark St; ☺5-11pm Sun-Thu, to midnight Fri & Sat; Ⓜ Red Line to Addison) Early-20th-century Cubs baseball great Mordecai Brown lends his name to this stylish bar at Hotel Zachary (p239). With a serious cocktail menu spotlighting vintage whiskeys, it's a far cry from Wrigleyville's standard sticky-floored boozers. Snacks like beer-battered cheese curds dusted with bonito and *togarashi* spice play wonderfully with high and low cuisine.

Opens three hours prior to Cubs home games.

Wrigley Field Experience

You'll experience more than just a game at Wrigley Field. A tangible sense of history comes alive at the 100-plus-year-old baseball park, thanks to the hand-turned scoreboard, iconic neon entrance sign and time-honored traditions that infuse each inning. Plus the streets around it erupt into one big party during games.

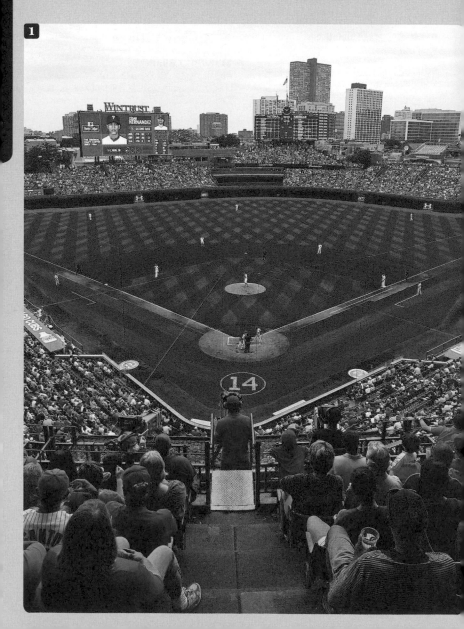

2

1. View of the Outfield
Wrigley Field is the second-oldest baseball park in the major league.

2. Scoreboard
The hand-turned scoreboard has barely changed since it was built in 1937.

3. Chicago Cubs player Ian Happ
Playing against Oakland Athletics in 2019; the Cubs won 10-1.

4. Wrigley Field Sign
The iconic neon sign is located directly over the main stadium entrance.

SMART BAR
CLUB

Map p314 (☑773-549-4140; www.smartbar chicago.com; 3730 N Clark St; tickets $5-15; ⊙10pm-4am Thu, Fri & Sun, to 5am Sat; MRed Line to Addison) Smart Bar is a long-standing, unpretentious favorite for dancing, located in the basement of the Metro rock club. The DJs are often more renowned than you'd expect the intimate space to accommodate. House and techno dominate the turntables.

SLUGGERS
SPORTS BAR

Map p314 (☑773-472-9696; www.sluggersbar. com; 3540 N Clark St; ⊙11am-2am Sun-Fri, to 3am Sat; MRed Line to Addison) Practice your home-run swing at Sluggers, a cheesy but popular bar and grill across from Wrigley Field. Sidestep the schnockered Cubs fans and giant-screen TVs and head to the 2nd floor, where there are four batting cages. Ten pitches cost $2.

LUCKY DORR
CRAFT BEER

Map p314 (☑773-388-8249; www.luckydorr. com; 1101 W Waveland Ave; ⊙4-11pm Mon-Thu, to midnight Fri & Sat, to 10pm Sun; MRed Line to Addison) Lucky Dorr, which stands about 20 paces from Wrigley Field, sends out its siren song to beer aficionados. The 20 taps pour brews by local makers such as Begyle, Moody Tongue, Whiner, Haymarket and Maplewood. Many of the beers are created exclusively for the bar, so you won't find them elsewhere. Weekly Meet the Brewer events celebrate new releases.

MURPHY'S BLEACHERS
SPORTS BAR

Map p314 (☑773-281-5356; www.murphys bleachers.com; 3655 N Sheffield Ave; ⊙11am-2am; MRed Line to Addison) It's a Cubs game prerequisite to beer up at this well-loved, historic watering hole, only steps away from the entrance to Wrigley Field's bleacher seats. Fans jam in like sardines on game day. A smattering of good local beers are on tap, or you can opt for the infamous $3 cheap can of mystery beer.

GMAN TAVERN
BAR

Map p314 (☑773-549-2050; www.gmantavern. com; 3740 N Clark St; ⊙3pm-2am Sun-Fri, to 3am Sat; MRed Line to Addison) The punk-rock jukebox, large, eclectic beer selection, and pierced-and-tattooed patrons make the GMan wonderfully different from the surrounding sports bars. Bands and comedy shows often play in the back room. For years the bar was Gingerman Tavern; new owners took over and dubbed it GMan, though long-standing patrons still use the original name. A splendid spot to pass an evening.

☆ ENTERTAINMENT

★CONSTELLATION
LIVE MUSIC

Off Map p314 (www.constellation-chicago.com; 3111 N Western Ave, Roscoe Village; ⊙6pm-midnight Mon & Tue, 7pm-2am Wed, Thu & Sun, 6pm-2am Fri & Sat; ☐77) The producer of Pitchfork Music Festival (p22) opened this intimate club, which actually breaks down into two small venues inside. The city's hepcats come out of the woodwork for the progressive jazz and improvisational music. Many acts are free, most cost $10 to $15, and none costs more than $25.

★METRO
LIVE MUSIC

Map p314 (☑773-549-4140; www.metrochicago. com; 3730 N Clark St, Wrigleyville; ⊙box office noon-6pm Mon, to 8pm Tue-Sat; MRed Line to Addison) For more than three decades, the Metro has been synonymous with loud rock. Sonic Youth and the Ramones in the '80s. Nirvana and Jane's Addiction in the '90s. White Stripes and the Killers in the new millennium. Each night prepare to hear noise by three or four bands who may well be teetering on the verge of stardom.

MUSIC BOX THEATRE
CINEMA

Map p314 (☑773-871-6604; www.musicbox theatre.com; 3733 N Southport Ave, Lake View; MBrown Line to Southport) It hardly matters what's playing here; the Music Box itself is worth the visit. The restored theater dates from 1929 and looks like a Moorish palace, with clouds floating across the ceiling under twinkling stars. The art-house films are always first-rate and there's a midnight roster of cult hits like *The Big Lebowski*. A second, smaller theater shows held-over films.

SCHUBAS
LIVE MUSIC

Map p314 (☑773-525-2508; www.lh-st.com; 3159 N Southport Ave, Lake View; ⊙5pm-2am Mon-Thu, 2pm-2am Fri, 10:30am-3am Sat, 10:30am-2am Sun; MBrown Line to Southport) Set in an old Schlitz brewery building, Schubas presents twangy acoustic artists, plus indie rock acts on their way up (like the

National and Janelle Monáe in their early days). Bands play most nights in the cozy back-room club, which is noted for its great sound, thanks to the all-wood construction. A boisterous bar pours microbrews in the front room.

OTHERWORLD
THEATRE   THEATER

Map p314 (☎773-857-2116; www.otherworld theatre.org; 3914 N Clark St, Lake View; ⓂRed Line to Sheridan) It claims to be the world's first theater dedicated to science fiction and fantasy. There are two stages: a 120-seat main stage and the 40-seat black box, plus a bar. All main-stage shows are pay what you can. The theater also hosts sci-fi community events like cosplay meet-ups and game nights.

STRAWDOG
THEATRE COMPANY   THEATER

Map p314 (☎773-644-1380; www.strawdog.org; 1802 W Berenice Ave, North Center; ⓂBrown Line to Irving Park) The ensemble stages new works, reimagined classics and avant-garde musicals that get creative in their subject matter. Strawdog has received national attention for some of its works. The theater has two small performance spaces and a bar.

LAUGH FACTORY
CHICAGO   COMEDY

Map p314 (☎773-327-3175; www.laughfactory. com; 3175 N Broadway, Lake View; ⊗5pm-midnight Sun-Thu, to 2am Fri & Sat; ⓂRed, Brown, Purple Line to Belmont) Newbie comics line up hours in advance for Wednesday's open mike at the Laugh Factory. Such is the cachet of its parent LA club, where everyone from Richard Pryor to Sarah Silverman has tried out jokes. Expect lots of seasoned local stand-up acts the rest of the week.

MARTYRS'
                                           LIVE MUSIC

Map p314 (☎773-404-9494; www.martyrslive. com; 3855 N Lincoln Ave, North Center; ⊗6pm-1am Sun-Fri, to 2am Sat; ⓂBrown Line to Irving Park) Martyrs' is a small, catch-all venue where pretty much anything goes musically: a South American jazz improv band, a Tom Petty tribute band, a Mexican folk-music group. It also hosts occasional story-telling events and PechaKucha nights (an evening of fast-paced presentations by

artists, activists, chefs and other creatives). The venue serves mighty fine pub grub to boot.

EMERALD CITY
THEATRE COMPANY   THEATER

Map p314 (☎773-529-2690; www.emerald citytheatre.com; 2936 N Southport Ave, Lake View; ⓂBrown Line to Southport) It presents some of the most innovative plays for children in the country, from blockbusters such as *School House Rock Live* to lesser-known works like *Three Little Kittens* and *How I Became a Pirate*. Performances are at the group's on-site Little Theatre, as well as other theaters around town.

ANNOYANCE
THEATRE   COMEDY

Map p314 (☎773-697-9693; www.the annoyance.com; 851 W Belmont Ave, Lake View; ⓂRed, Brown, Purple Line to Belmont) A Chicago improv mainstay for more than 30 years, the Annoyance masterminds naughty and absurd shows, often musicals such as *Tiny Fascists: A Boy Scout Musical*. Performances take place on two stages nightly. The little lobby bar has good, cheap microbrews on tap.

VIC THEATRE
                                           LIVE MUSIC

Map p314 (☎773-472-0449; www.victheatre. com; 3145 N Sheffield Ave, Lake View; ⓂRed, Brown, Purple Line to Belmont) The Vic – a vintage 1912 vaudeville theater – now hosts big-name bands several nights a week, and second-run Hollywood and cult films on the off nights. Music fans dig the Vic's smallish (1300 capacity) size and great sight lines. Movie fans like the venue's Brew & View program, with pizzas and pitchers of beer on offer, and tickets for $5.

LOCAL SOUVENIRS

Lake View is a swell neighborhood to pick up unique Chicago souvenirs. Try the following:

Cubs Store For a hat, jersey, shot glass or anything with a Cubs logo.

Chicago Comics For a hand-drawn magazine made by a local artist.

Gramaphone Records (p123) For house music and other tracks by Chicago artists.

CSZ THEATER
COMEDY

Map p314 (☑773-549-8080; www.cszchicago.com; 929 W Belmont Ave, Lake View; ☺shows from 8pm Mon & Wed-Fri, from 6pm Sat, from 7pm Sun; MRed, Brown, Purple Line to Belmont) The signature show here is ComedySportz. The gimmick? Two teams compete to make you laugh. The show is totally improvised, with the audience dictating the action. A referee moderates and the wittiest team 'wins'. The comedy is profanity- and vulgarity-free, so all ages are welcome. Adults can bring in alcohol from the lobby bar. Prime-time weekend shows are $25.

BEAT KITCHEN
LIVE MUSIC

Map p314 (☑773-281-4444; www.beatkitchen.com; 2100 W Belmont Ave, Roscoe Village; ☺4pm-2am Mon-Fri, 11:30am-3am Sat, 11:30am-2am Sun; ☑77) Everything you need to know is in the name – entertaining beats traverse a spectrum of sounds and the kitchen turns out better-than-average dinners. Dine early in the front of the house, since service is unhurried. Music in the homely back room can be funky or jammy, but a crop of Chicago's smart, broadly appealing songwriters dominates the calendar.

🛍 SHOPPING

Shops for kitschy hipsters and rock-and-roll types cluster around Clark and Belmont Sts, along with several big box stores. Naughty stuff sells in Boystown. Southport Ave between Belmont and Irving Park Rd has designer and upscale wares.

★CHICAGO COMICS
BOOKS

Map p314 (☑773-528-1983; www.chicagocomics.com; 3244 N Clark St, Lake View; ☺noon-8pm Mon, Tue, Thu & Fri, 11am-8pm Wed & Sat, noon-7pm Sun; MRed, Brown, Purple Line to Belmont) This emporium is frequently cited as one of the nation's best comic-book stores. Old Marvel *Superman* back issues share shelf space with hand-drawn works by cutting-edge local artists such as Chris Ware, Ivan Brunetti and Dan Clowes (who lived here during his early *Eightball* days). Plenty of toys and T-shirts for sale, too.

CUBS STORE
GIFTS & SOUVENIRS

Map p314 (☑773-975-3636; 3637 N Clark St, Wrigleyville; ☺11am-7pm) This slick shop outside Wrigley Field has every Cubs-logoed item you could dream of. Browse two stories of official team paraphernalia, including an entire wall of hats, plus jerseys, jackets, flip-flops, shot glasses, toys and wall hangings. Fun interactive photo ops allow you to insert yourself into the batter's box or the outfield.

HOLLYWOOD MIRROR
VINTAGE

Map p314 (☑773-404-2044; www.hollywoodmirror.com; 812 W Belmont Ave, Lake View; ☺11am-8pm Mon-Thu, to 9pm Fri & Sat, to 7pm Sun; MRed, Brown, Purple Line to Belmont) Who isn't tempted by a store whose windows beckon with a giant creepy clown face and wig-wearing dog mannequin in a velvet skirt? Hollywood Mirror features a vast sprawl of costumes, vintage clothing and leather jackets, as well as kitschy toys and disco balls. Friendly staff will help you find whatever it is you need.

UNABRIDGED BOOKSTORE
BOOKS

Map p314 (☑773-883-9119; www.unabridgedbookstore.com; 3251 N Broadway, Boystown; ☺10am-9pm Mon-Fri, to 7pm Sat & Sun; MRed, Brown, Purple Line to Belmont) This indie shop is known for its stellar gay and lesbian section (including gay fiction, gay parenting and queer spirituality), as well as travel, sci-fi and children's sections. Staff tape up notes on the shelves next to their recommendations.

GRAMAPHONE RECORDS

MUSIC

Map p314 (⌂773-472-3683; www.gramaphone records.com; 2843 N Clark St, Lake View; ◷noon-8pm Tue & Thu-Sat, to 6pm Sun; ⓜBrown, Purple Line to Diversey) Gramaphone is a favorite of DJs and electronic music fans. It carries a vast selection of new and old, popular and underground house, techno, hip-hop, juke, drum and bass, and more. The shop also sells record needles, slipmats and other DJ supplies, and has a host of info on upcoming events.

UNCLE DAN'S

SPORTS & OUTDOORS

Map p314 (⌂773-348-5800; www.udans.com; 3551 N Southport Ave, Lake View; ◷10am-7pm Mon-Sat, 11am-6pm Sun; ⓜBrown Line to Southport) This store offers top travel and outdoor gear for those looking to escape the concrete jungle, or at least get some abrasion-reinforced fleece to protect them from the elements. It's a relaxed place to buy hiking boots, camping supplies, backpacks and whatnot without the attitude that gear stores sometimes give off.

SPORTS WORLD

GIFTS & SOUVENIRS

Map p314 (⌂844-462-4422; www.sports worldchicago.com; 3555 N Clark St, Wrigleyville; ◷9am-5pm; ⓜRed Line to Addison) Located across from Wrigley Field, Sports World overflows with – that's right – sportswear. It carries all shapes and sizes of Cubs jerseys, T-shirts, sweatshirts and ballcaps, plus baby clothes and drink flasks. Bears and Blackhawks gear is available, too. Surprisingly, the prices aren't bad given the location.

MEN'S ROOM

CLOTHING

Map p314 (⌂773-857-0907; https://shop themensroom.com; 3420 N Halsted St, Boystown; ◷noon-midnight; ⓜRed Line to Addison) When the urge strikes for leather harnesses, fetish gear, handcuffs or sexy underwear, the Men's Room has the goods. It's a one-stop shop for fashion, grooming and fetish, as the helpful sign out front says. Fun T-shirts, too.

W82

SPORTS & OUTDOORS

Map p314 (⌂773-472-6868; www.w82.com; 3317 N Clark St, Lake View; ◷11am-8pm Mon-Sat, noon-6pm Sun; ⓜRed, Brown, Purple Line to Belmont) W82 is one-stop shopping for sporty board gear, whether you're into surfing, windsurfing, kiteboarding, snowboarding or skateboarding. It carries the requisite apparel labels, too (Quiksilver, Billabong, Split etc). Staff members are clued in to local boarding hot spots.

 # SPORTS & ACTIVITIES

CHICAGO RIVER CANOE & KAYAK

KAYAKING

Off Map p314 (⌂773-704-2663; www.chicagoriver paddle.com; 3400 N Rockwell St, North Center; kayaks per hour $15-20; ◷10am-6pm Mon-Fri, 9am-6pm Sat & Sun Jun-early Sep, Fri-Sun only May, rest of Sep & Oct; ⊟152) Paddling the river from here is less trafficky and more relaxing than paddling from downtown. Head north from the launch, and the current will help bring you back. Look for herons, mallards, deer and turtles en route. Star architect Jeanne Gang designed the zinc-and-slate boathouse.

SYDNEY R MAROVITZ GOLF COURSE

GOLF

Map p314 (⌂312-742-7930; www.cpdgolf.com; 3600 N Recreation Dr, Lake View; ⊟151) The nine-hole course enjoys sweeping views of the lake and skyline. It is very popular and in order to secure a tee time golfers cheerfully arrive at 5:30am. You can avoid that sort of lunacy by reserving in advance (either online or by phone; no extra fee). Fees are $29 to $32 in summer. You can also rent clubs here.

Andersonville & Uptown

ANDERSONVILLE | UPTOWN | WEST RIDGE

Neighborhood Top Five

1 **Clark Street** Ambling along this busy thoroughfare, popping into stylish shops by day and drinking and dining in gastronome eateries at night.

2 **Green Mill** (p133) Listening to jazz and sipping martinis with Al Capone's ghost in velvet booths amid the candlelit, art deco interior.

3 **Argyle Street** (p126) Slurping a savory bowl of pho and some bubble tea in the steamy-windowed shops of 'Little Saigon.'

4 **Neo-Futurist Theater** (p134) Watching 30 plays in 60 minutes at this off beat theater, where a dice throw determines your admission cost.

5 **Montrose Beach** (p135) Exploring the dunes and bird-filled 'magic hedge,' or lounging at the bar while watching sailboats float in the harbor.

For more detail of this area see Map p316

Explore Andersonville & Uptown

These northern neighborhoods are good for a delicious browse. Andersonville is an old Swedish enclave centered on Clark St, where timeworn bars mix with new foodie-destination restaurants, artsy boutiques, antique shops and gay and lesbian bars. The Swedish American Museum Center keeps the original inhabitants' legacy alive, but these residential streets are now home mostly to creative types and young professionals.

Just to the south, Uptown has a different feel. Argyle St runs through the heart of 'Little Saigon,' filled with Vietnamese restaurants serving pho and shops chockablock with exotic goods from the homeland. Several historic theaters cluster at N Broadway and Lawrence Ave, right near Al Capone's favorite speakeasy, the Green Mill.

Come here to stroll and window-shop, eat and drink and maybe see a show. Begin at the north end of Clark St in the afternoon, making your way down through the shops and cafes; divert to Argyle St as you head south, and eventually end up at the Green Mill for drinks and some live music. Or make a full day of it by starting either at Montrose Beach for surf and sand, or with a pleasant stroll through historic Graceland Cemetery.

Even further north, Devon Ave – a wild mash-up of Indian, Pakistani, Russian and Jewish shops and restaurants – offers a worthy detour for those with more time.

Local Life

➤ **Solstice party** In mid-June Andersonville harks back to its Swedish roots, and everyone gets together to dance around the maypole and eat lingonberries for **Midsommarfest** (www.andersonville.org/midsommarfest; N Clark St, Andersonville; suggested donation $10; ☺Jun; 🚻; Ⓜ Red Line to Berwyn).

➤ **Dog beach** When locals need to let their furry friends roam and splash, they unleash at Montrose Beach (p135). It is *the* four-legged scene.

➤ **Farmers market** Find fresh regional produce and mix with the locals at this compact summertime street market (p135).

Getting There & Away

➤ **The L** Take the Red Line to Berwyn (a half-mile east of Clark St) for Andersonville; to Argyle for Argyle St and 'Little Saigon'; and to Lawrence for the Green Mill.

➤ **Bus** Bus 22 travels along Clark St.

➤ **Car** Meter and on-street parking are available in Andersonville and Uptown, though it gets congested on weekends.

Lonely Planet's Top Tip

In addition to serving some of the neighborhood's best food, Hopleaf (p131) is a fantastic beer bar. Stop in before dinner and enjoy a hearty Trappist ale or an unusual microbrew from the 200-strong list. In summer sip it on the shady patio out back; in winter head for the fireplace.

✘ Best Places to Eat

➤ Passerotto (p127)

➤ Hopleaf (p131)

➤ Big Jones (p127)

➤ Vincent (p127)

➤ Hot 'G' Dog (p127)

For reviews, see p126.➡

🍷 Best Places to Drink

➤ Simon's Tavern (p131)

➤ Hamburger Mary's (p131)

➤ Marty's Martini Bar (p131)

➤ Big Chicks (p133)

➤ SoFo Tap (p133)

For reviews, see p131.➡

☆ Best Entertainment

➤ Green Mill (p133)

➤ Neo-Futurist Theater (p134)

➤ Chicago Magic Lounge (p134)

➤ Black Ensemble Theater (p134)

For reviews, see p133.➡

◉ SIGHTS

There aren't many traditional sights in these primarily residential neighborhoods, but Graceland Cemetery offers up some beautiful strolls and Argyle Street – aka Little Saigon – is good for a browse.

◉ Andersonville

SWEDISH AMERICAN MUSEUM CENTER   MUSEUM

Map p316 (☑773-728-8111; www.swedish americanmuseum.org; 5211 N Clark St; adult/child $4/3; ◷10am-4pm Mon-Fri, from 11am Sat & Sun; ☒22, ⓜRed Line to Berwyn) The permanent collection at this small storefront museum focuses on the lives of the Swedes who originally settled Chicago. Check out the items people deemed important enough to bring with them on their journey to America: butter churns, traditional bedroom furniture, religious relics and more. The children's section lets kids climb around on a steamship and milk fake cows.

◉ Uptown

GRACELAND CEMETERY   CEMETERY

Map p316 (☑773-525-1105; www.graceland cemetery.org; 4001 N Clark St; ◷8am-4pm Mon-Fri, from 9am Sat & Sun; ⓜRed Line to Sheridan) The final resting place for some of the biggest names in Chicago history, including architects Louis Sullivan and Ludwig Mies van der Rohe and retail magnate Marshall Field. Most of the notable tombs lie around the lake, in the northern half of the cemetery's 121 acres. Pick up a map at the entrance to navigate the swirl of streets.

Many of the memorials relate to the lives of the dead in symbolic and touching ways. National League founder William Hulbert lies under a baseball. Daniel Burnham, who did so much to design Chicago, gets his own island. George Pullman, the railroad car magnate who sparked so much labor unrest, lies under a hidden fortress designed to prevent angry union members from digging him up. Power couple Bertha and Potter Palmer (whose dry-goods business eventually became the Marshall Field company) also have a doozy of a memorial.

ARGYLE STREET   AREA

Map p316 (btwn N Broadway & Sheridan Rd; ⓜRed Line to Argyle) Many residents of this area, also known as 'Little Saigon,' arrived as refugees from the Vietnam War and subsequently filled the storefronts with lunch spots serving pho, bakeries pouring bubble tea, and shops with exotic goods from the homeland. The pagoda-shaped Argyle L station, painted in the auspicious colors of green and red, puts you in the heart of it.

HUTCHINSON STREET DISTRICT   ARCHITECTURE

Off Map p316 (ⓜRed Line to Sheridan) Homes here were built in the early 1900s and represent some of the best examples of Prairie School architecture in Chicago. Many residences – including 839 Hutchinson St – are the work of George W Maher, a famous student of Frank Lloyd Wright. Also of note are 817 Hutchinson St and 4243 Hazel St.

✗ EATING

Andersonville offers an international array of eateries, with a couple of trendy options. Uptown's 'Little Saigon' brings on the noodle houses.

✗ Andersonville

★LOST LARSON   BAKERY $

Map p316 (☑773-944-0587; www.lostlarson.com; 5318 N Clark St; baked goods $4.50-7; ◷7am-7pm Wed-Sun; ☒22, ⓜRed Line to Berwyn) Renowned pastry chef Bobby Schaffer has opened one of Andersonville's newest spots, a Scandi-influenced bakery with an appropriately minimalist, elegant design. Wheat is milled on-site and local ingredients used for delicious pastries such as lingonberry-almond cake, cardamom buns and white-chocolate-marzipan duchess cake, plus loaves of honey-oat, spelt and potato breads. *Chicago* magazine voted its chocolate croissant the best in town.

DEFLOURED   BAKERY $

Map p316 (☑773-234-5733; www.defloured bakery.com; 1477 W Balmoral Ave; baked goods $1-4.25; ◷11am-7pm Wed-Fri, 9am-4pm Sat & Sun; ☒22, ⓜRed Line to Berwyn) Celiacs, rejoice! Defloured is an entirely gluten-free bakery that believes everyone should be able to indulge in ooey-gooey down-home sweet treats like cupcakes, lemon bars, cream puffs, Whoopie Pies, Snickerdoodles and carrot cake. Dairy-free and vegan options also available.

★PASSEROTTO
KOREAN $$

Map p316 (⌖708-607-2102; www.passerotto chicago.com; 5420 N Clark St; small plates $9-16; ◷5-10pm Tue-Thu, to 11pm Fri & Sat; ☐22, ⓂRed Line to Berwyn) Korean American chef Jennifer Kim showcases the food of her childhood through the influences of Italian cooking at Andersonville's hottest new restaurant. The regularly changing menu features sharing plates of varying sizes, from raw Atlantic fluke or bay scallops to *ddukbokki* lamb ragu and *kalbi* short ribs for two ($38). Finish with Tuscan biscotti dipped in Italian raisin wine. Bookings advised.

BIG JONES
AMERICAN $$

Map p316 (⌖773-275-5725; www.bigjones chicago.com; 5347 N Clark St; mains $14-29; ◷11am-9pm Mon-Thu, to 10pm Fri, 9am-10pm Sat, 9am-9pm Sun; ☐22, ⓂRed Line to Berwyn) Warm, sunny Big Jones puts sustainable 'Southern heirloom cooking' on the menu, mixing dishes from New Orleans, the Carolina Lowcountry and Appalachia. Locals flock in for the seasonal menu that might include chicken and dumplings, crispy catfish, or shrimp and grits. The decadent, biscuit-laden brunch draws the biggest crowds. It's best to reserve in advance.

JIN JU
KOREAN $$

Map p316 (⌖773-334-6377; www.jinjurestaurant. com; 5203 N Clark St; mains $12-26; ◷5-9:30pm Sun, Tue & Wed, to 10pm Thu, to 11pm Fri & Sat; ⓂRed Line to Berwyn) Jin Ju throws a culinary curveball by tempering Korean food to Western tastes. The minimalist candlelit interior echoes softly with downbeat techno, and the stylish 30-something clientele enjoys mains like *haemul pajon* (a fried pancake stuffed with seafood) and *kalbi* (beef short ribs). Try a cucumber- or lychee-flavored 'soju-tini' made with soju (a Korean spirit distilled from sweet potatoes).

ANDIE'S
MEDITERRANEAN $$

Map p316 (⌖773-784-8616; www.andieschicago. com; 5253 N Clark St; mains $14-20; ◷4-10:30pm Mon-Thu, 11am-11pm Fri & Sat, 10:30am-10pm Sun; ☑ ♿; ⓂRed Line to Berwyn) Friendly, reliable Andie's has anchored Andersonville's restaurant row from the get-go, and it still

UPTOWN POETRY SLAM

A long-running event, **Uptown Poetry Slam** (Map p316; www.greenmilljazz. com; 4802 N Broadway, Uptown; cover charge $7; ◷7-10pm Sun; ⓂRed Line to Lawrence) birthed the 'performance poetry' genre, and it's still going strong every Sunday night at the Green Mill (p133). Founder Marc Smith continues to host the rollicking event. Watch shaky first-timers take the mike from 7pm to 8pm; a featured guest raps verse afterward, and the slam competition begins in earnest at 9pm. Get your snapping fingers ready.

draws crowds for Mediterranean comfort food such as kabobs, moussaka, smooth hummus, dill rice and much more, with lots of gluten-free and vegetarian/vegan options on offer. There's also a kids menu.

VINCENT
BISTRO $$$

Map p316 (⌖773-334-7168; www.vincent chicago.com; 1475 W Balmoral Ave; mains $23-38; ◷dinner 5:30-10pm Tue-Thu, 5-11pm Fri & Sat, 5-10pm Sun, brunch 11am-2pm Sat & Sun; ☐22, ⓂRed Line to Berwyn) Casual sophistication oozes from this cozy, candlelit bistro tucked down an Andersonville side street. A local crowd of older gay men and young families with small kids enjoy the changing-nightly menu, which ranges from bone-marrow spaetzle to braised lamb to pan-roasted chicken. The *moules-frites* (mussels and fries) – with Prince Edward Island (PEI) mussels prepared five different ways – are among the best in town.

✕ Uptown

HOT 'G' DOG
AMERICAN $

Map p316 (⌖773-209-3360; www.hotgdog.com; 5009 N Clark St; hot dogs $3-5, specialty sausages $7.50-9; ◷10:30am-8pm Mon-Sat, to 4pm Sun; ☑; ⓂRed Line to Argyle) The Garcia brothers (hence the 'G') learned the gourmet-sausage trade from famed Chicago bratmaster 'Hot Doug' Sohn. This is the place to bite into, say, a smoked elk sausage with garlic sauce and bacon cheddar cheese, or alligator sausage with shrimp remoulade. Or just go old-school with a regular Chicago-style hot dog (veggie version available). Cash only.

The Northern Neighborhoods – Andersonville & Uptown

Uptown's 'Little Saigon' and European-vibed Andersonville are both prime for delicious browsing. Locals linger at cafes and bars long after they should be on their way, and dinners at Andersonville's collection of restaurants are events to be savored. Uptown also has a clutch of historic music venues, including Al Capone's favorite jazz club.

1. Green Mill Jazz Club (p133)
Leon Bridges performing at the Green Mill.

2. Mural, Argyle Street (p126).
This area became known as Little Saigon after refugees from the Vietnam War settled in the neighborhood.

3. Andersonville (p126)
The ornate details of a building in Andersonville hint at its history in the former Swedish enclave.

4. Simon's Tavern (p131)
An Andersonville musicians' watering hole since 1934.

WORTH A DETOUR

DEVON AVENUE

Known as Chicago's 'International Marketplace,' Devon Ave in West Ridge, is where worlds collide. Indian, Pakistani, Georgian, Russian, Cuban, Israeli – you name the global culture and someone from the group has set up a shop or eatery along the street. It's a fun destination for browsing.

Devon at Western Ave is the main intersection. Indian sari and jewelry shops start near 2600 W Devon; to the west they give way to Jewish and Islamic goods stores, while to the east they trickle out into a gaggle of electronics and dollar stores. It's a good place to stock up on low-cost cell-phone necessities, luggage and other travel goods. Or just buy an armful of jangly bangles.

While you're here, you've got to stay for a meal. The best curry in the city simmers in Devon's aromatic restaurants. Vegetarians will find scads of options. Local favorites include the following:

Udupi Palace (Off Map p334; ☑773-338-2152; www.udupipalacetogo.com; 2543 W Devon Ave; mains $8-15; ☺11:30am-9:30pm; ☑; ☑155) This bustling all-vegetarian South Indian restaurant serves toasty, kite-sized *dosas* (crepes made with rice and lentil flour) stuffed with all manner of vegetables and spices, along with an array of curries. The room gets loud once it packs with Anglo hipsters and a young Indian crowd.

Mysore Woodlands (Off Map p334; ☑773-338-8160; www.mysorewoodlands.info; 2548 W Devon Ave; mains $10-17; ☺11:30am-9pm Sun-Thu, to 10pm Fri & Sat; ☑; ☑155) Another South Indian all-veg favorite, where friendly servers deliver well-spiced curries, dosas and *iddlies* (steamed rice-lentil patties) in the spacious, clattering room.

Sabri Nihari (Off Map p334; ☑773-465-3272; www.sabrinihari.com; 2502 W Devon Ave; mains $12-16; ☺noon-11pm; ☑155) Fresh, fresh meat and vegetable dishes, distinctly seasoned, set this Pakistani place apart from its competitors on Devon. Try the 'frontier' chicken, which comes with a plate of freshly cut onions, tomatoes, cucumber and lemon, and enough perfectly cooked chicken for two. For dessert, check out the *kheer,* a creamy rice pudding.

Devon's epicenter is about 9 miles northwest of downtown. Take the Red Line to Loyola and transfer to bus 155 (Devon), or take the Brown Line to Western and transfer to bus 49B (North Western).

TIZTAL CAFE
BREAKFAST $

Map p316 (☑773-271-4631; 4631 N Clark St; mains $8-14; ☺8am-3pm; ☑22) Everyone from hipsters nursing hangovers to moms nursing babies piles in to family-run Tiztal for brunch. The chorizo scrambles, gravy-slathered biscuits and country-fried steak are house favorites, along with oatmeal shakes and fresh fruit juices. At the time of research the restaurant was just finishing up a renovation and reopening, to the collective relief of the neighborhood.

TANK NOODLE
VIETNAMESE $

Map p316 (☑773-878-2253; www.tank-noodle.com; 4953 N Broadway; mains $10-21; ☺8:30am-10pm Mon, Tue & Thu-Sat, to 9pm Sun; ☑; ☒Red Line to Argyle) The crowds come to this popular, spacious utilitarian eatery for banh mi (served on crunchy fresh baguette rolls) and the pho, which is widely regarded as

the city's best. The 200-plus-item menu sprawls on from there and includes stir-fried noodles, catfish and squid dishes, and a rainbow array of bubble teas and a good vegetarian selection.

TASTE OF LEBANON
MIDDLE EASTERN $

Map p316 (☑773-334-1600; 1509 W Foster Ave; wraps $3-4; ☺11am-8pm Mon-Sat; ☑; ☑22, ☒Red Line to Berwyn) Locals rave about this little storefront restaurant serving up chicken or beef shawarma, lamb kabobs, falafel or stuffed grape leaves wrapped in lavash bread – so much so that it was voted Best Middle Eastern Restaurant in the annual *Chicago Reader* poll. It doesn't get much more cheap and cheerful than this.

NHA HANG VIETNAM
VIETNAMESE $

Map p316 (☑773-878-8895; 1032 W Argyle St; mains $8-14; ☺8:30am-10pm Mon & Wed-Sat, to 9pm Sun; M Red Line to Argyle) Little Nha Hang may not look like much from the outside, but it offers a huge menu of authentic, well-made Vietnamese dishes. It's terrific for slurping pho and eating clay-pot catfish, and for appetizers such as *banh xeo* (a crispy pancake with shrimp, pork and vegetables).

BA LE SANDWICHES VIETNAMESE $
Map p316 (✆773-561-4424; www.bale sandwich.com; 5014 N Broadway; sandwiches $6-9; ☺7:30am-9pm; ✐; M Red Line to Argyle) Ba Le serves Saigon-style banh mi sandwiches, with pâté, BBQ pork, sautéed chicken or shrimp on fresh baguettes made right here (vegetarian and vegan versions with tofu and mock beef also available). There are a few tables to eat at, or a case full of premade rolls and salads ready to grab for a picnic in the park.

TWEET AMERICAN $
Map p316 (✆773-728-5576; www.tweet.biz; 5020 N Sheridan Rd; mains $8-16; ☺8:30am-3pm; ☎✐; M Red Line to Argyle) ✎ Decadent, reimagined breakfast standards hit the tables at this cozy morning spot in a stunning art deco building. The Havarti omelet folds in green apple slices while the country Benedict adds two poached eggs and a thick slab of sausage alongside biscuits and gravy. Most ingredients are organic, and there's loads of gluten-free and vegetarian/vegan options too. Cash only.

HAI YEN VIETNAMESE $
Map p316 (✆773-561-4077; www.haiyen restaurant.com; 1055 W Argyle St; mains $10-15; ☺10:30am-10pm Mon, Tue, Thu, to 10:30pm Fri, 9:30am-10:30pm Sat, 9:30am-10pm Sun; M Red Line to Argyle) Many dishes at this warm Argyle St eatery require some assembly, pairing shrimp, beef or squid with rice crepes, mint, Thai basil and lettuce. For an appetizer, try the *goi cuon,* fresh rolls of vermicelli rice noodles with shrimp, pork and carrots. Order sparingly, or ask your server for help – some menu options are large enough to feed an army.

★**HOPLEAF** EUROPEAN $$
Map p316 (✆773-334-9851; www.hopleaf.com; 5148 N Clark St; mains $9-32; ☺noon-10pm Sun-Thu, to 11pm Fri & Sat; ☐22, M Red Line to Berwyn) A cozy, European-like tavern, Hopleaf draws crowds for its Montreal-style smoked brisket, cashew-butter-and-fig-jam sandwich, ubercreamy macaroni and Stilton cheese, and the house-specialty *frites* (fries) and beer-broth-soaked mussels. It also pours 200 types of brew (with around 60 on tap), emphasizing craft and Belgian suds. (The bar stays open several hours after the kitchen closes.)

🍷 DRINKING & NIGHTLIFE

Andersonville is known for its awesome beer bars and low-key LGBT+ drinking spots found along or off Clark St. Uptown has stylish lounges around Broadway and Lawrence Ave.

📍 Andersonville

★**SIMON'S TAVERN** BAR
Map p316 (✆773-878-0894; 5210 N Clark St; ☺11am-2am Sun-Fri, to 3am Sat; ☐22, M Red Line to Berwyn) An Andersonville mainstay since 1934, Simon's is a dimly lit musicians' watering hole. The jukebox rocks an eclectic menu ranging from St Vincent to James Brown to Nas to Depeche Mode. In winter, in homage to its Swedish roots, Simon's serves *glögg* (spiced wine punch). A giant neon fish holding a martini glass marks the spot. Cash only.

MARTY'S MARTINI BAR COCKTAIL BAR
Map p316 (✆773-561-6425; 1511 W Balmoral; ☺5pm-2am Sun-Thu, from 4pm Fri, 4pm-3am Sat; ☐22, M Red Line to Berwyn) A pocket-sized cocktail bar decorated with gilt-framed mirrors and Toulouse-Lautrec posters, Marty's is known for its various takes on the classic martini in two sizes, including 'dessert martinis' (such as chocolate hazelnut) and the popular 'dirty bird,' which features olive juice and blue-cheese-stuffed olives made in-house every day.

HAMBURGER MARY'S BAR
Map p316 (✆773-784-6969; www.hamburger marys.com/chicago; 5400 N Clark St; ☺11:30am-11pm Mon-Fri, from 10:30am Sat & Sun; ☐22, M Red Line to Berwyn) The Chicago outpost of this campy, gay-friendly San Francisco-based chain serves well-regarded burgers and weekend brunch in the downstairs restaurant, but the action's on the rowdy, booze-soaked patio. Next door is its

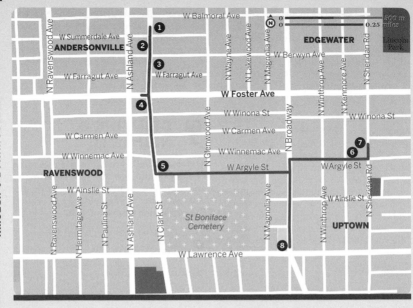

Local Life
Mixing It Up in Andersonville & Uptown

The formerly Swedish enclave of Andersonville is a vibrant neighborhood where long-standing businesses mix with new foodie restaurants, antique shops and gay bars. Adjacent Uptown is a whole different scene, with historic jazz houses such as the Green Mill and the popular restaurants of 'Little Saigon.' Both areas are prime for strolling, window-shopping, eating and drinking.

❶ Big Jones

Big Jones (p127) offers a menu of 'Southern heirloom cooking' in its airy dining room, with popular draws including crawfish étouffée and shrimp and grits. Be prepared to fight the throng of locals on weekend mornings, who flock here for an indulgent brunch.

❷ Lost Larson

A new, design-forward bakery, Lost Larson (p126) harks back to Andersonville's immigrant past with Scandinavian pastries – cardamom buns, lingonberry-almond cake – and breads made from wheat milled right in-house. The chocolate croissant alone is worth the trip.

❸ Andersonville Galleria

Have a wander through Andersonville Galleria (p134), where several dozen kiosks of locally made art, crafts and food are spread out for sale over three floors. Support local artisans while finding that perfect souvenir gift.

❹ Woolly Mammoth

Satisfy your morbid leanings at Woolly Mammoth Antiques & Oddities (p134), where cases are stuffed with all manner of the macabre: creepy doll heads, taxidermied animals, the logbook from an insane asylum, and more.

❺ Hot 'G' Dog

Hot 'G' Dog (p127) is the place to sample, say, a chicken-apple-cranberry hot dog with whiskey cheese and pecans. But if you're feeling a bit less gourmet you can also try a good ol' Chicago-style dog. The chefs formerly worked at Hot Doug's famed brat shop.

❻ Nha Hang Vietnam

Humble eatery Nha Hang Vietnam (p130) dazzles the tastebuds with delicious,

'nano-brewery' pub Andersonville Brewing Company, which makes its own beer and turns on the HDTVs for sports fans (it stays open a bit later).

🍷 Uptown

SOFO TAP GAY
Map p316 (☏773-784-7636; www.thesofotap. com; 4923 N Clark St; ◷5pm-2am Mon-Thu, from 3pm Fri, noon-3am Sat, noon-2am Sun; 🐾; Ⓜ Red Line to Argyle) SoFo is a normal neighborhood bar with a sweet dog-friendly patio. Then again, there are also raucous live game shows and rock and soul karaoke. And if you happen in on Friday night, the vast majority of the male crowd will be shirtless for Bear Night.

BIG CHICKS GAY & LESBIAN
Map p316 (☏773-728-5511; www.bigchicks.com; 5024 N Sheridan Rd; ◷4pm-2am Mon-Fri, from 8:30am Sat, from 10am Sun; 🛜; Ⓜ Red Line to Argyle) Despite the name, both men and women (queer and otherwise) frequent Big Chicks, with its weekend DJs, fun dance floor, art displays and next-door organic restaurant Tweet (p131), where weekend brunch packs 'em in. Cash only.

LA COLOMBE COFFEE
Map p316 (☏773-942-7090; www.lacolombe. com; 5158 N Clark St; ◷6:30am-7pm Mon-Fri, from 7am Sat & Sun; 🛜; 🚌22, Ⓜ Red Line to Berwyn) The giant windows of this industrially fitted-out corner shop afford an excellent vantage for people-watching over an espresso or cold-brew coffee. It's one of several Chicago branches; you'll find another one in **Wicker Park** (Map p318; ☏872-829-3681; 1552 N Damen Ave; ◷6:30am-7pm Mon-Fri, from 7am Sat & Sun; Ⓜ Blue Line to Damen).

☆ ENTERTAINMENT

★GREEN MILL JAZZ
Map p316 (☏773-878-5552; www.greenmilljazz. com; 4802 N Broadway, Uptown; ◷noon-4am Mon-Fri, to 5am Sat, 11am-4am Sun; Ⓜ Red Line to Lawrence) The timeless – and notorious – Green Mill was Al Capone's favorite speakeasy (a trap door behind the bar accessed tunnels for running booze and escaping the feds). Sit in one of the curved booths and feel his ghost urging you on to another

Exterior shot of Big Chicks bar and Tweet restaurant (p131)

authentically made dishes. Try the steaming-hot pho or the clay-pot catfish.

❼ Big Chicks
Iconic bar Big Chicks is a mainstay of the Chicago queer community, though its doors are open to all. Stop by for DJs, dancing, local artwork on the walls and a welcoming vibe from a diverse crowd.

❽ Green Mill
The timeless Green Mill earned its notoriety as Al Capone's favorite speakeasy. Sit in one of the curved leather booths and play gangster with a dirty martini. Nightly performances by local and national jazz musicians.

martini. Local and national jazz artists perform nightly; on Sunday is the nationally acclaimed poetry slam (p127). Cash only.

If you're around on a Friday evening, drop by at 5pm for the Flipside show, with music played on the classic Hammond B3 organ on a small stage behind the bar. FYI, Capone's designated booth is the one at the end of the bar, on the northern side – the only seat in the house that has a view of both the front and side doors.

★NEO-FUTURIST THEATER THEATER

Map p316 (☑773-878-4557; www.neofuturists. org; 5153 N Ashland Ave, Uptown; ☺11:30pm Fri & Sat, 7pm Sun; ☐50, ⓜRed Line to Berwyn) The Neo-Futurists are best known for their show *The Infinite Wrench,* in which the hyper troupe makes a manic attempt to perform 30 original plays in 60 minutes. Admission costs $10 to $15 – you pay $9 plus the roll of a six-sided die.

The group puts on plenty of other original works that'll make you ponder and laugh simultaneously. Well worth the northward trek, but prepare to wait in line. A limited number of pricier tickets are available online in advance. The small theater has 150 seats.

★CHICAGO MAGIC LOUNGE LIVE PERFORMANCE

Map p316 (☑312-366-4500; www.chicagomagic lounge.com; 5050 N Clark St, Uptown; tickets $10-55; ☺5-11pm Mon-Wed, to midnight Thu, to 2am Fri & Sat, 1:30-3pm Sun; ☒; ☐22, ⓜRed Line to Argyle) Hidden behind a wall of laundry machines is the secret entrance to Chicago's only purpose-built magic lounge. See amazing feats of prestidigitation seven days a week in two theater spaces and a 1930s-style bar (where you can drink without a show ticket). On Monday and Tuesday a jazz band plays while performers roam between tables doing close-up magic.

A menu of small plates is also available. On Sunday afternoons there's a family show, aimed at children ages five and up.

BLACK ENSEMBLE THEATER THEATER

Map p316 (☑773-769-4451; www.blackensemble theater.org; 4450 N Clark St, Uptown; ⓜBrown Line to Montrose) This well-established group saw its fledgling production of *The Jackie Wilson Story* attract wide attention and national tours. The focus here has long been on original productions about the African American experience through mostly his-

torical, biographical scripts. Musical revues pay homage to legends such as Chuck Berry or Aretha Franklin.

🛍 SHOPPING

Shops offering antiques, books, clothing and locally made arts and crafts line up along Clark St.

★PROVISIONS ALCOHOL

Map p316 (☑773-944-0978; 4812 N Broadway, Uptown; ☺11am-9pm Mon-Thu, to 10pm Fri & Sat, to 6pm Sun; ⓜRed, Purple Line to Lawrence) An impressive and thoughtfully curated collection of beer, wine and spirits, especially the flavored bitters and the prodigious amount of small-batch indie whiskies from around the US. It's a great place to find that special tipple to round out your home bar. You can also find gourmet condiments and foodstuffs here.

★ANDERSONVILLE GALLERIA ART

Map p316 (☑773-878-8570; www.andersonville galleria.com; 5247 N Clark St, Andersonville; ☺11am-7pm Mon-Sat, to 6pm Sun; ⓜRed Line to Berwyn) Over a hundred indie vendors sell their fair-trade and locally made artisan wares in kiosks spread over three floors. Sweets, coffee, clothing, handbags, paintings, photography, jewelry – it's a smorgasbord of cool, crafty goods in a community-oriented marketplace. A great place for gifts that support Chicagoland artists.

WOOLLY MAMMOTH ANTIQUES & ODDITIES ANTIQUES

Map p316 (☑773-989-3294; www.woolly mammothchicago.com; 1513 W Foster Ave, Uptown; ☺noon-7pm Wed-Sun, from 1pm Mon, from 3pm Tue; ⓜRed Line to Berwyn) Part morbid curiosity shop, part eerie art installation. Creepy doll heads, a stuffed groundhog wearing a Superman cape, death masks, Victorian medical instruments – it's all here, and then some. Set designers often come here for props. There's even an original drawing done by serial killer John Wayne Gacy...of Adolf Hitler. Creepy.

WOMEN & CHILDREN FIRST BOOKS

Map p316 (☑773-769-9299; www.womenand childrenfirst.com; 5233 N Clark St, Andersonville; ☺11am-7pm Mon & Tue, to 9pm Wed-Fri, 10am-7pm Sat, 11am-6pm Sun; ☒; ⓜRed Line to Berwyn) An Andersonville mainstay, this feminist independent bookstore has been around for more than 35 years. Book signings and author events happen most weeks at the welcoming shop, which features fiction and nonfiction by and about women, a big selection of gay and lesbian titles and scads of children's books. Every Wednesday morning at 10:30am there's free storytelling for the kids.

ANDERSONVILLE
FARMERS MARKET   MARKET

Map p316 (www.andersonville.org; W Berwyn Ave, btwn N Clark St & N Ashland Ave, Andersonville; ⊙Wed 3-8pm May-Aug, to 7pm Sep–mid-Oct; 🚌22, MRed Line to Berwyn) 🌱 This top-notch farmers market supports local producers, with all items for sale grown, raised or made within 200 miles. Besides local fish, meat, fruit and veg, you'll find honey, eggs, cheese, bread, baked goods and cut flowers. Street-food vendors sell tasty snacks and sometimes there's live music.

BROWN ELEPHANT   VINTAGE

Map p316 (📞773-271-9382; www.brownelephant. com; 5404 N Clark St, Andersonville; ⊙11am-7pm; 🚌22) Set inside a massive former movie theater built in 1915, this resale shop has an ocean of browsable wares: racks and racks of clothing, furniture, electronics, housewares, furniture and even art. Plus you're shopping for a good cause – all proceeds go to support LGBT+ health initiatives at the Howard Brown Health group of medical clinics.

STRANGE CARGO   CLOTHING

Map p316 (📞773-327-8090; www.strangecargo. com; 5216 N Clark St, Andersonville; ⊙11am-7pm Mon-Sat, to 5pm Sun; MRed Line to Berwyn) This retro store stocks hipster wear, platform shoes, wigs and a mind-blowing array of kitschy T-shirts. Staff will iron on decals of Harry Caray, Mike Ditka, the city skyline or other local touchstones, as well as Obama, the Smurfs and more – all supreme souvenirs.

MIDDLE EAST
BAKERY & GROCERY   FOOD & DRINKS

Map p316 (📞773-561-2224; www.middleeast bakeryandgrocery.com; 1512 W Foster Ave, Andersonville; ⊙9am-8pm Mon-Sat, 11am-5pm Sun; 🚌22, MRed Line to Berwyn) Northsiders love this small deli-market for its cases filled with fresh, housemade Middle Eastern food: tubs of smoky roasted-eggplant dip and creamy hummus, za'atar-seasoned

flatbread, spinach or lamb and potato pies, baklava and semolina honey cake. The shop also sells marinated olives, nuts, dried fruits, olive oils, teas and other imported grocery items.

🏃 SPORTS & ACTIVITIES

★MONTROSE BEACH   BEACH

Off Map p316 (www.cpdbeaches.com; 4400 N Lake Shore Dr, Uptown; 🚌146) One of the city's best beaches. You can rent kayaks, stand-up paddleboards and Jet Skis; sometimes you'll see surfers and kitesurfers, and anglers frequently cast here. Watch sailboats glide in the harbor over some waterside snacks or a drink at the Dock Bar and Grill. A wide, dog-friendly beach with a curving breakwater abuts the main beach to the north.

Swimming is allowed only when lifeguards are on duty (11am to 7pm) during beach season, which runs from Memorial Day through Labor Day.

KAYAK CHICAGO   KAYAKING

Off Map p316 (📞312-852-9258; www.kayak chicago.com; 4400 N Lake Shore Dr, Uptown; ⊙10am-7pm Jun-Aug; 🚌146) Rents kayaks and stand-up paddleboards for $30 per hour or $80 per day; double kayaks are also available. Staff can provide lessons. The main season is Memorial Day through Labor Day but Kayak Chicago is open in September in fine weather.

It's located in the southeast corner of Montrose Beach, with another branch at North Avenue Beach in Lincoln Park.

Lincoln Square & Ravenswood

LINCOLN SQUARE | RAVENSWOOD | NORTH CENTER

Neighborhood Top Five

1 **Malt Row** (p142) Swigging triple India Pale Ales, *rauchbiers* and passionfruit ales in the taprooms of the many breweries near each other in Ravenswood's old factory corridor.

2 **Goosefoot** (p141) Dining in the Michelin-starred but casual-vibed eatery that cooks wildly creative tasting menus.

3 **Lincoln Ave** (p145) Perusing the cool, quirky lineup of stores along the neighborhood's main thoroughfare, like Gene's Sausage Shop with its festive rooftop beer garden.

4 **Old Town School of Folk Music** (p144) Seeing an intimate folk or world-music concert at the long-standing venue, or learning to do it yourself via guitar or banjo classes.

5 **Huettenbar** (p143) Knocking back a German lager, black beer or wheat beer amid alpine murals and wood-paneled walls at this kitschy bar.

For more detail of this area see Map p334

Explore Lincoln Square & Ravenswood

Lincoln Square is perfect for an afternoon or evening. Lincoln Ave is the main vein, though Western and Lawrence Aves are bountiful, too. Cute shops and cafes line up one after the other, and it's all easily walkable. Take the Brown Line train to Western for the thick of it; it's a half-hour ride from downtown Chicago.

Ravenswood's Malt Row works best for a late afternoon or evening stroll, since some breweries don't open until 4pm or so. It's easiest to start in the south and work your way northwest (the food options work out better this way). Take the Brown Line train to Irving Park, and you're steps from Begyle Brewing, the first suds maker in the 2-mile lineup.

It's much more local than touristy in these areas, so while you may encounter crowds, it's rarely jam-packed – unless there's a beery festival going on, and then it is teeming.

Local Life

→ **Midday beer** You'll usually find a group of dedicated beer enthusiasts hanging out in the taprooms at Begyle Brewing (p143), Dovetail Brewing (p144) and Empirical Brewery (p144) in the afternoon.

→ **Market browse** From June through October, Lincoln Square hosts two farmers markets each week in the lot at Lincoln and Leland Aves (adjacent to the L station at Western). The first is Tuesday morning from 7am to 1pm. The second is Thursday evening from 4pm to 8pm. Both brim with fruit, vegetables, doughnuts, éclairs and other sweet baked goods.

→ **Summer tunes** Free jazz, folk and world music concerts take place at Giddings Plaza (at Lincoln Ave and Giddings St) on Thursdays in summer from 6:30pm to 9pm. They coincide with the Thursday farmers market, and many locals make a night of it.

Getting There & Away

→ **L Train** Brown Line to Western for cafes and shopping; Brown Line to Irving Park or Damen for Malt Row.

→ **Bus** Bus 50 runs along Damen Ave as far as Foster Ave (as close as you'll get on public transportation to the breweries on Balmoral Ave).

→ **Car** Street parking can be tough to find; try Sunnyside Ave. There are parking lots near the L station at Western and on Lincoln Ave (across the street from Bistro Campagne).

Lonely Planet's Top Tip

Check out the 'events' section of the Lincoln Square Ravenswood Chamber of Commerce website (www.lincolnsquare.org/events) for daily details on restaurant specials – such as the Tuesday all-you-can-eat mussels at Bistro Campagne (p141) – and happy hours at local pubs. It's a great way to find out what will be going on when you visit.

Best Places to Eat

→ Goosefoot (p141)
→ Luella's Southern Kitchen (p140)
→ Band of Bohemia (p141)
→ Elizabeth (p141)
→ Spacca Napoli (p141)

For reviews, see p140.

Best Places to Drink

→ Spiteful Brewing (p143)
→ Begyle Brewing (p143)
→ Half Acre Balmoral Tap Room (p143)
→ Northman (p143)
→ Huettenbar (p143)
→ Empirical Brewery (p144)

For reviews, see p141.

Best Places to Shop

→ Gene's Sausage Shop (p145)
→ Merz Apothecary (p145)
→ Timeless Toys (p145)
→ Koval Distillery (p145)

For reviews, see p145.

Local Living – Lincoln Square & Ravenswood

Lincoln Square is an old German enclave that has blossomed into a stylish eating, drinking and shopping destination. Next-door Ravenswood is mostly residential, except for an industrial corridor of bygone factories that have morphed into modern breweries, where drinkers from all over the city come to raise a glass.

2

SERHII CHRUCKY / ALAMY STOCK PHOTO ©

1. Rosehill Cemetery (p140)
Interior of the Horatio May chapel.

2. Half Acre Lincoln Tap Room (p144)
Half Acre was one of the leaders of Chicago's craft-brewing movement.

3. Spiteful Brewing (p143)
Spiteful Lager from Spiteful Brewing.

4. Gene's Sausage Shop (p145)
The market shop with its rooftop beer garden has a European atmosphere to it.

4

TRIBUNE CONTENT AGENCY LLC / ALAMY STOCK PHOTO ©

3

TRIBUNE CONTENT AGENCY LLC / ALAMY STOCK PHOTO ©

⊙ SIGHTS

There are no sights here, unless you're a fan of cemeteries, in which case Rosehill Cemetery offers an intriguing walkabout.

ROSEHILL CEMETERY   CEMETERY
Map p334 (📞773-561-5940; 5800 N Ravenswood Ave, Ravenswood; ⊙8am-4pm; 🚇84) The entrance gate to Chicago's largest cemetery is worth the trip alone. Designed by WW Boyington (the architect who created the Water Tower on Michigan Ave), the entry looks like a cross between high Gothic and low Disney. Inside you'll see the graves of plenty of Chicago bigwigs, from Chicago mayors and a US vice president to meat-man Oscar Mayer.

You'll also find some of the weirdest grave monuments in the city, including a postal train and a huge carved boulder from a Civil War battlefield in Georgia. More than one ghost story started here; keep an eye out as night falls.

✗ EATING

Lots of foodie hot spots have staked out claims along Lincoln, Western and Lawrence Aves, alongside old-world European cafes. It's all pretty casual. Even the Michelin-starred restaurants occupy unobtrusive storefronts. Go further west on Lawrence, and you'll run into a slew of global restaurants serving authentic Vietnamese, Bosnian, Brazilian, Italian and other cuisines.

✗ Lincoln Square

CHUBBY WIENERS   HOT DOGS $
Map p334 (📞773-769-1394; www.chubby wieners.com; 4652 N Western Ave; mains $4-8; ⊙11am-8pm Tue-Thu, to 9pm Fri & Sat, to 5pm Sun; 🚇Brown Line to Western) This hot-dog joint beside the L track has a sign that's launched a thousand Instagram posts. Take the requisite photos while you wait for your Chubby Dog, an extrathick weenie served Chicago-style (with tomatoes, onions, relish and pickle). Add crispy, fresh-cut fries to any order.

NHU LAN BAKERY   VIETNAMESE $
Map p334 (📞773-878-9898; 2612 W Lawrence Ave; sandwiches $4-8; ⊙7:30am-7pm Mon &

Wed-Sun; 🚇Brown Line to Western) Vietnamese banh-mi sandwiches are the name of the game here. Baguettes are the base for the French-inspired concoction, and Nhu Lan bakes its own daily using rice flour. The resulting loaves are perfectly light, crisp and ready to cushion your protein pick (pork, beef, chicken or tofu), boosted by the zing of cucumbers, cilantro, jalapeños, and pickled carrots and daikon.

★LUELLA'S
SOUTHERN KITCHEN   SOUTHERN US $$
Map p334 (📞773-961-8196; www.luellassouthern kitchen.com; 4609 N Lincoln Ave; mains $16-24; ⊙5-10pm Mon, 11:30am-10pm Tue-Fri, 10am-10pm Sat, 10am-8pm Sun; 🚇Brown Line to Western) You could easily walk right by this modest storefront without realizing the rich, buttery glory that awaits inside. The chef reworks his great-grandmother Luella's recipes that she brought from Mississippi when she came to Chicago in the 1940s. There's chunky shrimp in creamy grits, fluffy buttermilk biscuits, and chicken and waffles with bourbon-tinged maple syrup. It's a BYOB, counter-service ambience.

RESTAURANT
SARAJEVO   BOSNIAN $$
Off Map p334 (📞773-275-5310; www.restaurant sarajevo.com; 2701 W Lawrence Ave; mains $15-20; ⊙noon-9pm Mon-Thu, to 11pm Fri & Sat, to 7pm Sun; 🚇Brown Line to Rockwell) Family-owned Sarajevo serves homemade Bosnian cuisine with Italian, Greek, Turkish and Mediterranean influences. Specialties include ćevapčići – skinless sausages made from minced beef and lamb, which are stuffed into fresh pita and served with onion and kaymak (a Balkan-style clotted cream) – and pljeskavica, a spiced meat patty.

It's BYOB with a small corkage fee (waived if you reserve ahead).

CAFE SELMARIE   CAFE $$
Map p334 (📞773-989-5595; www.cafeselmarie. com; 4729 N Lincoln Ave; mains $14-20; ⊙8am-9pm Tue-Thu, to 10pm Fri & Sat, 9am-9pm Sun; 🚇Brown Line to Western) Selmarie has been serving the Lincoln Square neighborhood cakes, tortes, quiches, tomato bisque soup and turkey-and-Brie sandwiches for more than 35 years. The European-style cafe remains a communal hangout for locals of all ages. It's lovely for an unfussy bite and glass of wine, or for coffee and pastries.

★GOOSEFOOT   AMERICAN $$$

Off Map p334 (☑773-942-7547; www.goosefoot.
net; 2656 W Lawrence Ave; tasting menu $145;
☺6-8:30pm Wed-Sat; Ⓜ Brown Line to Rockwell)
Michelin-starred Goosefoot serves a cutting-edge, modern American tasting menu
that never fails to surprise. For instance,
your dessert – a vanilla-truffle-cherry-pink-
peppercorn ice-cream cone – will arrive in
a toy goose-foot-shaped holder surrounded
by moss. Prepare for around six courses of
richly textured, amazing-looking food. It's
BYOB, with most people buying a bottle at
Goosefoot's wine shop next door. Reservations required.

ELIZABETH   AMERICAN $$$

Map p334 (☑773-681-0651; www.elizabeth-
restaurant.com; 4835 N Western Ave; multicourse menus $175-200; ☺5:30-9:30pm Tue-Sat;
Ⓜ Brown Line to Western) Michelin-starred
Elizabeth will blow your mind. Chef Iliana
Regan describes her dishes as 'new gatherer' cuisine, meaning she uses ingredients
that are foraged or hunted. Fried lichens
or deer broth might result. The tasting
menu (around 10 courses) follows different
themes throughout the year, such as Harry
Potter, Julia Child or Game of Thrones. Reservations required.

BISTRO CAMPAGNE   FRENCH $$$

Map p334 (☑773-271-6100; www.bistro
campagne.com; 4518 N Lincoln Ave; mains $23-
34; ☺5:30-9pm Mon-Thu, to 10pm Fri, 5-10:30pm
Sat, 11am-9pm Sun; Ⓜ Brown Line to Western)
Chicago has a lot of French bistros sprinkled around, but not many perfect the balance of fine yet unfussy dining in a sophisticated but welcoming ambience the way
Campagne does. The stained-glass-filled
Lincoln Square favorite plates such classics
as beef bourguignon, chocolate soufflé and
mussels (all you can eat on Tuesdays) alongside fat wines.

Reservations are useful, especially if
there's a concert at the nearby Old Town
School of Folk Music (p145).

✕ Ravenswood

BANG BANG PIE & BISCUITS   AMERICAN $

Map p334 (☑773-530-9020; www.bangbang
pie.com; 4947 N Damen Ave; pie slices $5, mains
$7-12; ☺8am-4pm; 🛜; Ⓜ Brown Line to Damen)
The name doesn't lie: Bang Bang serves pie,
both sweet and savory, but even better are
the biscuits – fluffy masses that come with
bacon, avocado or other sandwich fixings,
or ladled with gravy. Seats are at a premium in the small space. Scope out the couch
by the fireplace or long communal table toward the back. Bang Bang's main branch is
in Logan Square (p168).

SPACCA NAPOLI   PIZZA $$

Map p334 (☑773-878-2420; www.spacca
napolipizzeria.com; 1769 W Sunnyside Ave; pizzas $15-18; ☺11:30am-9pm Tue-Thu, to 10pm Fri
& Sat, noon-9pm Sun; Ⓜ Brown Line to Montrose)
You might walk by this plain-looking restaurant and wonder why so many families,
older couples and millennials are thronging
it. The answer: Neapolitan-style pizza. The
crust is light and delicate, the toppings are
minimal and the flavors shine. The grilled
baby octopus appetizer and reasonably
priced wines add to the attraction. Gluten-
free crusts are available. Make reservations.

BAND OF BOHEMIA   AMERICAN $$$

Map p334 (☑773-271-4710; www.bandof
bohemia.com; 4710 N Ravenswood Ave; mains
$26-40; ☺5-10pm Tue-Fri, 10am-2pm & 5-10pm
Sat, 10am-2pm & 5-9pm Sun; Ⓜ Brown Line to Damen) Band of Bohemia is the first brewpub
to earn a Michelin star. You can see what's
cooking in the open kitchen: maybe roasted hen with woodsy vegetables, or braised
short rib with kimchi and fermented plum.
The five beers on tap, brewed to match the
food, contain peculiar ingredients such as
jasmine rice and celery seeds.

🍷 DRINKING & NIGHTLIFE

**Beer lovers will want to hit up
Ravenswood Ave, where a bunch of
breweries have opened north of Irving
Park Rd. In Lincoln Square, trendy pubs
inhabit much of the 'hood, though old
German stalwarts remain the local
favorites. Lincoln Ave holds the majority;
Western and Lawrence Aves have their
share as well.**

🍺 Lincoln Square

NORTHMAN   BAR

Map p334 (☑773-935-2255; www.thenorthman.
com; 4337 N Lincoln Ave; ☺5pm-midnight Mon,

🏃 Neighbourhood Walk
Malt Row Breweries

START BEGYLE BREWING
END HALF ACRE BALMORAL TAP ROOM
LENGTH 2 MILES; FOUR HOURS

What happens when you have scads of old industrial buildings sitting vacant when Chicago's brewery boom is taking off? Malt Row is born – a stretch of six breweries and a distillery conveniently lined up along a 2-mile path.

Start at **1 Begyle Brewing** (opposite), set in a 1930s-era, redbrick factory. The humble taproom is a community clubhouse where neighbors from the surrounding homes pop in to hobnob over heady ales. Walk north a block on Ravenswood Ave to **2 Dovetail Brewing** (p144). In a vintage redbrick plant, this one pours smoky *rauchbier*, cherry *lambic* and other European-style brews.

Continue north on Ravenswood Ave. Commuter trains whistle by on the embankment to your right, and you'll see community gardens planted along the wall. Stay the course until you reach Sunnyside Ave, and then turn right. Cross under the tracks to **3 Spacca Napoli** (p141) for a crisp-crusted pizza.

Retrace your steps to Ravenswood Ave's west side, and after a few blocks you'll arrive at **4 Band of Bohemia** (p141), a Michelin-starred brewpub that uses jasmine rice, coriander and other odd ingredients in its food-focused beers.

Walk to Lawrence Ave and turn right. Go under the tracks to get on Ravenswood Ave's east side again. You'll pass loads of apartment buildings and houses before arriving at **5 Koval Distillery** (p145), an organic whiskey and liqueur maker.

Head north to Foster Ave and turn left. **6 Empirical Brewery** (opposite) awaits, a comfy spot to play board games and sample experimental beers. Continue west on Foster to Damen Ave and turn right. Stay on Damen for a quarter mile to Balmoral Ave and turn left. Here you'll find **7 Spiteful Brewing** (opposite), offering strong-ass India Pale Ales (IPAs) in its rock-and-roll garage taproom, and **8 Half Acre** (opposite), a destination brewery for its hop-forward suds and lively beer garden.

to 2am Tue-Fri, noon-3am Sat, noon-2am Sun; MBrown Line to Montrose) The Northman gives the neighborhood beer scene a twist by focusing on cider. Around 20 taps flow with tart, fermented creations from the US, England, France and Spain, and there's a long list of calvados (apple or pear brandies), as well. The low-lit, dark-wood pub feels like it has been plucked from the English countryside.

HUETTENBAR — BAR

Map p334 (☑773-561-2507; www.huettenbar. com; 4721 N Lincoln Ave; ⊙2pm-2am Mon-Fri, noon-2am Sat & Sun; MBrown Line to Western) Pay homage to Lincoln Square's German roots at the stalwart Huettenbar. The kitschy, wood-paneled ambience is straight out of the Black Forest. So are the fresh beers flowing from the taps. A crisp *kölsch* from Frankfurt and a seat by the big open front windows on a warm night, and you're practically a local.

SIXTH — COCKTAIL BAR

Map p334 (☑773-360-6499; www.thesixthbar. com; 2202 W Lawrence Ave; ⊙5pm-midnight Tue-Thu, to 2am Fri & Sat, 2-10pm Sun; MBrown Line to Western) Chic, dimly lit and reminiscent of a downtown bar more than a neighborhood corner bar, the Sixth blows minds with its playful cocktails. You might sip whimsical drinks such as the Spaceman Spiff, a mezcal-based concoction lifted from a smoke-filled bowl, and the Silly Rabbit, a gin cocktail served alongside a glass of Trix-inspired ice cubes.

SPYNERS — LESBIAN

Map p334 (☑773-784-8719; 4623 N Western Ave; ⊙11am-2am Sun-Fri, to 3am Sat; MBrown Line to Western) Spyners is a full-on dive bar beloved by lesbians and karaoke fans. The latter flock in Thursday, Friday and Saturday to belt out tunes in a welcoming environment. Lady-loving ladies enjoy low-priced beers throughout the week. It's a fun scene regardless of your sexual orientation. Look for the Michelob Light sign to find the unmarked entrance.

🍺 Ravenswood

★SPITEFUL BREWING — MICROBREWERY

Map p334 (☑773-293-6600; www.spiteful brewing.com; 2024 W Balmoral Ave; ⊙4-10pm Mon-Wed, to 11pm Thu, noon-midnight Fri & Sat,

11am-10pm Sun; 🛜🍽; 🚊50) Spiteful's taproom has a rock-and-roll, DIY vibe. Two home brewers launched the brand, and they now operate out of a renovated garage. The concrete floored, exposed-ductwork place has a long bar where you can belly up for hard-hitting pale ales, IPAs and double IPAs.

HALF ACRE BALMORAL TAP ROOM — BREWERY

Map p334 (☑773-754-8488; www.halfacrebeer. com; 2050 W Balmoral Ave; ⊙4-10pm Tue, to 11pm Wed & Thu, 11am-midnight Fri & Sat, 10am-10pm Sun; 🛜🌭🍽; 🚊50) The original Half Acre on Lincoln Ave (p144) got so popular it had to expand to this hulking facility on Balmoral Ave. Now it has become a destination brewery, where beer lovers go to try everything from passion-fruit ales to milk sugar IPAs and chocolate raspberry imperial stouts. It's always a happening scene, especially the picnic-table-dotted beer garden in summer.

The kitchen makes good pizzas and sandwiches, and there's even a kids' menu. Tours ($10) take place on Sundays at 1pm. Note the entrance is through the parking lot on Rascher Ave (which is one block north of Balmoral).

★BEGYLE BREWING — MICROBREWERY

Map p334 (☑773-661-6963; www.begylebrewing. com; 1800 W Cuyler Ave; ⊙noon-9pm Mon-Thu, to 10pm Fri, 11am-10pm Sat, noon-8pm Sun; 🛜🍽; MBrown Line to Irving Park) Tucked in a warehouse by the train tracks, Begyle's little taproom is a community hub. Friends play cards at one table, an old guy chills with his dog next to them, while work mates discuss business nearby. The blond and wheat ales are mainstays of the 15 beers on tap, but there are also some monster stouts and triple IPAs.

They come in 5oz pours and pints, and you can bring in your own food to eat alongside them. Brewery tours ($10) take place at noon on Saturday and include generous samples.

EMPIRICAL BREWERY — MICROBREWERY

Map p334 (☑773-293-7896; www.empirical brewery.com; 1801 W Foster Ave; ⊙noon-10pm Tue-Thu, to midnight Fri & Sat, to 8pm Sun; 🛜🍽; MBrown Line to Damen) Hobnob with neighborhood folks in Empirical's no-frills taproom: play board games, hit the pinball machine, pet the locals' dogs. There's a

LOCAL KNOWLEDGE

LINCOLN SQUARE CELEBRATIONS

Lincoln Square knows how to put on a great shindig. If you happen to be in Chicago in June, July or September, join the locals kicking up their heels and tossing back their drinks.

Mayfest (www.mayfestchicago.com) The beer sloshes in steins and everyone dances around the maypole at Mayfest, held over four days in early June to celebrate the community's German heritage.

Square Roots (www.squareroots.org) It's a three-day neighborhood bash in mid-July with suds from local breweries and music stages curated by the Old Town School. It takes place on Lincoln Ave between Montrose and Wilson Aves.

German-American Oktoberfest (www.germanday.com) Break out the lederhosen and grab a seat in the beer tent at this three-day party in mid-September. The highlight is the big parade – the same one in which Ferris Bueller sang 'Danke Schoen' in the famed film.

science-geek theme at play, not only in the signature beers' names (Electron Smash pale ale, Cold Fusion cream ale), but also in the one-off, experimental brews Empirical makes weekly, anything from a kettle-soured ale to an imperial rye stout.

DOVETAIL BREWING   MICROBREWERY
Map p334 (☑773-683-1414; www.dovetail brewery.com; 1800 W Belle Plaine Ave; ⊙4-11pm Mon, noon-10pm Tue-Thu, noon-11pm Fri, 11am-11pm Sat, noon-8pm Sun; 🐾🍴; MⒷBrown Line to Irving Park) Dovetail brews Belgian- and German-style beers. Smoky *rauchbier*, yolky-orange wheat beer, fruity *lambics* and sweet tasting spelt beer flow from the taproom's 16 handles. Three-beer flights are parceled out in glass beakers. Warm pretzels and German sausages make fine accompaniments. By day Dovetail is a beer geek hangout; at night the blond-wood room draws a trendier crowd. Tours ($15) take place every Saturday at 11am and include three beers.

🍷 North Center

**HALF ACRE LINCOLN
TAP ROOM**   BREWERY
Map p334 (☑773-248-4038; www.halfacrebeer. com; 4257 N Lincoln Ave; ⊙11am-11pm Tue, Wed & Sun, to midnight Thu, to 1am Fri & Sat; 🐾; MⒷBrown Line to Montrose) Half Acre was one of the leaders of Chicago's craft brewing movement, concocting the deliciously hoppy Daisy Cutter Pale Ale and selling it in cans. The beer earned a cult following, and now local suds fanatics practically live in the exposed-brick and rustic-wood tap

room, sucking down the strong 'core' brews and limited-batch 'adventure' beers.

An upscale pub-grub menu (with an emphasis on eclectic burritos) accompanies the beer lineup. Tours ($10) take place at 11am on Saturdays; reservations are not accepted, so arrive early. While Half Acre opened a larger brewery and tap room (p143) a couple of miles north near Rosehill Cemetery, the Lincoln brewery is the original site and the one where more of the experimental beers are made.

GLOBE PUB   PUB
Map p334 (☑773-871-3757; www.theglobepub. com; 1934 W Irving Park Rd; ⊙11am-midnight Sun-Wed, to 2am Thu-Sat; MⒷBrown Line to Irving Park) This warm, dark-oak pub is ground zero for English soccer and rugby fanatics, since it shows all the international league games on satellite TV. It even opens at 6am for big matches so patrons can watch the action live. The kitchen cooks up a traditional English breakfast daily and the taps flow with ales from the homeland.

☆ ENTERTAINMENT

**★OLD TOWN SCHOOL
OF FOLK MUSIC**   LIVE MUSIC
Map p334 (☑773-728-6000; www.oldtown school.org; 4544 N Lincoln Ave, Lincoln Square; ♿; MⒷBrown Line to Western) You can hear the call of the banjos from the street outside this venerable institution, where major national and international acts such as Richard Thompson and Joan Baez play when they come to town. Old Town also hosts

superb world-music shows, including every Wednesday at 8:30pm when they're free (or a $10 donation).

DAVIS THEATER
CINEMA

Map p334 (☑773-769-3999; www.davistheater.com; 4614 N Lincoln Ave, Lincoln Square; ☺4:30pm-1am Mon-Fri, 11am-2am Sat, 11am-1am Sun; Ⓜ Brown Line to Western) Thanks to a renovation, the century-old Davis has burnished its deco charm while adding modern amenities such as stadium seating and state-of-the-art sound. The first-run theater also attached a bar-restaurant called Carbon Arc, named after the carbon arc lamps in old film projectors, serving fancy snacks (Thai mussels, duck-and-bean stew) and craft beers that you can take into the movie.

CORN PRODUCTIONS
COMEDY

Map p334 (☑773-650-1331; www.cornservatory.org; 4210 N Lincoln Ave, North Center; Ⓜ Brown Line to Irving Park) Though Corn occasionally stages something serious, most of its productions are kitschy, inexpensive and feature improv or sketch comedy. There's no bar, but you're welcome to bring in your own alcohol. Cash only at the box office.

🛍 SHOPPING

Cute new boutiques mingle with long-standing apothecaries, record shops and toy stores on Lincoln Ave.

★GENE'S SAUSAGE SHOP
FOOD & DRINKS

Map p334 (☑773-728-7243; www.genessausage.com; 4750 N Lincoln Ave, Lincoln Square; ☺9am-8pm Mon-Sat, to 4pm Sun; Ⓜ Brown Line to Western) As if the hanging sausages, ripe cheeses and flaky pastries lining the shelves at this European market weren't enough, Gene's also rocks a rooftop summer beer garden. Sit at communal picnic tables and munch hot-off-the-grill bratwursts while sipping worldly brews from the tap.

TIMELESS TOYS
TOYS

Map p334 (☑773-334-4445; www.timelesstoyschicago.com; 4749 N Lincoln Ave, Lincoln Square; ☺10am-6pm Mon-Wed & Sat, to 7pm Thu & Fri, to 5pm Sun; Ⓜ Brown Line to Western) This charming independent shop is better described for what it does *not* carry – no Barbies, Harry Potter books or trendy kiddie togs. Instead you'll find high-quality, old-fashioned toys, many of which are made in Germany or other European countries. Have fun playing with the bug magnifiers, microscopes, glitter balls and wooden spinning tops.

MERZ APOTHECARY
COSMETICS

Map p334 (☑773-989-0900; www.merzapothecary.com; 4716 N Lincoln Ave, Lincoln Square; ☺9am-6pm Mon-Sat; Ⓜ Brown Line to Western) Merz is a true turn-of-the-century European apothecary. Antique pharmacy jars contain herbs, homeopathic remedies, vitamins and supplements, and the shelves are stacked high with skin care, personal care, bath and aromatherapy products from around the world. Lavender toothpaste, calendula ointment, cypress tree soap – you'll find it here. Merz expanded into the building next door for its higher-end wares.

KOVAL DISTILLERY
DRINKS

Map p334 (☑312-878-7988; www.koval-distillery.com; 5121 N Ravenswood Ave, Ravenswood; ☺2-7pm Mon-Fri, 1-6:30pm Sat, 2-5pm Sun; Ⓜ Brown Line to Damen) Koval distills organic, small-batch whiskey and gin in the shiny copper tanks that you see inside. It also makes ginger, jasmine, walnut and other unique liqueurs. The shop in front sells them; you can sample the wares before buying.

The distillery also offers hour-long tours ($10) on Wednesday, Saturday and Sunday, and weekly cocktail classes. The website has the schedule.

BOOK CELLAR
BOOKS

Map p334 (☑773-293-2665; www.bookcellarinc.com; 4736 N Lincoln Ave, Lincoln Square; ☺10am-9pm Mon & Wed-Sat, noon-6pm Tue & Sun; Ⓜ Brown Line to Western) The independent Book Cellar is an integral part of the Lincoln Square neighborhood. Local book groups hold their meetings here, and authors do readings several nights per week, while the cafe pours wine and beer to add to the festivities.

CHOPPING BLOCK
FOOD & DRINKS

Map p334 (☑773-472-6700; www.thechoppingblock.com; 4747 N Lincoln Ave, Lincoln Square; ☺10:30am-9:30pm Mon-Fri, 9:30am-9:30pm Sat, 9:30am-7:30pm Sun; Ⓜ Brown Line to Western) Let's say your recipe calls for Hungarian cinnamon, gray sea salt and Balinese long pepper. Instead of throwing up your hands in despair after searching the local grocery store and then calling for a pizza delivery, stop in here for specialty foods, high-end cookware and hard-to-find utensils.

Wicker Park, Bucktown & Ukrainian Village

WICKER PARK | BUCKTOWN | UKRAINIAN VILLAGE | WEST TOWN | EAST VILLAGE

Neighborhood Top Five

❶ Milwaukee Avenue (p162) Trawling for treasures – an old Devo record, a vintage pillbox hat, steel-toed boots, a mustachioed disguise kit – in the shops along the half-mile stretch between Damen and Ashland Aves.

❷ Hideout (p159) Hearing an alt-country band, snap-ping your fingers to a poetry slam or singing along with a Meatloaf tribute band in one of Chicago's coolest venues.

❸ Matchbox (p158) Squeezing into the teeny bar for a gimlet, sidecar or other retro cocktail.

❹ 606 (p153) Strolling on high through the neighborhood past hip restaurants, clackety L trains and locals' backyards via this elevated trail.

❺ Quimby's (p160) Perusing the zines and getting the lowdown on the city's underground culture.

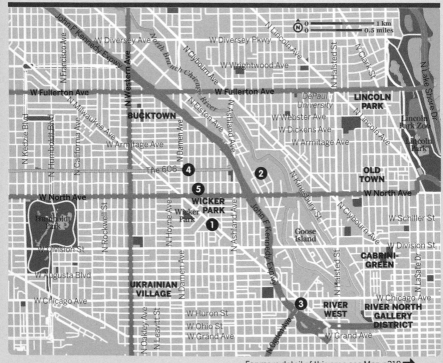

For more detail of this area see Map p318 ➡

Explore Wicker Park, Bucktown & Ukrainian Village

For a taste of trendy young Chicago, wander along Milwaukee Ave near Damen Ave in Wicker Park on a Friday night. You'll pass booming bars, packed restaurants and stages hosting indie rock on one side of the street and underground author readings on the other. By Saturday morning the scene shifts to the dozens of cool vintage stores, in-the-know record shops and buzzing brunch spots. Buttressed by the slightly fancier Bucktown and slightly scruffier Ukrainian and East Villages, this neighborhood has a lot happening, so strap on some comfy kicks and take it block by block.

Milwaukee, North and Damen Aves are the main veins through these neighborhoods, along with Division St – once a polka-bar-lined thoroughfare known as the 'Polish Broadway,' it's now stuffed with trendy restaurants, dive bars and crafty boutiques.

Save for a number of art galleries, this area holds few conventional sights, but you could easily while away the day shopping and the night eating and drinking. And it's definitely Chicago's best 'hood for rock clubs, with the Hideout and Empty Bottle leading the cool-cat pack.

Local Life

➡ **Group soup** Crowds gather at the Hideout on Wednesdays in winter for Soup & Bread (p154), a hobnobbing dinner series where local foodies, musicians and artists take turns making, well, soup and bread.

➡ **Bar crafts** The Handmade Market (p162) brings out the local crafting community to the Empty Bottle each month.

➡ **Vinyl freaks** Crate diggers find their bliss near the corner of Milwaukee and Ashland Aves, where Reckless Records (p160), Shuga Records (p161) and Dusty Groove (p160) all hover.

Getting There & Away

➡ **The L** Blue Line to Damen for Bucktown and northern Wicker Park; Blue Line to Division for southern Wicker Park; Blue Line to Chicago for Ukrainian Village.

➡ **Bus** Bus 72 runs along North Ave; bus 70 along Division St; bus 66 along Chicago Ave; bus 50 along Damen Ave; and bus 73 along Armitage Ave.

➡ **Car** Meter and free on-street parking are at a premium in Wicker Park and Bucktown; you'll find more spots available in Ukrainian Village.

Lonely Planet's Top Tip

In summer the neighborhood throws excellent street festivals with big-name bands. Watch for Do Division (www.do-division streetfest.com) in early June; Green Music Fest (www.greenmusicfest chicago.com) in mid-June; West Fest (www.westfest chicago.com) in early July; and the Hideout Block Party (www.hideoutchicago.com) – the best of the bunch – in early September.

Best Places to Eat

➡ Dove's Luncheonette (p151)

➡ Irazu (p149)

➡ Schwa (p152)

➡ Pub Royale (p152)

➡ Small Cheval (p149)

➡ Boeufhaus (p153)

For reviews, see p149.➡

Best Places to Drink

➡ Matchbox (p158)

➡ Danny's (p155)

➡ Violet Hour (p155)

➡ Rainbo Club (p158)

➡ Remedy (p155)

➡ Forbidden Root (p158)

For reviews, see p154.➡

Best Places to Shop

➡ Reckless Records (p160)

➡ Quimby's (p160)

➡ Una Mae's (p161)

➡ Wicker Park Secret Agent Supply Co (p161)

➡ Virtu (p161)

For reviews, see p160.➡

WICKER PARK, BUCKTOWN & UKRAINIAN VILLAGE

◉ SIGHTS

There aren't many traditional sights here, though art galleries, onion-domed churches, a couple of national/ethnic museums and writer Nelson Algren's house keep it interesting. Walking or cycling the 606 trail is an excellent way to spend an afternoon.

INTUIT: THE CENTER FOR
INTUITIVE & OUTSIDER ART   GALLERY

Map p318 (☑312-243-9088; www.art.org; 756 N Milwaukee Ave, River West; $5; ⊙11am-6pm Tue, Wed, Fri & Sat, to 7pm Thu, noon-5pm Sun; Ⓜ Blue Line to Chicago) Behold this small museum's collection of naive and outsider art from Chicago artists, including rotating mixed-media exhibits and watercolors by famed local Henry Darger (p99). In a back room the museum has re-created Darger's awesomely cluttered studio apartment, complete with balls of twine, teetering stacks of old magazines, an ancient typewriter and a Victrola phonograph. The gift shop carries groovy jewelry (such as pencil-eraser necklaces), bags and wallets made from recycled material, and art books.

UKRAINIAN INSTITUTE
OF MODERN ART   MUSEUM

Map p318 (☑773-227-5522; www.uima-chicago. org; 2320 W Chicago Ave, Ukrainian Village; suggested donation $5; ⊙noon-4pm Wed-Sun;

🖳66) Founded in 1971, this collection acts as the westernmost anchor to a string of West Town art galleries (p150). Two rooms display a permanent collection of colorful paintings and sculpture (which rotates a few times per year) as well as provocative temporary exhibits, done in various media. While most artists are Ukrainian, plenty of other locals get wall space, too.

UKRAINIAN
NATIONAL MUSEUM   MUSEUM

Map p318 (☑312-421-8020; http://ukrainian nationalmuseum.org; 2249 W Superior St, West Town; $5; ⊙11am-4pm Thu-Sun; 🖳66) Across from one of the Ukrainian Village's larger churches, this small museum packs in a massive amount of information about the history, culture and politics of Ukraine and its people. Exhibits include dozens of beautiful, intricately decorated eggshells (known as *pysanky*), plus traditional costumes from various regions of the country, Cossack weaponry and Ukrainian handicrafts and instruments. Somber displays relate the history of Stalin's engineered famine that killed millions of Ukrainian peasants and of the 2004 'Orange Revolution.'

POLISH MUSEUM
OF AMERICA   MUSEUM

Map p318 (☑773-384-3352; www.polishmuseum ofamerica.org; 984 N Milwaukee Ave, Noble Square; adult/child $10/8.50; ⊙11am-4pm Mon,

---

CHURCHES OF UKRAINIAN VILLAGE & WEST TOWN

Take a minute to wander by these beauties – just look for the majestic domes popping out over the neighborhood's treetops.

St Nicholas Ukrainian Catholic Cathedral (Map p318; ☑773-276-4537; www.st nicholaschicago.org; 835 N Oakley Blvd; 🖳66) The less traditional of the main churches. Its 13 domes represent Christ and the Apostles. The intricate mosaics – added to the 1915 building in 1988 – were inspired by the Cathedral of St Sophia in Kyiv.

Sts Volodymyr & Olha Church (Map p318; ☑312-829-5209; www.stsvo.org; 2245 W Superior St, West Town; 🖳66) Traditionalists from nearby St Nicholas split over liturgical differences and built this showy church in 1975. It only has five domes, but makes up for it with a massive mosaic of the conversion of Grand Duke Vladimir of Kyiv to Christianity in AD 988.

Holy Trinity Russian Orthodox Cathedral (Map p318; ☑773-486-6064; www.holy trinitycathedral.net; 1121 N Leavitt St; 🖳70) This creamy structure looks like it was lifted straight out of the Russian countryside. But this 1903 stunner – with its octagonal dome, front bell tower, and stucco and wood-framed exterior – was actually designed by famed Chicago architect Louis Sullivan. Czar Nicholas II helped fund the church, which is now a city landmark. Tours of the gilded interior are offered twice a month on Saturdays at noon.

Tue & Fri-Sun, to 7pm Wed; Ⓜ Blue Line to Division) If you don't know Pulaski from a pierogi, this is the place to get the scoop on Polish culture. Founded in 1935, it's one of the oldest ethnic museums in the country, and crammed with traditional Polish costumes, WWII artifacts, ship models and folk-art pieces, as well as rotating exhibits from Polish and Polish American artists. Entrance is on Augusta Blvd.

The curator can give you a personalized tour, since you'll likely be the only one here. It's a fine opportunity to learn about the Poles who helped shape Chicago, which has one of the world's largest Polish communities. (Casimir Pulaski, by the way, was a Polish hero in the American Revolution, known as the 'father of the American cavalry,' while a pierogi is a Polish dumpling.)

WICKER PARK
PARK

Map p318 (www.chicagoparkdistrict.com; 1425 N Damen Ave, Wicker Park; ⊘6am-11pm; Ⓜ Blue Line to Damen) The neighborhood's favorite green space is home to softball fields, a children's water playground, a winter ice rink, an active dog park, and indoor and outdoor movies. If you're here anytime from May through September, stop by to see a 16-inch softball game in action. Chicago invented the game a century ago; it uses the same rules as normal softball, but with shorter games, a bigger, squishier ball and no gloves or mitts on the fielders. There's a league that plays in the park on Sundays.

NELSON ALGREN'S HOUSE
HISTORIC SITE

Map p318 (1958 W Evergreen Ave, Wicker Park; Ⓜ Blue Line to Damen) On the 3rd floor of this apartment building writer Nelson Algren created some of his greatest works about life in the once down-and-out neighborhood. A plaque marks the spot, though unfortunately you can't go inside. Algren won the 1950 National Book Award for his novel *The Man with the Golden Arm,* about a drug addict hustling on Division St near Milwaukee Ave (a half-mile southeast).

✖ EATING

Trendy restaurants open almost every day, with many serving nouveau takes on classic comfort food. Division St is a bountiful vein of snazzy bistros and pubs, many of which have sidewalk seating.

✖ Wicker Park & Bucktown

★MARGIE'S CANDIES
DESSERTS $

Map p318 (✆773-384-1035; www.margiesfine candies.com; 1960 N Western Ave, Bucktown; sundaes from $6; ⊘9am-midnight Sun-Thu, to 1am Fri & Sat; ♿; Ⓜ Blue Line to Western) Margie's has held court at Bucktown's edge for more than 90 years, scooping ice cream sundaes into giant clamshell bowls for everyone from Al Capone to the Beatles (check the wall photos). Admire the marble soda fountain and the booths with mini-jukeboxes, but the star is the hot fudge – unbelievably thick, rich and bountiful, and served in its own silver pot.

★IRAZU
LATIN AMERICAN $

Map p318 (✆773-252-5687; www.irazuchicago. com; 1865 N Milwaukee Ave, Bucktown; mains $7-16; ⊘11:30am-9:30pm Mon-Sat; ✍; Ⓜ Blue Line to Western) Chicago's lone Costa Rican eatery turns out burritos bursting with chicken, black beans and fresh avocado, and sandwiches dressed in a heavenly, spicy-sweet vegetable sauce. Wash them down with an *avena* (a slurpable milkshake in tropical-fruit flavors). For breakfast, the *arroz con huevos* (peppery eggs scrambled into rice) relieves hangovers. Irazu is BYOB with no corkage fee. Cash only.

STAN'S DONUTS
BAKERY $

Map p318 (✆773-360-7386; www.stansdonuts chicago.com; 1560 N Damen Ave, Wicker Park; doughnuts $2-5; ⊘6:30am-9pm Sun-Wed, to 10pm Thu, to 10:30pm Fri & Sat; Ⓜ Blue Line to Damen) In a field rich with contenders, Stan's may just have Chicago's best doughnuts. Staff are always super nice, the retro vibe rocks, and the Biscoff pockets (cookie butter inside a frosted square doughnut) and lemon-pistachio old-fashioned doughnuts are glorious. There are over 30 flavors on the menu – though many sell out by afternoon – including some gluten-free and vegan options.

SMALL CHEVAL
BURGERS $

Map p318 (www.smallcheval.com; 1732 N Milwaukee Ave, Wicker Park; burgers $9-10; ⊘11am-midnight Mon-Sat, to 10pm Sun; Ⓜ Blue Line to Damen) Maybe you've heard of Au Cheval, the foodie-adored West Loop joint with two-hour waits for its famed burgers, once crowned the nation's best by *Bon Appétit*?

LOCAL KNOWLEDGE

WEST TOWN ART GALLERIES

Various neighborhoods west of the river are great places to seek out emerging talent. Besides the galleries listed below, you'll find quite a few more along Chicago Ave, stretching from about 1400 to 2300 W.

Flat Iron Building (Map p318; www.flatironchicago.com; 1579 N Milwaukee Ave, Wicker Park; M Blue Line to Damen) Several artists live and work in this landmark building and host a monthly First Friday open house, where there's reasonably priced art on offer for purchase. Keep an eye on fliers around Wicker Park detailing the latest shows and open houses.

Document Gallery (Map p318; 262-719-3500; http://documentspace.com; 1709 W Chicago Ave, West Town; ⊙11am-6pm Tue-Sat; 66, M Blue Line to Chicago) Exhibitions of contemporary photography, film and media-based works by emerging national and international artists.

Monique Meloche Gallery (Map p318; 773-243-2129; www.moniquemeloche.com; 951 N Paulina St, West Town; ⊙11am-6pm Tue-Sat; M Blue Line to Division) Tastemaker Meloche has an eye for emerging artists. Her gallery features provocative paintings, neon and mixed media from local and international artists, with an emphasis on artists of color.

This pared-down kid sibling is a festive little shack serving up nothing but burgers. And boozy milkshakes, cocktails and beer. Wait time is minimal, and there's plenty of patio seating beneath the rumbling L.

BIG STAR MEXICAN $
Map p318 (773-235-4039; www.bigstarchicago. com; 1531 N Damen Ave, Wicker Park; tacos $2.50-4; ⊙11:30am-1:30am Sun-Fri, to 3am Sat; ; M Blue Line to Damen) This former gas station is now a taco-serving honky-tonk bar from big-name Chicago chef Paul Kahan. The place gets packed but it's worth the wait – pork belly in tomato-*guajillo* chili sauce and mole-spiced carrots drizzled with date-infused yogurt accompany the whiskey- and agave-based cocktail list. Vegan options available. If the table-studded patio is too crowded, order from the walk-up window.

HANDLEBAR INTERNATIONAL, VEGETARIAN $
Map p318 (773-384-9546; www.handlebar chicago.com; 2311 W North Ave, Wicker Park; mains $10-14; ⊙10am-midnight Mon-Thu, to 12:30am Fri, 9am-12:30am Sat, 9am-midnight Sun; ; M Blue Line to Damen) The cult of the bike messenger runs strong in Chicago, and this clamorous restaurant-bar is a way station for tattooed couriers and locals who love the microbrew-centric beer list and the vegetarian/vegan comfort-food menu (which includes some fish dishes), such as West African ground-nut stew and fried avocado tacos. In summer head to the festive beer garden out back.

DIMO'S PIZZA PIZZA $
Map p318 (773-525-4580; www.dimospizza. com; 1615 N Damen Ave, Wicker Park; slices/pies from $4.50/14; ⊙11am-2am Sun-Thu, to 3am Fri, to 4am Sat; ; M Blue Line to Damen) This late-night Wicker Park standby serves up slices and pies of thin-crust pizza with both standard and inventive toppings: macaroni and cheese, chicken and waffles, or BBQ chicken with bacon, cheddar and ranch dressing. Vegans can choose from half a dozen options. The daily Dimo special ($9) – a shot of bourbon, a PBR tallboy and a slice – can't be beat.

FURIOUS SPOON RAMEN $
Map p318 (773-687-8445; www.furiousramen. com; 1571 N Milwaukee Ave, Wicker Park; ramen bowls $9-15; ⊙11am-1am Sun-Thu, to 2am Fri & Sat; ; M Blue Line to Damen) Perch yourself at the long, high wooden tables and delve into a giant bowl of ramen, made with vegetable, chicken, pork or spicy beef broth and stuffed with meats, vegetables, fried tofu, egg and shredded nori. For some real kick, opt for the chili-infused noodles. There are several other locations around town, including in the Loop at Revival Food Hall (p58).

NATIVE FOODS CAFE VEGAN $
Map p318 (773-489-8480; www.nativefoods. com; 1484 N Milwaukee Ave, Wicker Park; mains $10-13; ⊙11am-10pm; ; M Blue Line to Damen) Entirely plant-based versions of comfort-food classics beckon at this sunny corner

fast-casual spot right on Wicker Park's main shopping strip. Plow into double cheeseburgers, fried-chicken sandwiches, macaroni and cheese, nacho fries and fish tacos, as well as various rice and veggie bowls, salads and wraps, all cruelty-free. There's another branch downtown in the Loop (p59).

VIENNA BEEF FACTORY
STORE & CAFE
AMERICAN $

Off Map p318 (☑773-435-2277; www.viennabeef. com; 2501 N Damen Ave, Bucktown; mains $3-6.50; ☺8am-4pm Mon-Fri, 10am-3pm Sat; ☑50) A true Chicago hot dog uses a Vienna Beef weenie, and there's no better place to indulge than right at the source – the company's HQ cafe. Grab a tray, go through the line, then chow down with local construction workers. The shop counter at the front sells well-priced cases of franks and superb meaty T-shirts, posters and condiments.

MILK & HONEY
CAFE $

Map p318 ` (☑773-395-9434; www.milkand honeycafe.com; 1920 W Division St, Wicker Park; mains $7-11; ☺7am-4pm Mon-Fri, from 8am Sat & Sun; ☑Blue Line to Division) A bright, stylish cafe, Milk & Honey has become the hangout du jour for discerning neighborhood socialites. Waffles and pancakes in different flavors (peanut butter and banana, chocolate chips and strawberries) rock the breakfast menu; thick-cut BLTs and crab-cake baguettes please the lunch crowd. The fireplace and small list of beer and wine soothe when the weather blows.

LETIZIA'S
NATURAL BAKERY
BAKERY $

Map p318 (☑773-342-1011; www.superyummy. com; 2144 W Division St, Wicker Park; sandwiches $7-8, pizzas from $6; ☺6am-7pm Mon-Sat, from 7am Sun; ☎; ☑70, ☑Blue Line to Division) Early risers can get their fix of fantastic baked goods here starting at 6am, and everyone else can swing by at a more reasonable hour for Letizia's crunchy, toasty panini, mini gourmet pizzas and cups of mind-expanding coffee. The expansive patio with plush seats wins kudos in summer.

SULTAN'S MARKET
MIDDLE EASTERN $

Map p318 (☑773-235-3072; www.chicagofalafel. com; 2057 W North Ave, Wicker Park; mains $4-10; ☺10am-10pm Mon-Sat, to 9pm Sun; ☑; ☑Blue Line to Damen) Steps from the Blue Line, this Middle Eastern spot is a neighborhood favorite for meat-free delights such as falafel sandwiches, spinach pies and a sizable salad bar. Carnivores can enjoy, too; many swear by the chicken and lamb shawarma and the baked *kefta* (spiced lamb) kabob. Cash only.

LAZO'S TACOS
MEXICAN $

Map p318 (☑773-486-3303; www.lazostacos. com; 2009 N Western Ave, Bucktown; tacos $2.50-3.50, mains $7-16; ☺24hr; ☑Blue Line to Western) The west side's quintessential taco stop after a long night of drinking. Also great for quesadillas, burritos, tortas and hangover-curing breakfasts.

★DOVE'S
LUNCHEONETTE
TEX-MEX $$

Map p318 (☑773-645-4060; www.doveschicago. com; 1545 N Damen Ave, Wicker Park; mains $13-22; ☺9am-10pm Mon-Thu, to 11pm Fri, 8am-11pm Sat, 8am-10pm Sun; ☑Blue Line to Damen) Sit at the retro counter for Tex-Mex plates of pork-shoulder posole and buttermilk fried chicken with chorizo-verde gravy. Dessert? It's pie, of course – maybe horchata, lemon cream or peach jalapeño, baked by Hoosier Mama (p152). Soul music spins on a record player, tequila flows from the 70 bottles rattling behind the bar, and presto: all is right in the world.

ENOTECA ROMA
ITALIAN $$

Map p318 (☑773-772-7700; www.facebook.com/ enotecaroma; 2146 W Division St, Wicker Park; mains $18-29; ☺5-10pm Mon-Thu, to 11pm Fri & Sat, 4:30-9:30pm Sun; ☑Blue Line to Damen) Candlelit and cozy, family-run Enoteca Roma feels like an old country *ristorante*. Specialties include venison bolognese lasagna, polenta served piping-hot table-side, bruschetta flights and handmade pastas such as pear-ricotta ravioli – all best consumed on the starry back patio in summer. During the day, sibling eatery Letizia's Natural Bakery serves up toasty panini, lemon tarts and lattes next door.

MINDY'S HOT
CHOCOLATE
AMERICAN $$

Map p318 (☑773-489-1747; www.hotchocolate chicago.com; 1747 N Damen Ave, Wicker Park; mains $16-27; ☺lunch 11:30am-2pm Wed-Fri, brunch 10am-2pm Sat & Sun, dinner 5:30-10pm Sun & Tue-Thu, to midnight Fri & Sat; ☑Blue Line to Damen) 'Come for dessert, stay for dinner' might be the motto of award-winning pastry chef Mindy Segal's mod restaurant.

WICKER PARK, BUCKTOWN & UKRAINIAN VILLAGE EATING

With five kinds of hot chocolate available, along with cakes, cookies, pies and mini brioche doughnuts, you may forget to order the striped sea bass, meatball hoagie and other seasonally changing mains on offer. It's a great date-night place.

PIECE   PIZZA $$

Map p318 (📞773-772-4422; www.piecechicago. com; 1927 W North Ave, Wicker Park; small pizzas from $14; ⊙11am-10:30pm Mon-Thu & Sun, to 12:30am Fri & Sat; 🖋; Ⓜ Blue Line to Damen) The thin, flour-dusted crust of 'New Haven–style' pizza at this spacious Wicker Park microbrewery offers a welcome reprieve from the city's omnipresent deep-dish version. The best is the white variety – a sauceless pie dressed simply in olive oil, garlic and mozzarella – which makes a clean pairing with brewer Jon Cutler's award-winning beer. (Cheese-free versions are available too.)

LE BOUCHON   FRENCH $$$

Map p318 (📞773-862-6600; www.lebouchonof chicago.com; 1958 N Damen Ave, Bucktown; mains $23-32; ⊙lunch 11:30am-2:30pm Mon-Sat, dinner 5:30-10pm Mon-Thu, 5-11pm Fri & Sat; 🚌50, 73) A Bucktown mainstay for over 25 years, this small bistro has a warm, French-cafe atmosphere where conversation buzzes over clinking wineglasses. The menu offers a full run of Gallic classics: escargots with garlic and parsley butter, a seafood-stuffed bouillabaisse, sirloin steak *frites*, duck cassoulet, salad Niçoise with tuna and quail egg, and cheese-topped French onion soup. *Bon appétit!*

SCHWA   MODERN AMERICAN $$$

Map p318 (📞773-252-1466; www.schwa restaurant.com; 1466 N Ashland Ave, Wicker Park; 9-course menu $140; ⊙5:30-9:30pm Tue-Sat; Ⓜ Blue Line to Division) Chef Michael Carlson once worked at Lincoln Park's Alinea (p104), which is apparent in his avant-garde, nine-course menu that redefines American comfort food via such dishes as apple-pie soup or quail egg, truffle and ricotta ravioli. The chefs also act as servers, and the intimate room is bookended by black wood floors and a mirrored ceiling. Make reservations well in advance.

MIRAI SUSHI   JAPANESE $$$

Map p318 (📞773-862-8500; www.miraisushi. com; 2020 W Division St, Wicker Park; maki $6-12, small plates $8-26; ⊙5-10pm Wed, Thu & Sun, to 11pm Fri & Sat; 🖋; Ⓜ Blue Line to Damen) This high-energy restaurant has a higher-energy saki lounge upstairs; both are packed with young locals enjoying some of Wicker Park's freshest sushi. From the trance-hop electronic music to the young, black-clad staff, Mirai is where connoisseurs of sashimi and *maki* (rolled sushi) throw back sake cocktails between savory morsels of yellowtail and soft-shell crab tempura lightly fried to perfection.

✖ Ukrainian Village & East Village

★HOOSIER MAMA
PIE COMPANY   PIES $

Map p318 (📞312-243-4846; www.hoosiermama pie.com; 1618 W Chicago Ave, East Village; slices $5-6; ⊙8am-7pm Tue-Fri, 9am-5pm Sat, 10am-4pm Sun; 🚌66, Ⓜ Blue Line to Chicago) Soothing 1950s pastels and antique pie tins set the Americana vibe at Paula Haney's celebrated pie shop, where hand-rolled, buttery-flaky crust is plumped full with fruit or creamy fillings. Favorites include sour-cream Dutch cranberry, banana cream, chocolate chess (aka 'brownie pie') and apple-blueberry-walnut. A handful of savory pies tempt, but let's not kid ourselves – we're here for the sweet stuff.

PUB ROYALE   INDIAN $

Map p318 (📞773-661-6874; www.pubroyale.com; 2049 W Division St, Ukrainian Village; mains $12-18; ⊙5pm-1am Mon-Wed, to 2am Thu, 4pm-2am Fri, 11am-3am Sat, 11am-1am Sun; Ⓜ Blue Line to Damen) Loud and fun with brightly painted wood cutouts of Indian gods on the walls, Royale serves distinctive Anglo-Indian pub grub. Sit at a booth or one of the communal tables and tear into lamb dumplings, hot-spiced chicken or cashew-coconut eggplant curry, washed down with great beers, ciders and Pimm's Cup–inspired cocktails or boozy mango lassis.

TAKITO KITCHEN   MEXICAN $

Map p318 (📞773-687-9620; www.takitokitchen. com; 2013 W Division St, Ukrainian Village; tacos $4, shared plates $7.50-9.50; ⊙5-9pm Tue, to 10pm Wed & Thu, 11am-10:30pm Fri & Sat, to 8pm Sun; 🚌50, 70) Found along the hip run of bars and restaurants on Division St, Takito Kitchen has a menu of tasty new twists on Mexican food that's 100% gluten-free. Munch on crispy fish, chicken *al pastor*

THE 606 TRAIL

••

Like NYC's High Line, Chicago's **606** (Map p318; www.the606.org; Wicker Park/Bucktown; ☺6am-11pm; Ⓜ Blue Line to Damen) is an urban-cool elevated path along an old train track. Cycle or stroll past factories, smokestacks, clattering L trains and locals' backyard affairs for 2.7 miles between Wicker Park and Logan Square. It's a fascinating trek through Chicago's socioeconomic strata: moneyed at the east, becoming more industrial and immigrant to the west. The trail parallels Bloomingdale Ave, with access points every quarter mile.

The entrance at Churchill Field (1825 N Damen Ave) is a handy, sculpture-laden place to ascend. For those wanting to cycle, there's a Divvy bike-share station a few blocks from the trail's eastern end at the corner of N Marshfield Ave and W Cortland St.

Top spots to take a break along the way (from east to west) include the following:

Mindy's Hot Chocolate (p151) Exit at Damen.

Irazu (p149) Exit at Milwaukee.

Donut Delight (p171) Exit at California.

Parson's Chicken & Fish (p168) Exit at Humboldt.

and pork-belly tacos and shared plates like hearts of palm salad and shrimp ceviche while you experiment with the tequila-forward cocktail menu.

LA PASADITA
MEXICAN $

Map p318 (☏773-278-2130; www.pasadita.com; 1140 N Ashland Ave, East Village; mains $4-12.50; ☺10am-1am Sun-Thu, to 3:30am Fri & Sat; Ⓜ Blue Line to Division) The national press crowned La Pasadita's burrito as one of America's 10 best. They are absolutely behemoth and delicious, with mouthwateringly good carne asada. But cheapos prefer the fat tacos, two of which will make a nice meal; or else go for a basket of 'chachos,' La Pasadita's take on nachos topped with grilled steak or chicken ($9).

BLACK DOG GELATO
GELATO $

Map p318 (www.blackdogchicago.com; 859 N Damen Ave, East Village; gelato from $2.50; ☺noon-11pm Tue-Sun Apr-Aug, 2-10pm Tue-Sun Sep-Nov; Ⓜ Blue Line to Division) All hail the oddball masterpieces on this little shop's ever-changing menu. Will it be the goat's cheese cashew caramel flavor or the sassafras rum raisin? What about the bacon-studded, booze-tinged, chocolate whiskey gelato bar? Or the apple-cider sorbet, or the blueberry French toast, or the sesame fig chocolate chip, or... Black Dog is also at the Loop's Revival Food Hall (p58).

ROOTS
PIZZA $$

Map p318 (☏773-645-4949; www.rootspizza. com; 1924 W Chicago Ave, East Village; small pizzas from $14; ☺11am-midnight Sun-Thu, to 2am Fri, to 3am Sat; ☏; 🚌66) This purveyor of Quad Cities–style pizza (distinguished by a malty-crust pie snipped into thin strips) encourages guests of all ages to let their hair down, handing kids balls of dough for stretching and squashing and winning over adults with grown-up toppings like Korean fried chicken, duck sausage and butter chicken. There's a commendable roster of Midwestern beer and cider.

BITE CAFE
INTERNATIONAL $$

Map p318 (☏773-395-2483; www.bitecafe chicago.com; 1039 N Western Ave, Ukrainian Village; mains lunch $10-14, dinner $12-21; ☺9am-midnight Mon-Thu, to 1am Fri, 8am-1am Sat, 8am-midnight Sun, closed 4-5pm Sat & Sun; ☏; 🚌49) Join the shaggy rockers reading graphic novels and eating cinnamon streusel French toast for breakfast, grilled Gouda-and-white-cheddar sandwiches for lunch or ribeye with fried plantains for dinner. Many dishes can be made vegan on request. The small room is industrial-chic, with sky-blue chairs around plain wood tables, and funky artwork peppering exposed-brick walls.

BOEUFHAUS
STEAK $$$

Map p318 (☏773-661-2116; www.boeufhaus. com; 1012 N Western Ave, Ukrainian Village; mains $32-52; ☺11am-3:30pm & 5:30pm-close Tue-Sat, 5:30-10pm Sun; 🚌49) Chicago has many steakhouses, but none like European-style Boeufhaus in Ukrainian Village. Sit in a snug banquette and carve into dry-aged steaks and appetizers such as the beloved short-rib beignets or *cavatelli* (small pasta shells) with spicy *merguez* sausage.

LOCAL KNOWLEDGE

SOUP & BREAD DINNERS

The Hideout (p159) hosts a groovy dinner series at 5:30pm on Wednesday. From January to late March, Soup & Bread (www.soupandbread.net) offers a free meal of – yes – homemade soup and bread. Local foodies, musicians and artists take turns making the wares. Donations are collected and go to local food banks.

From late June until early September, the action morphs into a cookout and Veggie Bingo. You pay a few bucks to play, and winners receive organic produce as prizes. Proceeds support community gardens.

These jolly shindigs attract a big crowd, so don't be late.

Capacity is small, so reserve well ahead. Need more meat? Take some to go from the rustic butcher and deli counter.

✕ West Town

FLO   MEXICAN $
Map p318 (☏312-243-0477; www.flochicago. com; 1434 W Chicago Ave, Noble Square; mains $12-17; ◷8:30am-10pm Tue-Thu, to 11pm Fri, 9am-11pm Sat, 9am-3pm Sun; ☏; Ⓜ Blue Line to Chicago) Think you've had a good breakfast burrito before? Not until you've eaten here. The Southwestern-bent dishes, cozy atmosphere and jovial staff draw hordes of late-rising neighborhood hipsters on the weekend. Tart, potent margaritas, chicken mole and fish tacos take over after dark, but the breakfast foods are the main draw.

BARI FOODS   DELI $
Map p318 (☏312-666-0730; www.bariitalian subs.com; 1120 W Grand Ave; sandwiches $6-10; ◷8am-6:30pm Mon-Fri, to 6pm Sat, to 2pm Sun; ☏65, Ⓜ Blue Line to Grand) This Italian grocery store and butcher cuts a mean salami. If you're planning a picnic, drop by and pick up a 9in sub sandwich or two (the Italian meatball is particularly scrumptious) and a limoncello tiramisu.

PODHALANKA   POLISH $
Map p318 (☏773-486-6655; 1549 W Division St, Noble Square; mains $6-16; ◷9am-8pm Mon-Sat,

10am-7pm Sun; Ⓜ Blue Line to Division) In the old 'Polish Downtown' is this hole-in-the-wall holdover, a true mom-and-pop joint (with owner Helena up front and husband Jerry in the kitchen). Enjoy massive portions of potato pancakes, pierogi, pork stew and other Polish fare on red vinyl seats as Pope JP2 stares from the wall, surrounded by shelves of classic Polish-themed kitsch. Cash only.

MR BROWN'S
LOUNGE   JAMAICAN $$
Map p318 (☏773-278-4445; www.mr brownslounge.com; 2301 W Chicago Ave; mains $11-22; ◷11am-midnight Tue-Thu, to 2am Fri, to 3am Sat, to 10pm Sun; ☏66) Named after a Jamaican folklore tale that Bob Marley adapted into a song, this bar-restaurant cooks up such Jamaican staples as curried goat, jerk chicken and (on weekends) stewed oxtail, along with American riffs such as 'island-style' macaroni and cheese. Wash it down with a spiced-rum punch. DJs spin reggae and dance-hall tunes on weekends.

KENDALL COLLEGE
DINING ROOM   MODERN AMERICAN $$$
Map p318 (☏312-752-2328; www.kendall.edu; 900 N North Branch St, Goose Island; 3-course menus lunch/dinner $18/29; ◷hours vary; ☏8, Ⓜ Blue Line to Grand) The School of Culinary Arts at Kendall College has turned out a host of local cooking luminaries – this classy space with river and skyline views is where they honed their chops. Students prepare and serve inventive contemporary American dishes, with forays into French and international fusion styles, all of which come with white-glove service at fantastic value. The Monday Night Dinner series offers a five-course banquet dinner ($39) from various international cuisines. Call ahead for reservations (and note the hours vary depending on the school term schedule). It's located on Goose Island, west of the Old Town area.

🍷 DRINKING & NIGHTLIFE

Milwaukee, Damen, Division and Chicago Aves burst with cocktail lounges and chic bars, while authentically retro mom-and-pop joints thrive quietly on the neighborhood's side streets.

🍸 Wicker Park & Bucktown

★ VIOLET HOUR
COCKTAIL BAR

Map p318 (☑773-252-1500; www.theviolethour. com; 1520 N Damen Ave, Wicker Park; ⊗6pm-2am Sun-Fri, to 3am Sat; MBlue Line to Damen) This nouveau speakeasy isn't marked, so look for the wood-paneled building with a full mural and a yellow light over the door. Inside, high-backed booths, chandeliers and long velvet drapes provide the backdrop to elaborately engineered, award-winning seasonal cocktails with droll names. As highbrow as it sounds, friendly staff make Violet Hour welcoming and accessible.

DANNY'S
BAR

Map p318 (☑773-489-6457; 1951 W Dickens Ave, Bucktown; ⊗7pm-2am Sun-Fri, to 3am Sat; MBlue Line to Damen) Danny's comfortably dim, dog-eared ambience is perfect for conversations over an early pint, before DJs arrive to stoke the dance party later on. It winds through several rooms in a vine-covered brick building that looks more like a house than a bar, filled with twenty- and thirty-somethings getting their moves on. Prepare for lines on weekend nights. Cash only.

ROYAL PALMS SHUFFLEBOARD CLUB
BAR

Map p318 (☑773-486-8682; www.royalpalms chicago.com; 1750 N Milwaukee Ave, Wicker Park; ⊗5pm-midnight Mon-Thu, to 2am Fri, noon-2am Sat, noon-10pm Sun; ☐56) A hop, skip and a shuffle away from the 606 trail (p153) is this Brooklyn import that combines hipster cocktails and beer with leisurely games of full-court shuffleboard ($40 per hour) on 10 courts. Various local food trucks serve snacks on a rotating weekly schedule. The rooftop deck is lovely in summer, though you'll have to shout over the thundering L.

EMPORIUM
BAR

Map p318 (www.emporiumchicago.com; 1366 N Milwaukee Ave, Wicker Park; ⊗5pm-2am Mon-Thu, from 3pm Fri, noon-3am Sat, noon-2am Sun) Test your joystick skills at this large bar filled with '80s and '90s standup arcade games – everything from Donkey Kong to Tron to NBA Jam – as well as pinball and

skeeball. Twenty-four beers on tap (many local or regional) keep you hydrated, while live music several nights per week offers something besides 8-bit entertainment.

REMEDY
BAR

Map p318 (☑773-698-7715; www.remedybar chicago.com; 1910 N Milwaukee Ave, Bucktown; ⊗4pm-4am Sun-Fri, to 5am Sat; MBlue Line to Western) Situated on the western edge of Bucktown, Remedy is a newer addition to Chicago's slate of bars open until 4am (5am on Saturday). But despite the coveted late-night liquor license, it endeavors to be an 'anytime' establishment, courting the line between casual and classy.

There are craft cocktails – the Asshattan (rye, Italian vermouth, yellow chartreuse, sour cherry maraschino and Angostura bitters) won best cocktail in town in the *Reader's* 2017 Best of Chicago poll – and local beer, fancy light fixtures and a loud jukebox, a cozy fireplace and massive fish tank. When you're undecided what type of bar you're in the mood for, this neighborhood spot offers a remedy.

WORMHOLE COFFEE
COFFEE

Map p318 (☑773-661-2468; www.thewormhole. us; 1462 N Milwaukee Ave, Wicker Park; ⊗7am-9pm; 🛜; MBlue Line to Damen) The Wormhole is pretentious in an endearing way. Consider drinks such as 'cool but rude' (a latte with fresh ginger and curry sauce) or the peanut butter koopa troopa (peanut mousse, chocolate and coffee); pompous, but also cutely delicious. Laptop-wielding students and hipsters caffeinate at broad tables and old couches amid 1980s movie kitsch. The music is kickin', too.

DEBONAIR SOCIAL CLUB
CLUB

Map p318 (☑773-227-7990; www.debonair socialclub.com; 1575 N Milwaukee Ave, Wicker Park; ⊗9pm-2am Tue & Wed, from 10pm Thu, from 8pm Fri, 8pm-3am Sat; MBlue Line to Damen) It's mostly a younger, hipster crowd dancing their asses off at Debonair to '80s new wave, hip-hop, house, trap, drum and bass, and new electro. The main action takes place on the upstairs floor. The downstairs floor is less hot and packed, though still grooving. Check the website for album parties and other events.

To the Heart of Wicker Park, Bucktown & Ukrainian Village

Bucktown and Wicker Park beckon to the southwest with vintage shops and DJ-spinning lounges, while Ukrainian Village gives hipsters an edgier playground next door. You can visit the neighborhoods' ethnic museums and art galleries, but what you're really here for is the food, drink and window browsing.

SERHII CHRUCKY / ALAMY STOCK PHOTO ©

JIM NEWBERRY / ALAMY STOCK PHOTO ©

1. Reckless Records (p160)
Considered by many to have the best independent vinyl and CD collections in Chicago.

2. Wicker Park (p149)
The locals favorite green space in the Wicker Park neighborhood.

3. Ukrainian Village (p146)
Typical residential architecture of the Ukrainian Village.

4. The Hideout (p159)
Saxophonist Akira Sakata performing at the Hideout, one of Chicago's hippest venues.

THOMAS BARRAT / SHUTTERSTOCK ©

📍 Ukrainian Village & East Village

★ INNERTOWN PUB   BAR

Map p318 (📞773-235-9795; 1935 W Thomas St, East Village; ⏰3pm-2am Sun-Fri, to 3am Sat; Ⓜ Blue Line to Division) A holiday-light-festooned moose head and a life-size statue of Elvis overlook the crowd of artsy regulars playing pool and drinking on the cheap at this lovably divey, kitsch-filled watering hole (and former 1920s speakeasy). The bartenders enjoy mixing up unconventional cocktails and DJs spin new wave and other tunes a few nights per week.

QUEEN MARY   BAR

Map p318 (www.queenmarytavern.com; 2125 W Division St, Ukrainian Village; ⏰5pm-2am Sun-Fri, to 3am Sat; Ⓜ Blue Line to Division) Making waves when it opened in Wicker Park in 2015 in a sea of sports bars, Queen Mary is a neighborhood tavern inspired by the British Royal Navy. It's named after building owner Mary Kafka, who, alongside her husband, ran a Polish dive bar in the same spot during the 1970s.

Following a family tragedy, Mary shut down the business and it remained empty for nearly 40 years. Enter Heisler Hospitality, the visionary restaurateurs behind Bad Hunter, Pub Royale (p152), Estereo and other respected Chicago establishments, who befriended Mary and revitalized the watering hole. It now teems with nautical charm: the original mahogany bar dominates the space, and warm wood paneling and exposed brick line the walls.

On the menu are gin- and rum-based cocktails that riff on 'British maritime drinking traditions,' including a navy-strength old-fashioned, daily rum grog and shareable tea-based punch, plus fortified wines and beer. Take a seat in a high-backed booth, replete with life-preserver cushions, and you'll feel as if you've sailed away to another place and time.

FORBIDDEN ROOT   MICROBREWERY

Map p318 (📞312-929-2202; www.forbiddenroot.com; 1746 W Chicago Ave, East Village; ⏰11:30am-midnight Mon-Fri, 11am-1am Sat, 11am-10pm Sun; 🚌66, Ⓜ Blue Line to Chicago) Forbidden Root is a 'botanical brewery' that uses roots, bark, spices, fruit and flowers to make eclectic beers such as Wildflower Pale Ale

(with marigold and elder) and Snoochie Boochies, a double IPA with a sweet orange aroma. The weird mash-ups are delicious and the on-site brewery changes things up regularly. The cool space is done up with farm-industrial decor.

GOLD STAR BAR   BAR

Map p318 (📞773-227-8700; 1755 W Division St, East Village; ⏰4pm-2am Sun-Fri, to 3am Sat; Ⓜ Blue Line to Division) A century-old vestige from the days when Division St was 'Polish Broadway,' the Gold Star remains a divey winner, drawing a posse of bike messengers and other bartenders talking shop for cheap beer, free popcorn and a great metal-and-punk jukebox.

RAINBO CLUB   BAR

Map p318 (📞773-489-5999; 1150 N Damen Ave, Ukrainian Village; ⏰4pm-2am Sun-Fri, to 3am Sat; Ⓜ Blue Line to Damen) The center for Chicago's indie elite during the week, the boxy, dark-wood 1930s Rainbo Club has an impressive semicircular bar and one of the city's best photo booths. The service is slow and the place goes a little suburban on weekends, but otherwise it's a fun place to hang out with artsy locals quaffing $2 PBR drafts. Cash only.

OLA'S LIQUOR   BAR

Map p318 (📞773-384-7259; 947 N Damen Ave, East Village; ⏰7am-2am Mon-Fri, to 3am Sat, 11am-2am Sun; 🚌50) This classic 'slashie' – the term for a combination bar/liquor store – has hours catering to third-shift locals and the most indomitable night owls. Order the advertised *zimne piwo* (Polish for 'cold beer') and blast some tunes on the juke in the same language.

📍 West Town

★ MATCHBOX   BAR

Map p318 (📞312-666-9292; www.facebook.com/matchboxchicago; 770 N Milwaukee Ave, River West; ⏰3pm-2am Sun-Fri, to 3am Sat; Ⓜ Blue Line to Chicago) Lawyers, artists and bums all squeeze in for retro cocktails. It's as small as – you got it – a matchbox, with about a dozen bar stools; everyone else stands against the back wall. Barkeeps make the drinks from scratch. Favorites include the pisco sour and the ginger gimlet, ladled from an amber vat of homemade ginger-infused vodka.

WICKER PARK, BUCKTOWN & UKRAINIAN VILLAGE DRINKING & NIGHTLIFE

LUSH WINE & SPIRITS
WINE BAR

Map p318 (☏312-666-6900; www.lushwineand
spirits.com; 1412 W Chicago Ave, Noble Square;
☺noon-10pm Sun-Thu, to 11pm Fri & Sat; Ⓜ Blue
Line to Chicago) Lush is a local mini-chain that
is part wine shop and part wine bar, special-
izing in smaller vineyards and organic wines.
Buy a bottle on one side, then take it over to
the other and sit at butcher-block tables in a
decibel-friendly, Euro-style ambience. It's all
very economical, especially during the free
tastings on Sunday from 2pm to 5pm.

BEAUTY BAR
CLUB

Map p318 (☏312-226-8828; www.thebeautybar.
com; 1444 W Chicago Ave, Noble Square; ☺7pm-
2am Mon-Fri, to 3am Sat, 9pm-2am Sun; Ⓜ Blue
Line to Chicago) The interior is a restored
late-1960s beauty salon from New Jersey.
'Martinis & Manicures' is the shtick; get
your nails done for $20 on Saturday (to
1am) or $15 on every other night except
Tuesday (to midnight). Genre-spanning
DJs spin nightly and live performers (drag
queens, comedians) entertain, too. It's part
of a chain with outposts in several US cities.

☆ ENTERTAINMENT

**Unsurprisingly for such a hip area, the
northwestern neighborhoods have
a bevy of choices for an evening's
entertainment. You'll find venues for
indie rock, hip-hop and other popular
genres, as well as a few of Chicago's
smaller independent theater companies.**

★ HIDEOUT
LIVE MUSIC

Map p318 (☏773-227-4433; www.hideout
chicago.com; 1354 W Wabansia Ave, West Town;
tickets $5-15; ☺4pm-midnight Mon-Thu, to 2am
Fri, 6pm-3am Sat, hours vary Sun; ☐72) Hidden
behind a factory past the edge of Bucktown,
this two-room lodge of indie rock and alt-
country is well worth seeking out. The owners have nursed an outsider, underground
vibe, and the place feels like your grandma's
rumpus room. Music and other events (talk
shows, literary readings, comedy etc) take
place nightly. On Mondays there's a great
open-mike poetry night (p160).

★ DAVENPORT'S PIANO BAR CABARET
LIVE MUSIC

Map p318 (☏773-278-1830; www.davenports
pianobar.com; 1383 N Milwaukee Ave, Wicker Park;
☺7pm-midnight Mon, Wed & Thu, to 2am Fri & Sat,
6-11pm Sun; Ⓜ Blue Line to Damen) Old standards get new interpretations and new songs
are premiered at Davenport's, a magnet for
the local theater crowd. The front room
is a fun, inclusive (read: sing-along) place
with an open mike on Monday nights that
attracts everyone from shower singers to
professional actors; the back room stages
cabaret shows with a cover and two-drink
minimum.

HOUSE THEATRE
THEATER

Map p318 (☏773-769-3832; www.thehouse
theatre.com; 1543 W Division St, Noble Square;
Ⓜ Blue Line to Division) This exhilarating
company presents a mix of quirky, funny,
touching shows written by up-and-coming playwrights – magic, music and good
old-fashioned storytelling usually tie in
somehow. House typically performs at the
on-site **Chopin Theatre** (☏773-278-1500;
www.chopintheatre.com), but sometimes it
turns up in offbeat locations (such as a hotel
room) as well. The company also stages an
annual ballet-free version of *The Nutcracker*.

EMPTY BOTTLE
LIVE MUSIC

Map p318 (☏773-276-3600; www.empty
bottle.com; 1035 N Western Ave, Ukrainian Village;
☺5pm-2am Mon-Wed, from 3pm Thu & Fri, from
11am Sat & Sun; ☐49) Chicago's music insid-
ers fawn over the Empty Bottle, the city's
scruffy, go-to club for edgy indie rock, jazz
and other beats that's been a west-side institution for almost three decades. Monday's show is often a freebie by a couple of
up-and-coming bands. Cheap beer, a photo
booth and good graffiti-reading in the
bathrooms add to the dive-bar fun.

One Saturday per month the space hosts
local arts and crafts vendors at the Handmade Market (p162).

PHYLLIS' MUSICAL INN
LIVE MUSIC

Map p318 (☏773-486-9862; 1800 W Division St,
Wicker Park; ☺4pm-2am Mon-Fri, 3pm-3am Sat,
from noon Sun; Ⓜ Blue Line to Division) One of
Chicago's all-time great dives, this former
Polish polka bar features live performances nightly – often scrappy up-and-coming
bands, sometimes a poetry slam or comedy.
It's hit-and-miss for quality, but you've got to
applaud them for taking a chance. Don't like
the sound? Slip outside to the bar's basketball court for relief. The brewskis are cheap,
to boot.

WICKER PARK, BUCKTOWN & UKRAINIAN VILLAGE ENTERTAINMENT

LOCAL KNOWLEDGE

WEEDS POETRY NIGHT

Verse comes in all shapes and sizes at the long-standing weekly **Monday night event** (Map p318; www.facebook.com/WeedsPoetry; Hideout, 1354 W Wabansia St, West Town; by donation; ⊙9:30pm Mon; 🚌9, 72), now at the Hideout (p159). A cast of delightfully eccentric poets get on the mike to vent about love, sex, war, booze, urban living and pretty much everything in between. Some of it rhymes, some of it rambles, but it all makes for a pretty cool scene.

CHICAGO DRAMATISTS THEATRE
THEATER

Map p318 (📞312-633-0630; www.chicagodramatists.org; 1105 W Chicago Ave, River West; ⓂBlue Line to Chicago) For a visit to the heart of Chicago's dramatic scene, step into this small, functional theater space, a testing ground for Chicago's new playwrights and plays, which has sent more than a few works on to Broadway (such as Keith Huff's *A Steady Rain*). The Monday Night Drama series features public readings of works-in-progress and other special events ($10).

SUBTERRANEAN
LIVE MUSIC

Map p318 (📞773-278-6600; www.subt.net; 2011 W North Ave, Wicker Park; ⊙7pm-2am Sun-Fri, 6pm-3am Sat; ⓂBlue Line to Damen) A trendy crowd comes to Subterranean, which looks slick inside and out. The main room upstairs draws good indie rock, funk and hip-hop bands; Thursday is reggae night. The downstairs lounge hosts smaller shows, DJ dance parties and popular open-mike events, including a long-standing hip-hop open-mike night on Tuesday.

🛍 SHOPPING

Milwaukee Ave offers a trove of hip vintage fashion, book and record shops. Damen Ave's shops are a bit more upscale, with perfume, children's clothing and artisanal gifts on offer.

⭐RECKLESS RECORDS
MUSIC

Map p318 (📞773-235-3727; www.reckless.com; 1379 N Milwaukee Ave, Wicker Park; ⊙10am-10pm Mon-Sat, to 8pm Sun; ⓂBlue Line to Damen) Chicago's best indie-rock record and CD emporium lets you listen to everything before you buy. There's plenty of elbow room in the big, sunny space, which makes for happy hunting through the new and used bins. DVDs and cassette tapes, too. Stop by for flyers and listing calendars of the local live-music and theater scene.

⭐QUIMBY'S
BOOKS

Map p318 (📞773-342-0910; www.quimbys.com; 1854 W North Ave, Wicker Park; ⊙noon-9pm Mon-Thu, to 10pm Fri, 11am-10pm Sat, noon-7pm Sun; ⓂBlue Line to Damen) The epicenter of Chicago's comic and zine worlds, Quimby's is one of the linchpins of underground literary culture in the city. Here you can find everything from crayon-powered punk-rock manifestos to slickly produced graphic novels. It's a groovy place for cheeky literary souvenirs and bizarro readings.

⭐TRANSIT TEES
GIFTS & SOUVENIRS

Map p318 (www.transittees.com; 1371 N Milwaukee Ave, Wicker Park; ⊙9:30am-8pm Mon-Fri, from 11am Sat, 11am-6pm Sun) If you want to take a bit of Chi-town home with you, check out these locally made, Chicago-inspired wares – souvenirs with style. Just about anything that can be emblazoned with the iconic two blue stripes and four red stars is: throw pillows, socks, engraved tumblers, suspenders and, of course, T-shirts. Plus there are transit maps, Chicago posters and street signs.

DUSTY GROOVE
MUSIC

Map p318 (📞773-342-5800; www.dustygroove.com; 1120 N Ashland Ave, East Village; ⊙10am-8pm; ⓂBlue Line to Division) Old-school soul, Latin beats, American gospel, bass-stabbing hip-hop, every flavor of jazz – if it's funky, Dusty Groove (which also has its own record label) stocks it. Flip through stacks of vinyl, or get lost amid the tidy shop's CDs. Be sure to check out the bargain basement, with boxes full of 50¢ records.

WICKER PARK SECRET AGENT SUPPLY CO
GIFTS & SOUVENIRS

Map p318 (📞773-772-8108; www.826chi.org; 1276 N Milwaukee Ave, Wicker Park; ⊙11am-6pm Mon-Sat, noon-5pm Sun; ♿; ⓂBlue Line to Division) This place sells 'espionagical wares' (aka crazy spy and detective gear): mustache disguise kits, underwater voice amplifiers, Sherlock Holmes deerstalker hats

– it's loads of smart fun. Creative books and games for children also fill the shelves. Better yet: profits support the after-school writing and tutoring programs for kids that take place on-site at nonprofit group 826CHI.

UNA MAE'S
CLOTHING

Map p318 (📞773-276-7002; www.unamaes chicago.com; 1528 N Milwaukee Ave, Wicker Park; ⏰noon-8pm Mon-Fri, from 11am Sat, noon-6pm Sun; Ⓜ Blue Line to Damen) It's a fine spot to browse for a pillbox hat or a classic houndstooth-check jacket. Along with its vintage wares, Una Mae's has a collection of new, cool-cat designer duds, accessories and shoes for both men and women.

VIRTU
ARTS & CRAFTS

Map p318 (📞773-235-3790; www.virtuchicago. com; 2035 N Damen Ave, Bucktown; ⏰11am-7pm Tue-Fri, 10am-6pm Sat, 11am-5pm Sun; 🚌50, 73) 'Come In, We're Awesome' says the sign on the front door. Gregarious owner Julie has been running this Bucktown boutique for two decades and it's become a neighborhood favorite for its wonderful variety of mainly handmade objects, many from women artisans: textiles and clothing, ceramics and housewares, precious and semiprecious jewelry, stationery, candles and more. They're perfect for thoughtful gifts.

MOTH
CLOTHING, HOMEWARES

Map p318 (📞872-802-4408; www.mothchicago. com; 2008 N Damen Ave, Bucktown; ⏰11am-6pm Tue-Sat, noon-5pm Sun; Ⓜ Blue Line to Damen) Japanese and Nordic design share similar features, including clean lines, minimal adornments and references to the natural world. So when former architect and frequent traveler Catherine Becker decided to open her Bucktown boutique, it made sense to blend these two design traditions. Moth stocks beautiful, hard-to-find art, clothing, textiles and artisan housewares from Scandinavia, Finland and Japan.

WITT-CENTURY MODERN
VINTAGE

Map p318 (📞773-904-7074; www.wcmod.com; 1136 N Milwaukee Ave, Noble Square; ⏰11:30am-7:30pm Mon, Wed & Fri-Sun; Ⓜ Blue Line to Division) This well-curated vintage shop in Noble Square stocks a selection of beautiful modern furniture and home decor, from teak credenzas to vintage Eames chairs to abstract and surrealist art. The emphasis is on mid-century American and Danish design with a playful splash of '70s. The shop can ship to anywhere in the continental US.

KOKOROKOKO
VINTAGE

Map p318 (📞773-252-6996; www.kokorokoko vintage.com; 1323 N Milwaukee Ave, Wicker Park; ⏰noon-8pm Mon-Fri, from 11am Sat, 11am-7pm Sun; Ⓜ Blue Line to Division) The smell of incense greets you as you walk in to peruse the array of Bionic Woman lunch boxes, celebrity-saint pillar candles, New Kids on the Block trading cards, authentic trucker hats and racks of vintage men's and women's clothing (average price per shirt or jacket around $20). The shop is a neighborhood favorite.

SHUGA RECORDS
MUSIC

Map p318 (📞773-278-4085; www.shugarecords. com; 1272 N Milwaukee Ave, Wicker Park; ⏰10am-10pm Mon-Sat, to 8pm Sun; Ⓜ Blue Line to Division) The smallish shop carries lots of soul and funk vinyl, plus a bit of everything else, from stoner doom to Native American ballads. It's also a great place to find local and regional bands, including those on the store's own label. Prices typically hover around $20 per record.

BUFFALO EXCHANGE
CLOTHING

Map p318 (📞773-227-9558; www.buffalo exchange.com; 1478 N Milwaukee Ave, Wicker Park; ⏰11am-8pm; Ⓜ Blue Line to Damen) You can buy, sell or trade your duds at this well-regarded secondhand clothing shop for men and women. Part of a national chain, the Wicker Park outpost has a good selection of designer wares mixed in with the everyday shirts, jackets and jeans on the packed racks.

MILDBLEND SUPPLY CO
CLOTHING

Map p318 (📞773-772-9711; www.mildblend.com; 1342 N Milwaukee Ave, Wicker Park; ⏰11am-7pm Mon-Sat, noon-6pm Sun; Ⓜ Blue Line to Division) Stacks and racks of premium denim fill this roomy shop, which feels a bit like a country store, albeit one stocked with leather boots, fashionable women's jackets and artisanal men's grooming products. Staff will hem any jeans you buy at the sewing machines on-site.

MYOPIC BOOKS
BOOKS

Map p318 (📞773-862-4882; www.myopicbook store.com; 1564 N Milwaukee Ave, Wicker Park; ⏰9am-11pm; Ⓜ Blue Line to Damen) Myopic is one of the city's oldest and largest used

---

LOCAL KNOWLEDGE

VINTAGE THRIFT SHOPS

The stretch of Milwaukee Ave between Division and North Aves holds the mother lode of vintage and thrift shops, with some funky shoe stores and T-shirt shops thrown in for good measure. Within a half-mile you'll pass around eight hot spots, including US #1, Una Mae's (p161), Kokorokoko (p161) and **Ragstock** (Map p318; ☑773-252-4880; www.ragstock.com; 1461 N Milwaukee Ave, Wicker Park; ◷11am-8pm Mon-Sat, 10am-7pm Sun; ⓜBlue Line to Damen). And at Buffalo Exchange (p161), if you have some suitably fashionable threads of your own to trade in, you don't even need cash.

---

bookstores, with stacks upon stacks of tomes (about 70,000 by the shop's count). It rambles through three floors and hosts poetry readings (on occasional Saturday evenings) and experimental music (most Monday evenings). Staff is hard-core about the rules here – no picture taking, no phones etc – so mind your manners.

T-SHIRT DELI
CLOTHING

Map p318 (☑773-276-6266; www.tshirtdeli.com; 1739 N Damen Ave, Wicker Park; ◷11am-7pm Mon-Fri, to 6pm Sat, to 5pm Sun; ⓜBlue Line to Damen) The 'deli' part is taken seriously here: after cooking (ie ironing a retro design on) your T-shirt, it's wrapped in butcher paper and served to you with potato chips. Choose from heaps of shirt styles and decals: Chairman Mao, Sean Connery, Patty Hearst and a red-white-and-blue bong are but the beginning. 'Mystery meat' packages ($5) let you try your luck.

PENELOPE'S
CLOTHING

Map p318 (☑773-395-2351; www.shoppenelopes.com; 1913 W Division St, East Village; ◷11am-7pm Mon-Sat, noon-6pm Sun; ☒70, ⓜBlue Line to Division) Penelope's is a warm boutique for twenty- and thirty-somethings. It offers both men's and women's fashions (they're new, but look thrift-store-bought) along with housewares, baby and kid clothes, jew-

elry and nifty gifty things. It has expanded next door to a twin shop called Gemini (get it?), with similar items but focusing more on upscale men's and women's clothes and accessories.

US #1
VINTAGE

Map p318 (☑773-489-9428; 1460 N Milwaukee Ave, Wicker Park; ◷noon-7pm; ⓜBlue Line to Damen) Rack after rack of '70s bowling, Hawaiian and western-wear shirts, leather motorcycle jackets, cowboy boots and secondhand jeans (including big-name brands) cram this vintage shop. It's like someone raided a rock star's closet and put the contents up for sale. Alas, the goods don't come cheap, and the owner can be cantankerous with those who aren't serious about buying.

HANDMADE MARKET
ARTS & CRAFTS

Map p318 (☑773-276-3600; www.handmadechicago.com; 1035 N Western Ave, Ukrainian Village; ◷noon-4pm 2nd Sat and last Sun of the month Oct-Apr; ☒49) Held on the second Saturday and last Sunday of each month of the colder half of the year, this event at the Empty Bottle (p159) showcases Chicagoland crafters who make funky glass pendants, knitted items, handbags, scarves, journals, greeting cards and more. The bar serves drinks throughout the event so you can sip while you shop.

🏃 SPORTS & ACTIVITIES

RED SQUARE SPA
BATHHOUSE

Map p318 (☑773-227-2284; www.redsquarechicago.com; 1914 W Division St, Wicker Park; $35; ◷10am-11pm Mon-Thu, to midnight Fri, 7am-midnight Sat, 7am-11pm Sun; ☒50, 70, ⓜBlue Line to Division) This historic 1906 bathhouse was renovated in 2011 and is today a full-featured *banya* with tattooed twenty-somethings taking a *shvitz* (steam bath) right alongside portly old Russian men. There are both gender-segregated and mixed-sex facilities with saunas, steam rooms and hot tubs; massages and spa treatments are available, as is a full bar and a menu of Russian food.

Logan Square & Humboldt Park

LOGAN SQUARE | HUMBOLDT PARK | AVONDALE

Neighborhood Top Five

❶ Chowhound hot spots (p168) Dining at one of the esteemed little storefront restaurants that's making big foodie news, such as Giant.

❷ Humboldt Park (p165) Strolling around the lagoon, lounging on the beach, checking out the free arts center and munching Puerto Rican snacks in the sprawling green space.

❸ Rosa's Lounge (p173) Hearing a fret-bending set by local blues musicians in unvarnished environs.

❹ Busy Beaver Button Museum (p165) Perusing thousands of oddball badges – including one from George Washington's campaign – on display in an unusual office building.

❺ Galerie F (p165) Getting the lowdown on the street art scene, and then heading out to browse Logan Square's murals.

For more detail of this area see Map p322 ➡

Lonely Planet's Top Tip

Many of the area's best restaurants are small, and it's tough to get a seat by walking in. Luckily, most places take reservations, though you'll need to book at least a few weeks in advance (especially for weekend seats). Otherwise try to arrive right at opening time. At Kuma's Corner (p171) and Longman & Eagle (p169), which don't take reservations, you can order meals at the bar if you snag a seat.

✖ Best Places to Eat

- Giant (p169)
- Ground Control (p168)
- Spinning J (p171)
- Parachute (p172)
- Pretty Cool Ice Cream (p170)
- Fat Rice (p169)

For reviews, see p168.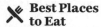

☙ Best Places to Drink

- Metropolitan Brewing (p173)
- Cole's (p172)
- Lost Lake (p172)
- Revolution Brewing (p172)
- Scofflaw (p172)

For reviews, see p172.➡

🔒 Best Places to Shop

- Katherine Anne Confections (p173)
- Peach Fuzz (p173)
- Wolfbait & B-girls (p173)

For reviews, see p173.➡

LOGAN SQUARE & HUMBOLDT PARK

Explore Logan Square & Humboldt Park

Sights are few and far between in Logan Square and Humboldt Park. You're mostly here to eat, drink and see a show. Plan on at least an evening in the neighborhood, and maybe an afternoon, to boot.

Logan Square has the most action and is a fine place to begin. Milwaukee Ave is the heart of it, chockablock with coffee roasters, bohemian little restaurants, thrifty cocktail lounges and artsy music clubs. Nighttime is when the action peaks; expect lots of company on your evening out. And expect lots of construction: Logan is gentrifying big-time, and new buildings are rising up all around.

Humboldt Park, to the south, is rougher around the edges. It's still heavily Puerto Rican, as the giant flag sculptures and island-food cafes along Division St attest. The eponymous park is the area's focal point. Pockets of cool-cat bakeries and coffee bars fringe it to the south, especially along California Ave. Afternoon is the best time to visit.

Streetwise restaurants, microbreweries and clubs have also popped up in Avondale. The slightly scruffy neighborhood sits next door to Logan Square, and it was only a matter of time before hip spots spilled over.

Local Life

➡ **Corner bar** To slake your thirst like a neighborhood regular, plop down on a barstool at Archie's Iowa Rockwell Tavern (p173).

➡ **Jibarito meal** Join the Puerto Rican folks chitchatting in Spanish in between bites of their *jibarito* sandwich at Papa's Cache Sabroso (p171).

➡ **Patio party** When the weather warms, everyone hangs out on the patio at Parson's Chicken & Fish (p168).

Getting There & Away

➡ **L Train** Blue Line to Logan Square or California for Logan Square; Blue Line to Belmont for Avondale.

➡ **Bus** For Humboldt Park destinations, you'll need a bus. Bus 70 travels along Division St, bus 72 along North Ave and bud 73 along Armitage Ave.

➡ **Car** Street parking isn't bad, although it can get tight around Logan Square.

⊙ SIGHTS

This is not an area full of big-ticket attractions. A couple of freebies – the Busy Beaver Button Museum and National Museum of Puerto Rican Arts & Culture (p168) – are worth a peek. So are the area's murals and the street art displays at Galerie F. Or join the locals hanging out at the lagoons and gardens in Humboldt Park.

bage Patch Kids to Big Rock Point Nuclear Plant.

They're fascinating to browse (especially Washington's button), and the hipster office staff are totally gracious about letting you gawk over their desks where the framed cases hang. Heaps more buttons are preserved in drawers that you're welcome to pull out and examine. Ring the doorbell to enter. And don't forget to pick up your souvenir button before you leave!

⊙ Logan Square

★GALERIE F   GALLERY
Map p322 (☑872-817-7067; www.galeriefchicago. com; 2415 N Milwaukee Ave; ⊙11am-6pm Mon & Thu-Sun; ⓂBlue Line to California) Galerie F is exactly the type of laid-back, ubercool gallery you'd expect to find in Logan Square. It specializes in rock-and-roll gig posters, printmaking and street art. Walk into the bright, open space and browse – the vibe here is totally welcoming. Dip into the basement to listen to records, play chess or just linger in the sitting area.

★BUSY BEAVER
BUTTON MUSEUM   MUSEUM
Map p322 (☑773-645-3359; www.button museum.org; 3407 W Armitage Ave; ⊙10am-4pm Mon-Fri; ☐73) FREE Even George Washington gave out campaign buttons, though in his era they were the sew-on kind. Pin-back buttons came along in 1896. Badge-making company Busy Beaver chronicles its history in displays holding thousands of the little round mementos. They tout everything from Dale Bozzio to Bozo the clown, Cab-

⊙ Humboldt Park

HUMBOLDT PARK   PARK
Map p322 (www.chicagoparkdistrict.com; 1440 N Humboldt Dr; ⊙6am-11pm; ☐70, 72) This 207-acre park, which lends its name to the surrounding neighborhood, comes out of nowhere and gobsmacks you with Mother Nature. A lagoon brushed by native plants takes up much of the green space, and birdsong flickers in the air. The 1907 Prairie School boathouse is the park's centerpiece, home to a cafe and free cultural events. The flowery Formal Garden, National Museum of Puerto Rican Arts & Culture (p168), and Chicago's only inland beach are other highlights. The park was built in 1869 and named for German naturalist Alexander von Humboldt. Landscape architect Jens Jensen gave it its 'prairie style' design, using native plants and stone, in the early 1900s. The park has gone through some rough times since then, and has only come into its own again in the past decade or so. While it's family filled by day, it's still pretty rough and best avoided at night (unless there's a free outdoor movie or music event happening).

(Continued on page 168)

STREET ART VIEWS

Logan Square and Humboldt Park are popular areas for street artists to do their thing. Top places to glimpse the works:

➡ Take the L train to the California stop, and then walk southeast on Milwaukee Ave for a half-mile or so. You'll pass several cool murals, including **Greetings from Chicago** (Map p322; 2226 N Milwaukee Ave, Logan Square; ⓂBlue Line to California) and a waggish **Robin Williams** rendering (2047 N Milwaukee Ave, Logan Square; ⓂBlue Line to California).

➡ You could also just stay on the L and gape out the window as the train travels between the Logan Square and Damen stations. Clowns, monsters, leprechauns, monkeys and Simpsons characters flash by on rooftops and walls around the tracks.

➡ In Humboldt Park, walk along the half-mile stretch of Division St between Western and California Aves – aka the Paseo Boricua (p168) – and you'll see the Puerto Rican Doors project. The eye-catching paintings on 16 different storefronts celebrate Latin culture and identity.

Hipster Haven at Logan Square & Humboldt Park

Whenever something new and cool opens – be it a craft whiskey maker, a pop-up sausage restaurant, a thrifty gin lounge, a record shop with an attached video-game museum – it opens here. And even though it's the hottest 'hood in town, it remains refreshingly low-key.

HENRYK SADURA / SHUTTERSTOCK ©

STEVEGER / GETTY IMAGES ©

1. Prairie School Boathouse (p165)
The 1907 Prairie School boathouse is the centerpiece of Humboldt Park.

2. National Museum of Puerto Rican Arts & Culture (p168)
Located in the former horse stables of Humboldt Park.

3. Smoque (p169)
Pork spare ribs from barbecue restaurant Smoque.

4. Formal Garden (p165)
This Prairie-style garden in Humboldt Park was designed in 1908 by landscape architect Jens Jensen.

PHOTOCUISINE RM / ALAMY STOCK PHOTO ©

(Continued from page 165)

Street vendors and food trucks sell fried plantains, meat dumplings and other Puerto Rican specialties around the park's edges. Many congregate on Kedzie Ave at North Ave and at Hirsch St – sniff them out for a picnic. For more in-depth explorations, including the park's wee waterfall, wind turbine and picnic island, download the free audio tour at www.chicagoparkdistrict.com/parks-facilities/humboldt-park-audio-tour.

NATIONAL MUSEUM OF PUERTO RICAN ARTS & CULTURE MUSEUM

Map p322 (☑773-486-8345; www.nmprac.org; 3015 W Division St; ⊙10am-5pm Tue-Fri, to 2pm Sat; ☐70) FREE The museum fills the old horse stables in Humboldt Park. It's worth a stroll inside to see what free art and cultural exhibits are showing. These might include paintings by Afro Caribbean artists or vintage posters from Puerto Rico's early days as a US territory.

PASEO BORICUA AREA

Map p322 (Division St, btwn Western Ave & Mozart St; ☐70) The Paseo Boricua, aka Puerto Rican Promenade, is a half-mile-long stretch of Division St where many Puerto Rican shops and restaurants do business. It's marked at either end by an enormous **Puerto Rican flag sculpture** (Map p322; cnr N Mozart & W Division Sts, ☐70) that arches over the road; the eastern flag stands beside Artesian Ave, while the western one is at Mozart St. Striking murals cover many of the storefronts.

EATING

Logan Square is the city's inventive foodie mecca. Restaurants tend to be small in size but big on creativity and accolades. Many serve modern comfort food, and many are reasonably priced. Milwaukee Ave is the main vein. Puerto Rican cafes and the *jibarito* sandwich are Humboldt Park's claim to fame. It's also getting gastronomic: the area around California and Augusta Aves has seen several hot spots fire up.

✕ Logan Square

★GROUND CONTROL VEGETARIAN $

Map p322 (☑773-772-9446; www.groundcontrol chicago.com; 3315 W Armitage Ave; mains $10-12; ⊙5-10pm Tue-Thu, 5-11pm Fri, 11am-11pm Sat, 11am-9pm Sun; ☑; ☐73) Ground Control is an industrial, trippy mural-clad restaurant with pinball machines and craft beer on tap. That it's meat-free is incidental. The dishes play off Asian, Latin and Southern flavors, like the Nashville hot tofu, sweet-potato tacos and wasabi portobello sandwich. It's super delicious, and there's always a cool-cat crowd.

PARSON'S CHICKEN & FISH AMERICAN $

Map p322 (☑773-384-3333; www.parsonschicken andfish.com; 2952 W Armitage Ave; mains $8-16; ⊙11am-midnight Mon-Fri, 10am-midnight Sat & Sun; ⓜBlue Line to California) Parson's fries its chicken skin hard, so the super juicy flesh underneath comes as a surprise. Everyone eats outdoors at picnic tables under striped umbrellas. This is *the* neighborhood hot spot when the weather warms, and the negroni slushies slide down with ease. Battles at the ping-pong table get fierce. No reservations.

CHICAGO DINER VEGETARIAN $

Map p322 (☑773-252-3211; www.veggie diner.com; 2333 N Milwaukee Ave; mains $10-14; ⊙11am-10pm Mon-Thu, 11am-11pm Fri, 10am-11pm Sat, 10am-10pm Sun; ☑; ⓜBlue Line to California) Chicago's favorite, long-standing vegetarian restaurant expanded from Lake View and opened this fancier branch in Logan Square. Poutine, meatloaf, barbecue chicken and milkshakes are all on the menu, plus cocktails in the light-wood, exposed-brick digs. Anything on the menu can be made vegan, and there are gluten-free options as well.

BANG BANG PIE & BISCUITS AMERICAN $

Map p322 (☑773-276-8888; www.bangbangpie. com; 2051 N California Ave; pie slices $5, mains $7-12; ⊙7am-7pm Mon-Fri, 9am-4pm Sat & Sun; ☎; ⓜBlue Line to California) The namesake pie comes in several varieties daily. Check the blackboard for coffee custard, spiced apple plum, chocolate peanut butter and more creamy, fruity goodness. Bang Bang's hulking biscuits likewise earn raves, especially after a slathering with the condiment bar's jams. Chicken pot pies, cheddar grits and candied bacon biscuit sandwiches satisfy savory tastes.

CELLAR DOOR PROVISIONS AMERICAN $$

Map p322 (☑773-697-8337; www.cellardoor provisions.com; 3025 W Diversey Ave; mains $20-26; ⊙8am-3pm Wed, Thu & Sun, 8am-3pm &

SMOQUE
....

This **barbecue joint** (Off Map p322; ☑773-545-7427; www.smoquebbq.com; 3800 N Pulaski Rd, Irving Park; mains $10-23; ⊗11am-9pm Sun & Tue-Thu, to 10pm Fri & Sat; 🚻; Ⓜ Blue Line to Irving Park) is all about slow-cooked meats. The baby-back and St Louis–style ribs are what line 'em up: they're smoked over oak and applewood and soaked in a tangy, slightly sweet sauce. Brisket and pulled pork aren't far behind in awesomeness. Brisket-flecked baked beans, cornmeal-crusted mac 'n' cheese, freshly cut fries and citrusy coleslaw round things out. Smoque is a couple of miles northwest of Logan Square. BYOB.

5:30-9pm Fri & Sat; Ⓜ Blue Line to Logan Square) A cafe by day and bistro by night, Cellar Door's teeny space only has about 20 seats. The rotating menu of bright, seasonal dishes might include carrot ravioli, spicy lamb with smoked tomatoes or creamed mushrooms and dumplings. There's always awesomely crusty bread. Choose your wine from the shop next door ($10 corkage fee). Book ahead.

LONGMAN & EAGLE   AMERICAN $$
Map p322 (☑773-276-7110; www.longman andeagle.com; 2657 N Kedzie Ave; mains $16-28; ⊗9am-2am; Ⓜ Blue Line to Logan Square) Hard to say whether this shabby-chic tavern is best for eating or drinking. Let's say eating, thanks to its beautifully cooked comfort foods such as duck egg hash for breakfast, wild-boar sloppy joes for lunch, and smoked trout stew with Brie and pickles for dinner. There's a whole menu of small plates and whiskeys too. No reservations.

LULA CAFE   AMERICAN $$
Map p322 (☑773-489-9554; www.lulacafe.com; 2537 N Kedzie Blvd; mains $16-28; ⊗9am-11pm Mon, Wed, Thu & Sun, to midnight Fri & Sat; 🖉; Ⓜ Blue Line to Logan Square) 🍴 Funky, arty Lula led the way for Logan Square's dining scene, and appreciative neighborhood folks still crowd in for the seasonal, locally sourced menu. Even the muffins are something to drool over, and that goes double for lunch items like pasta *yiayia* (*bucatini* pasta with Moroccan cinnamon, feta and garlic) and dinners including steamed flounder with wild fennel and parsnip.

PAULIE GEE'S   PIZZA $$
Map p322 (☑773-360-1072; www.pauliegee.com/ logan-square; 2451 N Milwaukee Ave; pizzas $15-18; ⊗5:30-10pm Mon-Thu, 5:30pm-2am Fri, 11am-2pm & 5pm-2am Sat, 11am-2pm & 5-10pm Sun; 🖉; Ⓜ Blue Line to California) At this buzzy, candlelit space – an outpost of the well-known Brooklyn pizzeria – diners huddle over chunky wooden tables while digging into

creatively topped thin-crust pies. There's a big list of vegan options (using vegan cheese and housemade vegan sausage) and a detour into Detroit-style pan pizza (with a thick, cheesy crust) that might just be the best thing on the menu.

★GIANT   AMERICAN $$$
Map p322 (☑773-252-0997; www.giantrestaurant. com; 3209 W Armitage Ave; small plates $14-19; ⊗5-10:30pm Tue-Sat; 🚌73) This wee storefront eatery produces huge flavors in its heady comfort food. Dishes like the king-crab tagliatelle, biscuits with jalapeño butter and sweet-and-sour eggplant have wowed the foodie masses, and rightfully so. The small plate portions mean you'll need to order a few dishes to make a meal. Well-matched cocktails and wine add luster to the spread. Reserve ahead.

FAT RICE   FUSION $$$
Map p322 (☑773-661-9170; www.eatfatrice.com; 2957 W Diversey Ave; mains $20-32; ⊗5:30-10pm Tue, 11am-2pm & 5:30-10pm Wed-Sat, 11am-3pm Sun; Ⓜ Blue Line to Logan Square) Fat Rice won a Beard Award for its dishes, which are inspired by the flavors of Macau, a former Portuguese territory off China's coast. The unconventional food mixes Chinese, Portuguese, Indian and Southeast Asian influences. The namesake dish shows the spirit: a layered bowl of crisped jasmine rice, curried chicken, prawns, garlicky sausages, steamed clams, hard-boiled eggs and pickled chilies.

✖ Humboldt Park

★SPINNING J   BAKERY $
Map p322 (☑872-829-2793; www.spinningj.com; 1000 N California Ave; mains $9-12; ⊗7am-9pm Tue-Fri, 8am-9pm Sat & Sun; 🚌52) Retro-cute as can be, little Spinning J harks back to a 1950s soda fountain, with a line of counter stools and a smattering of booths where you can sip egg creams and malts made

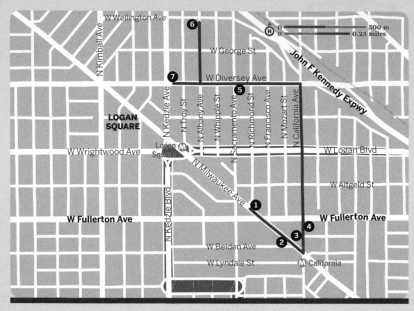

Local Life
A Night Out in Logan Square

Logan Square is the 'it' neighborhood for new and cool. But it's also refreshingly low-key, since it's somewhat off the beaten path. Art displays, Beard Award–winning kitchens and dive bars chock-full of local color dot the leafy boulevards. Try to arrive early in the evening to take advantage of the shops and galleries.

❶ Whistler

It's easy to walk right by the Whistler (p173). Its sign is unobtrusive, but the art in the window is not. The nifty space is part gallery and part venue for local indie bands, jazz combos and DJs. There's never a cover charge, but it's your job to buy a snazzy cocktail to fund the performances.

❷ Cole's

Who can resist a dimly lit dive bar with free entertainment? Not the neighborhood's young and thrifty. They pile in to Cole's (p172) to play pool and suck down microbrews in the neon-bathed front room, and to listen to bands and hoot at open-mike comedy on the back-room stage.

❸ Revolution Brewing

Revolution Brewing (p172) is always buzzing. It was one of the first breweries on the scene, and ever since it has served as the neighborhood clubhouse. The beers kick

butt, like the Anti-Hero IPA and berry-tinged Freedom of Press sour. Several are absurdly strong, so order the bacon-fat popcorn with fried sage to steady yourself.

❹ Pretty Cool Ice Cream

Vegans, kids, frozen-dairy fans and popsicle lovers all trod in for the novelties at **Pretty Cool Ice Cream** (Map p322; ☎773-697-4140; www.prettycoolicecream.com; 2353 N California Ave; ice-cream bars $3-5; ⊙11am-11pm May-Sep, reduced hours Oct-Apr; 🚲; Ⓜ Blue Line to California). There's something for everyone in addictive flavors like strawberry buttermilk, coffee pretzel toffee and matcha mint. No scoops though – all treats come on a stick.

❺ 6 Fat Rice

Tiny Fat Rice (p169), purveyor of Macanese cuisine, is crazy popular. It's been that way for a while, but after the chef won a James Beard Award in 2018 the furor picked

Fat Rice (p169)

with housemade syrups in flavors like Thai tea and bay rum cola. Classic sandwiches, hearty soups and sweet and savory pies also please the artsy-crafty patrons.

PAPA'S CACHE SABROSO   PUERTO RICAN $

Map p322 (☑773-862-8313; www.papascache. com; 2517 W Division St; mains $9-15; ⊙11am-9pm Mon-Thu, to 10pm Fri & Sat; ⧉70) Homey, family-run Papa's is a favorite of the local Puerto Rican community. Specialties are roasted chicken (as you can see from the birds slow-turning on spits) and *jibarito* sandwiches (garlic-mayo-slathered steak or chicken between slices of fried plantain 'bread'). The *jibarito* is a Chicago invention, and Papa's small, island-y cafe is a terrific place to try one. The restaurant will make a vegetarian version, with fried tomatoes and peppers, for those who don't eat meat. BYOB.

DONUT DELIGHT   BAKERY $

Map p322 (☑773-227-2105; www.facebook.com/donutdelightinc; 1750 N California Ave; doughnuts & sandwiches $2.25-6; ⊙10am-6:30pm Tue & Wed, 8am-6:30pm Thu-Sat, 8am-4pm Sun; ⧁Blue Line to California) The beauty of this little shop – besides the yummy, yeasty, perfectly sweet original glazed doughnuts – is its location right smack off the 606 trail (p153). Exit at California, head down the ramp, and you're there. Simple sandwiches, coffee drinks, smoothies and magazine-strewn tables also await. Hours can be erratic.

up even more. Hopefully you scored a reservation to chow on the Portuguese-Chinese-Indian food mash-up.

❻ Small Bar

Its ace jukebox, affordable food menu and kindly staff make this unpretentious little corner **bar** (Map p322; ☑773-509-9888; www.theoriginalsmallbar.com; 2956 N Albany Ave, Avondale; ⊙4pm-2am Mon-Fri, noon-2am Sat & Sun; ⧁Blue Line to Belmont) an easygoing place to spend an evening in the neighborhood. The mirror behind the bar dates back to 1907.

❼ Lost Lake

Lost Lake (p172) recreates a flawless South Seas vibe, and locals line up to get in on the tiki action. The bamboo decor, insane collection of rum and nationally acclaimed cocktails made with exotic ingredients are pure magic.

✖ Avondale

KUMA'S CORNER   BURGERS $

Map p322 (☑773-604-8769; www.kumas corner.com; 2900 W Belmont Ave; mains $14-17; ⊙11:15am-midnight Mon-Wed, to 1am Thu, to 2am Fri & Sat, 11:45am-midnight Sun; ⧉77) Ridiculously busy and head-bangingly loud, Kuma's attracts the tattooed set for its monster 10oz burgers, each named for a heavy-metal band and hefted onto a pretzel-roll bun. There's a vegan burger and mac 'n' cheese menu for those who don't eat meat, and beer and bourbon for all. Expect a line.

PARACHUTE   KOREAN $$$

Off Map p322 (☑773-654-1460; www.parachute restaurant.com; 3500 N Elston Ave; mains $22-32; ⊙5-10pm Tue-Thu, to 11pm Fri & Sat; ⧁Blue Line to Belmont) Michelin-starred Parachute puts an American spin on Korean street-food classics like mackerel and barbecued onion

LOGAN SQUARE & HUMBOLDT PARK EATING

bibimbap (mixed vegetables and rice). The ambience is like a dinner party in your friend's retro-cool kitchen. There are only 40 seats, so reserve ahead; you can do so 30 days in advance. Walk-ins fare best before 6pm.

🍷 DRINKING & NIGHTLIFE

Hipster dive bars, thriving microbreweries, gin lounges and tiki bars mix it up in this area's rich trove of boozers. Milwaukee Ave between the Logan Square and California L stations is richly layered. Armitage Ave near the intersection with Kedzie Ave also has several excellent bars.

🍸 Logan Square

LOST LAKE   COCKTAIL BAR
Map p322 (☑773-293-6048; www.lostlaketiki. com; 3154 W Diversey Ave; ☺5pm-2am Mon-Fri, 4pm-3am Sat, 4pm-2am Sun; ⓜBlue Line to Logan Square) Take a seat under the bamboo roof by the banana-leaf wallpaper inside this trendy tiki bar, and swirl a Mystery Gardenia or other tropical drink made from one of 275 rums behind the bar. Lost Lake has won many national accolades for its cocktails. Expect a wait.

SCOFFLAW   COCKTAIL BAR
Map p322 (☑773-252-9700; www.scofflaw chicago.com; 3201 W Armitage Ave; ☺5pm-2am Mon-Fri, 11am-3am Sat, 11am-2am Sun; ⓠ73) Scofflaw is a gin joint – literally. The bar specializes in boutique, small-batch gins mixed into gimlets, martinis and other cocktails that get creative with juniper. It's mostly a 30-something crowd sipping from mismatched glassware and relaxing in vintage French armchairs by the fireplace. That may sound preciously hipster, but the cozy bar's vibe is more rebellious thrift store.

REVOLUTION BREWING   BREWERY
Map p322 (☑773-227-2739; www.revbrew.com; 2323 N Milwaukee Ave; ☺11am-1am Mon-Fri, 10am-1am Sat, 10am-11pm Sun; ⓜBlue Line to California) Raise your fist to Revolution, an industrial-chic brewpub that fills glasses with heady beers such as the Eugene porter and Anti-Hero IPA. The brewmaster here led the way for Chicago's huge craft beer scene, and his suds are top-notch. Haute pub grub includes a pork belly and egg sandwich and bacon-fat popcorn with fried sage.

★COLE'S   BAR
Map p322 (☑773-276-5802; www.coleschicago. com; 2338 N Milwaukee Ave; ☺5pm-2am Mon-Fri, 4pm-3am Sat, 4pm-2am Sun; ⓜBlue Line to California) Cole's is a dive bar with nifty free entertainment. Young scenesters flock in to shoot pool and swill Midwest microbrews (Bell's, Two Brothers) in the front room. Then they head to the back-room stage where bands and DJs do their thing. On Wednesday the popular open-mike comedy takes over from 9:30pm.

MAPLEWOOD BREWERY & DISTILLERY   MICROBREWERY
Map p322 (☑773-270-1061; www.maplewood brew.com; 2717 N Maplewood Ave; ☺4pm-midnight Tue-Fri, noon-2am Sat, 11am-midnight Sun; ⓠ76) Maplewood looks sexier than most taprooms with its heavy chandeliers and high-back seats, but that doesn't deter bearded brewer types from lining up for American Beer Fest winners like Charlatan, a citrusy American pale ale, and Fat Pug, a roasty oatmeal stout. Maplewood also makes whiskey and gin, so there's a lengthy cocktail menu too, including many made with beer.

BILLY SUNDAY   COCKTAIL BAR
Map p322 (☑773-661-2485; www.billy-sunday. com; 3143 W Logan Blvd; ☺5pm-2am Mon-Fri, 5pm-3am Sat, 3pm-1am Sun; ⓜBlue Line to Logan Square) Classy cocktails are Billy's thing. Spiced kola nut, rhubarb sherbet and pineapple bitters are among the ingredients shaken and stirred into the high-end gins, bourbons and other booze. Old-timey portraits hang on the walls; sconces give the small room a warm glow.

🍸 Humboldt Park

ARCHIE'S IOWA ROCKWELL TAVERN   BAR
Map p322 (☑872-206-5119; 2600 W Iowa St; ☺2pm-2am Sun-Fri, to 3am Sat; ⓠ66) From the Hamm's beer sign over the door to shots of Malört (Chicago's infamous, vile-tasting liquor) and mounted fish on the wall, Archie's has all the hallmarks of a quintessential, old-school Chicago corner tavern. Put some Bob Seger on the jukebox and join the regulars enveloped in the room's neon glow for a game of pool or cards. Dogs welcome.

♟ Avondale

★METROPOLITAN
BREWING
MICROBREWERY

Map p322 (☑773-754-0494; www.metrobrewing.com; 3057 N Rockwell St; ☺4-10pm Mon, to 11pm Tue-Thu, to midnight Fri, noon-midnight Sat, noon-10pm Sun; ☑77) An elder of the local beer scene, Metropolitan has expanded into a striking, retrofitted old tannery overlooking the Chicago River. The floor-to-ceiling windows provide water views, while the tables made of salvaged wood provide a place to put your slew of German-style lagers.

LATE BAR
CLUB

Map p322 (☑773-267-5283; www.latebarchicago.com; 3534 W Belmont Ave; ☺10pm-4am Tue-Thu, 8pm-4am Fri, 8pm-5am Sat; ☑Blue Line to Belmont) Late Bar is off the beaten path on a forlorn stretch of Belmont Ave surrounded by auto-repair shops and Polish bars, though it's easy to get to via the L train. Two DJs opened the club, and its weird, new-wave vibe draws fans of all stripes: mods, hooligans, rockers, punks, goths and more. Saturday's Planet Earth alt/postpunk dance nights are popular.

☆ ENTERTAINMENT

★WHISTLER
LIVE MUSIC

Map p322 (☑773-227-3530; www.whistlerchicago.com; 2421 N Milwaukee Ave, Logan Square; ☺6pm-2am Mon-Thu, 5pm-2am Fri-Sun; ☑Blue Line to California) Hometown indie bands, jazz combos and DJs rock this wee, arty bar most nights. There's never a cover charge, but you'd be a schmuck if you didn't order at least one of the swanky cocktails or craft beers to keep the scene going.

★ROSA'S LOUNGE
BLUES

Map p322 (☑773-342-0452; www.rosaslounge.com; 3420 W Armitage Ave, Logan Square; tickets $10-20; ☺8pm-2am Tue-Sat; ☑73) Rosa's is an unadorned, real-deal blues club that brings in top local talent and dedicated fans to a somewhat derelict Logan Square block. Get ready to dance. At night a taxi or rideshare is probably the best way to get here.

PROP THTR
THEATER

Off Map p322 (☑773-742-5420; www.propthtr.org; 3502 N Elston Ave, Avondale; ☑Blue Line to Belmont) This long-running storefront venue presents original plays and fresh stage adaptations of literary works by writers from Nabokov to William S Burroughs. The well-executed productions are typically provocative and dark in theme. Prop also hosts the annual fringe Rhinoceros Theater Festival in February.

🛍 SHOPPING

Logan Square's and Humboldt Park's far-flung indie shops brim with hand-rolled truffles, stylish clothes, gender-neutral toys, letterpress stationery and vintage home goods.

★KATHERINE
ANNE CONFECTIONS
CHOCOLATE

Map p322 (☑773-245-1630; www.katherine-anne.com; 2745 W Armitage Ave, Logan Square; hot chocolate from $5; ☺11am-7pm Tue & Wed, to 9pm Thu & Fri, 10am-9pm Sat, 11am-5pm Sun; ☑Blue Line to California) Hot chocolate in unexpected flavors like tea and cookies and brown butter is the fan favorite at this shabby-chic boutique. While you await your elixir of choice, watch owner Katherine Duncan and her troop of hip chocolatiers roll truffles and stir up salted caramels in the open kitchen just beyond the register.

PEACH FUZZ
TOYS

Map p322 (☑312-785-1442; www.littlepeachfuzz.com; 1005 N California Ave, Humboldt Park; ☺10am-6pm Wed-Fri, 11am-6pm Sat & Sun; ☑52) This sunny, pastel-colored children's shop markets itself as inclusive. Browse the shelves for wood blocks, progressive children's books, kite-making kits, shark-design lunch boxes and other high-quality toys from around the world. Be sure to seek out the secret reading room with its rainbow ceiling.

WOLFBAIT & B-GIRLS
FASHION & ACCESSORIES

Map p322 (☑312-698-8685; www.wolfbaitchicago.com; 3131 W Logan Blvd, Logan Square; ☺10am-7pm Mon-Sat, to 4pm Sun; ☑Blue Line to Logan Square) Old ironing boards serve as display tables, and tape measures, scissors and other designers' tools hang from vintage hooks. You get that crafting feeling as soon as you walk in, and indeed, Wolfbait & B-girls sells the wares (dresses, handbags and jewelry) of local indie designers.

West Loop & Near West Side

GREEKTOWN | LITTLE ITALY | NEAR WEST SIDE | WEST LOOP

Neighborhood Top Five

1 **Starry food** (p182) Forking into a decadent meal by a celebrity chef at one of the district's mega-hot restaurants, like Stephanie Izard's Girl & the Goat.

2 **Fancy cocktails** (p186) Swirling a magical drink at the champagne bars, rooftop bars and distilleries that mix in the 'hood; Aviary is an exemplar of the genre.

3 **Greektown** (p179) Exploring the tavernas, bakeries and shops along Halsted St and indulging in flaming cheese, honeyed sweets and carafes of wine; Artopolis shows how it's done.

4 **Carrie Secrist Gallery** (p178) Wandering around the old warehouses to find art hubs such as this contemporary haven.

5 **Randolph Street Market** (p188) Browsing the monthly market for antiques and indie fashion, then lingering for the live bands and alfresco street party.

For more detail of this area see Map p324 ➡

Explore West Loop & Near West Side

Start in West Loop. It's akin to New York City's Meat-packing District, with chic restaurants, clubs and galleries inhabiting former meat-processing plants. By day it's a thriving business zone, where Google, McDonald's and other companies have shiny new complexes and hip young workers bustle amid latte shops. But by evening the area really shines, as people leave work and head for the haute eateries, swanky cocktail lounges and rooftop bars. Stroll along the main veins of W Randolph St and W Fulton Market (this core is also called the Fulton Market District). An evening meal or drink here is a must. The galleries and street art are the only sights.

The Near West Side includes the neighborhoods of Greektown (along Halsted St, steps from West Loop's hubbub) and Little Italy (along Taylor St, which is further flung). Neither has much in the way of sights, but gustatory tourists will revel in the delicious offerings during an afternoon or evening visit.

Local Life

➡ **Tube socks and tacos** Maxwell Street Market (p188) draws a local crowd of junk hounds and Mexican-street-food fans.

➡ **Pastrami for politicos** Chicago politicians get their sandwich fix at Manny's Deli (p180); listen in for good gossip.

➡ **Taylor Street treats** Little Italy's Sweet Maple Cafe (p179) and Scafuri Bakery (p179) are homey, family-run spots that keep residents coming back for more.

➡ **Lou Mitchell's** Yes, tourists flock here (p181), but it's also a place where a dedicated group of regulars linger at the counter to drink coffee and discuss life with the waitstaff.

Getting There & Away

➡ **L Train** Green, Pink Lines to Morgan or Clinton for West Loop; Blue Line to UIC-Halsted for Greektown; Pink Line to Polk or Blue Line to Racine for Little Italy.

➡ **Bus** For United Center (p187), buses 19 (game-day express) and 20 run along Madison St. Bus 8 travels along Halsted St through Greektown.

➡ **Taxi** West Loop and Greektown are only 1.25 miles west of the Loop, making them a fairly cheap ride. Cabs and rideshares are easy to hail in the neighborhoods.

➡ **Car** It can be tough to find parking in West Loop and Greektown, but valets abound. Street parking is pretty easy in Little Italy.

Lonely Planet's Top Tip

Check out the B_Line (http://blinechicago.com), a mile-long street art corridor that stretches along W Hubbard St between Halsted and Carpenter Sts. More than three dozen murals decorate the walls that flank the Metra train tracks here, including a sweet one of DJ Frankie Knuckles (the local who popularized house music).

✖ Best Places to Eat

➡ Girl & the Goat (p182)
➡ Lou Mitchell's (p181)
➡ Monteverde (p181)
➡ Publican Quality Meats (p181)
➡ Mario's Italian Lemonade (p179)

For reviews, see p178.➡

🍷 Best Places to Drink

➡ RM Champagne Salon (p185)
➡ CH Distillery (p185)
➡ Waydown (p186)
➡ Aviary (p186)
➡ Goose Island Fulton Street Brewery (p185)

For reviews, see p183.➡

🛍 Best Places to Shop

➡ Open Books (p187)
➡ Randolph Street Market (p188)
➡ Athenian Candle Co (p188)
➡ H Mart (p187)

For reviews, see p187.➡

WEST LOOP & NEAR WEST SIDE

Chicago Frontier – West Loop & Near West Side

In West Loop chic restaurants, clubs and galleries poke out between meat-processing plants left over from the area's industrial days, while in the Near West Side development continues as new buildings rise rapidly. This edgy and flashy neighborhood also provides its fair share of eating and drinking reasons for visiting.

1. Mary Bartelme Park (p178)

The Misting Gate entrance to the park features five offset, stainless-steel arches designed by Site Design Group.

2. Girl & the Goat (p182)

Stephanie Izard's flagship restaurant.

3. Haymarket Square (p178)

The *Haymarket Memorial*, by Mary Brøgger, marks the spot where the labor movement began.

4. Artopolis Bakery & Cafe (p179)

Enjoy Greek classics such as baklava while savoring a wine at the streetside bar.

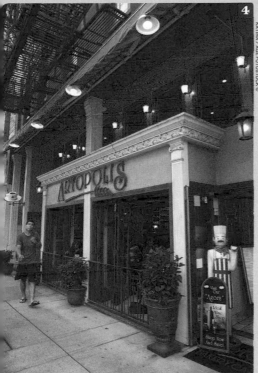

◉ SIGHTS

Several galleries (p180) pop up in West Loop, and the B_Line (p175) offers a swath of murals along the train tracks. Otherwise there's not much here for sightseeing.

KAVI GUPTA GALLERY   GALLERY

Map p324 (☑312-432-0708; www.kavigupta. com; 835 W Washington Blvd, 2nd fl, West Loop; ☺10am-6pm Tue-Fri, 11am-5pm Sat; Ⓜ Green, Pink Line to Morgan) Gupta represents contemporary, mid-career artists who work in various mediums, including painting, sculpture, collage and film. Intriguing new exhibitions take place every few months. Call to confirm the gallery is open before you visit, as it sometimes closes when a show is being installed. Three other galleries also occupy the building.

CARRIE SECRIST GALLERY   GALLERY

Map p324 (☑312-491-0917; www.secristgallery. com; 835 W Washington Blvd, 1st fl, West Loop; ☺10:30am-6pm Tue-Fri, 11am-5pm Sat; Ⓜ Green, Pink Line to Morgan) Secrist's contemporary gallery has been around for more than a quarter century. The big, open space hosts about six different exhibitions per year, both solo and group shows of provocative painters, photographers, filmmakers and artists working in other mediums. It's one of West Loop's coolest galleries. The building is also home to three other galleries.

MARS GALLERY   GALLERY

Map p324 (☑312-226-7808; www.marsgallery. com; 1139 W Fulton Market, West Loop; ☺noon-6pm Wed & Fri, to 7pm Thu, 11am-5pm Sat; Ⓜ Green, Pink Line to Morgan) This pop-art gallery is pure fun, from the colorful, cartoony prints and paintings to the building's offbeat history (it was an egg factory and then a club where the Ramones played). Weird bonus: it sits atop an energy vortex.

MARY BARTELME PARK   PARK

Map p324 (115 S Sangamon St, West Loop; Ⓜ Blue Line to UIC-Halsted) The neighborhood's stroller-pushing families and dog-walking hipsters get their exercise in Mary Bartelme Park. Five off-kilter stainless-steel arches form the gateway into the park; kids play in the mist the sculptures release in summer. Grassy mounds dot the park and provide good lookout points to view the Willis Tower rising in the distance.

The Green City farmers market sets up in the park on Saturday mornings from June through October and draws a big crowd.

OLD ST PATRICK'S CHURCH   CHURCH

Map p324 (☑312-648-1021; www.oldstpats. org; 700 W Adams St, West Loop; Ⓜ Blue Line to Clinton) A Chicago fire survivor, this 1852 church is one of the city's oldest. Old St Pat's is best known for its World's Largest Block Party, a weekend bash in late June with a solid lineup of big-name rock bands on stage. The event is famed for matchmaking: more than 100 couples have met in the crowd and eventually married.

Such social programs have certainly boosted Old St Pat's membership, which has gone from four (yes, four) in 1983 to thousands three decades later. The domed steeple signifies the Eastern Church; the spire signifies the Western Church. There's a beautifully restored Celtic-patterned interior.

HAYMARKET SQUARE   HISTORIC SITE

Map p324 (Desplaines St, btwn Lake & Randolph Sts, West Loop; Ⓜ Green, Pink Line to Clinton) The odd bronze statue of guys on a wagon marks the spot where the world's labor movement began. So the next time you take a lunch break or go home after your eight-hour workday, thank Haymarket Sq, which you're now standing upon. Striking factory workers held a meeting here on May 4, 1886. Bombs, deaths, anarchists and hangings ensued.

The statue is meant to depict the speaker's platform at the rally.

BATCOLUMN   SCULPTURE

Map p324 (600 W Madison St, West Loop; Ⓜ Green, Pink Line to Clinton) Artist Claes Oldenburg – known for his gigantic shuttlecocks in Kansas City and oversized cherry spoon in Minneapolis – delivered this 96ft, baseball-bat-like sculpture to Chicago in 1977. It stands in front of the Harold Washington Social Security Center.

✖ EATING

West Loop booms with celebrity-chef restaurants. Stroll along W Randolph St, W Lake St and W Fulton Market and take your pick: Michelin-starred eateries, foodie diners, Korean barbecue spots,

WORTH A DETOUR

GARFIELD PARK CONSERVATORY

Built in 1907, these **two acres** (Off Map p322; ☎773-638-1766; www.garfieldconservatory.org; 300 N Central Park Ave, East Garfield Park; ⊗9am-5pm Thu-Tue, to 8pm Wed; Ⓜ Green Line to Conservatory) FREE under glass are a lovely spot to while away a few hours sauntering around rooms of palms, ferns, orchids and koi-filled ponds. Between May and October the 10 acres of outdoor grounds are open, including the lily pool, a carnivorous plant bog and the Monet Garden, which is based on the impressionist painter's flower patch at Giverny, France. The Demonstration Garden shows urbanites how to grow veggies, keep bees and compost in city plots.

Kids can get dirty with roots and seeds in the indoor Children's Garden. Newer halls contain displays of seasonal plants that are especially spectacular in the weeks before Easter.

Garfield Park is about four L stops west of West Loop. The L station is a stone's throw from the conservatory's front door. If you drive, lock up: the surrounding neighborhood isn't the safest.

European-style bistros. **Greektown extends along S Halsted St, Little Italy along Taylor St.**

✖ Greektown

MELI CAFE
BREAKFAST $

Map p324 (☎312-454-0748; www.melicafe.com; 301 S Halsted St; mains $12-16; ⊗7am-3pm; Ⓜ Blue Line to UIC-Halsted) Meli is the Greek word for 'honey,' and it's apt for this sweet breakfast spot. Cage-free eggs served over a bed of potatoes, spinach-and-feta omelets, seasonal berry crepes and the decadent French toast (made from challah bread dipped in vanilla-bean custard) start the day off right. Meli has a few outposts around town.

ARTOPOLIS BAKERY & CAFE
GREEK $

Map p324 (☎312-559-9000; www.artopolischicago.com; 306 S Halsted St; mains $10-18; ⊗8:30am-11pm Sun-Thu, to 12:30am Fri & Sat; Ⓜ Blue Line to UIC-Halsted) Artopolis is one of the city's top bakeries – many of the nearby Randolph St restaurants get their bread here, and locals often pop in to ogle the pastries glistening in the cases. It's also a cafe-bar that opens onto the street, with wine-laden tables along the front. Wood-fired pizzas, spinach-and-feta pies and roasted chicken top the menu.

MR GREEK GYROS
GREEK $

Map p324 (☎312-906-8731; www.mrgreekgyros.com; 234 S Halsted St; mains $6-12; ⊗8am-4am; Ⓜ Blue Line to UIC-Halsted) 'The Mr' is a classic gyros joint. While the fluorescent lighting and plastic decor may lack charm, the gyros have a beauty of their own. Carnivores: this is definitely your place in the 'hood for late-night eats, as the UIC students and club go-ers will attest.

✖ Little Italy

SWEET MAPLE CAFE
AMERICAN $

Map p324 (☎312-243-8908; www.sweetmaplecafe.com; 1339 W Taylor St; mains $10-14; ⊗7am-2pm; Ⓜ Blue Line to Racine) The creaking floorboards, matronly staff and soulful home cookin' lend the Sweet Maple Cafe the bucolic appeal of a Southern roadside diner. The signature dishes – inch-thick banana (or, seasonally, peaches and cream) pancakes, cheddar grits and fluffy biscuits that come smothered in spicy sausage gravy – earn the superlatives of locals.

The egg dishes, sturdy muffins and lunch sandwiches are done with equal aplomb.

MARIO'S ITALIAN LEMONADE
DESSERTS $

Map p324 (☎312-201-6760; www.mariositalianlemonade.com; 1068 W Taylor St; cups $2-5; ⊗10am-midnight May-Sep; Ⓜ Blue Line to Racine) At this cheerful box of a shop, super Italian ice comes loaded with big chunks of fresh fruit, which keeps crowds lining up throughout the summer. The owners have been serving the slushy goodness-in-a-cup for a half-century. Lemon tops the list.

SCAFURI BAKERY
BAKERY $

Map p324 (☎312-733-8881; www.scafuribakery.com; 1337 W Taylor St; baked goods $2-4, sandwiches $7; ⊗7am-4pm Tue-Sun; Ⓜ Blue Line to

WEST LOOP GALLERIES

West Loop is Chicago's stronghold for edgy, contemporary art that earns international acclaim. Most galleries are well established. See www.chicagogallerynews.com for listings. Favorites include:

Carrie Secrist Gallery (p178) More than 25 years of provocative solo and group shows in a cavernous space.

Mars Gallery (p178) Pop art in a cheery loft that sits on top of an energy vortex.

Kavi Gupta Gallery (p178) Ambitious exhibitions across mediums that sometimes spill over to the satellite warehouse.

Racine) Exposed brick walls and sepia-hued family photos lend a cozy atmosphere to this spot, the second coming of a bakery that occupied this Little Italy address for more than a century. Revived by the founder's great-grandniece in 2013, the bakery today offers southern Italian classics such as pine-nut cookies and freshly filled cannoli alongside all-American treats like apple-cider doughnuts.

AL'S #1 ITALIAN BEEF   SANDWICHES $

Map p324 (☑312-226-4017; www.alsbeef.com; 1079 W Taylor St; mains $6-10; ☺9am-11pm Mon-Thu, to midnight Fri, 10am-midnight Sat; ⓂBlue Line to Racine) Piled high with savory beef that soaks through the thick bun, Al's sandwich is one of Chicago's culinary hallmarks. This is the original location of the local chain, which has now spread beyond the city. Note there's not much seating at the no-frills joint – just a handful of counter stools, plus a few outdoor seats in warm weather. Cash only.

TUFANO'S VERNON PARK TAP   ITALIAN $$

Map p324 (☑312-733-3393; www.tufanos restaurant.com; 1073 W Vernon Park Pl; mains $12-23; ☺11am-9:30pm Tue-Thu, to 10:30pm Fri, 4-10:30pm Sat, 3-9pm Sun; ⓂBlue Line to Racine) A family-run classic on a leafy residential street, Tufano's serves old-school Italian fare for modest prices. Blackboards carry a long list of daily specials, say, pasta with garlic-crusted broccoli or lemon chicken. Amid the celebrity photos on the wall you'll see lovely shots of owner Joey DiBuono, his family and their patrons through the decades since 1930. Cash only.

CHEZ JOEL   FRENCH $$$

Map p324 (☑312-226-6479; www.chezjoelbistro. com; 1119 W Taylor St; mains $21-28; ☺11:30am-9pm Tue-Thu, to 10pm Fri, 4-10pm Sat, 3-9pm Sun;

ⓂBlue Line to Racine) Whether you're dining outside under the oak tree or tucked in a cozy corner inside, the atmosphere and exceptional French fare make Chez Joel a romantic favorite, though an odd duck among this predominantly Italian stretch of Taylor St. The menu is anchored by bistro favorites including duck leg confit and coq au vin, complemented by an extensive wine list.

ROSEBUD   ITALIAN $$$

Map p324 (☑312-942-1117; www.rosebud restaurants.com; 1500 W Taylor St; mains $24-36; ☺11am-10:30pm Mon-Thu, to 11:30pm Fri, noon-11:30pm Sat, noon-10pm Sun; ⓂPink Line to Polk) This location in Little Italy is the first branch of an empire of quality Italian restaurants that has spread throughout the city. It is popular with politicos and old-school Taylor St Italians, who slurp down colossal piles of pasta and chicken Parmesan soaked in red sauces. Bring a big appetite.

✖ Near West Side

MANNY'S DELI   DELI $$

Map p324 (☑312-939-2855; www.mannysdeli. com; 1141 S Jefferson St; mains $11-18; ☺7am-3pm Mon, 7am-8pm Tue-Sat, 8am-3pm Sun; ⓂBlue Line to Clinton) Chicago's politicos and seen-it-all senior citizens get in the cafeteria-style line at Manny's for the towering pastrami and corned-beef sandwiches, matzo-ball soup, potato pancakes and other deli staples. Know what you want before you join the fast-moving queue.

The newspaper clippings on the wall provide a dose of city history – or you could just eavesdrop on the table next to you to hear deals being brokered that could be tomorrow's front-page story.

✕ West Loop

★LOU MITCHELL'S
BREAKFAST $

Map p324 (☑312-939-3111; www.loumitchells.com; 565 W Jackson Blvd; mains $9-14; ☺5:30am-3pm Mon, to 4pm Tue-Fri, 7am-4pm Sat, to 3pm Sun; ♿; ⓂBlue Line to Clinton) A relic of Route 66, Lou's brings in elbow-to-elbow locals and tourists for breakfast. The old-school waitstaff deliver big fluffy omelets and thick-cut French toast with a jug of syrup. They call you 'honey' and fill your coffee cup endlessly. There's often a queue to get in, but free doughnut holes and Milk Duds help ease the wait.

PUBLICAN QUALITY MEATS
DELI $

Map p324 (☑312-445-8977; www.publican qualitymeats.com; 825 W Fulton Market; mains $11-14; ☺10am-5pm Mon-Fri, 9am-6pm Sat, 9am-5pm Sun; ⓂGreen, Pink Line to Morgan) This butcher shop and 32-seat eatery is the casual, cheaper sibling to nearby Publican (p183). Grab a seat at a table in back and bite into a sandwich of delicately cured meat on just-baked bread. The lineup changes weekly, but might include the beefy meatball sandwich or thick-cut bacon, lettuce and tomato on sourdough. Also a tidy beer and wine list.

In summer the crowd spills out to streetside tables. Before leaving, browse the shelves of locally made condiments and spice mixes – great gifts for foodies.

GUS'S WORLD FAMOUS FRIED CHICKEN
SOUTHERN US $

Map p324 (☑312-733-1971; www.gusfried chicken.com; 847 W Fulton Market; mains $9-16; ☺11am-10pm Mon-Thu, to 11pm Fri & Sat, to 9pm Sun; ⓂGreen, Pink Line to Morgan) Sometimes you don't want a fancy-pants tasting menu or Tasmanian pepperberry cocktail in West Loop. Sometimes you just want fried chicken, mac 'n' cheese and a cold brew. In that case, Gus's is your place, where plastic plates hit the checker-clothed tables stacked with the light and crunchy, tender-juicy, hint-of-heat signature bird.

BONCI
PIZZA $

Map p324 (☑312-243-4016; https://bonciusa.com; 161 N Sangamon St; pizza per lb from $10; ☺11am-10pm Mon-Thu, to 11pm Fri & Sat, to 9pm Sun; ⓂGreen, Pink Line to Morgan) Chicago scored a major coup when it landed the first outpost of dough deity Gabriele Bonci's be-loved Roman pizzeria. Each day the diminutive shop bakes around a dozen of Bonci's 100-plus recipes, featuring unorthodox toppings such as spicy eggplant. Amiable staff lop long slices from your pie of choice with scissors, and calculate your tab based on the pizza's weight.

WISHBONE
SOUTHERN US $

Map p324 (☑312-850-2663; www.wishbone chicago.com; 161 N Jefferson St; mains $10-17; ☺7am-3pm Mon & Tue, to 9pm Wed & Thu, to 10pm Fri, 8am-10pm Sat, 8am-3:30pm Sun; ⓂGreen, Pink Line to Clinton) They call it 'Southern reconstruction cooking,' which means items such as corn muffins, cheese grits, fried chicken, buttermilk rolls and crawfish patties top the tables. It's a folksy, down-home, gravy-laden kind of place. Wacky chicken and egg artwork splashes across the walls in the lofty room. Weekend brunch is a big event.

★MONTEVERDE
ITALIAN $$

Map p324 (☑312-888-3041; www.monteverde chicago.com; 1020 W Madison St; mains $18-24; ☺5-10:30pm Tue-Fri, 11:30am-10:30pm Sat, 11:30am-9pm Sun; ⓂGreen, Pink Line to Morgan) Housemade pastas are the specialty here. They seem simple in concept, such as the *cacio whey pepe* (small tube pasta with pecorino Romano, ricotta whey and four-peppercorn blend), but the flavors are lusciously complex. That's why the light-wood tables in the lively room are always packed. Reserve ahead, especially for weekends, or try the bar or patio for walk-in seats.

AU CHEVAL
AMERICAN $$

Map p324 (☑312-929-4580; www.aucheval chicago.com; 800 W Randolph St; mains $13-19; ☺10am-1am Mon-Sat, 9am-midnight Sun; ⓂGreen, Pink Line to Morgan) People go crazy over Au Cheval's cheeseburger. It drips with a runny fried egg, melty cheddar and tangy dijonnaise, all stuffed into a super-fluffy bun. *Bon Appetit* crowned it America's best burger, and the little diner has been mobbed since. No reservations, so prepare to wait (best done at the neighboring bar; staff will text when your table is ready).

LITTLE GOAT
DINER $$

Map p324 (☑312-888-3455; www.littlegoat chicago.com; 820 W Randolph St; mains $13-20; ☺7am-10pm Sun-Thu, to midnight Fri & Sat; 🔊☑; ⓂGreen, Pink Line to Morgan) *Top Chef* winner Stephanie Izard opened this diner for the foodie masses across the street from her ever-booked main restaurant, Girl & the Goat. Scooch into a vintage booth and order off the all-day breakfast menu. Better yet, try lunch and dinner favorites like the goat sloppy joe with rosemary slaw or pork belly on scallion pancakes. Izard's flavor combinations rule. Heavenly smelling bread baked on-site and bottomless cups of strong coffee add to the awesomeness. It's wise to reserve ahead.

AVEC
MEDITERRANEAN $$

Map p324 (📞312-377-2002; www.avecrestaurant. com; 615 W Randolph St; mains $18-28; ⊘11:30am-2pm & 3:30-11pm Mon-Thu, 11:30am-2pm & 3:30pm-midnight Fri, 3:30pm-midnight Sat, 10am-2pm & 3:30-11pm Sun; Ⓜ Green, Pink Line to Clinton) Feeling social? This happening spot gives diners a chance to rub elbows at eight-person communal tables. The mini room looks like a Finnish sauna and fills with noisy chatter as stylish urbanites pile in. The bacon-wrapped dates are the menu's must-try; the paella and the sausage and mint-pesto calzone are other standouts, though the menu changes regularly.

Reservations are a good idea, but they're only taken during off-peak hours.

DUCK DUCK GOAT
CHINESE $$

Map p324 (📞312-902-3825; www.duckduck goatchicago.com; 857 W Fulton Market; mains $16-27; ⊘5-10pm Mon-Thu, 4:30-11pm Fri, 11am-11pm Sat, 11am-10pm Sun; Ⓜ Green, Pink Line to Morgan) This is the third West Loop hot spot helmed by star local chef Stephanie Izard, and it focuses on Chinese-inspired dishes. The vast menu sprawls across dim sums, soups, fried rice and main dishes. The thick, doughy, housemade noodles and Peking duck win raves. Eclectic cocktails like the Shanghai-Biscus, made with tequila and hibiscus syrup, add to the remarkable flavors.

The space is divided into several small dining rooms; a different East-meets-West vibe pervades each. A takeout window on the Peoria St side of the restaurant serves up Taiwanese desserts and street food in summer.

SAINT LOU'S ASSEMBLY
AMERICAN $$

Map p324 (📞312-600-0600; www.saintlous chicago.com; 664 W Lake St; mains $16-20; ⊘11am-3pm & 5pm-midnight Mon-Thu, to 2am Fri, 9am-2am Sat, 9am-midnight Sun; Ⓜ Green, Pink Line to Clinton) Casual Lou's pays homage to the area's meatpacking past, when 'meat and three' cafeterias – where you'd select a meaty main dish and three sides – were popular. This is the modern version, so take a seat in a retro blue-vinyl booth and choose among Peruvian-style chicken, chili-marinated sirloin steak, kimchi and collard greens, and other modern takes on nostalgic fare.

Cocktails, craft beers and booze-spiked ice-cream floats accompany the wares. The back patio and its boccie court see lots of action when the weather warms.

BAD HUNTER
AMERICAN $$

Map p324 (📞312-265-1745; http://badhunter. com; 802 W Randolph St; mains $13-20; ⊘11am-10:30pm Mon-Thu, to 11:30pm Fri, 10am-11:30pm Sat, 10am-10:30pm Sun; 🍴; Ⓜ Green Line to Morgan Station) 🍴 Bad Hunter describes itself as 'vegetable-focused,' so vegetarians will find plenty to sink their teeth into, such as buttery squash dumplings with candied hazelnuts and eggplant-and-fig pasta (though the menu changes seasonally). The flavors are bright and unique, and it's pretty upscale for vegetarian food in Chicago.

Note the menu isn't exclusively meat free: a handful of fish, chicken and beef dishes also emerge from the kitchen.

★GIRL & THE GOAT
AMERICAN $$$

Map p324 (📞312-492-6262; www.girlandthe goat.com; 809 W Randolph St; small plates $12-19; ⊘4:30-11pm Sun-Thu, to midnight Fri & Sat; 🍴; Ⓜ Green, Pink Line to Morgan) 🍴 Stephanie Izard's flagship restaurant rocks. The soaring ceilings, polished wood tables and cartoony art on the walls offer a convivial atmosphere where local beer and housemade wine hit the tables, along with unique small plates such as catfish with pickled persimmons. Reservations are difficult; try for walk-in seats before 5pm or see if anything opens up at the bar.

Goat dishes figure prominently, of course; Izard buys her signature meat from a local farm. If you can't get a seat here try Little Goat (p181), Izard's casual diner across the road.

SMYTH
AMERICAN $$$

Map p324 (📞773-913-3773; www.smythandthe loyalist.com; 177 N Ada St; tasting menus $95-225; ⊘5-10pm Tue-Sat; Ⓜ Green, Pink Line to Ashland) Smyth is a homey spot that's bagged a pair of Michelin stars for its seasonal tasting menus. Prepare to spend two to three hours making your way through five to 12 courses of elevated comfort food, say biscuits with ramp honey or lamb with juniper. Ingredients come from Smyth's partner farm, located about an hour south of the city. Reservations required.

Smyth is upstairs. The chef-owners also operate the casual, pub-like Loyalist in the basement. It's hailed for its burger, a fat patty with American cheese and pickled cucumbers on a toasted sesame seed bun, and its desserts, such as the hazelnut praline puff.

ROISTER   AMERICAN **$$$**
Map p324 (www.roisterrestaurant.com; 951 W Fulton Market; mains $24-34; ☺5-9pm Mon-Thu, 10am-2pm & 5-10pm Fri-Sun; Ⓜ Green, Pink Line to Morgan) Eat creations by molecular gastronomist Grant Achatz, the chef of three-Michelin-star Alinea (p104), on the (relative) cheap at Roister. The restaurant cooks wild riffs on comfort foods while a rip-roaring soundtrack blasts. Dishes change and defy easy description – like the 'whole chicken' served with thighs fried, breast roasted and the rest melded into a chicken salad – but they're all rich and playful. Reserve ahead.

BLACKBIRD   AMERICAN **$$$**
Map p324 (✆312-715-0708; www.blackbird restaurant.com; 619 W Randolph St; mains $33-42; ☺11am-2pm & 5-10pm Mon-Thu, 11am-2pm & 5-11pm Fri, 5-11pm Sat, 5-10pm Sun; Ⓜ Green, Pink Line to Clinton) ✐ This buzzy destination for Chicago's young and trendy perches atop best-of lists for its exciting, seasonal menu. The warm-ups – like cauliflower soup and poached lobster with black truffles – are a perfect introduction to the visionary mains, which pair well with the short, careful wine list. The best comes last: award-winning desserts à la chestnut cheesecake and roasted-cocoa-nib ice cream.

The chef offers a tasting menu (around 10 courses) from $140, and there's a three-course prix-fixe lunch for $25, which is a total steal. Reserve ahead.

NEXT   INTERNATIONAL **$$$**
Map p324 (✆312-226-0858; www.nextrestaurant. com; 953 W Fulton Market; multicourse menu from $225; ☺5-11:30pm Wed-Sun; Ⓜ Green, Pink Line to Morgan) Grant Achatz' West Loop restaurant remains one of the hottest tickets in town. And we mean it literally – you need a ticket to dine at Next, which operates like

a time machine. It started by serving an eight-course French meal from 1906 Paris, but every three months the whole thing changes: new era, new country, new menu, new decor.

Sign up for tickets at the website as early as possible. Prices vary by date, time and menu (early weekdays cost less than prime-time weekends), and you pay when you book. Check the Facebook feed for possible last-minute seats.

PUBLICAN   AMERICAN **$$$**
Map p324 (✆312-733-9555; www.thepublican restaurant.com; 837 W Fulton Market; mains $21-30; ☺3:30-10pm Mon-Thu, to 11pm Fri, 10am-11pm Sat, 9am-10pm Sun; Ⓜ Green, Pink Line to Morgan) ✐ Set up like a swanky beer hall with urbanites young and old sitting across from each other at long communal tables, Publican specializes in oysters, hams and fine suds – all from small family farms and microbrewers. So you'll know your pork shoulder is from Dyersville, Iowa; your orange-honey turnips from Congerville, Illinois; and your oysters from Bagaduce River, Maine.

Many locals think the weekend brunch is the best around – Publican does indeed know its bacon.

🍷 DRINKING & NIGHTLIFE

Fancy cocktails are West Loop's calling card. Distilleries, wine bars and coffee shops that take their lattes seriously also add to the scene. Most places hover around Randolph, Lake and Fulton Market streets. Further flung in the Near West Side's industrial landscape is a smattering of breweries.

💡 Near West Side

RHINE HALL DISTILLERY   DISTILLERY
Map p324 (✆312-243-4313; www.rhinehall. com; 2010 W Fulton St, ☺5-9pm Wed-Fri, 2-7pm Sat; Ⓜ Green, Pink Line to Ashland) A father-daughter team operates this cute-as-a-button distillery that specializes in fruit brandies. They source the apples, cherries, plums and other ingredients from the Great Lakes region. Sample the unusual wares in

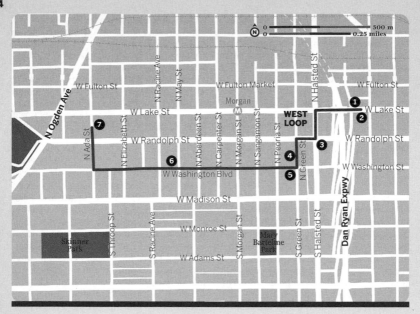

🏃 Local Life
West Loop Wander

West Loop has exploded in recent years with hotshot restaurants and condos carved from old meatpacking warehouses. While a few bloody-apron-clad workers remain, these days you're more likely to run into a Google employee toting a latte as you traverse the galleries and mega-stylish eateries inhabiting the industrial buildings.

❶ Saint Lou's Assembly

Saint Lou's Assembly (p182) draws a crowd for its 'meat and three' meals. The concept harks back to West Loop's factory past, when cafeterias served the combination to workers. Lou's offers a modern version of the meat main and three side dishes, along with cocktails and a rollicking patio with a boccie court.

❷ Open Books

Thrifty hipsters in need of a good read browse the gently used stacks at Open Books (p187). Hours slip by as they scan shelves that hold *Little House on the Prairie* next to Gwyneth Paltrow's latest cookbook next to a 1987 guidebook to Alaska. All proceeds go toward the nonprofit shop's literacy programs for local kids.

❸ Haymarket Pub & Brewery

Haymarket Pub & Brewery (p186) provides a nice dose of local history. It's located near where the 1886 Haymarket labor riot took place, and the brewery's suds often have affiliated names, such as the Mathias Imperial IPA (named after the first police officer to die in the melee) and the Speakerswagon Pilsner.

❹ Sawada Coffee

West Loop workers at Google, Uber and the district's other tech companies need to stay caffeinated, and Sawada Coffee (p186) provides the requisite lattes. The signature one is made with matcha (green tea powder) and poured exquisitely. Sawada's wi-fi, epicurean doughnuts and rustic-chic interior invite lingering.

Matcha latte, Sawada Coffee (p186)

⑤ Carrie Secrist Gallery

See what's showing at Carrie Secrist Gallery (p178). She has been organizing heady exhibitions of contemporary works for more than 25 years. Three other galleries share the building, so you can really dive into the local art scene.

⑥ Press Room

Follow the green neon 'Down for a Drink' sign to the Press Room (p186). The European-style wine bar is a convivial gathering spot for neighborhood dwellers. Join them for a glass of cava and plate of Spanish anchovies. It's located in the basement of a century-old publishing house, hence the name.

⑦ Smyth

It's totally worth it to reserve ahead and sink your teeth into the Michelin-starred tasting menu at Smyth (p182). But you have options if you don't get in. Smyth's sister restaurant the Loyalist sits in the basement, a neighborhood favorite for its mighty cheeseburger and rich desserts.

flights or cocktails in the minimalist little tasting room, or take a 45-minute tour (per person $10).

It's well off the beaten path in an industrial corridor, but super friendly and worth seeking out.

GOOSE ISLAND FULTON
STREET BREWERY   BREWERY

Map p324 (www.gooseisland.com; 1800 W Fulton St; ⊙2-8pm Wed & Thu, 2-9pm Fri, noon-9pm Sat, noon-6pm Sun; Ⓜ Green, Pink Line to Ashland) Goose Island – Chicago's first craft brewer, launched in 1988 – is now owned by Anheuser-Busch InBev, so technically it's no longer a craft brewer. But it still acts like one, making excellent small-batch beers at this facility. The swanky mod-industrial taproom pours 20 or so varieties; sample them via four-beer flights. Hour-long tours ($12) are available if you reserve in advance.

The bourbon-barrel-aged stouts have lots of starry-eyed devotees. The taproom doesn't serve food, but often food trucks are on-site or you can bring in food from neighborhood restaurants.

🍷 West Loop

★CH DISTILLERY   DISTILLERY

Map p324 (🖉312-707-8780; www.chdistillery. com; 564 W Randolph St; ⊙4-10pm Mon-Thu, to midnight Fri & Sat; Ⓜ Green, Pink Line to Clinton) This slick tasting room has a cool, naturalistic look with exposed concrete posts and knotty wood beams across the ceiling. Slip into a seat at the bar and watch the silver tanks behind the big glass window distilling the organic vodka and gin that go into your creative cocktail.

It's relatively small inside, and stylish workmates and couples tend to linger over charcuterie and cheese plates, so you might want to book ahead. Tours (per person $15) are available Saturday at 5:30pm and include a vodka drink.

CH also makes aquavit, amaro, coffee liqueur and Malört (Chicago's indigenous liquor that's famous for tasting awful). Most of it is produced at CH's larger production facility in Pilsen.

★RM CHAMPAGNE SALON   WINE BAR

Map p324 (🖉312-243-1199; www.rmchampagne salon.com; 116 N Green St; ⊙5pm-midnight Mon-Wed & Sun, 5pm-2am Thu-Sat, plus 11am-2pm Sat & Sun; Ⓜ Green, Pink Line to Morgan) This West

Loop spot is a twinkling-light charmer for bubbles. Score a table in the cobblestoned courtyard and you'll feel transported to Paris. In winter, the indoor fireplace and plush seats provide a toasty refuge.

WAYDOWN
ROOFTOP BAR

Map p324 (☎312-764-1919; www.acehotel.com; 311 N Morgan St, 7th fl; ⊙4pm-2am Mon-Fri, from 3pm Sat & Sun; Ⓜ Green, Pink Line to Morgan) The Ace Hotel's (p241) rooftop bar wins praise for several reasons. It provides terrific skyline views. It draws a superstylish crowd, but there's no velvet rope attitude. And it makes lovely cocktails with seasonal juices, vermouths and mezcals that aren't that pricey considering the neighborhood. Bands or DJs provide the soundtrack most nights.

On weekdays, enter via the hotel lobby and take the elevator up. On weekends enter through the door on the building's north side in the loading dock area.

AVIARY
COCKTAIL BAR

Map p324 (www.theaviary.com; 955 W Fulton Market; ⊙5pm-midnight Sun-Wed, to 2am Thu-Sat; Ⓜ Green, Pink Line to Morgan) The Aviary is a James Beard Award winner for best cocktails in the nation. The ethereal drinks are like nothing you've laid lips on before. Some arrive with Bunsen burners, others with a slingshot you use to break the ice. They taste terrific, whatever the science involved. It's wise to make reservations online. Drinks range between $21 and $29 each.

Various tasting menus let you sample the wares; some come with avant-garde, small-plate food pairings. The man behind the scene is Grant Achatz. Aviary sits beside his hot restaurant Next (p183), though the bar is more in spirit (pun!) with his Lincoln Park restaurant, Alinea (p104). Note the bar's entrance is actually on Morgan St.

PRESS ROOM
WINE BAR

Map p324 (☎331-240-1914; www.pressroomchicago.com; 1134 W Washington Blvd; ⊙4pm-midnight Mon-Sat; Ⓜ Green, Pink Line to Morgan) Groups of friends and couples on dates descend to the Press Room's snug basement digs to chitchat at candlelit tables over glasses of red, white and sparkling wines. More than 20 are available by the glass, along with a small cocktail and beer menu. The tranquil vibe is unusual – and much appreciated – in buzzing West Loop.

SAWADA COFFEE
COFFEE

Map p324 (☎312-754-0431; http://sawadacoffee.com; 112 N Green St; ⊙8am-5pm; 📶; Ⓜ Green, Pink Line to Morgan) This edgy coffee bar is somewhat disguised, tucked in a graffitied building (sharing a space with Green Street Smoked Meats). Prolific Chicago restaurateur Brendan Sodikoff collaborated with Japanese latte artist Hiroshi Sawada to serve espresso-based drinks and booze-spiked steamers, plus Sodikoff's popular Doughnut Vault doughnuts. The military latte, with green tea and cocoa powder, will fuel your day.

CRUZ BLANCA
MICROBREWERY

Map p324 (☎312-733-1975; www.cruzblanca.com; 904 W Randolph St; ⊙11am-midnight Tue-Fri, 10am-midnight Sat, 10am-9pm Sun; Ⓜ Green, Pink Line to Morgan) Revered chef Rick Bayless opened this quirky West Loop brewery inspired by beers people were drinking in Mexico City in the 1860s. Quaff fanciful renditions of German doppelbocks, Vienna lagers, wheat beers and wild-fermented sour beers. There are 12 brews on tap and several creative seasonal cocktails (heavy on tequila), as well as a small menu of foodie tacos.

HAYMARKET PUB & BREWERY
BREWERY

Map p324 (☎312-638-0700; www.haymarketbeer.com; 737 W Randolph St; ⊙11am-2am Sun-Fri, to 3am Sat; Ⓜ Green, Pink Line to Clinton) An early arrival on the West Loop scene, Haymarket remains nicely low-key. It doesn't try to win you over with uberhipness like many of its neighbors. Locals hang out in the cavernous, barrel-strewn space drinking fresh-from-the-tank recipes. The focus is on classic Belgian and German styles, but saisons, IPAs and barrel-aged barley wines fill glasses, too.

Five-beer flights let you sample among the 20-plus brews on offer, alongside house-made sausages, burgers and pizzas. Bands sometimes play later in the week. The brewery sits near Haymarket Square (p178), the historic labor riot site; hence the name.

CITY WINERY
WINE BAR

Map p324 (☎312-733-9463; www.citywinery.com; 1200 W Randolph St; ⊙11am-midnight; Ⓜ Green, Pink Line to Morgan) City Winery pours on the grape theme, with casks and tanks of wine everywhere you look. It's very Sonoma decor-wise, with a vine-strewn, open-air patio and exposed blond brick in the airy interior rooms. The menu sprawls through 400 reds and whites, including several housemade vintages that are on tap. Can't decide? Try a flight.

The winery also has a small theater that books well-known singer-songwriter types.

JOHNNY'S ICE HOUSE EAST SPORTS BAR

Map p324 (☑312-226-5555; www.johnnys icehouse.com; 1350 W Madison St; ⏱8pm-midnight; ⓜGreen, Pink Line to Ashland) Johnny's is an ice rink, which explains why you can practically see your breath in the upstairs bar. The wood-paneled, neon-lit room is prime for watching Blackhawks games and knocking back Labatts (Johnny's is supposedly the state's biggest seller of the beer). Hours can be erratic.

☆ ENTERTAINMENT

CHICAGO CHILDREN'S THEATRE THEATER

Map p324 (CCT; ☑773-227-0180; www.chicago childrenstheatre.org; 100 S Racine Ave, West Loop; tickets $22-40; ⓜBlue Line to Racine) CCT is dedicated exclusively to putting on quality productions for young audiences. Many plays are adapted from children's books, and many use puppets or music. The season usually consists of five productions that are a mix of world premieres and classics. Shows take place in the group's spiffy new facility known as the Station.

MB ICE ARENA ICE HOCKEY

Map p324 (☑312-455-7600; www.mbicearena. com; 1801 W Jackson Blvd, Near West Side; ⏱6am-2am; ⓜBlue Line to Illinois Medical District) Calling all ice hockey fans: this shiny arena, a stone's throw from United Center, is where the Blackhawks practice. You can watch the sessions for free. They're usually in the morning at 10am or 11am; check the website for the schedule. The rink also holds public skating sessions; skate rentals cost $4 per pair.

HOUSE OF VANS CONCERT VENUE

Map p324 (☑312-733-5270; www.houseofvans. com; 113 N Elizabeth St, West Loop; ⓜGreen, Pink Line to Morgan) Skateboard apparel maker Vans holds special events such as concerts and films in its West Loop warehouse. There's an indoor skate park for lessons and open skateboarding sessions. You need to RSVP online in advance for all events.

UNITED CENTER STADIUM

Map p324 (☑312-455-4500; www.unitedcenter. com; 1901 W Madison St, Near West Side; ⓠ19 or 20) This busy facility is Chicago's arena for big-name concerts and sporting events. The pro-hockey team the Blackhawks (www. nhl.com/blackhawks) and pro-basketball team the Bulls (www.nba.com/bulls) both play here from October through April. The slam-dunking Michael Jordan statue is a famed photo op; it's in the glass atrium on the building's eastern side.

The atrium also holds the box office, a cool Blackhawks/Bulls team shop and a couple of bars. On game days, there's a special express bus (bus 19) on Madison St that heads to the stadium.

🔒 SHOPPING

Chicago's two main markets are here. Big grocery chains hover around Halsted St. Interesting indie shops are few and far between.

★OPEN BOOKS BOOKS

Map p324 (☑312-475-1355; www.open-books.org; 651 W Lake St, West Loop; ⏱9am-7pm Mon-Sat, noon-6pm Sun; ♿; ⓜGreen, Pink Line to Clinton) Buy a used book here and you're helping to fund this volunteer-based literacy group's programs, which range from in-school reading help for grade-schoolers to book-publishing courses for teens. The jam-packed store has good-quality tomes and plenty of cushy sofas where you can sit and peruse your finds. Kids will find lots of imaginative wares. Books average around $5.

H MART FOOD & DRINKS

Map p324 (☑312-966-4666; www.hmart.com; 711 W Jackson Blvd, West Loop; ⏱9am-9pm Sun-Wed, to 10pm Thu-Sat; ⓜBlue Line to Clinton) Pop into this branch of the Asian grocery store chain when the urge strikes for fresh squid, fish balls, roasted chestnuts, banana chips or green tea Kit Kat bars. Vendors in the small food court sizzle spicy noodle dishes and Korean fried chicken to go with a slew of bubble teas.

GROOVE DISTRIBUTION MUSIC

Map p324 (☑312-997-2375; www.groovedis.com; 346 N Justine St, West Loop; ⏱noon-7pm Tue-Fri; ⓜGreen, Pink Line to Ashland) Whenever you're at a club, dancing to the beat, Groove is

NEAR WEST SIDE MARKETS

The neighborhood hosts a couple of stellar bazaars. They're a study in contrasts.

Maxwell Street Market (Map p324; www.maxwellstreetmarket.us; 800 S Desplaines St, Near West Side; ⊘9am-3pm Sun; Ⓜ Blue Line to Clinton) This is the working person's place. Every Sunday hundreds of vendors set up stalls that sell everything from Jesus statues to 10 packs of tube socks to power tools. The market has become a hot spot for foodies craving homemade churros, tamales and other Mexican noshes, and for folks seeking cheap clothing, electronics and junk galore. Don't let the name mislead you: the market is not actually on Maxwell St, though it was for decades until gentrification forced it onward. It now sprawls along Desplaines St. The city runs the market and adds to the festivities with free fitness classes and the occasional band or dance group performance.

Randolph Street Market (Map p324; ☑312-666-1200; www.randolphstreetmarket.com; 1340 W Washington Blvd, West Loop; $10-12; ⊘10am-5pm last weekend of month Feb-Dec; Ⓜ Green, Pink Line to Ashland) This monthly market is styled on London's Portobello Market and has become quite the to-do in town. It takes place inside the beaux-arts Plumbers Hall, where more than 200 antique dealers hock collectibles, costume jewelry, furniture, books, Turkish rugs and pinball machines. One of the coolest parts is the Indie Designer Fashion Market, where the city's fledgling designers sell their one-of-a-kind skirts, shawls, handbags and other pieces. In summer the action spills into the street with live bands, food vendors and a bar. A free trolley picks up patrons downtown by the Water Works Pumping Station hourly (on the half hour, May through September only). You can save a few bucks if you buy your ticket online.

likely the source of the music. The company provides record stores around the world with down-tempo, mash-ups, dubstep, nu jazz, cosmic disco and lots of that Chicago specialty – house – both on vinyl and CD. You can shop right in the warehouse, which is exactly what discerning DJs do.

BLOMMER CHOCOLATE STORE FOOD
Map p324 (☑312-492-1336; 600 W Kinzie St, West Loop; ⊘9am-5pm Mon-Fri, to 3pm Sat; Ⓜ Blue Line to Grand) Often in the Loop, a smell wafts through that's so enticing you'd almost shoot your own mother in the kneecaps to get to it. It comes from Blommer Chocolate Factory, which provides the sweet stuff to big-time manufacturers such as Fannie May and Nabisco. Luckily, the wee attached store sells a line of Blommer's own goodies straight to consumers.

The dark-chocolate-covered almonds reign supreme, and there's a sweet selection of retro candies such as Zots, Pop Rocks and Zagnut bars.

ATHENIAN CANDLE CO ARTS & CRAFTS
Map p324 (☑312-332-6988; www.athenian candle.com; 300 S Halsted St, Greektown; ⊘9:30am-6pm Mon, Tue & Fri, to 7pm Thu, to 5pm Sat; Ⓜ Blue Line to UIC/Halsted) Whether you're hoping to win at bingo, remove a jinx or fall in love, this Greektown store promises to help with its array of candles, incense, love potions and miracle oils. Though it's been making candles for Orthodox churches on-site since 1919, the owners aren't devoted to one religion: you'll find Buddha statues, Pope holograms, Turkish evil-eye stones and tarot cards.

Pilsen & Near South Side

PILSEN | NEAR SOUTH SIDE | CHINATOWN

Neighborhood Top Five

1 **Field Museum of Natural History** (p191) Sizing up Sue the T-rex, the towering totem poles and magnificent mummies at one of the world's foremost scientific research institutions.

2 **National Museum of Mexican Art** (p192) Admiring psychedelic paintings, polished altars and colorful folk art at the nation's largest Latinx arts center.

3 **Chinatown** (p196) Nibbling chestnut cakes and almond cookies in the bakeries, and shopping for trinkets and unusual food items in the shops.

4 **Pilsen Public Art Tours** (p201) Venturing out with local artists to see the neighborhood's superb murals and learning about their history as a traditional Mexican art form.

5 **Northerly Island** (p193) Walking or cycling around the wild, grassy island and checking out the birdlife en route.

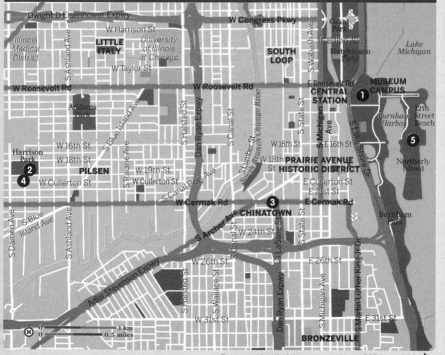

For more detail of this area see Map p328 and p330 ➡

PILSEN & NEAR SOUTH SIDE

Lonely Planet's Top Tip

In summer it's a good idea to buy advance tickets for the Shedd Aquarium (p192), the most popular of the Museum Campus attractions. It's less necessary for the Field Museum (opposite) unless there's an all-the-rage exhibit going on. For the Adler Planetarium (p193) and for the Shedd and Field in winter, there's no need for e-tickets. Save yourself the service charges.

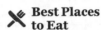

Best Places to Eat

➡ Pleasant House Pub (p196)

➡ Don Pedro Carnitas (p196)

➡ Qing Xiang Yuan Dumplings (p197)

➡ 5 Rabanitos (p197)

For reviews, see p196.➡

Best Places to Drink

➡ Alulu Brewery & Pub (p198)

➡ La Catrina Cafe (p198)

➡ Skylark (p198)

➡ Moody Tongue (p198)

For reviews, see p198.➡

Best Places to Shop

➡ Pilsen Community Books (p201)

➡ Knee Deep Vintage (p201)

➡ Pilsen Outpost (p201)

For reviews, see p200.➡

Explore Pilsen & Near South Side

Start at the Museum Campus to check off the big-ticket items first. The Field Museum of Natural History is the best of the bunch, though Shedd Aquarium draws more people. The Adler Planetarium is the third attraction. They each open early morning, a perfect time to visit. Expect crowds.

Spend the afternoon doing something more offbeat. Nature enthusiasts can head to Northerly Island, a prairie-grassed nature park abutting Museum Campus. Blues fans can make the pilgrimage further south to the old Chess Records site, a humble building where Muddy Waters and Howlin' Wolf plugged in their amps. History buffs will appreciate mansion-filled Prairie Ave between 16th and 20th Sts. It's a short distance to Chinatown, where steaming bowls of noodles and imported goods reward exploring.

To Chinatown's west lies Pilsen, the center of Chicago's Mexican community and a colorful, mural-splashed neighborhood. You could also spend the afternoon here poking around the taquerias and the impressive art museum, or checking out the copious street art. Chicago's hipster underground also calls Pilsen home, so you'll find some great bohemian bars and restaurants if you linger into the evening. While Pilsen can be crowded, it's more of a local scene than a touristy one.

Local Life

➡ **Blues heaven** Locals stop by Willie Dixon's Blues Heaven (p193) to see who's plugging in for the free Thursday-night concerts in summer.

➡ **Vintage jackpot** Local fashionistas scour 18th St's vintage shops in Pilsen. A smattering of good ones pop up in the mile-long stretch between Halsted St and Ashland Ave.

➡ **Ice-cream fix** All of Pilsen turns up at La Michoacana Premium (p197) on steamy evenings to get a lick of something cool, fruity and/or creamy.

Getting There & Away

➡ **Bus** Buses 130 (in summer) and 146 (year-round) go to the Museum Campus. Bus 1 goes to Prairie Ave's historic homes.

➡ **L Train** Red, Orange, Green Line to Roosevelt for Museum Campus. Red Line to Cermak-Chinatown for Chinatown.

➡ **Car** The Museum Campus boasts plenty of lot parking (from $19 per car on nonevent days). Meter parking is readily available in Near South Side; it can be a bit more difficult to find in Pilsen and Chinatown.

TOP SIGHT
FIELD MUSEUM OF NATURAL HISTORY

The mammoth Field Museum houses everything but the kitchen sink. The collection's rock star is Sue, the largest *Tyrannosaurus rex* yet discovered. She's 13ft tall and 41ft long, and menaces the 2nd floor with ferocious aplomb. The galleries beyond hold 30 million other artifacts, tended by a slew of PhD-wielding scientists, as the Field remains an active research institution.

The first dinosaur you'll encounter is a plant-eating titanosaur named Maximo, who rules over the main floor. He's even bigger than Sue. He's a cast (not real bones), so feel free to touch him. After communing with Max, head up to the Evolving Planet exhibit on the 2nd floor, where Sue lives with accompanying videos that show what life was like for her back in the day. You can learn about the evolution of various species and watch staff paleontologists clean up fossils in the lab.

'Inside Ancient Egypt' recreates an Egyptian burial chamber on two levels. The mastaba (tomb) contains 23 actual mummies and is a reconstruction of the one built for Unis-ankh, the son of the last pharaoh of the Fifth dynasty, who died at age 21 in 2407 BC. The relic-strewn bottom level is especially worthwhile.

Other displays that merit your time include the Hall of Gems and its glittering garnets, opals, emeralds, pearls and diamonds. The Northwest Coast and Arctic Peoples' totem-pole collection got its start with artifacts shipped to Chicago for the 1893 World's Expo. And the largest man-eating lion ever caught is stuffed and standing sentry on the basement floor. Preserved insects and birds, and Bushman, the cantankerous ape who drew crowds at Lincoln Park Zoo for decades, are also on display in all their taxidermic glory.

DON'T MISS

➡ Sue the T-rex
➡ Maximo the titanosaur
➡ Hall of Gems
➡ Totem poles
➡ Mummies
➡ Man-eating lions of Tsavo

PRACTICALITIES

➡ Map p328, F1
➡ 📞312-922-9410
➡ www.fieldmuseum.org
➡ 1400 S Lake Shore Dr, Near South Side
➡ adult/child $24/17
➡ ⊙9am-5pm
➡ 🚹
➡ 🚍146, 130

◉ SIGHTS

◉ Pilsen

★NATIONAL MUSEUM
OF MEXICAN ART
MUSEUM

Map p330 (☑312-738-1503; www.national museumofmexicanart.org; 1852 W 19th St; ☺10am-5pm Tue-Sun; ⓂPink Line to 18th St) FREE Founded in 1982, this vibrant museum – the largest Latinx arts institution in the US – has become one of the city's best. The vivid permanent collection sums up 1000 years of Mexican art and culture through classical paintings, shining gold altars, skeleton-rich folk art, beadwork and much more.

The turbulent politics and revolutionary leaders of Mexican history are well represented, including works about Cesar Chavez and Emiliano Zapata. Don't miss the psychedelic 'semen-acrylic' painting (that's, um, bodily fluids mixed with pigments). The museum also sponsors readings by top authors and performances by musicians and artists. October and November are busy months with lots of festive programs for Day of the Dead. The on-site store is a winner, with brightly painted Mexican crafts filling the shelves.

CHICAGO
ARTS DISTRICT
AREA

Map p330 (www.chicagoartsdistrict.org; S Halsted & W 18th Sts; ☐8) Pilsen's art galleries are known collectively as the Chicago Arts District. There are 20 or so studios, and they tend to be small, artist-run spaces with erratic hours. Many cluster around 18th and Halsted Sts. The best time to visit is on Second Fridays, when the galleries stay open from 6pm to 10pm on the second Friday of each month and welcome patrons with free wine, snacks, and freshly hung paintings and photos. Pick up a map at the office at 1945 S Halsted St.

◉ Near South Side

FIELD MUSEUM OF
NATURAL HISTORY
MUSEUM
See p191.

SHEDD AQUARIUM
AQUARIUM

Map p328 (☑312-939-2438; www.shedd aquarium.org; 1200 S Lake Shore Dr; adult/child $40/30; ☺9am-6pm Jun-Aug, 9am-5pm Mon-Fri, to 6pm Sat & Sun Sep-May; ♿; ☐146, 130) Top draws at the kiddie-mobbed Shedd Aquarium include the Wild Reef exhibit, where there's just 5in of Plexiglas between you and two-dozen fierce-looking sharks, and the Oceanarium, with its rescued sea otters. Note the Oceanarium also keeps beluga whales and Pacific white-sided dolphins, a practice that's increasingly frowned upon as captivity is stressful for these sensitive creatures.

General admission includes all of the aforementioned exhibits. The 4-D movies cost extra ($5 each). Lines can be very long here, especially in summer. Tickets pur-

---

LOCAL KNOWLEDGE

PILSEN MURALS

Pilsen is famous for its murals that splash across churches, schools and cafes throughout the neighborhood. Top spots to see them:

➡ The 16th Street railroad embankment unfurls a particularly rich vein, with 50 works by local and international artists adorning a 1.5-mile stretch between Wood and Halsted Sts. The Pink Line L train to 18th Street gets you within a few blocks of the strip's western end.

➡ Speaking of the 18th Street station: all of its walls and steps are painted with murals. The whole place is a work of art. The little stall inside sells churros that can fuel your browsing.

➡ A few blocks southwest is muralist Hector Duarte's house, which he has covered with his striking work **Gulliver in Wonderland** (Map p330; 1900 W Cullerton St; ⓂPink Line to 18th St) – a must see.

All of these are walkable, but there's a Divvy bike-share kiosk outside the 18th Street station (on Paulina St) that makes a mural-browsing trip even easier.

chased online at least one day in advance provide faster, priority entry (for a per order fee of $3).

ADLER PLANETARIUM
MUSEUM

Map p328 (☑312-922-7827; www.adler planetarium.org; 1300 S Lake Shore Dr; adult/child $12/8; ◎9:30am-4pm; 🖈; 🚊146, 130) Space enthusiasts will get a big bang (pun!) out of the Adler. There are public telescopes to view the stars (10am to 1pm daily, by the Galileo Cafe), 3-D lectures to learn about supernovas (in the Space Visualization Lab), and the Planet Explorers exhibit where kids can 'launch' a rocket. The immersive digital films cost extra (from $13 per ticket). The Adler's front steps offer Chicago's best skyline view, so get your camera ready.

There's also much to see outside the Adler, and for free. Check out the 12 sides of the 1930s building, one for each sign of the zodiac. Sculptor Henry Moore's sundial keeps time by the main entrance, while the bronze Copernicus statue lords it over the front median.

NORTHERLY ISLAND
PARK

Map p328 (1521 S Linn White Dr; 🚊146, 130) This hilly, prairie-grassed park has a walking and cycling trail, bird-watching, fishing and an outdoor venue for big-name concerts. It's actually a peninsula, not an island, but the Chicago skyline views are tremendous no matter what you call it. Stop in at the field house, if it's open, for tour information. Bicycles are available at the Divvy bike-share station by the Adler Planetarium. Note that parts of the trail are closed at times due to weather damage.

WILLIE DIXON'S BLUES HEAVEN
HISTORIC BUILDING

Map p328 (☑312-808-1286; www.bluesheaven. com; 2120 S Michigan Ave; adult/child $15/10; ◎noon-4pm Tue-Sat; Ⓜ️Green Line to Cermak-McCormick Pl) From 1957 to 1967, this humble building was Chess Records, the seminal electric blues label. It's now named for the bassist who wrote most of Chess' hits. Staff give hour-long tours of the premises. It's pretty ramshackle, with few original artifacts on display. Still, hard-core fans will get a thrill out of hearing stories from the heady era and walking into the studio where their musical heroes recorded. Free blues concerts rock the side garden on summer Thursdays at 6pm.

PRAIRIE AVENUE HISTORIC DISTRICT
ARCHITECTURE

Map p328 (🚊1) In the late 1800s, Prairie Ave between 16th and 20th Sts is where Chicago's millionaires lived in their mansions. Today the district is good for a stroll. Some of the homes have been preserved as museums, such as Glessner House and Clarke House. Others are intriguing to admire from the outside: William K Kimball House, Joseph G Coleman House (p196) and Elbridge G Keith House (p196).

GLESSNER HOUSE MUSEUM
MUSEUM

Map p328 (☑312-326-1480; www.glessnerhouse. org; 1800 S Prairie Ave; tours adult/child $15/8, admission Wed free; ◎tours 11:30am, 1pm & 2:30pm Wed-Sun; 🚊1) The 1887 John J Glessner House is the premier survivor of the Prairie Avenue Historic District. Much of the interior is reminiscent of an English manor house, with heavy wooden beams and other English-style details. Additionally, more than 80% of the current furnishings are authentic, thanks to the Glessner family's penchant for family photos. Tours (75 minutes) take it all in.

OLMEC HEAD NO 8
SCULPTURE

Map p328 (🚊146, 130) Staring out from the Field Museum's lawn, *Olmec Head No 8* is a replica of one of many sculptures the Olmec people carved in Veracruz, Mexico, c 1300 BC. Scholars believe the colossal heads are likenesses of revered Olmec leaders. This guy's noggin weighs in at 1700lb.

CLARKE HOUSE MUSEUM
MUSEUM

Map p328 (☑312-744-3316; www.clarkehouse museum.org; 1827 S Indiana Ave; ◎tours 1pm & 2:30pm Wed, Fri & Sat; 🚊1) FREE The Henry B Clarke House is the oldest structure in the city. When Caroline and Henry Clarke built the imposing Greek Revival home in 1836, log cabins were still the rage in Chicago residential architecture. The interior has been restored to the period of the Clarkes' occupation, which ended in 1872. One-hour tours delve into the family's life and times.

WILLIAM K KIMBALL HOUSE
HOUSE

Map p328 (1801 S Prairie Ave; 🚊1) Modeled after a 15th-century French château, the William K Kimball House dates from 1892. It now houses the US Soccer Federation, along with next-door Coleman House (p196).

Family-Friendly Pilsen & Near South Side

Where to begin for family fun? The Shedd Aquarium's tropical fish? The Field Museum's hulking dinosaurs? The Adler Planetarium's lunar landscape? If staying indoors gets to be too much, there's parkland and a beach nearby, and traditional Mexican art in the form of murals splashed all over Pilsen's buildings to gaze at.

2

HENRYK SADURA / SHUTTERSTOCK ©

4

STEVEGEER / GETTY IMAGES ©

1. Field Museum of Natural History (p191)

One of the largest, best-preserved Tyrannosaurus rex ever found is called Sue.

2. Adler Planetarium (p193)

Henry Moore's sundial sculpture is located at the entrance of the planetarium.

3. National Museum of Mexican Art (p192)

Calavera Catrina display at the largest Latinx arts institution in the US.

4. Pui Tak Center (p196)

Located in the heart of Chinatown this building was built in 1928.

3

JEFF GREENBERG / AGE FOTOSTOCK ©

JOSEPH G COLEMAN HOUSE   HOUSE

Map p328 (1811 S Prairie Ave; 🚇1) Part of the Prairie Avenue Historic District, the Romanesque 1886 Coleman House now serves as part of the headquarters for the US Soccer Federation.

ELBRIDGE G KEITH HOUSE   HOUSE

Map p328 (www.keithhousechicago.com; 1900 S Prairie Ave; 🚇1) This 1870 limestone beauty in the Prairie Avenue Historic District combines classical and French motifs. It's now a private event space.

CHICAGO WOMEN'S PARK   PARK

Map p328 (1801 S Indiana Ave; 🚇1) This lovely little park in the Prairie Avenue Historic District makes for a nice stroll thanks to its ornamental fountain, manicured gardens and winding footpaths.

⊙ Chinatown

Chicago's small but busy Chinatown is an easy 10-minute train ride from the Loop. Take the Red Line to the Cermak-Chinatown stop, which puts you between the neighborhood's two distinct parts: Chinatown Square (an enormous bi-level strip mall) unfurls to the north along Archer Ave, while Old Chinatown (the traditional retail area) stretches along Wentworth Ave to the south. Either zone allows you to graze through bakeries and shop for Hello Kitty trinkets.

HERITAGE MUSEUM
OF ASIAN ART   MUSEUM

Map p328 (📞312-842-8884; www.heritage asianart.org; 218 W 26th St; adult/child $8/free; ◷11am-5pm Tue-Sun; Ⓜ Red Line to Cermak-Chinatown) This little museum is criminally overlooked. The elegant permanent collection has jades, bronzes, lacquered furniture, porcelain bowls, silver teapots and other decorative arts from venerable cultures around Asia. Temporary exhibits change a few times per year; a recent one focused on carved Ojime beads from Japan.

PING TOM MEMORIAL PARK   PARK

Map p328 (W 19th St; Ⓜ Red Line to Cermak-Chinatown) Ping Tom stretches along the Chicago River and offers dramatic, bridge-strewn views of the skyline. Rent a kayak from the boathouse, or bring a picnic to eat under the willow trees. In summer, the Chi-

cago Water Taxi (www.chicagowatertaxi. com) runs a groovy boat to/from Michigan Ave (the dock is on the bridge's northwest side, by the Wrigley Building). It costs $5 one way ($6 on weekends).

The park's entrance is a bit tricky to find. Take either W 19th St or S Wells St to where they meet, and you'll see a small park sign pointing the way in toward the railroad overpass.

PUI TAK CENTER   ARCHITECTURE

Map p328 (2216 S Wentworth Ave; Ⓜ Red Line to Cermak-Chinatown) Built in 1928 and originally known as the On Leong Building, this grand structure is a fantasy of Chinese architecture that makes good use of glazed terra-cotta details. Note how the lions guarding the door have twisted their heads so they don't have to risk bad luck by turning their backs to each other. The building now houses a group that provides ESL classes and other community programs.

✖ EATING

Pilsen's 18th St teems with Mexican taquerias, tamale shops, hip gastropubs and modern American restaurants. Blue Island Ave is a similarly rich vein. Chinatown offers a densely packed smorgasbord of noodle houses, low-cost bakeries and dim sum places along S Wentworth Ave and in Chinatown Square.

✖ Pilsen

★PLEASANT HOUSE PUB   PUB FOOD $

Map p330 (📞773-523-7437; www.pleasant housepub.com; 2119 S Halsted St; mains $10.50-15; ◷10am-10pm Tue-Thu, to midnight Fri & Sat, to 10pm Sun; 🛜; 🚌8) Follow your nose to Pleasant House, which bakes tall, fluffy, savory pies. Daily flavors include chicken and chutney, steak and ale, or kale and mushroom, made with produce the chefs grow themselves. The pub also serves excellent UK and local beers to accompany the food. Friday is a good day to visit, when there's a fish fry.

★DON PEDRO CARNITAS   MEXICAN $

Map p330 (1113 W 18th St; tacos $2.50; ◷6am-6pm Mon-Thu, 5am-5pm Fri-Sun; Ⓜ Pink Line to

18th St) At this no-frills meat den, a man with a machete salutes you at the front counter. He awaits your command to hack off pork pieces and then wraps the thick chunks with onion and cilantro in a warm tortilla. You then devour the tacos at the tables in back. Goat stew and tripe add to the carnivorous menu. Cash only.

YVOLINA'S TAMALES MEXICAN $

Map p330 (☑312-731-3167; www.yvolinas.com; 814 W 18th St; mains $3-10; ⊘11am-6pm Mon-Wed & Fri, 10am-6pm Sat, 10am-5pm Sun; ☑; ☑8) This small storefront makes more than 30 types of tamales, including many in atypical, vegetarian flavors such as quinoa and lentil, eggplant and cheese, and spinach and mushroom. The mother-daughter chefs wrap the tamales in banana leaves instead of cornhusks, and use olive oil instead of lard. Carnivores, fear not: mole-sauced chicken, pork and beef options are plentiful, too.

TAQUERIA EL MILAGRO MEXICAN $

Map p330 (☑312-433-7620; 1923 S Blue Island Ave; mains $3.50-7; ⊘8am-7pm Mon-Thu, 7:30am-8pm Fri & Sat, 7:30am-7pm Sun; ☑Pink Line to 18th St) El Milagro is a classic. On one side it's a restaurant, with a cafeteria-style line for plates of beef stew simmering in tomato sauce or chicken in chocolate-y mole sauce. Mexican music plays above the clatter of locals hunkered down over their meals. On the other side it's a tortilla factory with a store to buy fresh packs of the goods.

LA MICHOACANA PREMIUM ICE CREAM $

Map p330 (☑312-226-9600; www.lamichoacana premlumpilsen.com; 1855 S Blue Island Ave; popsicles & ice-cream scoops $2-5.50; ⊘7am-11pm Mon-Thu, to midnight Fri-Sun; ☑Pink Line to 18th St) All of Pilsen is at this neon-pink ice-cream shop on warm nights. Huge, super creamy scoops in coconut, pistachio and Mexican sponge cake are one thing, but it's the bazillion flavors of *paletas* (popsicles) with big chunks of fruit or candy embedded in them that spark all the oohs and aahs (and Instagram snapshots).

5 RABANITOS MEXICAN $$

Map p330 (☑312-285-2710; www.5rabanitos. com; 1758 W 18th St; mains $15-17; ⊘11am-9pm Tue-Thu, 11am-10pm Fri, 9am-10pm Sat, 9am-9pm Sun; ☑; ☑Pink Line to 18th St) A storefront restaurant painted yellow, green and blue, 5 Rabanitos looks like any other taqueria on 18th St, except the chef learned his craft from renowned restaurateur Rick Bayless. Unusual spice combinations and addictive salsa and mole sauces make the dishes shine way beyond the norm. Try *torta ahogada*, a pork sandwich bathed in chili sauce. Several vegetarian options. BYOB.

DUSEK'S GASTROPUB $$$

Map p330 (☑312-526-3851; www.duseks chicago.com; 1227 W 18th St; mains $20-32; ⊘11am-1am Mon-Fri, 9am-1am Sat & Sun; ☑Pink Line to 18th St) Pilsen's hipsters gather under the pressed-tin ceiling of this dark, cozy tavern to fork into highbrow comfort food so delicious it has earned a Michelin star. Curried venison pie, chicken fried rabbit and pasta with wild boar sausage are among the changing dishes that hit the tables, alongside a terrific selection of local beers (ask about pairings).

✗ Chinatown

★QING XIANG YUAN DUMPLINGS DUMPLINGS $

Map p328 (☑312-799-1118; www.qxydumplings. com; 2002 S Wentworth Ave, Suite 103; mains $9-14; ⊘11:30am-9pm; ☑Red Line to Cermak-Chinatown) The name doesn't lie: it's all about dumplings in this bright room under bamboo lanterns. The dough pockets come steamed or pan-fried, in groups of 12 or 18, with fillings like lamb and coriander, ground pork and cabbage, sea whelk and leek, and some 30 other types. Bite into one and a hot shot of flavor erupts in your mouth.

RICOBENE'S ITALIAN $

Map p328 (☑312-225-5555; www.ricobenes pizza.com; 252 W 26th St; sandwiches $6-12, 7in pizzas from $9.50; ⊘9am-12:30am Mon-Thu, 9am-2am Fri, 10am-2am Sat, 10am-midnight Sun; ☑Red Line to Cermak-Chinatown) Ricobene's has been around for four-plus decades catering to construction workers, young families and other neighborhood types. While pizza and pasta take up most of the menu, everyone's really here for the breaded steak sandwich. The 2lb behemoth takes thin slices of beef, breads and deep-fries them, dips them in marinara sauce and plonks them in a fluffy bread roll.

CHIU QUON BAKERY & DIM SUM
BAKERY $

Map p328 (📞312-808-1818; www.cqbakery.com; 2253 S Wentworth Ave; pastries & snacks $1-4; ⏱7am-10pm) For a cheap à la carte lunch in Chinatown, this bright bakery has fluffy BBQ pork buns, bite-sized egg custard tarts, coconut and winter melon pastries and some dim-sum fare (shrimp dumplings, taro cake, sticky rice roll, steamed egg custard *bao*).

It's available to go, or to scarf down by the handful at the no-frills tables in back. Cash only.

CHI CAFE
CHINESE $

Map p328 (📞312-842-9993; www.chicafeonline. com; 2160 S Archer Ave; mains $9-16; ⏱8am-4am Sun-Thu, 24hr Fri & Sat; MRed Line to Cermak-Chinatown) Thanks to nearly nonstop hours and an enormous menu that has everything from Taiwanese-style fried turnip omelets to minced pork with spaghetti, beef hot pot and scallop congee, Chi Cafe's shiny lacquer tables bustle.

PHOENIX
DIM SUM $$

Map p328 (📞312-328-0848; www.chinatown phoenix.com; 2131 S Archer Ave; dim sum dishes $3-5; ⏱9am-10pm Mon-Fri, 8am-11pm Sat & Sun; MRed Line to Cermak-Chinatown) This big, modern, gilt-dragon-bedecked restaurant is a Chinatown stalwart known for reliable dim sum that's served all day. Small plates of *char siu bao* (barbecued pork buns), shrimp-filled rice noodles, egg custards and other popular dishes roll around the dining room in a seemingly endless parade of carts.

🍷 DRINKING & NIGHTLIFE

Pilsen has activist cafes, microbrewery taprooms and artsy dive bars, especially along 18th St, while the Near South Side has neighborhood pubs and leafy patios. Chinatown isn't much of a drinking destination, though it rocks for satisfying late-night, post-booze munchies.

🍷 Pilsen

⭐ALULU BREWERY & PUB
MICROBREWERY

Map p330 (📞312-600-9865; www.alulubrew.com; 2011 S Laflin St; ⏱5pm-2am Mon, Wed & Thu, 3pm-2am Fri & Sun, 3pm-3am Sat; MPink Line to 18th St) Pilsen's bohemians love this intimate brewpub and no wonder. Join them at the reclaimed wood tables for a flight and fancy pub grub like poutine with *merguez*-sausage gravy. The brewers play around with styles, so anything from a watermelon sour to coffee blond, wheat beer or Mexican lager may be pouring from the 20 taps when you visit.

⭐LA CATRINA CAFE
CAFE

Map p330 (📞312-434-4040; www.facebook. com/lacatrinacafeon18; 1011 W 18th St; ⏱7am-9pm Mon-Thu, 7am-6pm Fri, 8am-6pm Sat & Sun; 📶; MPink Line to 18th St) Activists, artists and students congregate here for the roomy window seats, soul-warming drinks and funky art exhibitions. It's a come-one, come-all kind of spot, prime for a Mexican hot chocolate, cinnamon-spiced coffee or Frida Kahlo–face cookie. A colorful mural marks the entrance.

MOODY TONGUE
MICROBREWERY

Map p330 (📞312-600-5111; www.moodytongue. com; 2136 S Peoria St; ⏱5-10pm Wed, 5-11pm Thu, 5pm-midnight Fri, noon-midnight Sat, noon-9pm Sun; 🚇8) A crackling fire, stylish glassware and, most of all, sophisticated brews featuring culinary ingredients such as black truffle and Oaxacan chocolate make this hidden-in-plain-sight Pilsen taproom more suited to an intimate aperitif than a wild night with your beer buds.

SKYLARK
BAR

Map p330 (📞312-948-5275; www.skylarkchicago. com; 2149 S Halsted St; ⏱4pm-2am Sun-Fri, to 3am Sat; 📶; 🚇8) The Skylark is a bastion for artsy guzzlers, who slouch in big booths sipping on strong drinks and eyeing the long room. They play pinball, snap pics in the photo booth and scarf down the kitchen's awesome tater tots. It's a good stop after the Pilsen gallery hop (a free arts event run by galleries, shops and studios). Cash only.

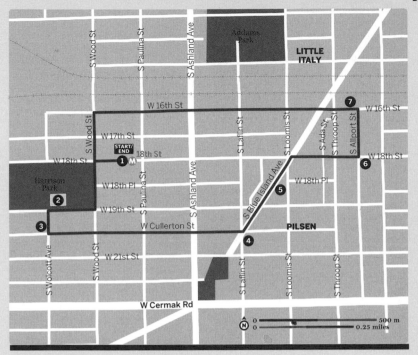

Neighborhood Walk
Pilsen Old & New

START 18TH STREET L STATION (PINK LINE)
END 18TH STREET L STATION
LENGTH 2 MILES; TWO HOURS

Pilsen mixes it up. On one hand it's a center of Mexican culture, with *paleta* (popsicle) shops and taquerias; on the other it's a hipster district, with vintage shops and brewpubs. Before either of these cultures arrived, Pilsen was home to Czech immigrants who named the area after a city in their homeland.

Start at the **❶ 18th Street L station**. Murals cover every inch of the walls and stairs. Aztec gods and skeletons predominate. Walk west on 18th St to Wood St and turn south, skirting the park. At 19th St turn west to reach the **❷ National Museum of Mexican Art** (p192). The vibrant collection is awesome and free.

Return to 19th St heading west, and turn south onto Wolcott Ave. In one block you'll arrive at the home of muralist Hector Duarte, who has covered the exterior with **❸ Gulliver in Wonderland** (p192), which

shows a Mexican immigrant trying to break free from barbed wire.

Head east on Cullerton St for four blocks to Laflin St, and turn south. Mosey over to **❹ Alulu Brewery & Pub** (opposite), an intimate hangout for Pilsen's young and stylish. Housemade suds and pub grub like beer cheese curds keep the place buzzing. It's a whole different scene a few blocks northeast on Blue Island Ave at **❺ La Michoacana Premium** (p197), a pink palace of gorgeous, fruit-studded *paletas*. Continue northeast to 18th St and turn east. Within a few blocks you'll arrive at **❻ Thalia Hall** (p200), an 1892 building patterned after Prague's opera house. Today it hosts rock bands.

Head north on Allport St for a block until it dead-ends at the **❼ train embankment**. This is a huge alfresco gallery for street art. Turn west on 16th St and follow the murals for three-quarters of a mile. At Wood St turn south, walk two blocks to 18th St, and head east. See the train station?

You've just looped your way through Pilsen.

WORTH A DETOUR

LAGUNITAS BREWING COMPANY

Enter this jovial **brewery** (Off Map p324; 312-767-9678; www.lagunitas.com; 2607 W 17th St; taproom noon-9pm Wed, Thu & Sun, to 10pm Fri & Sat; Pink Line to California) – the city's largest – via a blue glowing hallway with trippy art painted on the walls and the Willy Wonka theme song playing overhead. The beer-hall-esque taproom is a bit far flung, but fans make the trek for the free tours, hoppy suds and live music. IPAs and pale ales are the specialty.

Many of the brews have a high alcohol content that'll knock you on your butt if you're not careful. Grab a glass and settle in at the communal wood tables, maybe with a novel from the book exchange. Or walk out on the catwalks overlooking the production area (yes, you're allowed).

The schedule is quirky: tours happen daily, but the taproom is only open Wednesday through Sunday. Also, not all tours offer samples. The 1pm and 3pm jaunts on weekdays do; tours on weekends do not. If possible, take a tasting tour. The samples are generous and you get to hang out drinking in a weird purple room with video games, a piano and a giant blow-up eyeball.

The brewery is located in Douglas Park, west of Pilsen. It's about a half-mile walk from the L station through a pretty desolate industrial area. At night you're better off taking a taxi or rideshare.

Near South Side

VICE DISTRICT BREWING
MICROBREWERY

Map p328 (312-291-9022; 1454 S Michigan Ave; 4-11pm Tue-Thu, to midnight Fri, 2pm-1am Sat, to 9pm Sun; Green, Orange, Red Line to Roosevelt) Vice is a favorite gathering spot for neighborhood residents. The large, mod-industrial taproom is just right for a pint of black IPA or English-style bitter ale. Many drinkers stop in pre-Bears game. It's not far from Soldier Field, and it opens early (11am) on Sunday game days.

SPOKE & BIRD
CAFE

Map p328 (www.spokeandbird.com; 205 E 18th St; 7am-6pm; 1) The Near South Side has been begging for a leafy patio like the one at Spoke & Bird. Bonus: it's surrounded by several cool old manors in the Prairie Avenue Historic District (p193). Relax with a locally made brew and nifty cafe fare such as the sweet parsnip muffin or lamb barbecue sandwich.

ENTERTAINMENT

THALIA HALL
LIVE MUSIC

Map p330 (312-526-3851; www.thaliahallchicago.com; 1807 S Allport St, Pilsen; Pink Line to 18th St) Midsize Thalia hosts a cool-cat slate of rock, alt-country, jazz and metal concerts in an ornate 1892 hall patterned after Prague's opera house. A gastropub (p197) on the 1st floor, cocktail bar in the basement and punk piano saloon in the adjacent carriage house invite lingering before and after shows.

SOLDIER FIELD
FOOTBALL

Map p328 (847-615-2327; www.chicagobears.com; 1410 S Museum Campus Dr, Near South Side; 146, 130) The Bears, Chicago's NFL team, tackle at Soldier Field from September through January. Arrive early on game days and wander through the parking lots – you won't believe the elaborate tailgate feasts people cook up from the back of their cars.

DANCE CENTER AT COLUMBIA COLLEGE
DANCE

Map p328 (312-369-8330; https://dance.colum.edu; 1306 S Michigan Ave, Near South Side; Red, Orange, Green Line to Roosevelt) More than an academic institution, the Dance Center is one of the most focused collegiate modern-dance programs in the country and has carved out a fine reputation. The on-site theater attracts quality performers from beyond Chicago and hosts everything from tap jams to classical Indian dance.

SHOPPING

Pilsen's 18th St has funky vintage, record and bookstores interspersed with Mexican bakeries and mini-marts.

In Chinatown homewares, exotic foods and trinkets fill shops in Chinatown Square, a bi-level outdoor mall that spreads along Archer Ave, and on Wentworth Ave, a stone's throw south of the mall.

★PILSEN
COMMUNITY BOOKS
BOOKS

Map p330 (www.pilsencommunitybooks.org; 1102 W 18th St, Pilsen; ⊙11am-6pm Sun & Mon, to 9pm Tue-Sat; MPink Line to 18th St) Decorated with vintage typewriters and old card-catalog bureaus that serve as desks, this small store for new and used books charms. Sliding ladders provide access to the floor-to-ceiling bookshelves stacked with fiction, poetry, philosophy and lots of Spanish-language books. As part of the shop's community-focused mission, it gives free books to local schools.

PILSEN OUTPOST
ARTS & CRAFTS

Map p330 (☑773-830-4800; www.pilsen outpost.com; 1637 W 18th St, Pilsen; ⊙noon-8pm Wed-Fri, 11am-7pm Sat, 11am-5pm Sun; MPink Line to 18th St) This compact artist-run gallery and shop sells distinctive silk-screened T-shirts, zines, cards, posters and small paintings on canvas. Everything is locally made. Staff are terrifically welcoming.

KNEE DEEP VINTAGE
VINTAGE

Map p330 (☑312-850-2510; www.kneedeep vintage.com; 1219 W 18th St, Pilsen; ⊙noon-8pm Mon-Thu, 11am-8pm Fri & Sat, noon-6pm Sun; MPink Line to 18th St) Knee Deep offers a trove of vintage clothing for men and women. Browse the racks past the 1970s feather-print dresses and 1960s Hawaiian-style shirts until you spot that perfect 1950s faux-leopard-fur coat. The owner stocks a quality selection, and prices are reasonable though not cheap. The shop is in the Thalia Hall building.

AJI ICHIBAN
FOOD

Map p328 (☑312-328-9998; 2117a S China Pl, Chinatown; ⊙11am-8pm Mon-Thu, 11am-9pm Fri, 10am-9pm Sat, 10am-8pm Sun; MRed Line to Cermak-Chinatown) The front sign at this Asian snack and candy store says 'Munchies Paradise,' and so it is. Sweet and salty treats fill the bulk bins, from dried salted plums to chocolate wafer cookies, roasted fish crisps to fruity hard candies. It's all packaged in cool, cartoony wrappers, with plenty of samples out for grabs.

LOCAL KNOWLEDGE

CHINATOWN TOUR

Guides from the Chicago Chinese Cultural Institute offer **tours** (Map p328; ☑312-842-1988; www.chinatown tourchicago.com; Chinatown; 90min tours $15; ⊙10am Fri-Sun late-May–early Sep; MRed Line to Cermak-Chinatown) taking in the neighborhood's history, architecture and cultural highlights. Departure is from Chinatown Square by the animal statues (in front of 2126 S Archer Ave). You must reserve in advance.

🏃 SPORTS & ACTIVITIES

★PILSEN PUBLIC
ART TOURS
WALKING

(☑773-787-6847; www.ppat.space; Pilsen; 1hr tours per group $125) Murals are a traditional Mexican art form, and they're splashed all over Pilsen's buildings. Local artists and activists lead these highly recommended tours that take in the neighborhood's most impressive works. Call or go online to arrange an excursion (including meeting place and time).

BOATHOUSE AT PING TOM MEMORIAL PARK
KAYAKING

Map p328 (☑312-339-7669; www.rei.com/ping-tom-boathouse; W 19th St, Chinatown; per hr single/double $30/40; ⊙11am-7pm Mon-Fri, 8am-8pm Sat, 8am-7pm Sun Jun-Aug, 10am-6pm Sat & Sun May & Sep; MRed Line to Cermak-Chinatown) Outdoor outfitter REI rents kayaks from the cherry-red boathouse in Ping Tom Memorial Park (p196). It's a more relaxed paddle with less traffic than if you rent downtown.

SLEDDING HILL
SNOW SPORTS

Map p328 (☑312-235-7000; 1410 S Museum Campus Dr, Near South Side; ☐146, 130) The Park District operates a free, 33ft sledding hill on the southeast side of Soldier Field in winter; bring your own gear. A snow-making machine is fired up when the weather doesn't cooperate.

Hyde Park & South Side

HYDE PARK | BRIDGEPORT | BRONZEVILLE | SOUTH SIDE | KENWOOD

Neighborhood Top Five

❶ Museum of Science & Industry (p205) Exploring the U-boat, dollhouse, mock tornado and body slices at the largest science museum in the western hemisphere.

❷ Robie House (p204) Gawking at the eye-popping stained glass and horizontal design of Frank Lloyd Wright's Prairie-style masterpiece.

❸ Stony Island Arts Bank (p206) Seeing how creativity can reshape a downtrodden building in a one-of-a-kind cultural center.

❹ DuSable Museum of African American History (p207) Examining well-done exhibits that tell the story of Chicago's African American community at this small institution.

❺ Marz Community Brewing (p215) Sampling tea-infused wheat beers, ginger-tinged saisons, churro-flavored stouts and other wild creations alongside home brewers and artists.

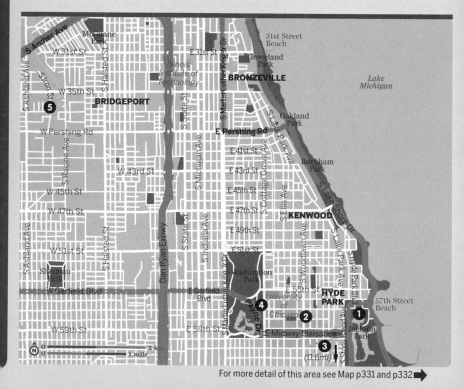

For more detail of this area see Map p331 and p332 ➡

Explore Hyde Park & South Side

The South Side is huge, but most sights are concentrated in three areas. Hyde Park is home to the crowd-favorite Museum of Science & Industry and University of Chicago. Start at 57th St and S University Ave, near Frank Lloyd Wright's Robie House. Walk east for the Museum of Science & Industry and Jackson Park; walk west for the DuSable Museum of African American History.

To the north is Bronzeville, the historic heart of Chicago's African American arts and cultural scene. A short distance west is Bridgeport, a traditionally Irish neighborhood that's now a cool pocket of hip restaurants and community taprooms. The White Sox also play here. Halsted St is the main commercial strip.

Beyond these areas, explorers will find neighborhoods that are slowly piecing things together in the shadow of some of the country's bleakest housing projects. Stony Island Arts Bank and Plant Chicago are good examples of positive transformation.

Local Life

→ **Arts block** Artist Theaster Gates and the University of Chicago worked together to launch the Arts Incubator (p208), Green Line Performing Arts Center (p216) and Peach's (p214) cafe on a forlorn strip of E Garfield Blvd, transforming it into a creative community hub.

→ **Farm fresh** The 61st Street Farmers Market (p216) brings together community dwellers for cooking demos, food sustainability workshops and Pleasant House pies.

→ **Third Fridays** The monthly open-studios night sponsored by Bridgeport Art Center (p209) and Zhou B Art Center (p209) is one of Chicago's coolest soirees.

Getting There & Away

→ **Bus** Bus 6 runs from State St in the Loop to Kenwood, Hyde Park, Jackson Park and beyond (it's express between 11th and 47th Sts). In summer, the Museum of Science & Industry has its own bus. Bus 8 motors along Halsted St for Bridgeport.

→ **Metra** Electric Line trains go from the Loop's Millennium Station to 47th St in Kenwood, to 51st-53rd, 55th-56th-57th and 59th St stations in Hyde Park, and to 63rd St in Jackson Park/Woodlawn.

→ **L Train** Green Line to 35th-Bronzeville-IIT for Bronzeville, to Garfield for the Arts Incubator. Red Line to Sox-35th for the ballpark.

→ **Car** Hyde Park can be tight for parking. Bridgeport and Bronzeville are usually fine.

Lonely Planet's Top Tip

Don't be put off by the distance of these southern neighborhoods from downtown. Many have good public transportation links, especially Hyde Park, and the sights, bookstores, bars and restaurants offer an authentic, exceptional slice of Chicago that's often overlooked. Bus 6 is your friend down here.

HYDE PARK & SOUTH SIDE

Best Places to Eat

→ Gorée Cuisine (p214)
→ Valois Restaurant (p212)
→ Duck Inn (p214)
→ Dat Donut (p214)
→ Kimski (p214)

For reviews, see p212.

Best Places to Drink

→ Marz Community Brewing (p215)
→ Whiner Beer Company (p215)
→ Maria's Packaged Goods & Community Bar (p215)
→ Cove Lounge (p215)
→ Bernice's Tavern (p215)

For reviews, see p214.

Best Places to Shop

→ Seminary Co-op Bookstore (p216)
→ 61st Street Farmers Market (p216)
→ 57th Street Books (p216)

For reviews, see p216.

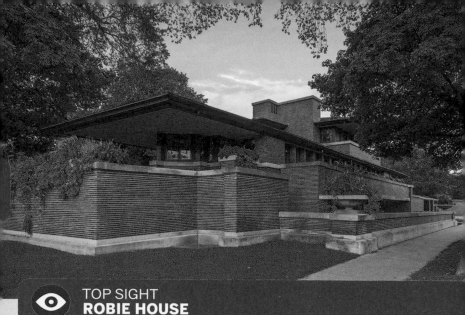

TOP SIGHT
ROBIE HOUSE

Robie House is one of the most famous dwellings in the world. Designed by Frank Lloyd Wright, it's the masterpiece of his Prairie style, and it is often listed among the most important structures in American architecture. The look is meant to reflect the Midwest's landscape – low-slung with long horizontal lines and lots of earth colors.

Frederick C Robie, a forward-thinking businessman who dealt in bicycle parts and early auto machinery, was only 28 years old when he commissioned Wright to build a modern house for his family. Wright designed it in his Oak Park studio between 1908 and 1909, but he wasn't around for the majority of the construction, as he had packed up and moved to Europe with his mistress by then. His associates finished the building, and the Robies moved into the home in 1910. Their residency was short-lived, however. After 14 months, financial and marital problems forced them to sell the house. It was threatened with demolition several times, until it became a landmark under Mayor Richard J Daley in the 1950s.

The house cost about $60,000 to build – furniture, light fixtures and 174 art glass windows included. The corner lot on which Robie House sits is three times as long as it is wide. This factored in to Wright's design, prompting him to envision the home as a set of long, narrow rectangles.

Docents tell the story during one-hour tours, run roughly every half-hour Thursday to Monday from June through October, and hourly otherwise. They go room to room explaining Wright's design concept in each space and how he achieved it. Note how the furniture repeats the building's forms, and how the colors link to the autumnal prairie palette.

DON'T MISS

→ Exterior view against the horizon

→ Stained glass everywhere

→ Cantilevered roofs

→ Fireplace

PRACTICALITIES

→ Map p332, C5

→ ☎312-994-4000

→ www.flwright.org

→ 5757 S Woodlawn Ave, Hyde Park

→ adult/child $18/15

→ ⊙10:30am-3pm Thu-Mon

→ 🚌6, Ⓜ Metra Electric Line to 59th St

TOP SIGHT
MUSEUM OF SCIENCE & INDUSTRY

Geek out at the largest science museum in the Western Hemisphere. Highlights include a WWII German U-boat nestled in an underground display, the life-size shaft of a coal mine, and the 'Science Storms' exhibit with a mock tornado and tsunami.

Level 1 holds the U-boat (pictured), which is pretty freaking impressive. It's given the Hollywood treatment with blue spotlights moving over it and dramatic music swelling in the background. An interactive kiosk lets you try to break codes. There's plenty more to see around the sub, but the highlight is going on board and touring the cramped quarters. Tours cost $18 extra ($14 for children); tickets are available at the exhibit-side kiosk (or at the main desk when you enter the museum). The Space Center with rockets and the Apollo 8 lunar module, the 'fairy castle' dollhouse and the Farm Tech exhibit with huge tractors to climb are other Level 1 highlights.

Level 2 rolls out lots of trains. Science Storms lets you conjure a mock tornado and simulate a tsunami rolling toward you. Or submerge into the realistic shaft of a coal mine ($12 extra for adults, $9 for children). The baby chick hatchery is also on this floor.

Level 3 hangs cool old German dive bombers and English Spitfires from the ceiling. 'You! The Experience' has a giant 3-D heart to walk through and the infamous body slices (cadavers displayed in half-inch-thick pieces) that have been scaring kids for decades.

The museum's main building served as the Palace of Fine Arts at the landmark 1893 World's Expo, which was set in surrounding Jackson Park (p206). When you've had your fill at the museum, the park makes an excellent setting to recuperate.

DON'T MISS

→ U-505 submarine
→ Fairy castle
→ Science Storms' tornadoes and tsunamis
→ Body slices

PRACTICALITIES

→ MSI
→ Map p332, F4
→ ☎773-684-1414
→ www.msichicago.org
→ 5700 S Lake Shore Dr, Hyde Park
→ adult/child $22/13
→ ⊙9:30am-5:30pm Jun-Aug, shorter hours Sep-May
→ 🚻
→ 🚍6 or 10, ⓂMetra Electric Line to 55th-56th-57th St

◉ SIGHTS

Hyde Park holds two top sights: the massive Museum of Science & Industry (p205) and Frank Lloyd Wright's Prairie-style masterwork Robie House (p204). Nearby, the underrated DuSable Museum of African American History (p207) and the Arts Incubator (p208) lie across Washington Park from each other. Nature-rich Jackson Park is also in the vicinity. Some 4 miles north, Bronzeville is dotted with African American history landmarks, as well as Mies van der Rohe architecture at the Illinois Institute of Technology (p209). A stone's throw west, Bridgeport offers a smattering of artists studios and galleries.

◉ Hyde Park

MUSEUM OF SCIENCE & INDUSTRY MUSEUM
See p205.

ROBIE HOUSE ARCHITECTURE
See p204.

★STONY ISLAND ARTS BANK GALLERY
(Off Map p332 (☎312-857-5561; www.rebuild-foundation.org; 6760 S Stony Island Ave, Greater Grand Crossing; ⊙hours vary; ⬛6) FREE Artist-activist Theaster Gates bought a tumbledown bank building for $1 in Chicago's neglected South Shore neighborhood, and transformed it into a fascinating African American cultural center and gallery. Staff give tours of the collections, including the 5000-album vinyl trove of local DJ Frankie Knuckles (the Godfather of House Music) and a roomful of racist 'negrobilia' items. Hours vary depending on season and exhibitions, so check the website before heading out.

PROMONTORY POINT PARK
Map p332 (5491 S Lake Shore Dr; ⬛6, MMetra Electric Line to 55th-56th-57th St) Runners, cyclists, swimmers, dog walkers and Hyde Park residents of all stripes rub shoulders on the Point, a 12-acre artificial peninsula that juts into Lake Michigan. The stone steps and castle-like field house are favorite hangouts; wedding receptions are often held in the latter because it's so pretty. Renowned landscape architect Alfred Caldwell designed the green space. The view of the Chicago skyline from here is sublime.

JACKSON PARK PARK
Map p332 (6401 S Stony Island Ave, Woodlawn; ⬛6, MMetra Electric Line to 59th or 63rd St) This 550-acre, lakefront green space is a gem. Designed by Frederick Law Olmsted, renowned creator of New York City's Central Park, it

---

KENWOOD'S FAMOUS HOMES
••

Kenwood, which abuts Hyde Park to the north, has had some famous residents whose homes you can stroll by:

Obama's House (Map p332; 5046 S Greenwood Ave; ⬛6, MMetra Electric Line to 51st-53rd St) Among the handsome manors lining S Greenwood Ave is the redbrick Georgian-style home at No 5046, where Barack Obama and his family lived from 2005 until he became president in 2008. The Obamas still own the house, though they chose to stay in Washington, DC, after his time in office. You can't go inside, and fences block the sidewalk, but you can get close enough for a photo.

Muhammad Ali House (Map p332; 4944 S Woodlawn Ave; ⬛6, MMetra Electric Line to 47th St) Muhammad Ali lived for a time in this large brick Tudor home, less than a block from his spiritual mentor Elijah Muhammad.

Elijah Muhammad House (Map p332; 4855 S Woodlawn Ave; ⬛6, MMetra Electric Line to 47th St) Muhammad, founder of the Nation of Islam, built the 21-room mansion at the corner of Woodlawn Ave and 49th St in 1971. Louis Farrakhan, the group's current leader, lives there now.

Muddy Waters' House (Off Map p332; 4339 S Lake Park Ave) Impromptu jam sessions with pals like Howlin' Wolf and Chuck Berry erupted in the front yard. Waters, of course, was Chicago's main bluesman, so everyone who was anyone came to pay homage. Waters lived here for 20 years, until 1974, but today the building stands vacant in a lonely, tumbledown lot. The big red X on the front means it's a candidate for demolition. A sign commemorates the spot. You'll need a car to get to this one.

comprises bird-rich lagoons, busy boat harbors, sweet-smelling meadows, the Garden of the Phoenix, a golf course (p216) and **63rd Street Beach** (Off Map p332; www.cpdbeaches. com; 6300 S Lake Shore Dr, Woodlawn; ⊘6am-11pm; 🚇6, Ⓜ Metra Electric Line to 63rd). Historically, it's where the city held the 1893 World's Expo, when Chicago introduced the world to wonders such as the Ferris wheel, moving pictures and the zipper. The Museum of Science & Industry (p205) sits in the park's northern reach. The new Barack Obama Presidential Center complex is set to open on the park's western edge between 60th and 63rd Sts sometime after 2021.

If you're looking for a nice walk, Jackson Park connects to Washington Park via a mile-long boulevard called the Midway Plaisance. The Plaisance itself is basically a park, home to an ice rink and college students kicking around soccer balls in the grassy expanse.

GARDEN OF THE PHOENIX   GARDENS
Map p332 (www.gardenofthephoenix.org⊘6am-11pm; 🚇6, Ⓜ Metra Electric Line to 59th St) **FREE** The enchanted Garden of the Phoenix floats in Jackson Park. Birds flit through the sunlight, turtles swim in the lagoons, and stonecut lanterns dot the exotic landscape, which feels worlds away from the city. Yoko Ono's sculpture *Sky Landing* – comprised of 12 large steel lotus petals – adds a groovy touch. It's all located on Wooded Island, behind the Museum of Science & Industry (p205).

HYDE PARK ART CENTER   GALLERY
Map p332 (📞773-324-5520; www.hydeparkart. org; 5020 S Cornell Ave, Kenwood; ⊘9am-8pm Mon-Thu, 9am-5pm Fri & Sat, noon-5pm Sun; 🚇6, Ⓜ Metra Electric Line to 51st-53rd St) Hyde Park Art Center shows contemporary works by Chicagoans – many of them students (current or graduated) of the center's classes. There's usually a couple of exhibitions going on simultaneously. Check the calendar for yoga sessions, educational workshops and other events.

WASHINGTON PARK   PARK
Map p332 (5531 S Martin Luther King Jr Dr; 🚇6, Ⓜ Metra Electric Line to 55th-56th-57th St) Famed landscape architect Fredrick Law Olmsted designed stately Washington Park. It hosts heaps of community festivals and athletic fields for teams playing cricket and 16in softball. The southern expanse is more peaceful, filled with lagoons, willowy trees and the enormous, forlorn *Fountain of Time*

sculpture by Lorado Taft, which has occupied the park's southeast corner for almost a century. The DuSable Museum of African American History is also here.

DUSABLE MUSEUM OF AFRICAN AMERICAN HISTORY   MUSEUM
Map p332 (📞773-947-0600; www.dusable museum.org; 740 E 56th Pl, Washington Park; adult/child $10/3, Tue free; ⊘10am-5pm Tue-Sat, noon-5pm Sun; 🚇6, Ⓜ Metra Electric Line to 55th-56th-57th St) This was the first independent museum in the country dedicated to African American art, history and culture. The collection features African American artworks and photography, permanent exhibits that illustrate African Americans' experiences from slavery through the Civil Rights movement, and rotating exhibits that cover topics such as Chicago blues music or the Black Panther movement. It's affiliated with the Smithsonian Institution. Free on Tuesdays.

UNIVERSITY OF CHICAGO   UNIVERSITY
Map p332 (www.uchicago.edu; 5801 S Ellis Ave; 🚇6, Ⓜ Metra Electric Line to 59th St) Faculty and students have racked up more than 80 Nobel prizes within U of C's hallowed halls. The economics and physics departments lay claim to most of the awards. The campus is well worth a stroll, offering grand Gothic architecture and free art and antiquities museums.

The university's classes first met on October 1, 1892. John D Rockefeller was a major contributor to the institution, donating more than $35 million. The original campus was constructed in an English Gothic style. Highlights of a walkabout include the sculpture-laden Rockefeller Memorial Chapel (p208), serene Bond Chapel (p209) and Henry Moore's bronze Nuclear Energy (p208) sculpture.

SMART MUSEUM OF ART   MUSEUM
Map p332 (📞773-702-0200; http://smartmuseum. uchicago.edu; 5550 S Greenwood Ave; ⊘10am-5pm Tue-Sun year-round, to 8pm Thu Sep–mid-Jun; 🚇6, Ⓜ Metra Electric Line to 55th-56th-57th St) **FREE** Named after the founders of *Esquire* magazine, who contributed the start-up money, this is the official fine-arts museum of the University of Chicago. The collection holds 5000 years' worth of works. Twentieth-century paintings and sculptures, Central European expressionism and East Asian art are the strong suits. De Goya, Warhol and Kandinsky are just a few of the big-name

WORTH A DETOUR

PULLMAN NATIONAL MONUMENT

A National Park Service site since 2015, **Pullman** (☏773-785-8901; www.nps.gov/pull; 11141 S Cottage Grove Ave; ⊙11am-3pm Tue-Sat, closed mid-Dec–mid-Feb; Ⓜ Metra Electric Line to 111th St-Pullman) **FREE** offers a rare look at a capitalist's fallen utopia.

George Pullman was a millionaire rail-car manufacturer, and he started his namesake community in 1880 to provide his workers with homes in a wholesome environment. He built houses, apartments, stores, a hotel and churches. The town's careful design was based on French models and featured an aesthetic unknown in workers' housing then or now. But business went sour in 1893 when an economic depression hit. Pullman cut workers' pay, though he didn't lower their rent. A violent strike ensued in 1894, and things were never the same afterward. Pullman died in 1897, and the town was sold off shortly thereafter.

Pullman's design and architecture make for a fascinating walkabout, and you'll learn about labor history and urban planning along the way. But be aware the site is a work in progress, and several buildings are still being refurbished. A new visitor center is set to open in the Clock Tower by late 2020. In the interim, the Historic Pullman Foundation (www.pullmanil.org) offers information and occasional walking tours; check the website for details.

The site isn't easy to reach, as it is located on the city's far south side. Metra's Electric Line train makes the trip in about 40 minutes from downtown's Millennium Station.

artists on offer. Frank Lloyd Wright's table and chairs mix in for good measure.

ARTS INCUBATOR   GALLERY

Off Map p332 (☏773-702-9724; www.facebook. com/pg/artspubliclife; 301 E Garfield Blvd, Washington Park; ⊙noon-6pm Wed-Fri; Ⓜ Green Line to Garfield) Artist-activist Theaster Gates, in conjunction with the University of Chicago, has revamped what was an abandoned 1920s terra-cotta building at the edge of Washington Park into a space for community-based art projects and exhibitions. It's worth popping in to see what's showing. Free yoga classes, knitting groups and other events take place regularly.

ORIENTAL INSTITUTE   MUSEUM

Map p332 (☏773-702-9514; www.oi.uchicago. edu; 1155 E 58th St; suggested donation $10; ⊙10am-5pm Tue & Thu-Sun, to 8pm Wed; ☐6, Ⓜ Metra Electric Line to 59th St) The University of Chicago's famed archaeologists – Indiana Jones supposedly was based on one – cram their headquarters with antiquities they've unearthed from Egypt, Nubia, Persia and Mesopotamia. King Tut is the star, standing 17ft tall, weighing 6 tons and lording over more mummies, clay tablets and canopic jars than you can shake a papyrus scroll at.

KAM ISAIAH ISRAEL   SYNAGOGUE

Map p332 (☏773-924-1234; www.kamii.org; 1100 E Hyde Park Blvd, Kenwood; ⊙by appointment 8:30am-4:30pm Mon-Fri; ☐6, Ⓜ Metra Electric Line to 51st-53rd St) The synagogue is a domed masterpiece in the Byzantine style with acoustics that are said to be perfect. Staff provide tours by appointment on weekdays; they're free, but donations are welcome. Outside, KAM's lawn has been transformed into a micro-farm that raises food for people in need on Chicago's south side.

NUCLEAR ENERGY   SCULPTURE

Map p332 (S Ellis Ave, btwn E 56th & E 57th Sts; ☐6, Ⓜ Metra Electric Line to 55th-56th-57th St) The nuclear age began at the University of Chicago: Enrico Fermi and his Manhattan Project cronies built a reactor and carried out the world's first controlled atomic reaction on December 2, 1942. The bronze *Nuclear Energy* sculpture, by Henry Moore, marks the spot where it blew its stack.

ROCKEFELLER
MEMORIAL CHAPEL   CHAPEL

Map p332 (☏773-702-2667; http://rockefeller. uchicago.edu; 5850 S Woodlawn Ave; ⊙11am-6pm Tue-Fri; ☐6, Ⓜ Metra Electric Line to 59th St) The building's exterior will send sculpture lovers into paroxysms of joy – the facade bears 24 life-size religious figures and 53 smaller ones, with even more inside. Check the website for times of carillon and tower tours ($5 donation requested). The chapel is also open on weekends during scheduled events.

BOND CHAPEL CHAPEL

Map p332 (1010 E 59th St; ⊘8am-4:45pm Mon-Fri; 🚇6, ⓂMetra Electric Line to 59th St) Built in 1926, the exquisite 150-seat chapel is worth a peek for its harmonious use of architecture, sculpture, woodcarvings and stained glass.

⊙ Bridgeport

BRIDGEPORT ART CENTER ARTS CENTER

Map p331 (⌨773-247-3000; www.bridgeportart.com; 1200 W 35th St; ⊘8am-6pm Mon-Sat, to noon Sun; 🚇8) The old Spiegel Catalog Warehouse holds more than 50 artists' studios. The best time to come is on the third Friday of the month when the studios open to the public for a big to-do between 7pm and 10pm. Galleries on the 3rd and 4th floors offer intriguing exhibits in a variety of media. The modern sculpture garden (along Racine Ave) is also worth a peek.

PALMISANO PARK PARK

Off Map p331 (2700 S Halsted St; ⊘6am-11pm; 🚇8) Opened on the site of an old limestone quarry, Palmisano Park unfurls an urban prairie landscape with great views of the Chicago skyline. Locals come here to fish for bluegill in the lagoon in summer and sled the hills in winter. The winding walkways, made of recycled construction debris, are great for a stroll anytime.

ZHOU B ART CENTER ARTS CENTER

Map p331 (⌨773-523-0200; www.zhoubartcenter.com; 1029 W 35th St; ⊘main exhibition spaces 10am-5pm Mon-Sat; 🚇8) Zhou B fills a massive old warehouse with galleries and studios and is the workplace of some 50 artists. The main exhibition spaces, on the 1st and 2nd floors, show contemporary paintings and sculpture by well-known international artists. The center also participates in the popular Third Friday Open Studios event from 7pm to 10pm.

PLANT CHICAGO FACTORY

Off Map p331 (⌨773-847-5523; www.plantchicago.org; 1400 W 46th St, Back of the Yards; ⊘10am-4pm Sat; 🚇9) The Plant occupies an enormous former meatpacking facility where a community of food producers is now engaged in a collaborative experiment to eliminate waste. Basically, each business housed in the Plant tries to make its waste somehow useful for another. For instance, used coffee from roaster Four Letter Word and spent grains from brewery Whiner Beer (p215) are compressed into bricks that fuel the ovens for Pleasant House's pizzas. Saturday tours (per person $10; see schedule) show how it's done.

UNION STOCKYARDS GATE HISTORIC SITE

Map p331 (850 W Exchange Ave, New City; 🚇8) The castle-like gate was once the main entrance to the vast stockyards where millions of cows and hogs met their ends each year. During the 1893 World's Expo the stockyards were a popular tourist draw, with nearly 10,000 people a day making the trek here to stare, awestruck, as the butchering machine took in animals and spat out blood and meat.

The value of those slaughtered in 1910 was an enormous $225 million. While sanitary conditions eventually improved from the hideous levels documented by Upton Sinclair, during the Spanish-American War American soldiers suffered more casualties because of bad cans of meat from the Chicago packing houses than because of enemy fire.

⊙ Bronzeville

ILLINOIS INSTITUTE OF TECHNOLOGY UNIVERSITY

Map p331 (IIT; ⌨312-567-7146; www.miessociety.org; 3201 S State St; ⓂGreen Line to 35th St-Bronzeville-IIT) A world-class leader in technology, industrial design and architecture, the IIT owes much of its look to Ludwig Mies van der Rohe, the famed mid-century architect who fled the Nazis in Germany for Chicago in 1938. From 1940 until his retirement in 1958, he designed 22 IIT buildings that reflected his tenets of architecture, combining simple, black-metal frames with glass and brick infills. SR Crown Hall is the rock star. Check the website to see if campus tours are being offered.

SR CROWN HALL ARCHITECTURE

Map p331 (3360 S State St; ⓂGreen Line to 35th-Bronzeville-IIT) The star of the Illinois Institute of Technology campus and Ludwig Mies van der Rohe's undisputed masterpiece is SR Crown Hall, appropriately home to the College of Architecture. The 1956 building, close to the center of campus, appears to be a transparent glass box floating between its translucent base and suspended roof. At night it glows from within like an illuminated jewel.

Lofty Heights in Hyde Park & South Side

Maybe it's the architecture that has inspired researchers at the University of Chicago to win more than 80 Nobel prizes. It's certainly grandiose, with Gothic spires soaring into the sky and thick, turreted buildings fronting leafy quadrangles. Frank Lloyd Wright's Prairie-style Robie House offers a more modern counterpoint.

STEVEGEER / GETTY IMAGES ©

CONCH MARTINEZ / SHUTTERSTOCK ©

1. Museum of Science & Industry (p205)

The Western Hemisphere's largest science museum has interactive displays offering hands-on experiences.

2. Dusable Museum of African American History (p207)

The United States' first independent museum dedicated to African American art, history and culture.

3. Robie House (p204)

The landmark Robie House was designed by Frank Lloyd Wright.

4. Garden of the Phoenix (p207)

An enchanting garden located in Jackson Park.

EQROY / SHUTTERSTOCK ©

VICTORY MONUMENT — MONUMENT

Map p331 (3500 S Martin Luther King Jr Dr; MGreen Line to 35th-Bronzeville-IIT) In the median of Martin Luther King Jr Dr, near 35th St, the Victory Monument was erected in 1928 in honor of the African American soldiers who fought in WWI. The figures include a soldier, a mother and Columbia, the mythical figure meant to symbolize the New World.

IDA B WELLS HOUSE — HOUSE

Map p331 (3624 S Martin Luther King Jr Dr; MGreen Line to 35th-Bronzeville-IIT) One of scores of Romanesque houses that date from the 1880s, the Ida B Wells House is named for its 1920s resident. Wells was a civil rights advocate who launched her career after being forcibly removed from a train for refusing to go to the segregated car. A crusading journalist, she investigated lynchings and other racially motivated crimes. The home is a private residence and not open to the public, though it's marked with a placard that outlines its significance.

SUPREME LIFE BUILDING — HISTORIC BUILDING

Map p331 (3501 S Martin Luther King Jr Dr; MGreen Line to 35th-Bronzeville-IIT) The 1930s Supreme Life Building was the spot where John H Johnson Jr, the publishing mogul who founded *Ebony* magazine, got the idea for his empire, which included *Jet* and other important titles serving African Americans. There's a little neighborhood visitor center that sells old albums and trinkets behind the bank here; enter from 35th St.

ROBERT W ROLOSON HOUSES — ARCHITECTURE

Map p331 (3213-19 S Calumet Ave; MGreen Line to 35th-Bronzeville-IIT) Examples of stylish architecture from the past can be found throughout Bronzeville, and you can see some fine homes along two blocks of Calumet Ave between 31st and 33rd Sts, an area known as 'the Gap.' The buildings here include Frank Lloyd Wright's only row houses, the Robert W Roloson Houses.

✖ EATING

Earthy cafes sprinkle Hyde Park. Bridgeport offers hipster chow. Head into the neighborhoods beyond, and soul food, barbecue, Senegalese dishes and doughnuts the size of a life preserver await. Establishments are very scattered, though 75th St near the intersection of S Martin Luther King Jr Dr does have a cluster of African American–owned eateries.

✖ Hyde Park

★VALOIS RESTAURANT — AMERICAN $

Map p332 (☑773-667-0647; www.valois restaurant.com; 1518 E 53rd St; mains $6-14; ◎5:30am-10pm; ☑6, MMetra Electric Line to 51st-53rd St) It's a mixed crowd at Valois. In fact, the clientele is so socioeconomically diverse that a U of C sociology professor wrote a well-known book about it, titled *Slim's Table*. It seems hot, fast, Southern-style dishes like catfish, biscuits and pot pies attract all kinds – even Barack Obama, who chowed here regularly when he lived in the neighborhood. Cash only.

SAUCY PORKA — FUSION $

Map p332 (☑872-244-3772; www.saucyporka.com; 1164 E 55th St; mains $8-13; ◎10:30am-9pm Sun-Thu, to 10pm Fri & Sat; ☑6) This airy, Asian-vibed eatery fuses flavors from Puerto Rico, Korea, Japan, China and Vietnam. Eclectic dishes result, such as the 'baco' (a cross between a steamed Chinese bao and taco), chorizo egg rolls and the signature 'saucy porka' banh mi sandwich (kimchi-topped pork carnitas on a French baguette). The fast-casual spot is a student favorite.

PLEIN AIR CAFE — CAFE $

Map p332 (☑773-966-7531; www.pleinaircafe.co; 5751 S Woodlawn Ave; mains $7-11; ◎7am-8pm Mon-Fri, 8am-6pm Sat & Sun; ☑6, MMetra Electric Line to 59th St) Natural light streams in the floor-to-ceiling windows that look out at Frank Lloyd Wright's famed Robie House (p204) next door. Order a quinoa-and-roasted-vegetable-packed grain bowl, spelt scone or egg-and-spinach pie off the wholesome menu. The rustic French farmhouse-inspired decor promotes lingering, as does the reading material at attached Seminary Co-op Bookstore (p216).

★GORÉE CUISINE — SENEGALESE $$

Off Map p332 (☑773-855-8120; www.goreecuisine.com; 1126 E 47th St, Kenwood; mains $11-19; ◎9am-10pm Mon-Wed, 8am-11pm Thu-Sun; MMetra Electric Line to 47th St) You'll feel transported to Dakar upon entering this tidy, white-curtained, cafe where spicy *yassa* chicken

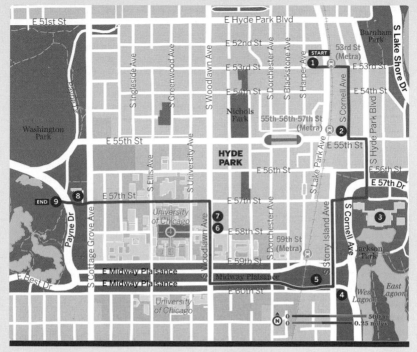

🏃 Neighborhood Walk
Hyde Park Highlights

START VALOIS RESTAURANT
END WASHINGTON PARK
LENGTH 3 MILES; FOUR HOURS

Local-favorite eats, African American history sites, eye-popping architecture, scholarly bookshops and famous parks pop up on this amble through the diverse community.

Start at ❶ **Valois Restaurant** (opposite), where neighborhood folks dig in to buttery, Southern-style dishes at the cafeteria tables. Head east on E 53rd St under the train tracks to S Cornell Ave, and turn south. After a couple of blocks you'll see a funky, geometric high-rise glinting in the sun. That's ❷ **Solstice on the Park**, an apartment designed by local starchitect Jeanne Gang.

Turn east on E 55th St, walk a block to S Hyde Park Blvd, and head south toward the ❸ **Museum of Science & Industry** (p205). It's the Western Hemisphere's largest science collection, complete with a submarine, space capsule and airplanes inside.

Walk west on E 57th St to S Stony Island Ave. Turn south and walk until you come to

E Midway Plaisance. Stand at the southeast corner (near 60th St), the site where the new Barack Obama Presidential Center will rise sometime after 2021. It's in the heart of historic ❹ **Jackson Park** (p206), developed as the site of the 1893 World's Fair, when Chicago introduced the world to zippers, Ferris wheels and Pabst Blue Ribbon beer.

Most of the fair's exhibits stood in the ❺ **Midway Plaisance**, a long, thin park, which is where you'll walk now (look for the sidewalk). In roughly a half-mile you'll arrive at S Woodlawn Ave; turn north toward the University of Chicago campus. At E 58th St Frank Lloyd Wright's masterwork ❻ **Robie House** (p204) sits unobtrusively on the corner. Browse the stacks at ❼ **Seminary Co-op Bookstore** (p216) next door, then continue north on Woodlawn Ave to E 57th St and turn west. In a half-mile you'll arrive at the ❽ **DuSable Museum of African American History** (p207), a gem that tells the South Side's story. Then you can explore surrounding ❾ **Washington Park** (p207) and its pretty lagoons, willowy trees and cricket fields.

(marinated in lemon and onion), *bissap* (hibiscus flower drink) and a slew of other Senegalese dishes hit the tables. If you're new to the cuisine, the friendly staff will help you order. Gorée offers a terrific, authentic, reasonably priced experience that's rare to find.

✕ Bridgeport

KIMSKI
FUSION $

Map p331 (☑773-823-7336; www.kimskichicago.com; 954 W 31st St; ☺5-11pm Tue-Sat, noon-9pm Sun; ☐8) This counter-service spot, a mod-looking addition to local bar Maria's (p215), has created a new culinary genre: KoPo, or Korean-Polish fusion. The owners created the mash-up in homage to their family backgrounds, resulting in some wild combinations. Maria's Standard tops a Polish sausage with 'kraut chi' (sauerkraut meets kimchi), while dill-scented potato pancakes get a twist from tamarispiked sour cream.

NANA
AMERICAN $

Map p331 (☑312-929-2486; www.nanaorganic.com; 3267 S Halsted St; mains $11-16; ☺10am-2:30pm Mon-Fri, 9am-4:30pm Sat & Sun; ☑; ☐8) 🍴 This convivial little gem has received multiple Michelin Bib Gourmand awards for great food offered at great value. It whips up yummy organic breakfasts (try the poached egg and chorizo 'nanadict') and sandwiches. Many dishes have a Latin twist, such as the chicken plantain sandwich with chipotle-lime mayonnaise.

DUCK INN
GASTROPUB $$$

Off Map 33100 (☑312-724-8811; www.theduckinnchicago.com; 2701 S Eleanor St; mains $22-31, 5-course tasting menu $85; ☺5-11pm Tue-Thu, 5pm-midnight Fri & Sat, 10am-midnight Sun; Ⓜ Orange Line to Ashland) This superb gastropub hides on a working-class block in Bridgeport. There's much to love here: the ubercool midcentury modern decor, the exquisite cocktails, oh, and the food, especially the signature roasted duck for two and the duck-fat hot dog. It's high-quality fare in a completely non-snooty environment.

✕ South Side

PEACH'S AT CURRENCY
EXCHANGE CAFÉ
CAFE $

Off Map p331 (☑312-300-4471; www.peachsexchange.com; 305 E Garfield Blvd, Washington Park; mains $7-14; ☺7am-3pm Mon-Sat; Ⓜ Green Line to Garfield) This former currency exchange, cleverly reconceived as a stylish cafe and community gathering spot by local activist-artist Theaster Gates, injects a commercial strip in under-resourced Washington Park with a dose of cool. The menu skews toward soulful dishes such as peach bourbon French toast, shrimp and cheese grits and caramel cupcakes.

DAT DONUT
BAKERY $

(☑773-723-1002; www.datdonut.com; 8251 S Cottage Grove Ave, Chatham; doughnuts & breakfast sandwiches $1-5; ☺24hr Mon-Sat, midnight-5pm Sun; Ⓜ Metra Electric Line to 83rd St) Point to what you want in the glass case, then a staff member will load it into the lazy Susan and spin it around to you. The device is hardly big enough to contain the shop's masterpiece – the Big Dat, a spongy glazed doughnut the size of a hubcap. Custard doughnuts, chocolate long johns and apple fritters also reign supreme.

LEM'S BAR-B-Q
BARBECUE $

(☑773-994-2428; www.lemsbarbq.com; 311 E 75th St, Greater Grand Crossing; mains $10-15; ☺1pm-1am Mon, Wed, Thu & Sun, to 3am Fri & Sat) Lem's is revered for its smoky-sauced rib tips, which come cushioned between a bed of fries and topping of white-bread slices. You'll need a car to get here. Cash only.

ORIGINAL SOUL
VEGETARIAN
VEGAN $$

(☑773-224-0104; www.originalsoulvegetarian.com; 203 E 75th St, Greater Grand Crossing; mains $7-13; ☺11am-8pm Mon-Thu, 8:30am-10pm Fri & Sat, 8:30am-8pm Sun; ☑) Finding soul food that meets the tenets of the vegan diet is such a rarity that the creative barbecue sandwiches and dinner plates at this comfy South Side place have earned a national reputation. It attaches to a juice bar, so you can get your wheatgrass fix, too. You'll need wheels to get here.

🍷 DRINKING & NIGHTLIFE

Hyde Park and Bridgeport both have long-standing, absolute gems for divey drinking with locals. Bridgeport also does beer well, thanks to a great microbrewery and community bar. Nightlife here is quite spread out.

🍷 Hyde Park

BUILD COFFEE
COFFEE

Off Map p332 (☑773-627-5058; www.buildcoffee. org; 6100 S Blackstone Ave, Woodlawn; ⊙8am-5:30pm Mon-Fri, from 9am Sat & Sun; ⬚6, ⓂMetra Electric Line to 63rd st) The cozy little room with found furniture and exposed brick walls is a great place to munch a sandwich, sip a rose cardamom latte with oat milk, and shop for zines and small-press books (it's a mini bookstore, as well).

COVE LOUNGE
BAR

Map p332 (☑773-684-1013; www.thecovelounge. com; 1750 E 55th St; ⊙11am-2am Sun-Fri, to 3am Sat; ⬚6, ⓂMetra Electric Line to 55th-56th-57th St) There's much to admire at the Cove: the worn swivel chairs at the bar, the jazzy jukebox, dart games and literary conversations. Add in the decent craft beer selection and Instagram-worthy Obama mural, and you can see why it has been a neighborhood mainstay for decades. A neon 'cocktail lounge' sign over the entrance marks the spot. Cash only.

JIMMY'S WOODLAWN TAP
BAR

Map p332 (☑773-643-5516; 1172 E 55th St; ⊙10:30am-2am Mon-Fri, 11am-3am Sat, 11am-2am Sun; ⬚6, ⓂMetra Electric Line to 55th-56th-57th St) Many of the geniuses of our age have killed brain cells right here in the Woodlawn Tap (also known as Jimmy's for the longtime owner). The place is dark and beery, and a little seedy. But for thousands of University of Chicago students craving pitchers of brew and heady conversation, it's home. Hungry? The Swissburgers are legendary. Cash only.

🍷 Bridgeport

⭐MARZ
COMMUNITY BREWING
MICROBREWERY

Off Map p331 (☑773-579-1935; www.marzbrewing. com; 3630 S Iron St, McKinley Park; ⊙noon-11pm Tue-Thu, to midnight Fri & Sat, to 10pm Sun; ⬚9) Marz started as a group of home brewers whose friends demanded more. The small brewery is known for its peculiar creations, such as Potion #1 (aged in absinthe barrels), Diliner Weisse (with fresh dill) and Churros Y Chocolate (milk stout brewed with cocoa nibs and cinnamon). The taproom is a gathering spot for local artists and beer buffs.

MARIA'S PACKAGED
GOODS & COMMUNITY BAR
BAR

Map p331 (☑773-890-0588; http://community-bar.com; 960 W 31st St; ⊙3pm-2am Mon-Thu, from noon Fri-Sun; ☎; ⬚8) Owner Ed works the cozy back-room bar furnished with vintage decor, while mom Maria works the front liquor store. Both offer an excellent craft-beer selection that draws local hipsters. Several taps flow with the oddball concoctions of Marz Community Brewing, which Ed also operates. They're perfect with Maria's grub, which comes from the family's Korean-Polish restaurant (Kimski) next door.

WHINER BEER COMPANY
MICROBREWERY

(☑312-810-2271; www.whinerbeer.com; 1400 W 46th St, Back of the Yards; ⊙4-11pm Wed-Fri, noon-11pm Sat, 1-8pm Sun; ⬚9) Barrel-aged beers rule at Whiner. Choose among wild saisons, Belgian wheat beers and Belgian dark ales in the rustic, softly lit taproom. A five-beer flight is the way to go, perhaps with a wood-fired pizza from the shop next door. Whiner is located in the Plant (p209), an experimental zero-waste facility, which provides an intriguing backdrop to the brewery.

BERNICE'S TAVERN
BAR

Map p331 (☑312-961-5516; 3238 S Halsted St; ⊙3pm-midnight Mon, 3pm-2am Wed-Fri, 11am-3am Sat, noon-midnight Sun; ⬚8, ⓂRed Line to Sox-35th St) A motley assemblage of local artists and neighborhood regulars haunts this workaday Bridgeport tavern, where the eclectic calendar includes wild, wacky bingo sessions on Wednesdays and country and blues bands on weekends. Order a Švyturys, a beer every bit as Lithuanian as the owners, and admire the kitschy knickknacks, which look like they've been around since time began. Cash only.

☆ ENTERTAINMENT

GREEN LINE PERFORMING
ARTS CENTER
PERFORMING ARTS

Off Map p332 (https://arts.uchicago.edu/apl/glpac; 329 E Garfield Blvd, Washington Park; ⓂGreen Line to Garfield) This stark-black, newly built venue opened in late 2018. It holds an 80-seat theater for music, dance and storytelling performances, and an outdoor courtyard for public programs and open-air film screenings. Much of the programming is free, including the First Mondays Jazz series, held the first Monday of every month.

HYDE PARK & SOUTH SIDE ENTERTAINMENT

GUARANTEED RATE FIELD
BASEBALL

Map p331 (☎866-769-4263; www.mlb.com/whitesox; 333 W 35th St, Bridgeport; MRed Line to Sox-35th St) The White Sox play in this modern stadium. They're the Cubs' South Side rivals. Tickets are usually cheaper and easier to get than at Wrigley Field; games on Sunday and Monday offer the best deals. The Sox also come up with more promotions (free T-shirts, fireworks etc) to lure fans. Sellouts aren't usually an issue; you can stroll up to the ballpark box office on game day and buy a ticket. The ballpark has a couple of cool features, such as the Craft Kave, where you sip your terrific microbrew practically on right field, and the pet check, which allows dog owners to bring Fido to the game and drop him off with a babysitter for a fee.

SHOPPING

Bookstores galore tempt from the streets around the University of Chicago campus. Heading further out you'll find farmers markets and crafty independent shops catering to African American consumers.

★SEMINARY CO-OP BOOKSTORE
BOOKS

Map p332 (☎773-752-4381; www.semcoop.com; 5751 S Woodlawn Ave, Hyde Park; ⊗8:30am-8pm Mon-Fri, 10am-6pm Sat & Sun; ☐6, MMetra Electric Line to 59th St) At awesomely academic Seminary Co-op, you might run into a Nobel laureate or three. Local scholars adore this place, where you'll find no less than eight versions of *War and Peace*. The shop sprawls through a sunny building next to Robie House (p204), and provides plenty of chairs on which to sit and read. Busy Plein Air Cafe (p212) is attached.

61ST STREET FARMERS MARKET
MARKET

Off Map p332 (☎773-241-6044; ⊗9am-2pm Sat) Shop for cheese, meat and eggs from family farms, as well as pies from Pleasant House Pub (p196). The small quality market also hosts cooking demonstrations, live music and food-sustainability workshops. From May through October it's held outdoors at 61st and Dorchester Sts; from November through April it moves indoors into the Experimental Station building at 6100 S Blackstone Ave.

BLACK MALL
ARTS & CRAFTS

(☎773-357-6154; www.facebook.com/theblackmall; 533 E 79th St, Greater Grand Crossing; ⊗10am-7pm Mon-Sat; MMetra Electric Line to 79th St) Walk around the big, open room where some 50 different African American vendors sell their jewelry, head wraps, dolls, T-shirts, purses, spice mixes, beauty products, pies and cakes. The space holds loads of free events as well.

57TH STREET BOOKS
BOOKS

Map p332 (☎773-684-1300; www.semcoop.com; 1301 E 57th St, Hyde Park; ⊗10am-8pm; ☐6, MMetra Electric Line to 55th-56th-57th St) As you descend the stairs to this basement-level shop you know you're in the right place. Its labyrinth of low-slung rooms makes up the kind of old-fashioned bookstore that goes way deeper than the popular titles. It has excellent staff picks. Seminary Co-op Bookstore is its sister shop.

POWELL'S
BOOKS

Map p332 (☎773-955-7780; www.powellschicago.com; 1501 E 57th St, Hyde Park; ⊗9am-11pm; ☐6, MMetra Electric Line to 55th-56th-57th) This leading store for used books can get you just about any title ever published. Shelf after heaving shelf props up the well-arranged stock. Staff sometimes put a box of free books outside by the entrance.

SPORTS & ACTIVITIES

MARGARET T BURROUGHS BEACH
BEACH

Off Map p331 (www.cpdbeaches.com; 3100 S Lake Shore Dr, Bronzeville; ⊗6am-11pm; ☐3) Named for Margaret T Burroughs, the prominent artist, poet, historian and founder of the DuSable Museum (p207), this beach is better known by its original name: 31st Street Beach. Whatever you call it, it's a fab strand with lots of families, great skyline views, a boat harbor, fishing dock and waterside cafe. It's one of the city's most underrated, amenity-laden beaches.

JACKSON PARK GOLF COURSE
GOLF

Off Map p332 (☎773-667-0524; www.cpdgolf.com; 6401 S Richards Dr, Woodlawn; ☐6, MMetra Electric Line to 63rd St) The district's only 18-hole course is moderately challenging. Public fees range from $32 to $35. Reservations are recommended. There's also a driving range.

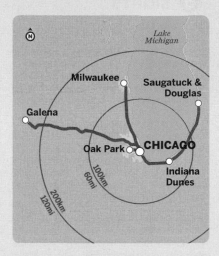

Day Trips from Chicago

Oak Park p218
Tour Frank Lloyd Wright's studio and see a slew of homes he designed for his neighbors. Ernest Hemingway's birthplace is here, too.

Indiana Dunes p219
Sunny beaches, woodsy trails, ranger-guided walks and towering sand dunes feature at this national and state park combination.

Milwaukee p221
Wisconsin's biggest city has a stellar lineup of beer, motorcycles, world-class art and a ballpark of racing sausages.

Saugatuck & Douglas p223
The artsy towns boom in summer thanks to their golden beaches, piney breezes, fruit pies and welcome-one, welcome-all mindset.

Galena p224
Quaint it is, with perfectly preserved, Civil War–era streets set amid rolling, cow-dotted hills by the Mississippi River.

Oak Park

Explore

This suburb next door to Chicago spawned two famous sons: novelist Ernest Hemingway was born here, and architect Frank Lloyd Wright lived and worked here for 20 years. The town's main sights revolve around the two men. For Hemingway, a low-key museum and his birthplace provide an intriguing peek at his formative years. For Wright, the studio where he developed the Prairie style is the big draw, as is a slew of surrounding houses he designed for his neighbors. Ten of them cluster within a mile along Forest and Chicago Aves (though gawking must occur from the sidewalk since they're privately owned).

The Best...

→ **Sight** Frank Lloyd Wright Home & Studio

→ **Place to Eat** Hemmingway's Bistro

→ **Place to Drink** Kinslahger Brewing Company

Top Tip

Explore on the cheap by buying an architectural site map ($4.35) from the Wright Home & Studio shop, which gives the locations of all Wright-designed homes in the area.

Getting There & Away

→ **Car** I-290 edges the town; exit on Harlem Ave. Take Harlem north to Lake St and turn right. There's a parking garage within a few blocks.

→ **Train** Metra commuter trains on the Union Pacific West Line stop at Oak Park on their Chicago–western suburbs route. Green Line trains also run to/from Chicago as part of the city's public transit system. The sights are walkable from the stations.

Need to Know

→ **Area Code** ✐708

→ **Location** 10 miles west of the Loop

→ **Tourist Office** (www.visitoakpark.com) A wealth of online info, but the physical visitors center has closed.

◉ SIGHTS

★FRANK LLOYD WRIGHT HOME & STUDIO   ARCHITECTURE

(✐312-994-4000; www.flwright.org; 951 Chicago Ave; adult/child $18/15; ◷10am-4pm) This is where Wright lived and worked from 1889 to 1909 and it's the first home he ever designed. Tour frequency varies, from every 20 minutes on summer weekends to every hour or so in winter. The hour-long walkthrough reveals a fascinating place, filled with the details that made Wright's style distinctive. The studio also offers guided neighborhood walking tours ($15) on Sundays; a self-guided audio version ($15) is available on other days.

ERNEST HEMINGWAY BIRTHPLACE   MUSEUM

(✐708-445-3071; www.ehfop.org; 339 N Oak Park Ave; adult/child $15/free; ◷1-5pm Wed-Fri & Sun, from 10am Sat Mar-Dec, 1-5pm Fri & Sun, from 10am Sat Jan & Feb) Despite Hemingway allegedly calling Oak Park a village of wide lawns and narrow minds, the town still pays homage to him by maintaining his childhood home as a museum.

NATHAN G MOORE HOUSE   ARCHITECTURE

(333 Forest Ave) During Wright's 20 years in Oak Park, he designed a whole heap of houses. Moore House (closed to the public) is particularly noteworthy. First built in 1895, it's Wright's bizarre interpretation of an English manor house. In his later years, Wright called the house 'repugnant' and said he had only taken the commission because he needed the money. He claimed that he walked out of his way to avoid passing it.

UNITY TEMPLE   ARCHITECTURE

(✐312-994-4000; www.flwright.org; 875 Lake St; tours $10-18; ◷9am-4:15pm Mon-Thu, to 3:15pm Fri, to 11:15am Sat) This architectural wonder from Frank Lloyd Wright was built in 1909 and reopened in 2018 after a five-year restoration. Explore at your leisure on a 30-minute self-guided look-around ($10 per person), or go on a 60-minute guided tour ($18 per person, with departures on the hour starting at 10am weekdays, 9am on Saturday).

✕ EATING & DRINKING

CITRINE CAFE MEDITERRANEAN $$

(📞708-948-7328; www.citrinecafe.com; 100 S Oak Park Ave; mains $18-36; ⏱4:30-10pm Mon-Thu, to 11pm Fri & Sat, 10:30am-2pm & 4-10pm Sun; 🛜) This Serbian–American venture offers a lovely, dimly lit bar and restaurant serving a melange of Mediterranean and Balkan-influenced fare. The beet and feta salad (red and golden beets, oranges, pistachios, arugula, blistered grapes, passionfruit vinaigrette) and salmon (arugula pesto, roasted cauliflower, pinenuts, gnocchi) scored high marks, but the incredible honeycomb baklava is worth the L ride from the city!

HEMMINGWAY'S BISTRO FRENCH $$$

(📞708-524-0806; www.hemmingwaysbistro. com; 211 N Oak Park Ave; mains $19-38; ⏱7am-10pm) Fork in to all the French classics – coq au vin, caussoulet, bouillabaisse – at this cozy little bistro across from the Ernest Hemingway Museum. If nothing else, drop in and sit at the bar for a glass of wine.

**KINSLAHGER
BREWING COMPANY** MICROBREWERY

(www.kinslahger.com; 6806 Roosevelt Rd; ⏱4-10pm Wed & Thu, to midnight Fri, noon-midnight Sat, to 5pm Sun) This gorgeous, retro, Prohibition-styled taproom was Oak Park's first, originally started in 2016 as a lager-only adventure (hence the name). Today, there are 15 taps offering a hodgepodge beyond artisanal lagers that focuses on crafted classics given both the traditional and modern treatment (the Baltic Porter is particularly recommended; pints from $7.50).

Indiana Dunes

Explore

In addition to being home to America's newest national park, sunny beaches, rustling grasses and woodsy campgrounds are the Indiana Dunes' claim to fame. The area is hugely popular on summer days with sunbathers from Chicago and towns throughout Northern Indiana. In addition to its beaches, the area is noted for its plant variety (over 1100 species, including everything from cacti to pine trees, sprout here) and birds (370 species). Sweet hiking trails meander up the dunes and through the woodlands.

The Best...

→ **Sight** Indiana Dunes National Park
→ **Place to Eat** Octave Grill
→ **Place to Drink** Flamingo Pizza

Top Tip

The Dunes can be visited on a day trip from Chicago. If you're looking to spend the night, Chesterton (the closest; popular for trainspotting) and Valparaiso (the most charming; food and drink hotbed) are both worthwhile small-town options.

Getting There & Away

→ **Car** The Indiana Toll Rd (I-80/90), I-94, Hwy 12, Hwy 20 and Hwy 49 all skirt the lakeshore. Look for large brown signs on the roads that point the way in to the Dunes.

→ **Train** The South Shore Line (www. mysouthshoreline.com) commuter train also services the area on its Chicago–South Bend route. The stops at Dune Park and Beverly Shores put you about a mile-and-a-half walk from the beaches.

Need to Know

→ **Area Code** 📞219
→ **Location** 45 miles southeast of the Loop
→ **Tourist Office** (📞219-395-1882; www. indianadunes.com; 1215 Hwy 49; ⏱8am-6pm Jun-Aug, 8:30am-4:30pm Sep-May)

⊙ SIGHTS

**INDIANA DUNES
NATIONAL PARK** NATIONAL PARK

(📞219-926-7561; www.nps.gov/indu; 1100 N Mineral Springs Rd, Porter; ⏱6am-11pm) FREE The Dunes, which became the USA's 61st national park in 2019, stretch along 15 miles of Lake Michigan shoreline. Swimming is allowed anywhere along the shore. A short walk away from the beaches, several hiking paths crisscross the dunes and woodlands. The best are the Bailly/Chellberg Trail (2.5 miles) that winds by a still-operating 1870s farm, and the Heron Rookery Trail

GET YOUR KICKS: ROUTE 66 IN ILLINOIS

America's 'Mother Road' kicks off in Chicago on Adams St, just west of Michigan Ave. Within a 3½-hour drive you can see some vintage bits. Sadly, most of the original Route 66 has been superseded by I-55 in Illinois, though the old road still exists in scattered sections often paralleling the interstate. Keep an eye out for brown 'Historic Route 66' signs, which pop up at crucial junctions to mark the way. Top stops include the following:

Gemini Giant (810 E Baltimore St, Wilmington) The first must-see rises from the corn-fields 60 miles south of Chicago in Wilmington. Here the Gemini Giant – a 28ft fiber-glass spaceman holding a rocket – stands guard outside the Launching Pad Drive In and makes a terrific photo op. To reach it, leave I-55 at exit 241, and follow Hwy 44 south a short distance to Hwy 53, which rolls into town.

Funks Grove (☑309-874-3360; www.funksmaplesirup.com; 5257 Old Rte 66, Shirley; ☺9am-5pm Mon-Sat, from 1pm Sun) FREE Drive 90 miles onward to see Funk's pretty, 19th-century maple-sirup farm (yes, that's sirup with an 'i'). It's in Shirley (exit 154 off I-55). Afterward, get on Old Route 66 – a frontage road that parallels the interstate here – and in 10 miles you'll reach...

Palms Grill Cafe (☑217-648-2233; www.thepalmsgrillcafe.com; 110 SW Arch St, Atlanta; mains $5-11; ☺10am-2pm Wed-Fri, to 3pm Sat & Sun) Pull up a chair at this diner in the throwback hamlet of Atlanta, where thick slabs of gooseberry, chocolate cream and other retro pies tempt from the glass case. Then walk across the street to snap a photo with Tall Paul, a sky-high statue of Paul Bunyan clutching a hot dog.

Cozy Dog Drive In (☑217-525-1992; www.cozydogdrivein.com; 2935 S 6th St; mains $2-6; ☺8am-8pm Mon-Sat) It's in Springfield, 50 miles down the road from the Palms Grill, and it's where the cornmeal-battered, fried hot dog on a stick was born.

For more information, visit the Route 66 Association of Illinois (www.il66assoc.org) or Illinois Route 66 Scenic Byway (www.illinoisroute66.org). Detailed driving directions are at www.historic66.com/illinois.

(2 miles), where blue herons flock (though there's no actual rookery) and native wild-flowers bloom.

INDIANA DUNES STATE PARK   STATE PARK

(☑219-926-1952; www.in.gov/dnr/parklake; per car Indiana/out of state $7/12; ☺7am-11pm) The state park is a 2100-acre, shoreside pocket within the national park (p219); it's located at the end of Hwy 49, near Chesterton. It has more amenities than the rest of the lakeshore, but also more regulation and crowds (plus the vehicle entry fee). Winter-time brings out the cross-country skiers; summertime brings out the hikers. Seven trails zigzag over the landscape; No 8 up Mt Tom rewards with Chicago skyline views.

✖ EATING & DRINKING

★OCTAVE GRILL   BURGERS $

(www.octavegrill.com; 105 S Calumet Rd, Chesterton; burgers $8.50-11.75; ☺3-10pm Mon-Fri, noon-11pm Sat, noon-9pm Sun; ☏) Octave Grill's burgers made with grass-fed beef and piled high with gourmet goodness were voted best in Porter County. Indeed, they are cooked to perfection, just juicy and greasy enough, and are chased with a won-derful selection of five rotating craft beers.

GREAT LAKES CAFE   DINER $

(☑219-883-5737; 201 Mississippi St, Gary; mains $5-12; ☺5am-2pm Mon-Fri, 6am-noon Sat; ♨) This colorful Greek family diner sits right in front of a steel mill, whose workers pile in for the cheap, hearty pancakes, chopped steak burgers, bacon-pecan brownies and whatever else features on the whiteboard of daily specials. It's located a short distance off the highway, before you reach the na-tional lakeshore (p219).

FLAMINGO PIZZA   BAR

(www.facebook.com/thebird403; 8341 Locust Ave, Gary; ☺11am-3am; ☏) Yes, you can get pizza (from $9), but the bar is what beck-ons: a cozy watering hole where you sit elbow-to-elbow with locals. The good beers (six taps, including Michigan's Bell's Brewery and Hammond's 18th Street Brewery) and near-lake perch are a bonus to the ambience. Located near West Beach.

☆ SPORTS & ACTIVITIES

3 DUNE CHALLENGE   HIKING

(www.indianadunes.com/3dc; 1600 N 25 E, Chesterton) One of the most popular activities in the state park, the 3 Dune Challenge is a great option for day-trippers and allows you to take in the park's three highest dunes: Mt Jackson (176ft), Mt Holden (184ft) and Mt Tom (192ft). The 1.5-mile, 552ft vertical climb affords beautiful views all the way to Chicago.

CAMP STOP GENERAL STORE   CYCLING

(☑219-878-1382; 2 W Dunes Hwy; bike rental per 3hr/day $12/20; ⊙9am-9pm Mon-Sat, to 7pm Sun late May-early Oct) The store serving the nearby Dunewood Campground also rents bikes. It's located across the tracks from the Beverly Shores train stop. From here, it's a short ride to the nearest beach. Be sure to turn left onto Lake Front Dr for a quick detour past the 'Century of Progress homes,' five offbeat remnants from the 1933 Chicago World's Fair.

🛏 SLEEPING

★RILEY'S RAILHOUSE   B&B $

(☑219-395-9999; www.rileysrailhouse.com; 123 N 4th St, Chesterton; d $120-160; ❄️🏠) Occupying a decommissioned 1914 freight station in Chesterton, this railway-themed boutique B&B offers a beautiful, fireplace-warmed lounge with discerning recycled design touches, a bar and a massive open kitchen from which Richard's awesome breakfast emerges. Modern rooms – inside both the depot and the parked antique rail cars – are comfortably appointed with locomotive-themed art. Two big Labradoodles hold down the fort.

DUNEWOOD CAMPGROUND   CAMPGROUND $

(☑219-395-1882; www.nps.gov/indu; Indiana Dunes National Lakeshore, Beverly Shores; tent & RV sites $25; ⊙Apr-Oct) These seasonal campsites at Indiana Dunes National Lakeshore (p219) are rustic (no electricity) and first come, first served (no reservations).

INDIANA DUNES NATIONAL PARK CAMPGROUND   CAMPGROUND $

(☑866-622-6746; www.camp.in.gov; Indiana Dunes National Lakeshore, Chesterton; tent & RV sites $23-33; ⊙year-round) These campsites are modern and close to the beach. Reserve in advance in summertime.

Milwaukee

Explore

Beer, brats and bowling? Of course Milwaukee has them. But attractions like the Calatrava-designed art museum, bad-to-the-bone Harley-Davidson Museum, and stylish eating and shopping 'hoods have added a groovy layer to Wisconsin's largest city. In summertime, festivals let loose revelry by the lake. And where else will you see racing sausages? Milwaukee rocks any time, but especially during weekends.

The Best...

➤ **Sight** Harley-Davidson Museum
➤ **Place to Eat** Comet Cafe
➤ **Place to Drink** Champion's

Top Tip

Many bars and restaurants host a traditional fish fry on Friday. Join locals celebrating the work week's end over a communal meal of beer-battered cod, french fries and coleslaw.

Getting There & Away

➤ **Car** Take I-90/94 west from downtown Chicago, and follow I-94 when it splits off. The interstate goes all the way into Milwaukee. Travel time is around two hours; tolls cost around $6.

➤ **Train** Traveling on **Amtrak** (www.amtrak.com; 433 St Paul Ave) is often the quickest mode given the snail-crawl pace of highway traffic. The Hiawatha train runs seven times per day to/from Chicago ($25 to $35, 1½ hours). The main station is downtown.

Getting Around

➔ **Bus** The Milwaukee County Transit System (www.ridemcts.com; fare $2.25) provides efficient local bus service. Bus 31 goes to Miller Brewery; bus 90 goes to Miller Park. Catch them along Wisconsin Ave.

Need to Know

➔ **Area Code** ✏414

➔ **Location** 92 miles north of Chicago

➔ **Tourist Office** (✆800-554-1448; www.visitmilwaukee.org)

⊙ SIGHTS

★**HARLEY-DAVIDSON MUSEUM** MUSEUM

(✏414-287-2789; www.harley-davidson.com; 400 W Canal St; adult/child $20/10; ⊙9am-6pm Fri-Wed, 9am-8pm Thu May-Sep, 10am-6pm Fri-Wed, 10am-8pm Thu Oct-Apr) Hundreds of motorcycles show the styles through the decades, including the flashy rides of Elvis and Evel Knievel. You can sit in the saddle of various bikes (on the bottom floor, in the Experience Gallery) and take badass photos. Even nonbikers will enjoy the interactive exhibits and tough, leather-clad crowds.

★**MILWAUKEE ART MUSEUM** MUSEUM

(✏414-224-3200; www.mam.org; 700 N Art Museum Dr; adult/child $19/free; ⊙10am-5pm Tue-Sun, to 8pm Thu) You have to see this lakeside institution, which features a stunning wing-like addition by Santiago Calatrava. It soars open and closed every day at 10am, noon and 5pm (8pm on Thursday), which is wild to watch; head to the suspension bridge outside for the best view. There are fabulous folk and outsider art galleries, and a sizeable collection of Georgia O'Keeffe paintings. A 2015 renovation added photography and new media galleries to the trove.

MILLER BREWING COMPANY BREWERY

(✏414-931-2337; www.millercoors.com; 4251 W State St; tours $10; ⊙10:30am-4:30pm Mon-Sat Jun-Aug, to 3:30pm Mon-Sat Sep-May) FREE Founded in 1855, the historic Miller facility preserves Milwaukee's beer legacy. Join the legions lined up for the free, hour-long tours. Though the mass-produced beer may not be your favorite, the factory impresses with its sheer scale: you'll visit the packaging plant where 2000 cans are filled each minute, and the warehouse where a half-million cases await shipment. And then there's the generous tasting session at the tour's end, where you can down three full-size samples. Don't forget your ID.

LAKEFRONT BREWERY BREWERY

(✏414-372-8800; www.lakefrontbrewery.com; 1872 N Commerce St; 45min tours $11; ⊙11am-8pm Mon-Thu, 11am-9pm Fri, 9am-9pm Sat, 10am-5pm Sun) Well-loved Lakefront Brewery, across the river from Brady St, has afternoon tours, but the swellest time to visit is on Friday night when there's a fish fry, 16 beers to try and a polka band letting loose. Tour times vary throughout the week, but there's usually at least a 2pm and 3pm walk-through (and often many more).

✗ EATING & DRINKING

COMET CAFE AMERICAN $

(✏414-273-7677; www.thecometcafe.com; 1947 N Farwell Ave; mains $9-15; ⊙10am-midnight Mon-Fri, from 9am Sat & Sun; 🛜✏) Students, young families, older couples and bearded, tattooed types pile in to the rock-and-roll Comet for gravy-smothered meatloaf, mac 'n' cheese, vegan gyros and hangover brunch dishes. It's a craft-beer-pouring bar on one side, and retro-boothed diner on the other. Be sure to try one of the giant cupcakes for dessert.

MILWAUKEE PUBLIC MARKET MARKET $

(✏414-336-1111; www.milwaukeepublicmarket.org; 400 N Water St; sandwiches $10-15; ⊙10am-8pm Mon-Fri, 8am-8pm Sat, 9am-6pm Sun; 🛜✏) Located in the Third Ward, the market's vendors sell cheese, chocolate, sandwiches, beer, tacos, frozen custard and more. Take them upstairs where there are tables and free wi-fi. See the website for occasional special events and cooking classes.

★**CHAMPION'S** BAR

(✏414-332-2440; www.championspub.com; 2417 N Bartlett Ave; ⊙3pm-2am Mon-Fri, from 1pm Sat, from 11:30am Sun; 🛜) Champion's is the perfect choice if you're looking for something quiet, friendly and authentic. It has been a neighborhood fixture since the 1950s and not much has changed since. You'll find friendly locals, New Glarus' own Spotted Cow on tap and a low-key beer garden out back for relaxing summer nights.

BEST PLACE BAR

(☎414-223-4709; www.bestplacemilwaukee.com; 901 W Junau Ave; ☺noon-6:30pm Sun, Mon & Wed-Fri, from 10:30am Sat) Join the locals knocking back beers and massive whiskey pours at this small tavern in the former Pabst Brewery headquarters. A fireplace warms the cozy, dark-wood room; original murals depicting Pabst's history adorn the walls. Staff give daily tours of the building ($10, including a 16oz Pabst or Schlitz tap brew).

🏃 SPORTS & ACTIVITIES

★**MILLER PARK** BASEBALL

(☎414-902-4400; www.brewers.com; 1 Brewers Way; ☺box office 9am-7pm Mon-Fri, 9am-5pm Sat, 11am-5pm Sun) From April through September, the National League Milwaukee Brewers play baseball at fab Miller Park, which has a retractable roof and real grass. Buy tickets online or at the stadium box office. The stadium is about 5 miles west of downtown. The Brewers Line bus runs there on game days; pick it up along Wisconsin Ave.

🛏 SLEEPING

★**AMBASSADOR** HOTEL $

(☎877-935-2189; www.ambassadormilwaukee.com; 2308 W Wisconsin Ave; r $119-139; P✳@☎) This renovated art deco gem, on the city's western side, near Marquette University, is an affordable central option. Architecture buffs will love all of those 'jazz age' period details, such as the polished marbled flooring in the lobby and the bronze elevator doors. The in-house restaurant exudes a 'supper club' vibe and the adjacent bar pours the perfect Wisconsin-style old-fashioned.

BREWHOUSE INN & SUITES HOTEL $$

(☎414-810-3350; www.brewhousesuites.com; 1215 N 10th St; r $199-249; P✳@☎) This 90-room hotel sits in the exquisitely renovated old Pabst Brewery complex. Each of the large chambers has steampunk decor, a kitchenette and free wi-fi. It's at downtown's far west edge, about a half-mile walk from sausagey Old World 3rd St and a good 2 miles from the festival grounds. Parking costs $28.

Saugatuck & Douglas

....

Explore

Saugatuck is one of Michigan's most popular resort areas, known for its strong arts community, numerous B&Bs and gay-friendly vibe. Douglas is its twin city a mile or so to the south, and they've pretty much sprawled into one. It's a touristy but funky place, with ice-cream-licking families, yuppie boaters and martini-drinking gay couples sharing the waterfront. Galleries and shops fill the compact downtown core. Weekends attract the masses.

....

The Best...

➡ **Activity** Saugatuck Chain Ferry
➡ **Place to Eat** Crane's Pie Pantry
➡ **Place to Drink** Saugatuck Brewing Company

....

Top Tip

Don't forget that Michigan is on Eastern Standard Time, one hour ahead of Chicago.

....

Getting There & Away

Most visitors drive to Saugatuck/Douglas. The I-196/US 31 whizzes by to the east, while the Blue Star Hwy goes into both towns. The closest Amtrak station is in Holland, about 12 miles north.

....

Need to Know

➡ **Area Code** ☎269
➡ **Location** 140 miles northeast of Chicago
➡ **Tourist Office** (www.saugatuck.com) Provides maps and more.

✕ EATING & DRINKING

CRANE'S PIE PANTRY, RESTAURANT & WINERY BAKERY $

(☑269-561-2297; www.cranespiepantry.com; 6054 124th Ave, Fennville; pie slices $4.50; ☺9am-8pm Sun-Thu, to 9pm Fri & Sat) Buy a bulging slice of fruit pie, or pick apples and peaches in the surrounding orchards. Crane's also makes hard ciders and wines (the sauvignon blanc wins praise). Tastings are available for $5 per four samples. You can even get a pie flight ($7), which consists of four small slices served in little jars.

Crane's is in Fennville, 3 miles south of Saugatuck on the Blue Star Hwy, then 4 miles inland on Hwy 89. It also operates a tasting bar in downtown Saugatuck that pours its wines and ciders.

PHIL'S BAR & GRILLE AMERICAN $$

(☑269-857-1555; www.philsbarandgrille.com; 215 Butler St, Saugatuck; mains $17-29; ☺11:30am-9:30pm Sun-Thu, to 10:30pm Fri & Sat) This humming pub turns out terrific broasted (combining broiling and roasting) chicken, fish tacos, lamb lollipops and gumbo in a cozy, wood-floored room.

SAUGATUCK BREWING COMPANY MICROBREWERY

(☑269-857-7222; www.saugatuckbrewing.com; 2948 Blue Star Hwy, Douglas; ☺11:30am-9pm Sun-Thu, to 10pm Fri, to 11pm Sat) Locals like to hang out and sip the housemade suds in this comfy pub. IPAs, stouts and fruity seasonal specialties like the blueberry lemonade shandy fill glasses; there's live music a few nights each week.

🏃 SPORTS & ACTIVITIES

SAUGATUCK CHAIN FERRY BOATING

(end of Mary St, Saugatuck; one way $2; ☺9am-9pm late May-early Sep) The best thing to do in Saugatuck is also the most affordable. Jump aboard the clackety chain ferry, and the operator will pull you across the Kalamazoo River.

MT BALDHEAD WALKING

(Saugatuck) Huff up the stairs of this 200ft-high sand dune for a stellar view. Then race down the other side to Oval Beach. Get here via the chain ferry; walk right (north) from the dock.

OVAL BEACH BEACH

(Oval Beach Dr, Saugatuck; ☺8am-10pm) Life guards patrol the long expanse of fine sand. There are bathrooms and concession stands, though not enough to spoil the peaceful, dune-laden scene. It costs $10 to park. Or arrive the adventurous way, via chain ferry and a trek over Mt Baldhead.

🛏 SLEEPING

★PINES MOTORLODGE MOTEL $$

(☑269-857-5211; www.thepinesmotorlodge.com; 56 Blue Star Hwy, Douglas; r $139-249; 🛜) Retro-cool tiki lamps, pinewood furniture and communal lawn chairs add up to a fun, social ambience amid the firs in Douglas.

BAYSIDE INN INN $$

(☑269-857-4321; www.baysideinn.net; 618 Water St, Saugatuck; r $165-320; 🛜) This former boathouse has 10 rooms on Saugatuck's waterfront. All have private bathrooms and decks.

Galena

••

Explore

Wee Galena spreads across wooded hillsides near the Mississippi River, amid rolling, barn-dotted farmland. Redbrick mansions in Greek Revival, Gothic Revival and Queen Anne styles line the streets, left over from the town's heyday in the mid-1800s, when local lead mines made it rich. Even with all the touristy B&Bs, fudge and antique shops, there's no denying Galena's beauty – 85% of its structures make up the Galena Historic District, which is on the National Register of Historic Places, and its Main St is about as Pleasantville-perfect as one gets. Throw in cool kayak trips and back-road drives, and you've got a lovely, slow-paced getaway. Over one million visitors come to the town each year; summer and fall weekends see the most action.

The Best...

→ **Sight** Ulysses S Grant Home
→ **Place to Eat** Fritz and Frites
→ **Place to Drink** Galena Brewing Company

Top Tip

There is a free **parking lot** (Bouthillier St) beside the old train depot (street parking in town is also free but limited to three hours). Most sights, shops and restaurants are walkable from here.

Getting There & Away

Hwy 20 rolls into Galena. Driving is the only way to get here. The closest transportation hubs are Chicago (165 miles southeast), Madison, WI (95 miles northeast), and Dubuque, IA (16 miles northwest).

Need to Know

→ **Area Code** ☑779
→ **Location** 165 miles northwest of Chicago
→ **Tourist Office** (☑815-776-9200; www.visitgalena.org; 123 N Commerce St; ☺10am-4pm)

👁 SIGHTS

ULYSSES S GRANT HOME HISTORIC SITE
(www.granthome.com; 500 Bouthillier St; adult/child $5/3; ☺9am-4:45pm Wed-Sun Apr-Oct, reduced hours Nov-Mar) The 1860 abode was a gift from local Republicans to the victorious general at the Civil War's end. Grant lived here until he became the country's 18th president. Docents take you through the house. Around 90% of the furnishings are original.

🍴 EATING & DRINKING

FRITZ AND FRITES EUROPEAN $$
(☑815-777-2004; www.fritzandfrites.com; 317 N Main St; mains $19-27; ☺4-9pm Tue-Sat, 9am-8pm Sun) This romantic little bistro serves a compact menu of both German and French classics. Dig in to escargot (snails) in garlic-herb butter or maybe a tender schnitzel.

ONE ELEVEN MAIN AMERICAN $$
(☑815-777-8030; www.oneelevenmain.com; 111 N Main St; mains $10-40; ☺4-8pm Mon & Thu, 11am-9pm Fri & Sat, 11am-8pm Sun) Pot roast, pork tenderloins and other Midwestern favorites arrive at the table, made with ingredients sourced from local farms.

GALENA BREWING COMPANY MICROBREWERY
(www.galenabrewery.com; 227 N Main St; ☺4-9pm Mon-Thu, 11am-11pm Fri & Sat, 11am-8pm Sun; 🛜) The original Red Stripe beer was brewed by Galena Brewing Company in the 1930s before a British investor whisked the recipe off to Jamaica. This isn't *that* Galena Brewing Company, but it still does decent – if unadventurous – craft brews (six core and six seasonal taps) and standard pub grub. Live music on Friday and Saturday nights.

🏃 SPORTS & ACTIVITIES

FEVER RIVER OUTFITTERS OUTDOORS
(☑815-776-9425; www.feverriveroutfitters.com; 525 S Main St; canoe rental 2/4hr $40/50, bike rental 2hr/day from $23/40; ☺9am-5pm Mon & Fri-Sun, Tue-Thu by appointment) Fever River rents canoes, kayaks, bicycles, paddleboards and snowshoes. It also offers guided tours, such as 12-mile bike trips ($45 per person, gear included) to a local winery and various paddling excursions.

STAGECOACH TRAIL SCENIC DRIVE
The Stagecoach Trail is a 26-mile ride on a narrow, twisty road en route to Warren. Pick it up by taking Main St northeast through downtown; at the second stop sign go right (you'll see a trail marker). And yes, it really was part of the old stagecoach route between Galena and Chicago.

SHENANDOAH RIDING CENTER HORSEBACK RIDING
(☑815-777-9550; www.theshenandoahridingcenter.com; 200 N Brodrecht Rd; 1hr ride $45) Saddle up at Shenandoah. It offers trail rides through the valley for all levels of riders. The stables are 8 miles east of Galena.

Sleeping

Chicago's lodgings rise high in the sky, many in architectural landmarks. Snooze in the building that gave birth to the skyscraper, in one of Ludwig Mies van der Rohe's boxy structures, or in a century-old art deco masterpiece. Huge business hotels, trendy boutique hotels and snazzy hostels blanket the cityscape too. But nothing comes cheap...

Seasons & Prices

The high-season apex is June to August, when festivals and tourism peak. But Chicago hosts loads of business conventions, so demand – and prices – can skyrocket during odd times the rest of the year too. Book well in advance to avoid unpleasant surprises. Prices are lowest December to February.

Hotels

Hotels seem to be on every corner in the Loop, Near North and the Gold Coast. All big-box chains have outposts (usually several) here. Most are geared to conventioneers. Groovy boutique hotels abound, as do uber-luxury hotels catering to rock stars and business tycoons.

B&Bs

Chicago has several B&Bs and they're typically cheaper than big hotels. Set in elegant old row houses and greystones, they cluster in Wicker Park and Lake View. They're generally casual, with self-serve breakfast. Many have two- to three-night minimum stays.

Hostels

Chicago has one Hostelling International (www.hiusa.org) property and several independent hostels that do not require membership. There has been a boom of the latter in fun, outlying neighborhoods such as Wicker Park and Wrigleyville. Browse listings at www.hostels.com and www.hostelworld.com. A handful of hip hostel-hotel hybrids have also opened around downtown.

SAVING STRATEGIES

In peak season it's hard to find a room for less than $275 per night. Here are a few ways to cut costs:

Ditch the car Most downtown properties charge $60 to $72 per night for parking. Lodgings in outlying neighborhoods, such as Lake View and Wicker Park, often have free or lower-cost parking lots (closer to $25 per night).

Bidding sites Try Priceline (www.priceline.com) or Hotwire (www.hotwire.com). 'River North' and 'Mag Mile' yield the most listings. Certain properties turn up often at well-reduced rates.

Free wi-fi While free wi-fi is common, many business-oriented hotels still charge for it ($10 to $15 daily).

Leave downtown Prices decrease as you move out to Lincoln Park, Lake View, Wicker Park and South Loop.

CHICAGO'S BIGGEST CONVENTIONS

When huge conventions trample through town, beware. You'll be competing with an extra 30,000 people or so for hotel rooms, which will skyrocket in price. In general, spring and fall are the busiest convention times. Check Choose Chicago's convention calendar (www.choosechicago.com/meeting-professionals/convention-calendar) to see what's on when. The following are some of the largest events, at which times room prices will make you weep:

➡ International Home & Housewares Show – three nights in mid-March.

➡ National Restaurant Association – three nights in mid-May.

➡ American Society of Clinical Oncologists (ASCO) – five nights in late May/early June.

➡ Radiological Society of North America – five nights in late November/early December.

Apartments

Apartment rentals are a good deal in Chicago, especially if your stay coincides with a big convention that ratchets up hotel prices. Chicago regulates and taxes rentals; homeowners have to register with the city. Airbnb (www.airbnb.com) and HomeAway (www.homeaway.com) are the main booking sites. Most listings range from $70 to $175 per night, getting more expensive as you head toward downtown. Popular neighborhoods for rentals where the value is usually better than a hotel include Near North, Lincoln Park, Lake View, Old Town and West Loop. Areas that are cheaper and great for their local vibe include Logan Square, Pilsen, Ukrainian Village, Chinatown, Andersonville and Lincoln Square. It's key to be near an L station, so ascertain this before booking.

Amenities

In-room wi-fi, air-conditioning and a private bathroom are standard, unless noted otherwise.

TOP-END

On-site concierge services, fitness and business centers, restaurants, bars and room service are all par for the course. There's often a fee for in-room wi-fi ($10 to $15), while it's free in the lobby. Breakfast is rarely included.

MIDRANGE

Rooms have a phone, cable TV and free wi-fi; many also have a mini-refrigerator, microwave and hairdryer. Often a small fitness center is on-site. Rates often include a continental breakfast.

BUDGET

Budget accommodations generally means hostels. Expect bunk-bed dorms, shared bathrooms, free wi-fi and continental breakfast. Staff often organize outings to local sights and entertainment venues.

Pets

A fair number of Chicago hotels allow pets, but many charge a $50 to $100 nonrefundable cleaning fee. Some places, however, not only permit pets, but waive fees and/or provide special programs for four-legged friends.

Useful Websites

Lonely Planet (www.lonelyplanet.com/hotels) Recommendations and bookings.

Chicago Bed & Breakfast Association (www.chicago-bed-breakfast.com) Represents around 11 properties.

Hotel Tonight (www.hoteltonight.com) National discounter with last-minute deals; book via the free app.

Choose Chicago (www.choosechicago.com) Options from the city's official website.

SLEEPING

NEED TO KNOW

Price Ranges

The following price ranges refer to a double room in high season (before taxes and tips).

$ less than $200

$$ $200–350

$$$ more than $350

Tax

Chicago's room tax is 17.4%.

Parking Costs

Figure on $60 to $72 per night downtown for in-and-out privileges.

Tipping

Hotel bellhops $2 per bag, minimum per cart $5.

Housekeeping staff $2 to $5 daily.

Parking valets $2 to $5 when you're handed back the keys.

Room service 15% to 20%.

Concierges Up to $20 (for securing last-minute restaurant reservations, sold-out show tickets etc).

Check-In & Check-Out Times

Normally 3pm for check-in and 11am for check-out. Many places will allow early check-in if the room is available (or will store your luggage if not).

Lonely Planet's Top Choices

Acme Hotel (p233) Downtown's grooviest boutique, complete with lava lights.

Ace Hotel (p242) Hipness in West Loop, including an in-room turntable or guitar.

Longman & Eagle (p241) Six wood-floored, vintage-stylish rooms that sit above a buzzy gastropub.

Fieldhouse Jones (p237) Sporty, companionable digs for an unrivaled Gold Coast price.

Publishing House Bed & Breakfast (p242) Eleven mid-century modern rooms named after Chicago writers.

Best By Budget:
$

Found Hotel (p233) Part hostel, part hotel with good-time common areas.

Wicker Park Inn (p241) Cozy B&B in the thick of Wicker Park's social scene.

Holiday Jones (p240) Good-value, off-the-beaten-path hostel with a sense of humor.

Freehand Chicago (p233) Super-hip hostel-hotel hybrid with spiffy, high-tech dorms.

Best By Budget:
$$

Hampton Inn Chicago Downtown/ N Loop (p230) The chain's much-loved amenities in retro, charismatic environs.

Majestic Hotel (p239) Handsome, English-manor-like property near the lake.

Hotel Lincoln (p238) Fun, from 'wall of bad art' kitsch to pedicab service.

Willows Hotel (p239) Peachy rooms fill the dapper little property.

Best By Budget:
$$$

Viceroy Chicago (p237) Chicago's newest luxury hotel wows with plush rooms, gracious amenities and attentive service.

Waldorf Astoria Chicago (p238) A name synonymous with classic hotel opulence lives up to its five-star reputation.

Fairmont (p232) Top-shelf accommodations a stone's throw from Millennium Park with unbeatable views.

Best For Families

Guesthouse Hotel (p240) Enormous modern suites with kitchen and laundry near Andersonville's hip shops and cafes.

Swissôtel Chicago (p232) Young guests will love specially dedicated family suites in a riverside location.

Wicker Park Inn (p241) Apartments with full kitchens in one of Chicago's most desirable residential neighborhoods.

Best Contemporary Cool

Sophy Hyde Park (p242) A truly novel-looking, art-focused hotel with a location not like the others.

Virgin Hotel (p230) Large rooms, clever and playful design, and a bed you can work from.

Sofitel Chicago Magnificent Mile (p237) Glassy high-rise with a minimalist vibe and international clientele.

Ivy Hotel (p233) Cozy boutique hotel with big soaking tubs in chic rooms.

Hotel Palomar (p233) Funky art, a rooftop pool and free wine social hour each evening.

Where to Stay

Neighborhood	For	Against
The Loop	Cool boutique and architectural hotels. Convenient for parks, festival grounds, museums and Theater District. Easy transportation to anywhere in the city.	Limited eating and drinking options after dark.
Near North & Navy Pier	The most hotel-packed 'hood. Bars, restaurants and big-box stores everywhere.	Lots of chain hotels. Can be crowded, noisy and pricey.
Gold Coast	Chichi environs. Close to downtown and the lakefront. Shopping bonanza at your doorstep.	Expensive.
Lincoln Park & Old Town	Characterful lodgings. Short walk to the park, zoo and beaches. Fun nightlife. Popular for apartment rentals.	A bit removed from downtown's sights.
Lake View & Wrigleyville	Distinct boutique hotels, B&Bs and apartments surrounded by rollicking bars, restaurants and music clubs.	Main areas can be congested and rowdy at night.
Andersonville & Uptown	Tranquility in a residential, gay-friendly neighborhood. Good for apartment rentals.	Far from the top-draw sights.
Lincoln Square & Ravenswood	Friendly neighborhood feel, walkable to pubs and cute shops. Good-value apartments (but no hotels in area).	Thirty-minute L ride from downtown and tourist sites.
Wicker Park, Bucktown & Ukrainian Village	Hostels and B&Bs away from the tourist masses. Area has a real neighborhood feel. Near buzzy nightlife and trendy shops.	About a 15-minute L ride to downtown and some properties are a 15-minute walk from the L station.
Logan Square & Humboldt Park	Authentic neighborhood vibe. Indie-cool cafes, bars and shops nearby. Few traditional lodgings, but popular for apartment rentals.	Isolated from downtown and the lakefront.
West Loop & Near West Side	Super-trendy hotels near super-trendy restaurants and nightlife. Lots of apartment rentals.	Can be costly.
Pilsen & Near South Side	Pilsen apartments have a great local vibe near restaurants and bars. Business hotels huddle at the convention center.	Convention center environs are dull.
Hyde Park & South Side	Low prices. One-of-a-kind properties.	Far-flung from downtown and just about everything else.

SLEEPING

🛏 The Loop

HI-CHICAGO
HOSTEL $

Map p302 (☎312-360-0300; www.hichicago. org; 24 E Congress Pkwy; dm $35-55; ✻@🛜; Ⓜ Brown, Orange, Purple, Pink Line to Library) Chicago's most stalwart hostel is immaculate, conveniently placed in the Loop, and offers bonuses such as a staffed information desk, free volunteer-led tours and discount passes to some sights. The simple dorm rooms have eight or 10 beds, and most have attached baths; others share hallway bathrooms. Dorms are segregated by gender.

The fully equipped kitchen allows for DIY meal-making, though there's also an excellent Cuban cafe (p58) just off the lobby. The giant common area buzzes with guests using the free wi-fi (available throughout the building), playing billiards or Ping-Pong and chatting up the concierge to plan their day. Linens are provided, but bring your own lock.

TRAVELODGE BY WYNDHAM
DOWNTOWN CHICAGO
HOTEL $

Map p302 (☎312-427-8000; www.wyndham hotels.com/travelodge; 65 E Harrison St; r $139-179; ✻@🛜; Ⓜ Red Line to Harrison) The Travelodge's mid-priced competitors in South Loop typically offer better quality with more amenities, but if you're just looking for the lowest rates in the neighborhood, Travelodge likely has them. What do you say about lackluster, motel-like rooms? Um, they're there. But hey, the wi-fi's free.

⭐VIRGIN HOTEL
HOTEL $$

Map p298 (☎312-940-4400; www.virgin hotels.com; 203 N Wabash Ave; r $240-380; Ⓟ✻@🛜🏊; Ⓜ Brown, Orange, Green, Purple, Pink Line to State/Lake) Billionaire Richard Branson transformed the 27-story, art deco Dearborn Bank Building into the first outpost of his cheeky new hotel chain. The airy, suite-like rooms have speedy free wi-fi, low-cost minibar items and a bed that doubles as a work desk. An app controls electronics including thermostat and TV. Guests receive earplugs, handy for dulling noise from nearby L trains.

⭐HAMPTON INN CHICAGO
DOWNTOWN/N LOOP
HOTEL $$

Map p298 (☎312-419-9014; www.hampton chicago.com; 68 E Wacker Pl; r $200-290; Ⓟ✻🛜; Ⓜ Brown, Orange, Green, Purple, Pink Line to State/Lake) This unique property with a central location makes you feel like a road-tripper of yore. Set in the 1928 art deco Chicago Motor Club Building, the lobby sports a vintage Ford and a cool USA mural map from the era. The dark-wood-paneled rooms strike the right balance of retro vibe and modern amenities. Free wi-fi.

It's near the river, Magnificent Mile shops and Millennium Park.

⭐HOTEL JULIAN
HOTEL $$

Map p298 (☎312-346-1200; www.hoteljulian chicago.com; 168 N Michigan Ave; r $200-400; Ⓟ➡✻🛜; Ⓜ Brown, Orange, Green, Purple, Pink Line to Washington/Wabash) Twelve stories in a 1912 office building now comprise one of the Loop's newest mod-luxe hotels. Large rooms are elegantly decorated with a slightly masculine retro-1930s vibe and feature king-sized captain's beds with Frette linens and leather headboards; espresso makers and 55in TVs – not to mention stunning views of Millennium Park through some of the city-view rooms.

RADISSON BLU AQUA HOTEL
HOTEL $$

Map p298 (☎312-565-5258; www.radisson blu.com/aquahotel-chicago; 221 N Columbus Dr; r $270-350; Ⓟ✻@🛜🏊; Ⓜ Brown, Orange, Green, Purple, Pink Line to State/Lake) Radisson Blu's sleek rooms occupy floors one to 18 of the rippling, 82-story Aqua Tower (p52), designed by local starchitect Jeanne Gang. Standard rooms are ample and clean-lined, with deco-style lamps and lounge chairs, thick marine-blue carpet, tall windows and big, aqua-hued bathrooms. Most rooms have pretty city or park views. Upgrading to a room with a balcony is worth it.

There's free wi-fi throughout. Service is top-notch, as is the fitness center with indoor and outdoor pools, a running track and half basketball court.

SILVERSMITH
HISTORIC HOTEL $$

Map p298 (☎312-372-7696; www.silversmith chicagohotel.com; 10 S Wabash Ave; r $200-350; Ⓟ✻@🛜; Ⓜ Red, Blue Line to Monroe) Designed by renowned architect Daniel Burnham's firm as a place for jewelers and silversmiths to ply their trade, this 1897 building's gem-inspired theme carries over to the current, vintage-cool design. Rooms are good-sized, with pearl-colored decor and ruby and gold accents. A cushioned seat nestles in each floor-to-ceiling window, prime for city watching.

The Art Institute, Millennium Park and CTA trains are steps away. Wi-fi is free. At times prices here become quite reasonable.

STAYPINEAPPLE

CHICAGO   HISTORIC HOTEL $$

Map p298 (☑312-940-7997; www.staypineapple. com; r $270-380; P ✳ 🕾🏊; Ⓜ Blue Line to Washington) Housed in the landmark 1890s Reliance Building (p53), a prototype for the modern skyscraper, this hotel's slick, historic design woos architecture buffs. Deco-style lights, iron-filigree stair railings and mosaic-tile floors prevail in the public areas. In the smallish rooms, big windows and pops of whimsical, bright-hued art liven up the warm wood decor. Free bicycles for zipping around town are handy.

A daily amenities fee ($15) offers guests wi-fi, coffee and cupcakes. History factoid: Al Capone's dentist (and partner in crime) used to drill teeth in Room 809.

BUCKINGHAM

ATHLETIC CLUB HOTEL   BOUTIQUE HOTEL $$

Map p298 (☑312-663-8910; www.thebuckingham club.com; 440 S LaSalle St; r $200-280; P ✳ 🕾🏊; Ⓜ Brown, Orange, Purple, Pink Line to LaSalle) On the 40th floor of the Chicago Stock Exchange building, this 21-room hotel isn't easy to find. The benefit if you do? It's quiet (on weekends and evenings especially) and has expansive views. Elegant rooms are so spacious they'd be considered suites elsewhere. Lots of freebies add to the excellence, including access to the namesake gym with lap pool.

There's free continental breakfast and free wi-fi, to boot.

BLACKSTONE HOTEL   HISTORIC HOTEL $$

Map p302 (☑312-447-0955; www.blackstone renaissance.com; 636 S Michigan Ave; r from $225; P ✳ @🕾🏊; Ⓜ Red Line to Harrison) This 1910 beaux-arts landmark is known as the 'hotel of presidents' (a dozen have slumbered here). The 23-story beauty now caters to an upmarket business crowd. Rooms are urban-stylish (downy bedding, monochrome bathrooms, abstract artworks); several have lake views (about $50 extra). The 5th-floor Art Hall features works by emerging local artists. Wi-fi costs $15 per day.

HOTEL MONACO   BOUTIQUE HOTEL $$

Map p298 (☑312-960-8500; www.monaco-chicago.com; 225 N Wabash Ave; r $269-399; P ✳ 🕾🏊; Ⓜ Brown, Orange, Green, Purple, Pink Line to State/Lake) The Monaco's rooms are large, with bold-red window curtains, geometric carpeting and curlicued dark-wood headboards; window nooks let you sit and watch the street action below. Amenities such as dog beds for pooches, child-safety kits for families, a fitness facility and free wi-fi ensure the Monaco draws a mixed crowd of business travelers and holidaymakers. There's a free wine happy hour each evening (as at all Kimpton-brand properties).

HILTON CHICAGO   HISTORIC HOTEL $$

Map p302 (☑312-922-4400; www.hilton.com; 720 S Michigan Ave; r $160-450; P ✳ @🕾🏊; Ⓜ Red Line to Harrison) They sure don't make 'em like they used to. When built in 1927, this was the world's largest hotel – practically a miniature city – with some 3000 rooms. After modern renovations that's now 1544, but the lobby's gilt grandeur and crystal-dripping class remain. Rooms are standard-issue, but beds are comfy. A lakeview upgrade costs about $30; wi-fi is $13 per day.

Anecdotes abound at the Hilton: in the 1940s it served as an army barracks, and at the height of the 1968 Democratic National Convention riots, police tossed protesters through the front plate-glass windows.

WIT   BOUTIQUE HOTEL $$

Map p298 (☑312-467-0200; www.thewithotel. com; 201 N State St; r $255-385; P ✳ @🕾; Ⓜ Brown, Orange, Green, Purple, Pink Line to State/Lake) One of the Loop's hottest properties, the design-savvy Wit draws holidaying hipsters and business travelers with its view-tastic rooms and swanky rooftop bar. The green-glass tower glints in a sweet spot between the Theater District and the river. Each chamber features vast windows and eco-amenities such as dual-flush toilets and energy-efficient heating and lighting.

Wi-fi is free in the lobby, though there's a fee for in-room service. The hotel is part of the Doubletree chain.

HOTEL BLAKE CHICAGO   BOUTIQUE HOTEL $$

Map p302 (☑312-986-1234; www.hotelblake. com; 538 S Dearborn St; r $169-339; P ✳ @🕾; Ⓜ Blue Line to LaSalle) The former Morton Salt headquarters building (1896) has found new life as a boutique hotel at the Loop's southern edge. It's a unique location midway between downtown's core and the

Museum Campus, though not much goes on in the evenings. The modern furnishings, set off by pops of red, are spread out in well-sized rooms, with huge bathrooms. Free wi-fi.

Breakfast is not included, but there's a good cafe on-site for omelets and creative French-toast dishes, with vegan and gluten-free options. If rates swing up to the high end of the spectrum, you'll probably get better bang for your buck elsewhere.

HOTEL ALLEGRO   HOTEL $$

Map p298 (📞312-236-0123; www.allegro chicago.com; 171 W Randolph St; r $249-359; P❄@🛜🐾; MBrown, Orange, Purple, Pink Line to Washington/Wells) Hotel Allegro is part of the fun and flirty Kimpton chain. The 483 rooms sport a retro 1920s luxury-cruise-ship look, with gold accents and funky patterned wallpaper and carpet. It's certainly dramatic, which makes sense for a hotel right next to the Cadillac Palace Theatre and its Broadway crowd.

Flat-screen TVs, free evening wine receptions and free yoga gear round out the stylish package. Wi-fi is $8 per day.

SWISSÔTEL CHICAGO   HOTEL $$

Map p298 (📞312-565-0565; www.swissotel chicago.com; 323 E Wacker Dr; r $239-319; P❄@🛜; MBrown, Orange, Green, Purple, Pink Line to Randolph) Water vistas are just part of the attraction at this triangular-shaped, mirrored-glass high-rise at the confluence of river and lake. Businessfolk like the rooms' ample, well-appointed workstations. Families love the oversized layouts, separate shower and tub, and special kids' suites with colorful furnishings and toys. The hotel shows up frequently on discount booking sites. Summer weekends sell out fast.

The newly renovated fitness center is a fine perk. A daily amenity fee ($15) covers wi-fi, morning coffee and shoeshines.

CAMBRIA HOTEL   HOTEL $$

Map p298 (📞312-763-3822; www.cambria chicagoloop.com; 32 W Randolph St; d $200-250; P⟳❄🛜) Hidden away on several floors of an office building, the Cambria's 199 rooms offer a host of small amenities: microwave, K-pod coffeemakers and refrigerators; USB charging ports; Bluetooth bathroom speakers and smart TVs.

There's also a guest lounge with pub games and a fitness center. The decor

doesn't exactly inspire but rooms are decently sized. A good midrange choice.

CENTRAL LOOP HOTEL   HOTEL $$

Map p298 (📞312-601-3525; www.centralloop hotel.com; 111 W Adams St; r $149-249; P❄@🛜; MBrown, Orange, Purple, Pink Line to Quincy) The Central Loop is in a good location (the name doesn't lie) and has good prices if you're stuck paying rack rates. It's accessorized for business-oriented guests; the smallish rooms are not so useful for families. A fine pub pours drinks downstairs. The owners have a similar property called **Club Quarters** (📞312-357-6400; 75 E Wacker Dr) at the Loop's northern fringe.

BEST WESTERN
GRANT PARK   HOTEL $$

Map p302 (📞866-360-5113; www.bwgrant parkhotel.com; 1100 S Michigan Ave; r $159-319; P❄@🛜; MRed, Green, Orange Line to Roosevelt) This basic Best Western attracts for its location near the Field Museum. A recent renovation has brought its rooms into the modern (though nondescript) era; king, queen and double-sized beds are all available, as are lake views. Outside convention time, it can be a definite bargain.

FAIRMONT   HOTEL $$$

Map p298 (📞312-565-8000; www.fairmont. com/chicago; 200 N Columbus Dr; r $285-575; P❄@🛜🐾; MBrown, Orange, Green, Purple, Pink Line to State/Lake) Millennium Park here you come – the 687 luxury rooms and suites here are a stone's throw away. Upgrade to a deluxe room to get a park or lake view. Those near the top of the hotel's 45 stories are the best. Accents such as Asian ceramics combine with French Empire chairs to create soft – if a bit stodgy – surrounds.

Allergy sufferers can book one of the 22 hypoallergenic rooms. Wi-fi costs $14 per day; a premium (faster) connection takes it up to $24.

PALMER HOUSE HILTON   HISTORIC HOTEL $$$

Map p298 (📞312-726-7500; www.palmerhouse hiltonhotel.com; 17 E Monroe St; r $185-535; P❄@🛜🐾; MRed, Blue Line to Monroe) Palmer House has been around since 1875 and the lobby still has an awe-inspiring opulence – Tiffany chandeliers, marble pillars, ceiling frescoes – that makes a look-see imperative. The 1600-plus guest rooms give off a more updated vibe: most are spacious, done up with playful chartreuse touches and geometric-print drapes and carpet. The Art Institute and Millennium Park are within spitting distance.

Chicago millionaire Potter Palmer set many worldwide records when he opened the property (first to use electric lighting, first to have in-room telephones, invention of the brownie...). Today it remains the nation's oldest hotel in continual operation. Its huge size makes it a convention favorite, which is why prices fluctuate wildly across the year. Wi-fi costs $12 per day.

🛏 Near North & Navy Pier

★FOUND HOTEL
CHICAGO
HOSTEL, HOTEL $

Map p304 (☑224-243-6863; www.foundhotels. com; 613 N Wells St, River North; dm $25-55, r $120-330; 🅿❄🖥; 🅼Brown, Purple Line to Merchandise Mart) Breezy Found Hotel joins the elevated hostel/casual-hotel brigade. The 60 rooms come in several configurations, including four-bed dorms with sturdy (and quite comfy) bunk beds, and private rooms with twin or queen beds – all with en-suite bathrooms. Rooms are small and plain, but who cares? The price is often right, and the common areas are where the fun is.

There's a TV lounge with whimsical, garage-sale decor and board games, a communal kitchen and a popular karaoke bar in the building's basement.

FREEHAND CHICAGO
HOSTEL, HOTEL $

Map p304 (☑312-940-3699; www.freehand hotels.com/chicago; 19 E Ohio St, River North; dm $35-55, r $220-310; ❄🖥; 🅼Red Line to Grand) 🍃 At this super-hip hostel-hotel hybrid, travelers split evenly between the four-person, bunk-bed dorms and private rooms. All feature warm woods, bright tiles and Central American–tinged fabrics. Everyone mingles in the totem-pole-filled common area and groovy Broken Shaker bar. The Freehand works best as a hostel, its dorms spiffier than most, with en-suite bathrooms and privacy curtains around each bed.

As a hotel, rooms are small and not great value. That said, the location *is* great, in the thick of trendy shops, restaurants and nightlife venues. A free continental breakfast is included for dorm dwellers only.

★ACME HOTEL
BOUTIQUE HOTEL $$

Map p304 (☑312-894-0800; www.acmehotel company.com; 15 E Ohio St, River North; r $170-

310; 🅿❄@🖥; 🅼Red Line to Grand) Urban bohemians love the Acme for its indie-cool style at (usually affordable) rates. The 130 rooms mix industrial fixtures with retro lamps, mid-century furniture and funky modern art. They're wired up with free wi-fi, good speakers, smart TVs and easy connections to stream your own music and movies. Graffiti, neon and a rock-and-roll elevator embellish the common areas.

Two frisky cocktail bars and a delicious bakery are on-site. The handy location puts you between the Michigan Ave shopping haven (a few blocks east) and the Theater District (about a half-mile south).

MOXY CHICAGO
DOWNTOWN
HOTEL $$

Map p304 (☑312-527-7200; http://moxy-hotels. marriott.com; 530 N LaSalle Dr, River North; r $224-299; 🅿❄🖥🖥; 🅼Red Line to Grand) When a hotel's front desk doubles as a bar, you know you're in for a good time. So it goes at Moxy, where the lobby is a communal area with a 24-hour taco joint and novelty-size Jenga and Connect Four games. The wee rooms feel bigger than they are thanks to floor-to-ceiling windows and a pegboard wall to hang items.

A folding table and folding chairs also save space. Some rooms overlook art installations and come with lightboxes that let you send messages to guests across the courtyard. For those not in the know, Moxy is Marriott's brand targeting millennials.

IVY HOTEL
BOUTIQUE HOTEL $$

Map p304 (☑312-335-5444; www.exploreivy. com; 233 E Ontario St, Streeterville; r $189-349; 🅿❄@🖥; 🅼Red Line to Grand) The 63-room Ivy parcels out its chambers so that there are just five per floor, making it feel exceptionally intimate. The sleek and chic rooms are decently sized and offer platform beds, large bathrooms with rainfall showers (plus soaking tubs in suites) and bamboo flooring. It often shows up on booking sites with good deals, so take advantage.

HOTEL PALOMAR
HOTEL $$

Map p304 (☑312-755-9703; www.hotelpalomar-chicago.com; 505 N State St, River North; r $249-409; 🅿❄@🖥🖥🖥; 🅼Red Line to Grand) This is another excellent property in the Kimpton chain, joining the Monaco (p231) and Allegro in the Loop. Note of distinction: the 17-story, 261-room Palomar has a green roof. Arty decor – little sculptures, original paintings on the wall – add to the fashionable but businesslike scheme. There's an indoor rooftop pool, free bicycles to use and a free wine hour each evening.

Wi-fi costs $13 per day, but it's free if you join Kimpton's loyalty program.

ALOFT CHICAGO
MAG MILE   HOTEL $$

Map p304 (☑312-429-6600; https://aloft-hotels.marriott.com; 243 E Ontario St, Streeter-ville; r $165-330; P ✱ @ 🛜 🏊 🐾; MRed Line to Grand) With 337 rooms spread over 19 floors, this is the world's largest Aloft. Colorful paintings scatter throughout in homage to the building's history as the original Museum of Contemporary Art site. The small, white-walled rooms are tech-savvy with a huge, wall-mounted TV. Perks include the indoor rooftop pool, fitness center, grab-and-go cafe and bar with live music.

The gleaming property opened in 2018. It's a sweet location a block from Michigan Ave and close enough to Garrett Popcorn (p79) to smell it. There's another Aloft (opposite) less than a mile west.

GODFREY HOTEL   HOTEL $$

Map p304 (☑312-649-2000; www.godfreyhotel chicago.com; 127 W Huron St, River North; r $195-325; P ⌂ ✱ @ 🛜; MRed Line to Chicago) The Godfrey's cubist-inspired exterior looks amazing. Inside, the large, mod-industrial rooms are more comfy than you'd think, with a snug bed, wet bar and ergonomic workstation. South-facing rooms offer swell city views. Guests are mostly the young and stylish. Request a room on a higher floor to avoid noise from the popular 4th-floor lounge. Free wi-fi.

KINZIE HOTEL   BOUTIQUE HOTEL $$

Map p304 (☑312-395-9000; www.kinziehotel. com; 20 W Kinzie St, River North; r $249-374; P ✱ @ 🛜 🐾; MRed Line to Grand) There's lots to love at the Kinzie beyond the modern-design-driven, blue-accented, good-sized rooms. A continental breakfast of pastries, fruit and yogurt is included daily, as is a reception offering hors d'oeuvres, beer and wine each evening. Rooms have speedy wi-fi and 42in HDTVs with loads of channels. It's all included in the nightly $15 'service fee' added to your bill.

AIRPORT HOTELS

Got an early flight to catch? Given the crazy Chicago traffic, or long L train commute (45 minutes from the Loop), resting your head at one of the dozens of airport hotels may be your best bet. Most run free 24-hour airport shuttles.

O'Hare Airport

Aloft Chicago O'Hare (☑847-671-4444; www.aloftchicagoohare.com; 9700 Balmoral Ave, Rosemont; r $149-239; P ✱ @ 🛜 🏊; MBlue Line to Rosemont) Expect the chain's usual petite, industrial-toned rooms and sociable lobby. It's nothing fancy, but perks include a small fitness room, indoor splash pool and quite a few restaurants and shops in the walkable vicinity. The L station is about a mile away. The hotel is 3.5 miles from the airport.

Hilton Chicago O'Hare Airport (☑773-686-8000; www.hilton.com; O'Hare International Airport; r $149-289; P ✱ @ 🛜 🏊; MBlue Line to O'Hare) It's attached to the airport via an underground tunnel. Relax in the sauna, take a refreshing dip in the indoor pool and then retire to your soundproofed contemporary room.

Midway Airport

Hilton Garden Inn (☑708-496-2700; www.hiltongardeninn.com; 6530 S Cicero Ave, Bedford Park; r $149-229; P ✱ @ 🛜 🏊; MOrange Line to Midway) The large rooms have comfy beds, a mini-refrigerator and microwave. Amenities include a small fitness center and pool. The hotel sits in the same complex as several other lodgings across the price spectrum.

Sleep Inn (☑708-594-0001; www.choicehotels.com; 6650 S Cicero Ave, Bedford Park; r $89-169; P ✱ @ 🛜; MOrange Line to Midway) Slightly cheaper than Hilton Garden Inn, but in the same complex. The basic, modular rooms are perfectly acceptable, if a bit thin-walled. Free hot breakfast is a nice touch.

The swell location puts you near the river, Michigan Ave shopping and House of Blues.

ALOFT CHICAGO
DOWNTOWN RIVER NORTH   HOTEL $$
Map p304 (☑312-661-1000; https://aloft-hotels. marriott.com; 515 N Clark St, River North; r $169-379; P ✳ @ ☎; M Red Line to Grand) This Aloft offers the chain's typical compact, efficiently designed, minimalist rooms. Each one features earthy colors, big windows, a work desk and 42in flat-screen TV. The clubby, game-filled lobby (another Aloft staple) is prime for mingling. So is Beatrix (p75), a popular comfort-food restaurant and bakery that's on-site. Wi-fi is free.

If the hotel is full, there's another, newer Aloft less than a mile away.

AC HOTEL
CHICAGO DOWNTOWN   HOTEL $$
Map p304 (☑312-981-6600; www.achotels. marriott.com; 630 N Rush St, River North; r $210-320; P ✳ @ ☎ ⌨; M Red Line to Grand) This eight-story property targets millennials and business travelers. The rooms, furnished in crisp shades of gray and white with hardwood floors, feel fresh and airy. Each has a multi-plug work space, free wi-fi and mini-refrigerator. It's a great location, within easy walking distance to loads of food and drink options. The small indoor pool and 4th-floor lounge add value.

Don't be put off by the small, drab lobby.

HOTEL FELIX   HOTEL $$
Map p304 (☑312-447-3440; www.hotelfelix chicago.com; 111 W Huron St, River North; r $159-269; P ✳ @ ☎; M Red Line to Chicago) 🖉 The 228-room, 12-story Felix is nothing fancy, though it does boast ecofriendly LEED certification (Leadership in Energy and Environmental Design). The modern, beige-toned rooms are small but efficiently and comfortably designed. It's more of a place for urban hipsters than families, but who doesn't enjoy soft Egyptian-cotton sheets, free wi-fi and a wine-soaked French cafe on-site?

INTERCONTINENTAL
CHICAGO   HOTEL $$
Map p304 (☑312-944-4100; www.icchicago hotel.com; 505 N Michigan Ave, Streeterville; r $269-389; P ✳ @ ☎ ⌨; M Red Line to Grand) The InterContinental is split in two. The Executive Tower's 315 rooms are its historic core. The spacious chambers are bright and clean lined, done up in whites, grays and jewel-toned accents. The Grand Tower is the hotel's newer portion. Its 477 rooms have spiffy fabrics and lots of USB ports for the many business travelers who stay here. Free wi-fi.

The ornate original tower was built in 1929 as the Medinah Athletic Club. Period architecture and decor grace the premises, best known for the mosaic-tiled indoor pool where Hollywood's Esther Williams swam. Ask the concierge for the audio tour that lets you explore the building.

BEST WESTERN
RIVER NORTH   HOTEL $$
Map p304 (☑312-467-0800; www.rivernorth hotel.com; 125 W Ohio St, River North; r $159-269; P ✳ @ ☎ ⌨; M Red Line to Grand) The well-maintained rooms have been freshened with a soothing slate palette, boxy lamps and other stylish decor. Add this to the low-cost parking (per night $25), indoor pool and sundeck overlooking the city, and you've found unusually good value for the area. Families, in particular, dig the straightforward, seven-story hotel given its proximity to several kid-friendly restaurants.

DOUBLETREE
MAGNIFICENT MILE   HOTEL $$
Map p304 (☑312-787-6100; www.doubletree magmile.com; 300 E Ohio St, Streeterville; r $179-329; P ✳ @ ☎ ⌨; M Red Line to Grand) Relax on your window seat and look out at the sliver of a lake view many rooms have here, near Navy Pier. The average-size rooms are sort of modern generic (ie white, black and gray decor, with ruby-red accents), but there is a large fitness room and a nifty rooftop outdoor pool. Wi-fi costs $10 per day per device.

The three-star property pops up at lower rates on discount booking websites quite often.

EMBASSY SUITES CHICAGO –
DOWNTOWN   HOTEL $$
Map p304 (☑312-943-3800; https://embassy suites3.hilton.com; 600 N State St, River North; ste $209-349; P ✳ @ ☎ ⌨; M Red Line to Grand) This hotel rises a mere half-mile west of its sibling the Embassy Suites Mag Mile (p236). It's the same deal – large rooms, free cooked-to-order breakfast, indoor pool etc – particularly beloved by families. The

Downtown property sometimes has slightly cheaper prices than the Mag Mile one.

EMBASSY SUITES CHICAGO – MAGNIFICENT MILE
HOTEL $$

Map p304 (☏312-836-5900; https://embassy suites3.hilton.com; 511 N Columbus Dr, Streeterville; ste $229-359; P❄@🛜🏊; MRed Line to Grand) The Embassy Mag Mile displays the chain's typical hallmarks: all the units are two-room suites (living room with sofa bed in front, bedroom in back); there's always a cooked-to-order bacon, egg and pancake breakfast each morning; there's free wine each evening; and there's an indoor, kiddie-mobbed pool. Families dig the location between Michigan Ave and Navy Pier.

It may leave little to the imagination, but this Embassy outpost does a fine job with all the basics.

HAMPTON INN & SUITES CHICAGO DOWNTOWN
HOTEL $$

Map p304 (☏312-832-0330; www.hampton suiteschicago.com; 33 W Illinois St, River North; r $199-289; P❄@🛜🏊; MRed Line to Grand) Horizontal-lined furniture and angular leaded-glass lamps give the lobby a Prairie School feel. The Frank Lloyd Wright influence is less apparent in the tidy, contemporary rooms. One-bedroom suites have full kitchens; all rooms have super-comfy beds. The 12-story property provides Hampton's requisite free wi-fi, a small indoor pool and hot (if spare) breakfast buffet. Families and older couples love it.

HILTON GARDEN INN CHICAGO DOWNTOWN
HOTEL $$

Map p304 (☏312-595-0000; www.hiltongarden inn.com; 10 E Grand Ave, River North; r $189-289; P❄@🛜🏊; MRed Line to Grand) Part of the stalwart chain, this outpost near the Magnificent Mile caters to business travelers, families and holidaying couples in equal measure. Rooms are decent sized and good quality, with free wi-fi. Meaty smells waft up from the Weber Grill restaurant downstairs. Rates vary wildly, so you may get a steal.

OHIO HOUSE MOTEL
MOTEL $$

Map p304 (☏312-943-6000; www.ohiohouse motel.com; 600 N LaSalle Dr, River North; r $159-289; P❄@🛜; MRed Line to Grand) First the good news about this retro 1960s motel: free parking! And a free hot breakfast if you book directly. And a great location close to

transportation and restaurants. Free wi-fi, too... Now the less-good news: the rooms are basic, kind of dingy and thin-walled. Still, it's full of character and often a bargain, particularly if you have a car.

PENINSULA CHICAGO
LUXURY HOTEL $$$

Map p304 (☏312-337-2888; www.peninsula. com; 108 E Superior St, River North; r from $450; P❄@🛜🏊; MRed Line to Chicago) The Peninsula is among Chicago's top addresses. Rich white-leather and ebony-wood furnishings dominate the large rooms. Marble bathrooms feature a soaking tub with inset TV. Floor-to-ceiling windows edge the 19th-floor pool, where you can swim and soak up skyline views after your hot-stone massage in the spa. This is where Hollywood stars check in when they come to town.

LANGHAM HOTEL
HOTEL $$$

Map p304 (☏312-923-9988; www.chicago. langhamhotels.com; 330 N Wabash Ave, River North; r from $450; P❄@🛜🏊; MRed Line to Grand) Early starchitect Ludwig Mies van der Rohe originally designed the 52-story, black-box building. His grandson remade the lower floors into the Langham in 2013. The megaswank, 316-room property features some of the biggest chambers in the city; they start at 516 sq ft and go up from there. Groovy sculptures and modern art dot the common areas.

The building's upper floors house the American Medical Association. There's free wi-fi throughout.

PARK HYATT CHICAGO
LUXURY HOTEL $$$

Map p304 (☏312-335-1234; www.hyatt.com/brands/park-hyatt; 800 N Michigan Ave, River North; r from $400; P❄@🛜🏊; MRed Line to Chicago) Want your room covered in rose petals, with candles lit and your bath water run? They've done it before at this ask-and-it-shall-be-granted luxury flagship of the locally based Hyatt chain. Rooms feature plush linens, soaking-tub-laden bathrooms and big windows with skyline views. C'mon – if it's good enough for U2 when they rock through town, you know it's got street cred.

🛏 Gold Coast

★FIELDHOUSE JONES
HOSTEL, HOTEL $

Map p308 (☏312-291-9922; www.fieldhouse jones.com; 312 W Chestnut St; r/apt from $125/180; P❄🛜; MBrown, Purple Line to

Chicago) This hip hotel occupies a vintage, redbrick dairy warehouse. It's great value for the Gold Coast, drawing a wide range of travelers – global backpackers, families – for its quality rooms and sociable common areas. There are standard hotel rooms, studios and one- and two-bedroom apartments, all with en-suite bathrooms, wi-fi and fun, sporty decor (dartboard wall art, old trophies etc).

Communal hangouts include the gymnasium-inspired lounge and coffee bar on the lobby level, and the game room – with Ping-Pong, air hockey and even slot-car racing! – in the basement. Parking costs $20.

SOFITEL CHICAGO
MAGNIFICENT MILE   HOTEL $$

Map p308 (☏312-324-4000; www.sofitel-chicago. com; 20 E Chestnut St; r $199-450; P❄@🖘; MRed Line to Chicago) The outside of the Sofitel looks like some state-of-the-art computing device, with a triangular glass tower leaning gracefully out into space. Inside, stylish staff members tend to stylish thirty- and forty-something guests, many European, who appreciate the minimalist vibe and sizable 400+ rooms (think blond wood and muted grays). The daily $12 amenities fee covers wi-fi, free coffee and more.

DRAKE HOTEL   HISTORIC HOTEL $$

Map p308 (☏312-787-2200; www.thedrakehotel. com; 140 E Walton St; r $230-360; P❄@🖘; MRed Line to Chicago) Queen Elizabeth, Princess Di, the Reagans, the Bushes, the Clintons, the late, great Aretha Franklin... Who *hasn't* stayed at the Drake since its 1920 opening? The elegant, chandelier-strewn grande dame anchors the northern end of Michigan Ave, near Oak Street Beach. While the public spaces are gilded eye-poppers, the 535 rooms are more everyday yet well-sized and comfy.

North-facing rooms have awesome lake views and are worth the extra cost. Guests tend to be older or members of the many weddings the Drake hosts. Wi-fi costs $13 per day (or is free for Hilton rewards members).

RAFFAELLO HOTEL   BOUTIQUE HOTEL $$

Map p308 (☏312-943-5000; www.chicago raffaello.com; 201 E Delaware Pl; r $179-319; P❄@🖘; MRed Line to Chicago) If only you could live in the creamy, silk-draped modernity of these rooms. Oh, wait, you can – they're condominiums, too. Suites

have microwaves and mini-refrigerators in marble cooking centers, plus roomy seating areas or separate living rooms. King and double rooms are smaller, but they have similar upscale amenities, such as rainfall shower heads and high-thread-count linens. Free wi-fi.

A smart rooftop lounge and Italian seafood restaurant tempt on-site. Parking costs $38 per night.

CLARIDGE HOUSE   BOUTIQUE HOTEL $$

Map p308 (☏312-787-4980; www.claridgehouse chicago.com; 1244 N Dearborn St; r $159-259; P❄@🖘🐾; MRed Line to Clark/ Division) Formerly the Indigo Hotel, the Claridge's 165 rooms underwent a full renovation in 2018. Standard queen rooms are still on the smallish size, but besides updated decor they now feature snazzy tablets that let you watch Netflix, listen to Spotify and order room service. There's a gym and a day spa on-site, too. Free wi-fi.

RESIDENCE INN
CHICAGO DOWNTOWN/
MAGNIFICENT MILE   HOTEL $$

Map p308 (☏312-943-9800; www.marriott.com; 201 E Walton St; ste from $249; P❄@🖘🐾; MRed Line to Chicago) What can we say about a generic extended-stay hotel? Studio, one-bedroom and two-bedroom suites are a bit dated but have all the extras traveling families want: DIY kitchens, laundry facilities, free wi-fi and hot breakfast buffet. Staff will even go grocery shopping for you. No pool though – sorry, kids (though Oak Street Beach is nearby).

★VICEROY CHICAGO   LUXURY HOTEL $$$

Map p308 (☏312-586-2000; www.viceroyhotels andresorts.com; 1118 N State St; d $275-450, ste from $550; P❄@🖘🐾; MRed Line to Clark/Division) The Gold Coast's newest luxury hotel, the Viceroy has 198 rooms and suites with art deco–inspired design elements with warm woods, gold accents and luxe furnishings. Blue-velvet curtains float across floor-to-ceiling windows with lake and skyline views; the restaurant, helmed by a Michelin-starred chef, features nautical yacht-club motifs. In summer you can use the rooftop dipping pool. Free wi-fi.

★WALDORF
ASTORIA CHICAGO   LUXURY HOTEL $$$

Map p308 (☏312-646-1300; www.waldorfastoria chicagohotel.com; 11 E Walton St; r from $400;

P✱@⛶✉✿; ⓂRed Line to Chicago) The Waldorf routinely tops the list for Chicago's best uber-luxury hotel. It models itself on 1920s Parisian glamour and, we have to admit, it delivers it in spades. Rooms are large – they have to be, to hold the fireplaces, the bars, the marble soaking tubs, the beds with 460-thread-count sheets and the fully wired work spaces and other techno gadgets.

There's a fancy gym with a lap pool, a high-rolling bar and a couple of spiffy restaurants. Wi-fi is free.

🛏 Lincoln Park & Old Town

CHICAGO GETAWAY HOSTEL
HOSTEL $

Map p310 (📞773-929-5380; www.getawayhostel.com; 616 W Arlington Pl, Lincoln Park; dm $22-30, r $50-100; P✱@⛶; 🖵22, ⓂBrown, Purple, Red Line to Fullerton) The fun, social Getaway Hostel attracts mostly a twenty-something crowd who strum the house guitars, lounge on the leather couches, sip beer on the patio and head out to nearby, nightlife-rich Clark and Halsted Sts. The rambling 1928 building, with over 200 rooms, was once a boarding house for single women. Continental breakfast and wi-fi are free.

Dorms are mixed sex, sleeping six to 12 people. The private rooms are small, basic and have either a full bathroom or a sink and toilet (or else share a bathroom down the hall). There's a large guest kitchen and coin-op laundry on-site.

HOTEL LINCOLN
BOUTIQUE HOTEL $$

Map p310 (📞312-254-4700; www.jdvhotels.com; 1816 N Clark St, Lincoln Park; r $150-399; P✱@⛶; 🖵22) The boutique Lincoln is all about kitschy fun, as the lobby's 'wall of bad art' and front desk patched together from flea-market dresser drawers attest. Standard rooms are small, but vintage-cool and colorful; many have sweet views. Leafy Lincoln Park and the city's largest farmers market (p98) sprawl across the street. The hotel's rooftop bar (p105) offers spectacular lake views.

A coffee bar in the lobby lets you fuel up in the morning and the attached restaurant serves breakfast and dinner daily. A hotel pedicab provides transport to nearby North Avenue Beach. A handful of free bicycles are also available on a first-come, first-served basis.

VILLA D'CITTA
B&B $$

Map p310 (📞312-771-0696; www.villadcitta.com; 2230 N Halsted St, Lincoln Park; r $179-399; P⛶; 🖵8, ⓂBrown, Purple, Red Line to Fullerton) Step into the old-world ambience of this 19th-century home and you may feel like you're a guest at an Italian count's country villa. The six rooms of this boutique hotel are plush and opulent (some have fireplaces); besides the hot breakfast, a fully stocked dream kitchen is available to guests 24/7. An outdoor hot tub rounds out the experience.

Stay in winter, especially midweek, for big discounts.

🛏 Lake View & Wrigleyville

WRIGLEY HOSTEL
HOSTEL $

Map p314 (📞773-598-4471; www.wrigley hostel.com; 3512 N Sheffield Ave, Wrigleyville; dm $30-60, r from $120; P✱@⛶; ⓂRed Line to Addison) This unobtrusive hostel, located in a converted apartment block, is practically within home-run distance of Wrigley Field (and its rowdy nightlife). The blue-and-green-painted dorms come in co-ed or women-only configurations with four to 10 beds. Small private rooms are also available. Bathrooms, some with vintage clawfoot tubs, are shared on each floor. There's free breakfast and free, strong-signaled wi-fi property-wide.

The common room rocks a pool table, leather couches, bar stools and a booming sound system. The hostel also organizes weekly movie nights and outings to local pubs.

OLD CHICAGO INN
B&B $

Map p314 (📞773-472-2278; www.oldchicagoinn.com; 3222 N Sheffield Ave, Lake View; r $135-190; ✱⛶; ⓂRed, Brown, Purple Line to Belmont) Sure the street din may seep into this century-old, 10-room greystone building, but that's the price you pay for being in a high-energy nightlife hub. Most of the chambers have wood floors and vintage accents; a few rooms share a bathroom. In addition to continental breakfast, you get a free dinner at the owner's pub, Trader Todd's, two doors down.

There's free wi-fi and on-street parking (though you may have to search a bit). Guests also have access to the small, jazzy speakeasy in the basement; it's open Thursday through Saturday.

VILLA TOSCANA
B&B $

Map p314 (☑773-404-2416; www.thevilla toscana.com; 3447 N Halsted St, Boystown; r $129-159; ✱☎; ⓂRed Line to Addison) This 1890s Victorian home sits smack on the busiest of Boystown streets. Wander through the leafy front garden and you're transported. Purple silks evoke Morocco in one room, toile recalls France in another. All eight diminutive rooms (five with private bath) are often booked, so plan ahead. Enjoy breakfast pastries on the rear sundeck in nice weather. Free wi-fi.

★WHEELHOUSE HOTEL
BOUTIQUE HOTEL $$

Map p314 (☑773-248-9001; www.wheelhouse hotel.com; 3475 N Clark St, Wrigleyville; r $250-350; Ⓟ✱☎; ⓂRed Line to Addison) A 2018 newbie, the Wheelhouse features 21 rooms in a restored greystone building not far from Wrigley Field. The smallish rooms have an earthy, urban loft feel, with exposed brick walls, cool vintage decor and bold shades of peach, yellow and blue; some even have bunk beds. The playful, baseball-tinged vibe extends to the lobby's wood-bat ceiling and scoreboard wall.

The hotel is full of character. There's a popular, Detroit-style pan pizza restaurant on the ground level and a speakeasy-style lounge in the basement. It's located on a busy stretch of Clark St, so noise can be an issue for light sleepers.

★MAJESTIC HOTEL
BOUTIQUE HOTEL $$

Map p314 (☑773-404-3499; www.majestic-chicago.com; 528 W Brompton Ave, Lake View; r $159-275; Ⓟ✱☎; ⬚151) Nestled into a row of residential housing, the Majestic is walking distance to Wrigley Field and Boystown and mere steps from the lakefront. From the lobby fireplace and dark-wood furnishings to the handsome, paisley-swirled decor, the interior has the cozy feel of an English manor. Free wi-fi and continental breakfast are included.

Rooms are slightly larger than those at sibling hotels, the City Suites (p240) and Willows (both also in the neighborhood), and the location is quieter and more remote.

HOTEL ZACHARY
HOTEL $$

Map p314 (☑773-302-2300; www.hotelzachary. com; 3630 N Clark St, Wrigleyville; r $250-425; Ⓟ✱☎✱; ⓂRed Line to Addison) Gleaming Hotel Zachary – named after Zachary Taylor Davis, the architect of Wrigley Field – opened in 2018 right across the street from the celebrated ballpark. Nods to baseball are subtle in the 173 stylish, natural-light-filled rooms: ivy-green headboards, baseball-glove-colored leather chairs, gray pinstripe carpet. On game days it's a high-energy scene, and it can be noisy into the wee hours.

Rooms with ballpark views cost extra and are worth it for big-time fans.

Hotel Zachary's lobby bar deserves a visit whether you're staying here or not. Head up to the 2nd floor (where the hotel reception is located), order a classic Manhattan or martini, and settle in to the library-like environs. Tables and armchairs are arranged in intimate clusters, bookshelves offer thick tomes on art, a sofa beckons by the fireplace – it's stately as can be, which is a rarity amid the Cubs madness.

WILLOWS HOTEL
BOUTIQUE HOTEL $$

Map p314 (☑773-528-8400; www.willows hotelchicago.com; 555 W Surf St, Lake View; r $170-285; Ⓟ✱☎; ⬚22) Small and stylish, Willows wins an architectural gold star. The chic lobby provides a swell refuge of overstuffed chairs by the fireplace, while the 55 rooms, done up in shades of peach and soft green, evoke a 19th-century French countryside feel. Free wi-fi and continental breakfast included. It's well located near loads of restaurants, bars and shops, and lakefront parklands.

BEST WESTERN HAWTHORNE TERRACE
HOTEL $$

Map p314 (☑773-244-3434; www.hawthorne terrace.com; 3434 N Broadway, Boystown; r $169-299; Ⓟ✱@☎✱; ⬚36) The earthy Hawthorne Terrace attracts the most mixed crowd of the neighborhood's hotels. Sporty Cubs fans check in next to gay groups, with everyone primed to go out and have some fun. Standard-issue furnishings fill the 83 rooms, but the free wi-fi, microwaves and mini-refrigerators are nice perks, along with the continental breakfast and a small fitness room.

The 1920s Federal-style structure blends in with the surrounding properties and looks more like a stately apartment building than a hotel, giving it a cool local vibe.

CITY SUITES HOTEL
BOUTIQUE HOTEL $$

Map p314 (☑773-404-3400; www.chicagocitysuites.com; 933 W Belmont Ave, Lake View; r $169-285; P✳🛜; MRed, Brown, Purple Line to Belmont) The colorful, art deco–tinged rooms and lobby buzzing just off Belmont Ave are vaguely reminiscent of a European city hotel. The L train races by quite near the building, so light sleepers should ask for a room away from the tracks. Perks include free wi-fi throughout, free continental breakfast and a pass to a nearby fitness club.

Compared with the Majestic (p239) and Willows (p239), the owners' other two properties close by, the City Suites skews toward a bit of a younger and livelier crowd.

HOTEL VERSEY
HOTEL $$

Map p314 (☑773-525-7010; www.hotelversey. com; 644 W Diversey Pkwy, Lake View; r $159-289; P✳@🛜; MBrown, Purple Line to Diversey) High-spirited Hotel Versey plays off two themes: the Cubs (Wrigley Field is a mile away) and music history (touring indie bands often stayed here during its earlier, more humble incarnation). Quirky art on the subjects livens up otherwise standard rooms. It's in a dandy location: an easy amble to the lakefront's parks and beaches, and a 15-minute bus ride to downtown.

Amenities include free wi-fi and access to a nearby LA Fitness center. Bars, restaurants and shops throng the area.

🛏 Andersonville & Uptown

HOUSE 5863
B&B $

Off Map p316 (☑773-682-5217; www.house5863. com; 5863 N Glenwood Ave, Edgewater; r $139-209; P✳@🛜; MRed Line to Thorndale) A modern, if modest, B&B located in an old apartment building. You'll find no frilly ruffles in the five rooms, just clean-lined furnishings and abstract art. Lounge on the black leather sofa in the common living room and watch the plasma TV, or use the free wi-fi throughout. The self-serve breakfast is a bountiful continental one.

GUESTHOUSE HOTEL
BOUTIQUE HOTEL $$

Map p316 (☑773-564-9568; www.theguesthousehotel.com; 4872 N Clark St, Uptown; ste $200-500; P😊✳@🛜🛎; ☐22, MRed Line to Lawrence) The Guesthouse is comprised of 25 elegant, condo-style suites, each with a full kitchen, washer-dryer and private balcony with BBQ grill. Choose from setups with one, two or three bedrooms; the more expensive suites have spa-jet tubs and fireplaces. A two- or three-night minimum stay is required, though exceptions are made for last-minute and off-season bookings. Great value for groups.

Gracious, friendly staff aim to please and can happily arrange grocery delivery. Andersonville's slew of bars and restaurants are a short walk up Clark St.

🛏 Wicker Park, Bucktown & Ukrainian Village

HOLIDAY JONES
HOSTEL $

Map p318 (☑312-804-3335; www.holidayjones. com; 1659 W Division St, East Village; dm/r from $28/76; 😊✳@🛜; MBlue Line to Division) Holiday Jones has an irreverent personality, with old steamer trunks turned stereo speakers comprising the front desk and cartoony posters lining the stairwell. Rooms are compact but tidy, with splashes of comforting plaid. Gender-segregated dorms have four to six bunk beds; private rooms available too. The large common room has couches and a flat-screen TV, plus free wi-fi and lockers.

The location rocks, near heaps of hip bars and eateries on Division St. If you don't feel like venturing out, an empanada restaurant that serves beer and wine is attached to the lobby. The hostel has the same owners as nearby Urban Holiday Lofts (p241), so check there if Holiday Jones is full.

WICKER PARK INN
B&B $

Map p318 (☑773-486-2743; www.wickerparkinn. com; 1331 N Wicker Park Ave, Wicker Park; r $180-200, apt $200-250; ✳🛜; MBlue Line to Damen) This classic brick row house is steps away from great restaurants and nightlife. The sunny rooms aren't huge, but all have hardwood floors, small desk spaces and soothing color schemes with bright splashes of floral wallpaper. Breakfast is rich in baked goods and fruit. Across the street, three apartments with kitchens provide a self-contained experience.

URBAN HOLIDAY LOFTS HOSTEL $

Map p318 (☑312-532-6949; www.urbanholiday lofts.com; 2014 W Wabansia Ave, Wicker Park; dm $25-40, r $79-115; ✳@🛜; MBlue Line to Damen) An international crowd fills the gender-segregated dorms (with four to eight beds) and private rooms of these converted loft condos; some rooms have private bathrooms. Exposed-brick walls, hardwood floors and bunks with plump bedding feature in all 21 rooms. It's close to the L station and in the thick of Wicker Park's nightlife. Continental breakfast is included. No elevator.

The common room bustles with folks using the kitchen facilities, shooting pool and playing arcade games. Loads of bars and cafes beckon in the surrounding blocks, and there's a gourmet supermarket on the ground floor, perfect for self-caterers who want to use the guest kitchen. If the hostel is full, try Holiday Jones, the sibling property in the neighborhood (on Division St).

RUBY ROOM INN $

Map p318 (☑773-235-2323; www.rubyroom.com; 1743-5 W Division St, East Village; r $139-200; ✳🛜; MBlue Line to Division) Take a meditation class, go on a guided intuitive journey or get your chakras massaged. Ruby Room is primarily a spa and 'healing sanctuary.' Nine simplified rooms are boiled down to the essence of comfort. No TVs, no telephones, no elevator, no breakfast. Instead, expect 500-thread-count sheets, pristine interiors, Malin + Goetz amenities, pillowtop mattresses and free wi-fi.

ROBEY HOTEL HOTEL $$

Map p318 (☑872-315-3050; www.therobey.com; 2018 W North Ave, Wicker Park; r from $240; P⊖✳🛜♨🏋; MBlue Line to Damen) Wicker Park's sole hotel is set in a 1929 art deco former office building. The 69 tower rooms run small but have comfy beds, lots of sunlight and great city views; the 20 annex loft rooms have a barebones-industrial vibe, with polished concrete floors and furniture made from pressed wood and metal pipes. Staff are friendly and there's free wi-fi.

There's a summer-only rooftop swimming pool and lounge, a top-floor cocktail bar and a full restaurant on the ground floor; guests can work out at the Bucktown Athletic Club next door. It's pricey for the area but the location can't be beat – the bars and restaurants of Wicker Park are at your feet and the L train is around the corner

(which means light sleepers might want to look elsewhere).

🛏 Logan Square & Humboldt Park

★LONGMAN & EAGLE INN $

Map p322 (☑773-276-7110; www.longmanand eagle.com; 2657 N Kedzie Ave, Logan Square; r $95-250; ✳🛜; MBlue Line to Logan Square) Check in at the tavern downstairs and then head to your wood-floored, vintage-stylish accommodations on the floor above. The six rooms aren't particularly soundproof, but after using your whiskey tokens in the bar, you probably won't care.

Artwork by local artists decorates each room.

🛏 West Loop & Near West Side

CHICAGO PARTHENON HOSTEL HOSTEL $

Map p324 (☑312-258-1399; www.chicago parthenonhostel.com; 310 S Halsted St, Greektown; dm/r from $28/69; ✳🛜; MBlue Line to UIC-Halsted) Guests young and old check in to this hostel in the heart of Greektown. It's a bit more out of the way and basic than other Chicago hostels; then again, prices are usually lower. Tidy dorms and private rooms come in myriad configurations; the typical single-sex dorm has eight beds with the bathroom down the hall.

While there's a common area, this is not a hostel known for its social ambience. The free continental breakfast at the restaurant next door is a nice start to the day. Dorm dwellers must pay $2 extra for towels. Wi-fi is free but spotty.

★ACE HOTEL HOTEL $$

Map p324 (☑312-548-1177; www.acehotel.com/chicago; 311 N Morgan St, West Loop; r $250-400; P✳🛜; MGreen, Pink Line to Morgan) Chicago's branch of the super-hip Ace chain rises up across the street from Google's shiny office. Hints of Frank Lloyd Wright, Ludwig Mies van der Rohe and other famed local architects show up in the mod, earthy design.

The 159 minimalist rooms are on the small side but have cool decor, including a turntable or Martin guitar in most.

Free wi-fi, 24-hour room service, a Stumptown Coffee Roasters cafe and a supreme-view rooftop bar are all part of the stylish package. Many of Chicago's best restaurants and bars are steps away.

★ PUBLISHING HOUSE
BED & BREAKFAST
B&B $$

Map p324 (📞312-554-5857; https://publishing housebnb.com; 108 N May St, West Loop; r $179-379; Ⓜ Green, Pink Line to Morgan) The building was indeed a publishing house more than a century ago, and it's now transformed so it looks like the stylish home of your coolest city friend. The 11 warm-toned rooms, each named for a Chicago writer, have hardwood floors, mid-century modern decor and original art on the walls. A fireplace and reading nooks fill the cozy common areas.

Breakfast is a full cooked affair with French press coffee. The location puts you steps from hot-spot restaurants and bars. Then again, you could just head to the atmospheric wine bar in the building's basement.

SOHO HOUSE CHICAGO
BOUTIQUE HOTEL $$$

Map p324 (📞312-521-8000; www.sohohouse chicago.com; 113 N Green St, West Loop; r $300-660; Ⓟ ❄ 🛜 🏊; Ⓜ Green, Pink Line to Morgan) Chicago's outpost of the members-only club for creative types opens its hotel to the masses. There are only 40 rooms in the century-old, former factory in the red-hot West Loop, but snag one and you'll settle in to a good-sized chamber with vintage decor, velvet couches and fluffy robes. Also access to the rooftop pool and gym with boxing ring.

🛏 Pilsen & Near South Side

HYATT REGENCY
MCCORMICK PLACE
HOTEL $$

Map p328 (📞312-567-1234; www.hyatt.com; 2233 S Martin Luther King Jr Dr, Near South Side; r $189-299; Ⓟ ❄ @ 🛜 🏊; Ⓜ Green Line to Cermack-McCormick Pl) If you're staffing a trade-show booth at **McCormick Place** (Map p328; 📞312-791-7000; www.mccormick place.com; 2301 S Martin Luther King Jr Dr), you can't beat the short walk to your bed in this attached hotel, where lobby monitors keep track of meeting schedules. However, if you're not a conventioneer, even the skyline views and comfy beds mightn't be reason enough to stay in this isolated 1258-room behemoth, 2.5 miles south of the Loop.

🛏 Hyde Park & South Side

LA QUINTA CHICAGO – LAKE SHORE
MOTEL $

Map p332 (📞773-324-3000; www.laquinta chicagolakeshore.com; 4900 S Lake Shore Dr, Kenwood; r $129-179; Ⓟ ❄ @ 🛜 🏊; 🚌6) The paint and decor are relatively fresh, but this four-story motel remains a bit scruffy (dimly lit, thin doors). Focus instead on the lakeside location, free parking and free shuttle that takes you to Michigan Ave downtown. The property is about a 15-minute walk from Hyde Park's restaurants and shops. Continental breakfast is included.

★ SOPHY HYDE PARK
BOUTIQUE HOTEL $$

Map p332 (📞773-289-1003; www.sophyhotel. com; 1411 E 53rd St, Hyde Park; r $229-329; Ⓟ ❄ 🛜; 🚌6, Ⓜ Metra Electric Line to 51st-53rd St) Hyde Park got its first boutique hotel in 2018, and it's a design winner. The 98 rooms have an artsy-hip look that feels truly fresh. Each is good-sized with hardwood floors, a record player and albums by local blues and rock musicians, plus an 8ft, bright-hued, abstract painting (by a local artist) that anchors the space. Free wi-fi, to boot.

The lobby with its double-sided fireplace and plush couches makes a nice hangout. The seasonal American restaurant on-site has a library-like look and bookshelves curated by neighborhood stores such as Powell's (p216).

BENEDICTINE B&B
B&B $$

Map p331 (📞773-927-7424; www.chicagomonk. org; 3111 S Aberdeen St, Bridgeport; r from $180; 🚌8) Monks run this B&B that consists of two simple apartments offering loads of space and kitchen facilities. One is a two-bedroom garden apartment with a deck and self-serve breakfast; the other is a three-bedroom loft with breakfast prepared by the monks. It's about a block from Maria's Packaged Goods & Community Bar (p215), and not far from Chinatown. Free parking.

Understand Chicago

Chicago Today

Downtown Chicago is thriving, with new skyscrapers, ambitious renovation projects and burgeoning industries. Meanwhile, other parts of the city struggle with entrenched poverty, gangs and violent crime. So there are two Chicagos, and the ever-present issue is how to bring the peripheral city up to the same standard as the booming core. But growth creates its own problems, like rising rents. Several gentrifying neighborhoods are trying to stop the process by taking matters into their own hands.

Best on Film

Ferris Bueller's Day Off (1986) A teen truant discovers the joys of the city, from Wrigley Field to the Art Institute.

The Untouchables (1987) Native son David Mamet wrote the screenplay for this nail-biter about Eliot Ness' takedown of Al Capone.

Widows (2018) Local novelist Gillian Flynn wrote this story about four women forced into a heist; features uncommon South Side locales.

The Blues Brothers (1980) Second City alums John Belushi and Dan Aykroyd star in the cult classic of two bluesmen on the run.

Best in Print

The Great Believers (Rebecca Makkai; 2018) National Book Award nominee about friendship and redemption set against the backdrop of the AIDS crisis in 1980s Chicago.

Chicago: A Novel (Brian Doyle; 2016) A young writer chronicles his time in the 'real Chicago' with a colorful cast of characters.

The Man with the Golden Arm (Nelson Algren; 1949) This tale of a drug-addicted kid on Division St won the 1950 National Book Award.

The Adventures of Augie March (Saul Bellow; 1953) Huck Finn–esque story of a destitute boy growing up in Depression-era Chicago.

Thriving Center

Chicago's core continues to develop. Gleaming hotels and condo towers are rising around downtown, like the 93-story Vista Tower, designed by star local architect Jeanne Gang and set to become the city's third-tallest skyscraper when it opens in 2020. Blue-chip companies such as McDonald's have relocated their headquarters to red-hot West Loop, and companies that already work there, like Google, are expanding.

Meanwhile, more people are moving to the area to live. West Loop recently became home to the highest concentration of millennials in the USA, thanks to heaps of slick new high-rises. Several civic projects have come to fruition, including multimillion-dollar L station upgrades at Washington/Wabash and Quincy, Navy Pier's transformation to be less carnival-like and more artsy, and the $60 million Navy Pier Flyover that fixes a dangerous bottleneck for cyclists. In 2018 Chicago's unemployment rate hit 4.1%, the lowest since the government started tracking it in 1976.

Divided City

Outlying neighborhoods, especially on the south and west sides, experience a different reality to Chicago's center. Here poverty and unemployment hold sway. Many of the middle-class African American families who once sustained these communities have left due to high rates of violent crime. Speaking of which: in 2018 there were nearly 560 homicides in Chicago, double that of New York City and Los Angeles. The upside, if there is one: the number is down from 650 homicides in 2017 and 762 homicides in 2016. A handful of south- and west-side neighborhoods account for the majority of killings, which are often triggered by gang-related rivalries. More than half of the victims are African American males aged between 16 and 41.

Some blame lax state gun laws for the problem. Others link it to Chicago's history of entrenched segregation, which has left generations of families stuck in poverty and vulnerable to the lure of gangs. It's a hard cycle to break. A recent study by the Great Cities Institute shows that while some 700,000 jobs are located within a 30-minute public transit ride from the Loop and north side areas, only 50,000 jobs are located within a 30-minute ride from the South Side.

Adding to the problem is mistrust between police and these communities, which came to a boil in the recent case of Laquan McDonald. McDonald was an African American teenager shot 16 times as he was walking away from a Chicago police officer. There were allegations of a cover-up and a 'code of silence' in which cops protected cops. It sparked all sorts of reforms in the police department, though many say the changes aren't happening quickly enough.

Gentrification Pushback

Chicago has long tried to figure out how to deal with gentrification. It's the classic story: as a neighborhood rises with cool bars, restaurants and arts, higher-income residents move in. Rents and property taxes go up, and then the original community members can no longer afford to live there. In neighborhoods such as Pilsen and Logan Square, strong community groups have formed to push back against this type of displacement. It's not that they want to stop the individual businesses from taking root, but that they want to stop uncontrolled development. They want more input and transparency in the process, and they want to ensure affordable housing is maintained as part of new building complexes.

Jackson Park in South Side is another area where the issue has come into play. The new Barack Obama Presidential Center, due for completion sometime after 2021, is the trigger. While most residents are thrilled to have the institution in their district, they want to ensure they don't get pushed out of the neighborhood if it starts to gentrify. They've asked for a community benefits agreement, a legally binding document that holds the developer to certain promises (such as local hiring, livable wages and/or retaining a percentage of affordable housing units). So far no agreement has been signed, but the parties involved – the Obama Foundation, the city council, the nearby University of Chicago and various community groups – continue to work together in good faith to find a resolution.

population per sq mile

CHICAGO   USA

✝ ≈ 90 people

if Chicago were 100 people

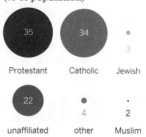

33 would be Caucasian
31 would be African American
29 would be Latinx
6 would be Asian
1 would be Native American & Alaska Native

belief systems
(% of population)

35 Protestant
34 Catholic
3 Jewish

22 unaffiliated
4 other
2 Muslim

History

Much of Chicago's past is downright legendary. You've probably heard about Mrs O'Leary's cow that kicked over a lantern that started the Great Fire that torched the city. And about a man named Al Capone who wielded a mean machine gun during an unsavory era of booze-fueled vice. And about the 'machine' that has controlled local politics for decades. Throw in the invention of the skyscraper and Ferris wheel, and you've got a whopper of a tale.

Early Days: Onions & Forts

The Potawatomi people were the first folks in town, and they gave the name 'Checagou' – or Wild Onions – to the area around the Chicago River's mouth. They weren't particularly pleased when the first settlers arrived in 1803. The newcomers built Fort Dearborn on the river's south bank, on marshy ground under what is today's Michigan Ave Bridge.

The Potawatomi's resentment toward their new neighbors mounted, and like many other tribes, they allied with the British against their common enemy during the War of 1812. That year, the Potawatomi killed 52 people fleeing Fort Dearborn. The killings took place near what is today Chicago Women's Park.

After the war ended, both sides let bygones be bygones for the sake of the fur trade.

Real Estate Boom

To see where Fort Dearborn once stood downtown, look for plaques in the sidewalk marking the spot at the corner of Michigan Ave and Wacker Dr.

Chicago was incorporated as a town in 1833, with a population of 340. Within three years land speculation rocked the local real estate market; lots that sold for $33 in 1829 now went for $100,000. Construction on the Illinois & Michigan Canal – a state project linking the Great Lakes to the Illinois River and thus to the Mississippi River and the Atlantic coast – fueled the boom. Swarms of laborers swelled the population to more than 4100 by 1837, and Chicago became a city.

Within 10 years, more than 20,000 people lived in what had become the region's dominant city. The rich Illinois soil supported thousands

TIMELINE	Late 1600s	c 1779	1803
	The Potawatomi people settle in. They paddle birchbark canoes, fish and ponder a name for the place. How about Checagou (Wild Onions), after the local plants growing here?	Jean Baptiste Point du Sable sails down from Québec and sets up a fur-trading post on the Chicago River. He is the city's first non-indigenous settler.	More settlers arrive and build Fort Dearborn at the river's mouth. The Potawatomi locals are not pleased by their new neighbors. They kill several settlers nine years later.

of farmers, and industrialist Cyrus Hall McCormick moved his reaper factory to the city to serve them.

In 1848 the canal opened. Shipping flowed through the area and had a marked economic effect on the city. A great financial institution, the Chicago Board of Trade, opened to handle the sale of grain by Illinois farmers, who now had greatly improved access to eastern markets.

Bring on the Bacon

By the end of the 1850s, immigrants had poured into the city, drawn by jobs on the new railroads that served the ever-growing agricultural trade. Twenty million bushels of produce were shipped through Chicago annually by then. The population topped 100,000.

Like other northern cities, Chicago profited from the Civil War, which boosted business in the burgeoning steel and toolmaking industries. In 1865, the same year the war ended, the Union Stockyards opened on the South Side. Chicago's rail network and the invention of the iced refrigerator car meant that meat could be shipped for long distances, satiating hungry carnivores all the way east to New York and beyond. The stockyards soon became the major meat supplier to the nation. But besides bringing great wealth to a few and jobs to many, the yards were also a source of water pollution.

Stop the Bacon!

The stockyard effluvia polluted not only the Chicago River but also Lake Michigan. Flowing into the lake, the fouled waters spoiled the city's source of fresh water and caused cholera and other epidemics that killed thousands. In 1869 the Water Tower and Pumping Station built a 2-mile tunnel into Lake Michigan and began bringing water into the city from there; it was hoped that this setup would skirt the contaminated areas. Alas, the idea proved resoundingly inadequate, and outbreaks of illness continued.

Two years later, engineers deepened the Illinois & Michigan Canal so they could alter the Chicago River's course and make it flow south, away from the city. The full project was completed in 1900. Sending waste and sewage down the reversed river provided relief for Chicago residents and helped ease lake pollution, but it was not a welcome change for those living near what had become the city's drainpipe.

Burn Baby Burn – Chicago Inferno

On October 8, 1871, the Great Chicago Fire started just southwest of downtown. Legend has it that a cow owned by a certain Mrs O'Leary

Historical Sites

Graceland Cemetery

Water Tower

Haymarket Square

Biograph Theater

Nuclear Energy sculpture

Pullman National Monument

HISTORY BRING ON THE BACON

The Chicago City Council officially passed a resolution in 1997 absolving the O'Leary family (and their cow) of blame for the Great Chicago Fire.

1837	1860	1865	1869
Chicago incorporates as a city (population 4100-plus). It's a happenin' place, having skyrocketed from just 340 people four years earlier. Within 10 years more than 20,000 call the city home.	The Republican Party holds its national political convention in Chicago and selects Abraham Lincoln, a lawyer from Springfield, IL, as its presidential candidate.	The Union Stockyards open. Thanks to new train tracks and refrigerated railcars, Chicago can send its bacon afar and becomes the world's butchering and meatpacking hub.	The city builds the Water Tower and Pumping Station to help bring clean water in from Lake Michigan, since pollution from the stockyards is contaminating the usual supply.

The Chicago History Museum has great photo archives you can browse online (https://images.chicagohistory.org). See Al Capone chatting with his lawyer, Babe Ruth at the old White Sox ballpark, the 1893 World's Fair Ferris wheel and Muddy Waters and other blues players doing their thing.

kicked over a lantern, which ignited some hay, which ignited some lumber, which ignited the whole town. The image of the hapless heifer has endured despite evidence that the fire was actually the fault of Daniel 'Peg Leg' Sullivan, who dropped by the barn on an errand, accidentally started the fire himself and then tried to blame it on the bovine.

However it started, the results were devastating. The fire burned for three days, killing 300 people, destroying 18,000 buildings and leaving 90,000 people homeless. The dry conditions and mostly wood buildings set the stage for the runaway conflagration. The primitive, horse-drawn firefighting equipment could do little to keep up. Almost every structure was destroyed or gutted in the area bounded by the river on the west, what's now Roosevelt Rd to the south and Fullerton Ave to the north.

Birth of the Skyscraper

Despite the human tragedy, the fire taught the city some valuable lessons – namely, don't build everything from wood. Chicago reconstructed with modern materials, and created space for new industrial and commercial buildings.

The world's best architects poured into the city during the 1880s and '90s to take advantage of the situation. They had a blank canvas to work with, a city giving them lots of money, and the green light to use their imaginations to the fullest. The world's first skyscraper soon popped up in 1885. Several other important buildings also rose during the era, spawning the Chicago School of architecture. Daniel Burnham was one of the premier designers running the show, and he encouraged architects to think big and go beyond traditional limits of design.

Labor Riots

Labor unrest had been brewing in the city for a while. In 1877, organized strikes began in the railroad yards as workers demanded an eight-hour workday and rest breaks. The police and federal troops broke up the strikes, killing at least 18 civilians and injuring hundreds more.

Flash forward a few years, and May 1 had become the official day of protest for Chicago's labor groups. On that day in 1886, thousands of workers went on strike, once again demanding an eight-hour workday. One of the focal points was the McCormick Harvesting Machine Works, which was then Chicago's largest factory. On May 3, fighting broke out between police and protesters at the site, and at least two workers were killed. In response, local anarchists called for a rally next day at Haymarket Square (in today's West Loop). When the speeches start-

1871	1880s	1885	1886
The Great Fire torches the entire inner city. Mrs O'Leary's cow takes the blame, though it's eventually determined that Daniel 'Peg Leg' Sullivan kicked over the lantern that started the blaze.	People start calling Chicago the 'Windy City' – not because of its blustery weather, but because of its big-mouthed local citizenry who constantly brag about the town's greatness.	The world's first steel-frame 'skyscraper,' the Home Insurance Building, rises up. It's 10 stories (138ft) tall and paves the way for big things to come.	Workers fight for an eight-hour workday and decent pay with a rally at Haymarket Sq. The police come, bombs explode, anarchists take the blame, and the labor movement is born.

ed to become inflammatory, the police intervened. Someone threw a bomb, which exploded and killed seven police officers.

The government reacted strongly to what became known as the Haymarket Riot. Eight anarchists were convicted of 'general conspiracy to murder' and four were hanged, although only two had been present at the incident and the bomber was never identified. A sculpture marks the square today.

The White City Debuts

The 1893 World's Expo marked Chicago's showy debut on the international stage. The event centered on a grand complex of specially built structures lying just south of Hyde Park. They were painted white and were brilliantly lit by electric searchlights, which is how the 'White City' tag came to be. Designed by architectural luminaries such as Daniel Burnham, Louis Sullivan and Frederick Law Olmsted, the fairgrounds were meant to show how parks, streets and buildings could be designed in a harmonious manner that would enrich the chaotic urban environment.

Open for only five months, the exposition attracted 27 million visitors, many of whom rode the newly built L train to and from the Loop. The fair offered wonders heretofore unknown to the world: long-distance phone calls, the first moving pictures (courtesy of Thomas Alva Edison's Kinetoscope), the first Ferris wheel and the first zipper. It was at this fair that Pabst beer won the blue ribbon that has been part of its name ever since.

The entire assemblage made a huge impact worldwide, and the fair's architects were deluged with commissions to redesign cities.

The Great Migration

Between 1910 and 1940 around two million African Americans moved from the rural South in what came to be known as the Great Migration. Chicago played a pivotal role in this massive population shift, both as an impetus and as a destination. Articles in the African American–owned and nationally circulated *Chicago Defender* proclaimed the city a workers' paradise and a place free from the horrors of Southern racism. These lures, coupled with glitzy images of thriving neighborhoods like Bronzeville, inspired thousands to relocate.

Chicago's African American population zoomed from 44,103 in 1910 to 109,458 in 1920 and continued growing. The migrants, often poorly educated sharecroppers with big dreams, found a reality not as rosy as promised. Employers were ready with the promised jobs, but many

Chicago Inventions

Roller skates (1884)

Ferris wheel (1893)

Hostess Twinkies (1930)

Pinball (1930)

Spray paint (1949)

Lava Lite lava lamps (1965)

House music (1977)

1890s	1893	1900	1908
Socialite Bertha Palmer makes trips to Paris, buying Monets, Renoirs and other impressionist works before they achieve acclaim. Her collection later forms the core of the Art Institute.	The World's Expo opens near Hyde Park, and Chicago grabs the global spotlight for the wonders it unveils, including the Ferris wheel, movies, Cracker Jack and Pabst beer.	In an engineering feat, Chicago reverses the flow of the Chicago River, forever antagonizing itself with its downstate neighbors as waste now streams in their direction.	Chicago Cubs win the World Series. But curses involving goats, fans named Bartman and general all-round cruddy teams keep them winless for the next 108 years.

CAPONE'S CHICAGO

Al Capone came to Chicago from New York in 1919. He quickly moved up the ranks and was the city's mob boss from 1924 to 1931, until Eliot Ness brought him down on tax evasion charges. Ness was the federal agent whose task force earned the name 'The Untouchables' because its members were supposedly impervious to bribes.

Prohibition fueled the success of the Chicago mob. Gangs made fortunes dealing in illegal beer, gin and other intoxicants. Infamous Capone sites to see include:

Green Mill (p133) The speakeasy in the basement was a Capone favorite.

Holy Name Cathedral (p71) Capone ordered a couple of hits that took place near the church.

Mt Carmel Cemetery (cnr Roosevelt & S Wolf Rds, Hillside) Capone is buried in this cemetery in suburban Hillside, west of Chicago. His simple gravestone reads, 'Alphonse Capone, 1899–1947, My Jesus Mercy.'

St Valentine's Day Massacre Site (p102) Capone's thugs killed seven members of Bugs Moran's gang here.

hoped to rid their factories of white unionized workers by replacing them with African Americans, which exacerbated racial tensions. Blacks were also restricted by openly prejudicial real estate practices that kept them from buying homes anywhere except for certain South Side communities. The South Side remains predominantly African American to this day.

Da Mayor No 1: Richard J Daley

In the 1930s Chicago's Democratic Party created the legendary 'machine' that would control local politics for the next 50 years. Its zenith of power began with the election of Richard J Daley in 1955. Initially thought to be a mere party functionary, Daley was reelected mayor five times before dying while still in office in 1976. With an uncanny understanding of machine politics and how to use it to halt dissent, he dominated the city in a way no mayor had before. His word was law, and the city council routinely approved all his actions, lest a dissenter find his or her ward deprived of vital city services.

Under 'the Boss's' rule, corruption was rampant. Several exposés by the press revealed that some police and politicians were in cahoots with various crime rings.

1929	1931	1933	1942
Prohibition conflict boils over when seven people are killed in a shoot-out between gangsters Al Capone and Bugs Moran. The day becomes known as the St Valentine's Day Massacre.	After years of running the Chicago Outfit and supplying the nation with illegal booze, Capone goes to jail for tax evasion.	Prohibition is repealed and beer flows again. The Democratic Party comes to power with a well-organized (and often corrupt) 'machine' that controls city politics for decades to come.	The first nuclear chain reaction occurs at the University of Chicago. Enrico Fermi and his Manhattan Project pals high-five each other for pulling it off – and not blowing up the city in the process.

Hippies & Riots Come to Town

In August 1968 Chicago hosted the Democratic National Convention, which degenerated into a fiasco of such proportions that its legacy dogged the city for decades.

With the war in Vietnam escalating and general unrest quickly spreading through the USA, the convention became a focal point for protest groups of all stripes. Enter Abbie Hoffman, Jerry Rubin, Rennie Davis, Tom Hayden, John Froines, Lee Weiner and David Dellinger – the soon-to-become 'Chicago Seven.' They called for a mobilization of 500,000 protesters to converge on Chicago. As the odds of confrontation became high, many moderate protesters decided not to attend. When the convention opened, there were just a few thousand young protesters in the city. But Mayor Daley and his allies spread rumors to the media to bolster the case for their aggressive preparations, including a claim that LSD would be dumped into the city's water supply.

The force amassed amounted to 11,900 Chicago police officers, 7500 Army troops, 7500 Illinois National Guardsmen and 1000 federal agents for the August 26 to 29 convention. The night before it began, police staged raids on protesters attempting to camp in Lincoln Park. They moved in with tear gas and billy clubs, singling out some individuals – including several news reporters – for savage attacks.

The action then shifted to Grant Park, across from the Conrad Hilton (now the Hilton Chicago), where the main presidential candidates were staying. Protesters attempted to march to the site, and the police again met them with tear gas and nightsticks and threw many protesters through the hotel's plate-glass windows. The media widely covered the incident, which investigators later termed a 'police riot.'

Polishing the Rust

In the early 1970s, the city's economy was hitting the skids. In 1971 financial pressures caused the last of the Chicago stockyards to close, marking the end of one of the city's most infamous enterprises. Factories and steel mills were also shutting down as companies moved to the suburbs or Southern USA, where taxes and wages were lower. Chicago and much of the Midwest earned the moniker 'Rust Belt,' describing the area's shrunken economies and rusting factories.

But two events happened in the 1970s that were harbingers of the city's more promising future. The world's tallest building (at the time) – the Sears Tower (later renamed Willis Tower) – opened in the Loop

HISTORY HIPPIES & RIOTS COME TO TOWN

Historical Reads

Boss: Richard J Daley of Chicago (Mike Royko)

Sin in the Second City (Karen Abbott)

Get Capone (Jonathan Eig)

The South Side (Natalie Y Moore)

1955	1960	1964	1968
Mayor Daley number one takes office, solidifying the Democratic Party's reign.	McCormick Place opens and is immediately hailed as the 'Mistake on the Lake.' More than 40 years later, nearby Soldier Field homes in on the title after its renovation.	The Rolling Stones come to jam with bluesman Muddy Waters at Chess Records. They consider the studio hallowed ground.	The Democratic National Convention debacle occurs. Around 27,000 police, army regulars and national guardsmen beat a few thousand hippie protesters.

in 1973, beginning a development trend that would spur the creation of thousands of high-paying white-collar jobs. And in 1976, the Water Tower Place shopping mall brought new life to N Michigan Ave.

The city's first female mayor – the colorful Jane Byrne – took the helm in 1979. Byrne's reign was followed by that of Harold Washington, Chicago's first African American mayor, in 1983. His legacy was the success of the African American politicians who followed him. Democrat Carol Moseley-Braun's election to the US Senate in 1992 can be credited in part to Washington's political trailblazing. Barack Obama is another name that comes to mind.

Da Mayor No 2: Richie M Daley

In 1989, Chicago elected Richard M Daley, the son of Richard J Daley, to finish the remaining two years of Harold Washington's mayoral term (Washington had died in office). Like his father, Daley had an uncanny instinct for city politics. He made nice with state officials, who handed over hundreds of millions of public dollars for O'Hare airport, Navy Pier and more.

Despite falling to the third-largest US city, population-wise, in the 1990 census (behind New York and LA), Chicago enjoyed a good decade in the '90s. In 1991 the Chicago Bulls won the first of six national basketball championships. And in 1996 a 28-year-old demon was exorcised when the Democratic National Convention returned to Chicago and went off without a hitch.

When you're on a roll, who else do you thank but the guy who seems to have made it all possible? Daley won his reelection bids in 1991, 1995, 1999, 2003 and 2007, pretty much by a landslide every time. That's not to say the guy didn't have issues, including the 2005 'Hired Truck scandal,' in which city staff had been accepting bribes in exchange for lucrative contracts. By 2011, Daley had enough; he chose not to run for reelection. He had been Chicago's mayor for a record-setting 22 years.

The Post-Daley Years

Enter Rahm Emanuel, Obama's former chief of staff, who took the mayoral reins from 2011 through 2018. Emanuel pledged change, transparency and an end to corruption when he came to office. But that's all easier said than done. While he did lots of good – bringing new businesses downtown, modernizing many city services, spearheading civic projects such as the Riverwalk – he also presided over an era of rising rates of violent crime, crises in the public schools, record tax increases and more. He decided not to seek reelection after his second term.

1973	1983	1989	2004
Chicago pops the last girder into the Sears Tower, which becomes the world's tallest building at 110 stories (1450ft) and remains the record holder for the next quarter century.	Harold Washington, Chicago's first African American mayor, wins election. He paves the way for other politicians down the road, like Barack Obama.	Mayor Daley number two takes office. His reign is highlighted by midnight bulldozings and shiny park unveilings. He ends up in charge of the city even longer than his father.	Millennium Park opens four years after the deadline and hundreds of millions of dollars over budget.

OBAMA-RAMA

Barack Obama, 44th President of the United States, is one of Chicago's most famous residents. He may not live in the city anymore, but he remains a mighty presence.

The former community organizer launched his political career in Chicago. He began by representing the Hyde Park/Kenwood district in the Illinois Senate in 1996. In 2000, he tried to kick it up a notch by running for a US House seat, but he went up against a highly entrenched local politician, and lost. So he regrouped and ran for a vacant US Senate seat in 2004. Bingo: he won in the largest landslide victory in Illinois history.

His career picked up steam from there big-time. First came the speech – a stirring oration Obama gave at the Democratic National Convention in Boston in 2004. Afterward, more than one pundit commented on Obama's presidential bearing; CNN called him a rock star. Public opinion was so high he decided to run for the White House. The pundits didn't really think he could do it. Remember, though, this is the guy who titled his 2006 book *The Audacity of Hope*.

By 2008, he'd won the highest office in the land – the first African American man in history to do so. He gave his acceptance speech in Grant Park, and Chicago was giddy with pride. He then left for Washington, DC. His eight years as president were marked by the economic stimulus package, the health-care-system overhaul, the legalization of gay marriage, and ups and downs to spare. Throughout his time in office, he and Michelle kept their home in Kenwood and would return to visit every once in a while. They still do, though their primary residence is in DC these days.

The Barack Obama Presidential Center is what keeps them connected to Chicago now. The sprawling complex of a museum, library, gardens and plaza is slated to be built in Jackson Park and completed sometime after 2021.

The most significant event of his tenure was the Laquan McDonald police shooting scandal, when cover-up allegations followed the delayed release of a video showing the teenager being shot 16 times by a Chicago policeman. Protesters took to the streets, saying it was yet another example of police misconduct and higher-ups in the city government sweeping it under the carpet. The mayor promised reforms in the police department to improve relations between the police and the African American and Latinx communities. Some have been implemented, but others have not.

Chicago's new mayor, Lori Lightfoot – a Democrat who was formerly the president of the Chicago Police Board and is the city's first openly LGBT mayor – took office in 2019 and is now tasked with these challenges.

2008	2011	2016	2019
Local boy Barack Obama stands in the electric air of Grant Park and gives his acceptance speech as elected President of the United States. Chicagoans swell with pride.	Mayor Richard M Daley leaves office after 22 years, having decided not to run for reelection. Rahm Emanuel, Obama's former chief of staff, takes the reins.	Cubs win the World Series – their first since 1908 – and the longest dry spell in US sports history ends. Some 5 million people attend the victory party.	Jason Van Dyke, the policeman who shot teenager Laquan McDonald 16 times, unleashing protests about police brutality, is sentenced to seven years in prison for second-degree murder.

Architecture

The Great Fire of 1871 sparked an architectural revolution in Chicago. It created a blank slate where new ideas could be tested. Daniel Burnham, one of the prime designers during the era, encouraged architects to think big and not be put off by traditional limits. The city has been a hotbed for skyscraper design ever since.

First Chicago School (1872–99)

Though the 1871 fire didn't seem like an opportunity at the time, it made Chicago what it is today. The chance to reshape the city's burned downtown drew young, ambitious architects including Dankmar Adler, Daniel Burnham, John Root and Louis Sullivan. These men saw the scorched Loop as a sandbox for innovation, and they rapidly built bigger, better commercial structures over the low roughshod buildings that went up immediately after the fire. These men and their colleagues made up the

Above: Auditorium Theatre (p65)

First Chicago School (some say they practiced the Commercial style), which stressed economy, simplicity and function. Using steel frames and elevators, their pinnacle achievement was the modern skyscraper.

The earliest buildings of the First Chicago School, such as the Auditorium Theatre (p65), used thick bases to support towering walls above. William Le Baron Jenney, the architect who constructed the world's first iron-and-steel-framed building in the mid-1880s, had a studio in Chicago, where he trained a crop of architects who pushed the city skyward through internal frames.

In the Loop, the Monadnock Building (p53) gives a practical sense of how quickly these innovations were catching on: the original northern half of the building consists of more traditional load-bearing walls measuring 6ft thick at ground level, while the southern half, constructed only two years later, uses the then-revolutionary metal frame for drastically thinner walls that go just as high.

No matter how pragmatic these First Chicago School architects were in their inspiration and motivation, the steel-framed boxes they erected rarely suffered from lack of adornment. Maverick firms like Adler & Sullivan and Burnham & Root used a simple, bold geometric language to rebuild downtown in style. Steel skeletons were clad in exterior masonry, often with highly decorative terra-cotta panels – which were, perhaps most importantly, fireproof – embellished with designs taken from neoclassicism or nature. When gazing up at these early skyscrapers, notice their strong vertical lines crossed grid-like by horizontal bands and topped by ledge-like ornamental cornices, contrasted with the sweeping lines of jutting bay windows, curved corners and grand entrances from the street.

> Fans of Frank Lloyd Wright can follow a self-guided trail around Illinois that takes in 13 Wright-designed buildings. Itineraries start in Chicago and head northwest to Rockford or southwest to Springfield. See Frank Lloyd Wright Trail (www.enjoyillinois.com/history/frank-lloyd-wright-trail).

Prairie School (1895–1915)

It was the protégé of Louis Sullivan, Frank Lloyd Wright, who would endow Chicago with its most distinctive style, the Prairie School. Wright, a spottily educated ladies' man from a Wisconsin farm town, was the residential designer for Adler & Sullivan until 1893, when his architectural commissions outside the firm led to his dismissal. Forced into his own practice, he eventually set up a small studio in suburban Oak Park and by 1901 had built 50 public buildings and private homes around the Chicago metro area.

Over the next 15 years, Wright's 'Prairie Houses' contrasted the grand edifices of the First Chicago School with more modest charms. His unique residential buildings emphasize low-slung structures with dominant horizon lines, hipped (shallowly sloped) roofs, overhanging eaves and unadorned open-plan spaces that mirrored the flat Midwestern landscape. To blend visually, such natural, neutral materials as brick, limestone and stucco were often used. Much in sympathy with the turn-of-the-20th-century arts-and-crafts style, Wright's 'organic architecture' was likewise anti-industrial, inspired by and aiming to exist harmoniously with nature.

Of all the Prairie Houses by Wright's hand, Robie House (p204) is the most dramatic and successful. It's a measuring stick by which all other buildings in the style are often compared, and is alone worth the trip to Hyde Park. A bit of Wright's early work is nearer to the city center – Bronzeville's Robert W Roloson Houses (p212), which were designed in 1894 while Wright still worked for Adler & Sullivan and are his only set of row houses; and the airy atrium of the Loop's landmark Rookery (p53). Wright's notable colleagues in the Prairie style include George W Maher, Walter Burley Griffin and Marion Mahony Griffin, the latter one of the USA's first licensed female architects.

Tiffany stained-glass dome, Chicago Cultural Center (p52)

Beaux Arts (1893–1920)

While the First Chicago School and Prairie School were forward-looking inventions that grew from the marshy shores of Lake Michigan, beaux arts – named for the École des Beaux-Arts in Paris – took after a French fad that stressed antiquity. Proud local builders like Louis Sullivan hated the style. Even so, these buildings are pleasing today for their eclectic mixed bag of classical Roman and Greek elements, including stately columns, cornices and facades crowded with statuary.

The popularity of the style was spurred on by the colossal French neoclassical structures of Daniel Burnham's 'White City,' built for the 1893 World's Exposition, which also erected the Palace of Fine Arts, now housing the Museum of Science & Industry (p205). After Burnham's smash hit at the Expo, beaux arts became the city's dominant architectural paradigm for the next two decades, making a welcome contrast to the dirty, overcrowded slums that had come with Chicago's urban expansion.

Beaux arts also propelled the 'City Beautiful' urban planning movement, for which Burnham was an evangelist. Published in 1909, Burnham's own *Plan of Chicago* called for a more splendorous, scenic and well-ordered cityscape. Although much of the Burnham Plan was never actually implemented, many public parks were reclaimed along the lakeshore and a network of diagonal streets newly built, both features that still define the city today.

The impressive echoes of Burnham's White City are evidenced in some of the city's best-known civic landmarks, including downtown's Art Institute (p49) and the Chicago Cultural Center (p278). The latter began in 1897 as the Chicago Public Library, housing a donated collection of some 8000 books sent by British citizens after the Great Fire

Carbide & Carbon Building

of 1871. (Many books were even autographed by the donors, including Queen Victoria, Charles Darwin and Alfred Lord Tennyson.) While the books have since been moved to the Harold Washington Library, the magnificent gilded ceilings, inlaid marble mosaics, stained-glass domes and classical details of the original beaux-arts building remain.

Art Deco (1920–39)

After the decline in popularity of beaux arts, Chicago's architects found inspiration from another French movement: art deco. The art-deco style may have been as ornamental as beaux arts, but instead of classical columns and statues, it took on sharp angles, geometric elements, reflective surfaces and a modern palette of blacks, silvers and greens.

Sadly, there are few remaining buildings in the Loop that characterize this style, which withered before WWII. An exception is the 1929 Carbide & Carbon Building, designed by Daniel Burnham's two sons, and now housing the St Jane Hotel. Check out the building's polished black granite, green terra-cotta and gold-leaf accented crown, rumored to be intended to look like a foil-wrapped champagne bottle. Another downtown deco landmark is the 1930 Chicago Board of Trade (p55), which remained the city's tallest skyscraper until 1965 when the Richard J Daley Center opened.

Second Chicago School (1946–79)

The city once again led the architectural world in the 1950s as German immigrant Ludwig Mies van der Rohe pioneered the Second Chicago School. Having previously drafted buildings in Europe alongside fellow German innovator Walter Gropius and Swiss-French modernist

Design geeks, take note: for one weekend in mid-October, the Chicago Architecture Center coordinates free tours of more than 200 architectural gems around the city, many of them normally off-limits to the public. The event is called Open House Chicago (www.openhouse chicago.org).

GREEN CHICAGO

Chicago has one of the highest numbers of LEED-certified (Leadership in Energy and Environmental Design) buildings in the country. Behemoths like theMart (aka the Merchandise Mart) and the Willis Tower have been retrofitted to meet LEED standards. The city boasts more than 500 green roofs, covering 5.5 million sq ft downtown and around. One covers City Hall, and Millennium Park is technically a green roof since it tops an underground parking garage. Chicago has also added protected bike lanes to busy streets and expanded its bike-sharing program to some 580 stations around town. It's now one of the nation's largest networks.

Le Corbusier, Mies was influenced by both Bauhaus and the International Style. Under Mies' direction, the steel frame that revolutionized Chicago's skyline once again became seminal, though now no longer hidden on the inside of walls.

The functional, stripped-bare style of the Second Chicago School was all about exposed metal and glass, and represents most people's image of the modern skyscraper. The Loop's best example of this is the **Chicago Federal Center** (Map p298; 219 & 230 S Dearborn St; Ⓜ Blue Line to Jackson), Mies' masterstroke, which demonstrates both the open, universal spaces and starkly minimalist vertical I beams he favored.

Chicago Architecture Today

In the last half of the 20th century, the Chicago architectural partnership of Skidmore, Owings & Merrill came to dominate the cityscape. Further developing Mies' ideas, they stretched the modern skyscraper even higher with the John Hancock Center (now known as 875 N Michigan) in 1969, and again in 1973 with the Sears Tower, which kept its crown as the world's tallest building for almost a quarter century. Now called the Willis Tower (p51), it remained the USA's tallest building until surpassed by NYC's One World Trade Center in 2013. Skidmore, Owings & Merrill continues to hold sway on the global stage, most recently as the designer of Dubai's Burj Khalifa, the world's tallest building since it opened in 2010.

The late '90s sparked a slew of development downtown, not all of it pretty. Local architects and developers were taken to task for betraying Chicago with a crop of unsightly condos and town-house developments. Blame the big, bad '80s, when downtown real estate prices were stratospheric, and largely unchecked development sprawled both north and south of the Loop.

So far, the 21st century has been marked by architectural triumphs – including Millennium Park (p46) and Frank Gehry's sculpted steel Pritzker Pavilion (p47) – and great controversies, such as love-it-or-hate-it Trump Tower, now the city's second-tallest building. Jeanne Gang's Aqua Tower (p52), with its spectacularly undulating wavelike balconies, was named the 2010 skyscraper of the year by Emporis, and she continues to build impressive structures all over the place. Her newest, most ambitious project is the 93-story Vista Tower in the Loop, which will become Chicago's third-tallest skyscraper when it's completed in 2020. Meanwhile the city remains one of the nation's leaders in ecofriendly, LEED-certified construction, helping to keep its architectural reputation sky-high.

The local public TV station offers a great, free mobile guide and audio tour of downtown architecture. It's available at http://interactive.wttw.com/loop.

Sports

Chicago is the USA's greatest sports town. There – we said it. Why? It's not because every professional sports team is winning championships these days, but because of the undying passion of the city's sports fans. Listen in at the office water cooler and the talk is all about the Bears or the Blackhawks. Eavesdrop on a conversation between neighbors as they tidy their yards, and the chatter revolves around the Cubs or the White Sox.

Many Teams, One Unified City of Fans

Almost every Chicagoan declares a firm allegiance to at least one of the city's teams, and the place goes absolutely nuts when one of them hits the big time. Take the Cubs' World Series win in 2016. It had been 108 years since the team won it all. A legendary curse supposedly hexed them from ever triumphing again. When it finally happened the city celebrated like never before. An estimated *five million* fans turned out to party with the team at the victory parade held a few days later.

When the Blackhawks won the Stanley Cup in 2015, some two million people poured into the city's streets for a raucous victory parade. And when the White Sox won the World Series in 2005? Similar scene, only with a ticker-tape parade that also included F-16 fighter planes, Journey's Steve Perry and Oprah, all strangely woven together.

Die-hard sports fandom is an accepted way of life here. This is a city that sees no conflict of interest in taking one of its most revered cultural icons – the Art Institute's lion sculptures – and plopping giant fiberglass Cubs helmets on them when the team wins big. The creatures also donned Blackhawks helmets, Bears helmets and White Sox caps when those teams played in the championships. Even the city's staid skyscrapers get into the spirit, arranging their window lights to spell 'Go Cubs' or 'Go Hawks' when those teams make a run for the championship play-offs.

Baseball

Chicago is one of only a few US cities to boast two Major League Baseball (MLB) teams. The Cubs are the North Side squad, with enthusiastic attendance year after year. The World Series win in 2016 after a 108-year drought – the longest losing streak in US sports history – has made the team more popular than ever. The White Sox are the working person's team on the South Side, and thumb their nose at all the hoopla across town.

The two ballparks are also a study in contrasts: traditional Wrigley Field (p111), aka 'the Friendly Confines,' is baseball's second-oldest park and is about as charming as they get. Guaranteed Rate Field (p216) is the new breed of stadium with modern amenities like a pet check, where you can drop off Fido, and fireworks exploding every time the Sox hit a home run after dark.

Chicago Sports Blogs

Bleed Cubbie Blue (www.bleed cubbieblue.com)

South Side Sox (www.south sidesox.com)

Windy City Gridiron (www. windycitygridiron. com)

Blog-A-Bull (www. blogabull.com)

Chicago Bulls play Philadelphia 76ers, United Center (p187)

Basketball

The Bulls, once the stuff of legend, haven't posed much of a threat since the late 1990s, when Michael Jordan led the team. Jordan, revered coach Phil Jackson and small forward Scottie Pippen were the core of a dynasty that won six NBA championships between 1991 and 1998. They helped popularize the NBA around the world. Since then the team, which plays at United Center (p187), has yo-yoed from awful to stellar to so-so and back to awful. But fans still journey to the stadium to take a photo with the famed dunking Jordan statue in the atrium.

Football

Once upon a time the Chicago Bears were one of the most revered National Football League (NFL) franchises. Owner and coach George Halas epitomized the team's no-nonsense, take-no-prisoners approach. The tradition continued with players such as Walter Payton, Dick Butkus and Mike Singletary and coach Mike Ditka. In 1986 the Bears won the Super Bowl with a splendid collection of misfits and characters, such as Jim McMahon and William 'the Refrigerator' Perry, who enthralled the entire city. The team has been up and down ever since. Their last championship appearance was in Super Bowl XLI in 2007 (they lost). No matter what, fans still fill the stands at sometimes snowy Soldier Field (p200).

Popular shops for team gear include the Cubs Store at Wrigley Field and its smaller branch in Near North (at 668 N Michigan Ave); the Blackhawks Shop in the Loop (at 333 N Michigan Ave); and the Blackhawks/Bulls Madhouse Store at United Center.

Hockey

After languishing at the bottom of Chicago's pro-sports pantheon for a few decades, the Blackhawks skated back into prominence with a

TOP CHICAGO SPORTS HEROES

Should you find yourself in a sports bar anywhere in the Windy City, a misty-eyed mention of any of the names below will help you bond with fellow drinkers.

Mike Ditka The Chicago Bears star (and current Chicago restaurateur), Ditka is the only person to have won a Super Bowl as a player, assistant coach and head coach. His mustache is legendary.

Michael Jordan The Chicago Bulls great ended his career of 15 seasons with the highest per-game scoring average in National Basketball Association (NBA) history.

Ryne Sandberg The Cubs second baseman played a record 123 consecutive games without an error. In 2005, he became the fourth Cubs player ever to have his number (23) retired.

Dick Butkus Elected to the Pro Football Hall of Fame in 1979, the Bears linebacker recovered a record-breaking number of fumbles during his career. *Sports Illustrated* once called him 'the Most Feared Man in the Game.'

Walter Payton This 1970s and '80s Chicago Bears great is ranked second on the National Football League (NFL) all-time rushing list, and fourth in all-time rushing touchdowns.

Ernie Banks Voted the National League's most valuable player (MVP) twice (1958 and '59) and a 14-time All-Star, 'Mr Cub' was the first player to have his number (14) retired by the Cubs. A statue of him stands near Wrigley Field's main entrance on Clark St.

Stan Mikita The Czech-born hockey star played his entire career (1959–80) with the Chicago Blackhawks, often alongside superstar teammate Bobby Hull, aka the 'Golden Jet,' considered one of hockey's all-time greats.

Ozzie Guillén Former White Sox coach and player known for his outspoken and politically incorrect comments, Ozzie nonetheless brought the World Series trophy to Chicago in 2005 – the first big baseball win in almost a century.

Theo Epstein The genius responsible for rebuilding the Cubs and bringing the team its first World Series in 108 years. He did what many thought was impossible – but he had done the impossible before when he was general manager of the Boston Red Sox, helping them win a championship after an 86-year dry spell.

young winning team and TV and radio deals that returned them to the mainstream. Oh, and they won the NHL's Stanley Cup in 2010, their first trophy since 1961 – and then repeated that feat in 2013 and 2015. The Hawks slap-shot pucks at United Center (p187). If you go to a game, be sure to arrive in time for the singing of the national anthem at the start. The raucous, ear-splitting rendition is a tradition.

Soccer

Thanks to support from the city's large Latinx and European communities, the city's soccer team, Chicago Fire, attracts a decent-sized fan base, despite being largely ignored by the mainstream media. The team has made the Major League Soccer (MLS) play-offs several times, and last won the championship in 1998. Watch 'em kick at suburban **Toyota Park** (☏888-657-3473; www.chicago-fire.com; cnr 71st St & Harlem Ave, Bridgeview; tickets $20-50; ☐Toyota Park Express).

Chicago Dining

For years epicures wrote off Chicago as a culinary backwater. Then little by little it changed. Inventive chefs set up shop, drawn by Chicago's lower costs compared to other big cities, and a citizenry hungry to try something new. Now the scene is bold enough that the James Beard Foundation chooses Chicago to host its annual awards ceremony. So get ready for a plateful. A rich clash of high gastronomy and comfort food is on the menu.

Current Scene

Plenty of meat gets carved in the city, a lasting legacy from when Chicago was the world's slaughterhouse capital. Steakhouses are a dime a dozen downtown, and new gastropubs and taverns with charcuterie menus seem to open weekly. That's not to say vegetarians and vegans don't get their due, with an increasing number of options, including Ground Control (p168) and Veggie Grill (p59).

The most interesting restaurants are out of downtown's core. They're in West Loop, the realm of celebrity chefs and big, stylish dining rooms, and in Logan Square, the domain of hot chefs in small, storefront spaces. Lincoln Square, Ravenswood, Bridgeport and Avondale also harbor wildly creative kitchens. These neighborhoods are really where the vanguard of chefs work, such as Iliana Regan of Michelin-starred Elizabeth (p141). She's known for her 'new gatherer' cuisine for which ingredients are foraged or hunted and might result in, say, deer bone broth or fried lichens.

John and Karen Shields, the husband-wife team at Smyth (p182), have earned two Michelin stars for their fancy, seasonal comfort food. They're part of the grow-your-own trend: all ingredients come from their farm near the city. Pleasant House Pub (p196) grows its own ingredients at an experimental zero-waste facility known as Plant Chicago (p209). Even celebrity chef Rick Bayless of Topolobampo/Frontera Grill (p76) cultivates his own herbs and edible flowers in his backyard garden in Bucktown.

If you're willing to trek further, immigrant enclaves dish out Vietnamese sandwiches and Thai noodles (Uptown), Mexican tacos and tortas (Pilsen), Swedish pastries (Andersonville), Indian and Pakistani curries (Far North Side's Devon Ave) and much more of the least expensive, most genuine dishes Chicago has to offer.

Food Blogs & Websites

Eater Chicago (http://chicago.eater.com)

LTH Forum (www.lthforum.com)

Fooditor (www.fooditor.com)

Smokin' Chokin' and Chowing with the King (http://chibbqking.blogspot.com)

Chicago's Best-Loved Specialties

Pizza

Deep-dish pizza is Chicago's most famous concoction. These behemoths are nothing like the flat circular disks known as pizza in the rest of the world. Chicago's thick-crusted pie stacks up like this: a fat and crumbly crust baked in a cast-iron pan (kind of like a skillet without a handle), capped by mozzarella, then toppings and sauce. Gino's East (p77), Pizano's (p59) and Lou Malnati's (p74) offer classic deep-dish.

Molecular gastronomy at triple-Michelin-starred restaurant Alinea (p104)

An adjunct to the genre is stuffed pizza. It's like deep dish on steroids, bigger and more decadent. Basically it's dough, with cheese on top, then another layer of dough atop that, plus toppings. Giordano's (p75) bakes a mighty one.

Pan pizza is the third contender. It's similar to deep dish, but the crust is baked differently so it's breadier, and it has a ring of caramelized cheese that crisps in the pan. Pequod's (p103) sets the standard for pan deliciousness.

Hot Dogs, Italian Beef & Jibaritos

No less iconic than deep-dish pizza is the Chicago-style hot dog. A real-deal specimen uses a local Vienna beef weenie and requires a poppy-seed bun and a litany of toppings (including onions, tomatoes, a dill pickle and neon-green relish). And remember rule *numero uno*: no ketchup! For gourmet versions (rabbit sausage with anchovy hazelnut butter sauce) along with stalwart classics, swing by Hot 'G' Dog (p127) in Andersonville.

Another renowned Chicago specialty is the Italian beef sandwich, which takes thin-sliced, slow-cooked roast beef that's sopped in natural gravy and *giardiniera* (spicy pickled vegetables), then heaps it all on a hoagie roll. Local Italian immigrants on the South Side invented it as a low-budget way to feed factory workers during the Depression era. Try it while you're here – Mr Beef (p75) makes a popular one – because you'll be hard-pressed to find one elsewhere on the planet.

Less well known, but equally messy and delicious, is the *jibarito* sandwich, developed at a local Puerto Rican eatery. It consists of steak covered in garlicky mayo and served between thick, crispy-fried plantain slices, which form the 'bread.' Many Latin American cafes in the

Iliana Regan, the chef at Elizabeth, wrote *Burn the Place: A Memoir* (2019) about her journey from foraging on the family farm to earning a Michelin star at her Lincoln Square restaurant. It also delves into her experience of being a gay female chef in a largely straight, male-dominated industry.

CHICAGO CHEFS TO KNOW

Rick Bayless He's everywhere: on TV, managing the organic garden where he grows the restaurants' herbs, and tending Xoco (p74), Topolobampo/Frontera Grill (p76) and Cruz Blanca (p186).

Grant Achatz Made 'molecular gastronomy' a culinary catchphrase at stratospherically priced Alinea (p104); his other hot spots include Roister (p183), Next (p183) and Aviary (p186).

Stephanie Izard Gaining fame as the first woman to win *Top Chef*, who then later became Iron Chef, this sustainable farm-to-table fan's Girl & the Goat (p182), Little Goat (p181) and Duck Duck Goat (p182) are West Loop landmarks.

Paul Kahan The son of a Chicago smokehouse and deli owner, this classically influenced chef makes waves at Dove's Luncheonette (p151), Avec (p182), Blackbird (p183), Publican (p183) and Big Star (p150), among others.

Humboldt Park neighborhood, such as Papa's Cache Sabroso (p171), have it on the menu.

Food Media

The trendsetter is *Check, Please!* (http://checkplease.wttw.com), a local TV program airing on Public Broadcasting Service (PBS) affiliate WTTW (Channel 11). For each episode it sends three dining citizens to three restaurants across the price spectrum to get their straightforward critiques. Then they all gather around a table and drink wine with the program's host to discuss. The show has been on since 2001, and it remains wildly popular. It gets flooded with thousands of applications from would-be food critics. Meanwhile, restaurants that are profiled often get deluged with hungry newcomers. See for yourself what locals have to say in the show's entertaining video archives online.

Chicago's Best (http://chicagosbesttv.com) is a similar TV program, only here locals write in and recommend bites for the show's hosts to try. Episodes are also archived online.

City of Chains

It's strangely fitting that Ray Kroc opened the first McDonald's franchise restaurant in a Chicago suburb, because today top-flight Chicago restaurateurs love to expand their turf to multiple locations. Sometimes – as is the case with Giordano's (p75) and Lou Malnati's (p74) pizzerias, high-class pasta kitchen Rosebud (p180) and addictive fried dough purveyor Stan's Donuts (p149) – it's a good thing. In general, though, secondary outlets of local franchises such as the Billy Goat Tavern (p77) are more like the unfortunate sequel to a great movie. When possible, stick with the original location.

Music & the Arts

Contrasts fuel the city's creative engine: high-concept installations occupy erstwhile warehouses, while poetry readings are nearly a contact sport. The city's dedication to populist ideals – most visible at free summer music festivals and in ubiquitous public art – lets artists push boundaries in front of unusually broad audiences. Few US cities can boast such engaging, affordable options for art lovers, and none can do so with such little pretension.

Music

The birthplace of electric blues and house music, Chicago also fosters a vibrant independent rock scene, boundary-leaping jazz cats and world-class orchestras and chamber groups. From top to bottom, local musicians embody the best characteristics of the city itself:

Above: Courtney Barnett performing at Taste of Chicago festival (p22)

they're resourceful and hardworking, sweating it out in muggy blues clubs, sunny outdoor amphitheaters, DIY punk bars and everyplace in between.

Chicago Blues

The most famous of Chicago's musical styles comes in one color: blue. After the Great Migration of African Americans out of the rural South, Delta bluesmen set up on Chicago's street corners and in the open-air markets of Maxwell St during the 1930s, when Robert Johnson first recorded 'Sweet Home Chicago.'

What distinguishes Chicago's regional blues style from Johnson's original ode is simple: volume. Chicago blues is defined by the plugged-in electric guitars typified by genre fathers Muddy Waters and Howlin' Wolf. Bluesmen from the 1950s and '60s, such as Willie Dixon, Junior Wells and Elmore James, and later champions like Buddy Guy, Koko Taylor and Otis Rush, became national stars.

These days, Chicago's blues clubs are still playing much the same song they were decades ago, but it's a proud one – synonymous with screaming guitars, rolling bass and R&B-inflected rhythms. For a modern take on the style listen to Shemekia Copeland, a powerful, award-winning vocalist who lives on the South Side and tours worldwide.

House Music

Chicago's other big taste-making musical export took root in the early '80s at a now-defunct West Loop nightclub called the Warehouse, where DJ Frankie Knuckles got tired of spinning disco and added samples of European electronic music and beats from that new-fangled invention, the stand-alone drum machine. Uninterested in appealing to commercial radio, the tracks used deep, pounding bass beats and instrumental samples made for dancing.

House music DJs such as Derrick Carter and Larry Heard revolutionized the form and huge second-wave stars like Felix da Housecat, DJ Sneak and acid-house artist Armando took Chicago's thump worldwide. The club scene was all about big beats, wild parties and drugged-out dancing until the late '90s, when police cracked down. In recent years, the house-music scene has matured, while still continuing to innovate.

The Rolling Stones hand-picked the tracks on *Confessin' the Blues* (2018), a compilation that features Howlin' Wolf, Muddy Waters, Chuck Berry, Big Bill Broonzy and more. Proceeds go to Willie Dixon's Blues Heaven – the former Chess Records, where the Stones had some transformative recording sessions.

Jazz, Folk, Rock, Hip-Hop & Gospel

For innovative, cutting-edge and avant-garde jazz, the name to know is AACM (aka the Association for the Advancement of Creative Musicians), a Chicago-based nonprofit organization formed in 1965 that has been a big inspiration for African American musicians. Contemporary jazz scene makers include saxophonist Ken Vandermark, a MacArthur 'genius' grant recipient, and Grammy-winning 'vocalese' singer Kurt Elling, who got his first big break at Uptown's Green Mill (though he now lives in New York).

Chicago's underground rock community has filled an important niche in recent decades with established indie labels such as Bloodshot, Thrill Jockey, Drag City and Touch & Go. The reigning king of Chicago rock is (arguably) still Wilco. Garage rock band Twin Peaks are current heroes making a mark on the scene.

For hip-hop, Common and Kanye West put Chicago on the map. Both grew up in the city, where Common's mom was a Chicago Public Schools principal, and Kanye's mom was head of Chicago State University's English department. They opened the door for fresh under-

Stony Island Arts Bank (p206)

ground names like Lupe Fiasco and Twista. Chance the Rapper is the native son headliner these days. Keep an eye out for his friend, hip-hop and soul singer Jamila Woods, who's on the rise.

Folk troubadours hold down open-mike nights and play at the North Side's Old Town School of Folk Music, while gospel choirs raise the roof at South Side churches. **Pilgrim Baptist Church** (Map p331; ☑312-842-5830; 3301 S Indiana Ave; Ⓜ Green Line to 35th-Bronzeville-IIT) in Bronzeville is considered the birthplace of gospel. Mahalia Jackson, Aretha Franklin and Mavis Staples (a current Chicago resident) were among the voices that let loose there before the church was destroyed in a fire.

Visual Arts

Nowhere is it easier to see the great chasms and curious bridges of the city's artistic ethos than in the visual arts. Take the work of painter and sculptor Kerry James Marshall, who uses elements of pop culture to confront racial stereotypes in contemporary society; or cartoonist Chris Ware, who draws graphic novels with architectural perfectionism. Photographer Dawoud Bey explores identity and racism in his portraits of African American subjects, while photographer Rashid Johnson evokes 19th-century photographic techniques and elements of hip-hop in his works. Dzine (pronounced 'design') draws inspiration from Chicago's graffiti movement and lowrider cars to create outdoor sculptural works, large-scale paintings and art installations that fuse high and low culture.

Such transgressive boundary crossings may well have rankled the fat-cat industrialists who raised marble halls for European art over a century ago, but Chicago's public has long embraced pioneering forms.

Printers Row Lit Fest (p22)

Consider society matron Bertha Palmer, who fostered the city's artistic edge in the late 1800s when she collected impressionist paintings in Europe that later became the Art Institute's core. Since then, Chicago's artists have contributed to every major international movement – from Archibald Motley Jr's portraits of roaring South Side jazz clubs in the 1920s to today's locals such as Theaster Gates, an installation artist, University of Chicago professor and founder of the Stony Island Arts Bank (p206) and Arts Incubator (p208).

Chicago's five gallery districts show more of the current scene. River North is the most entrenched, where top international names show off their works; it also has the largest concentration of galleries. West Loop is a hotbed of edgy, avant-garde art that garners international praise. Bucktown and Wicker Park are rife with alternative spaces and emerging talent. Pilsen hosts several small, artist-run spaces that have erratic hours. And the South Side neighborhood of Bridgeport has become a player with cool-cat galleries in a warren of old warehouses on W 35th St.

Best Chicago Nonfiction Books

....

One More Time,
Mike Royko

....

Working, Studs
Terkel

....

The Devil in the
White City, Erik
Larson

....

Sin in the Second
City, Karen Abbott

Literature & Spoken Word

Nelson Algren is perhaps the city's most famous writer. He lived in Wicker Park (p149) and wrote about the underbelly: drunks, sex workers, drug addicts and street toughs. He won the 1950 National Book Award for *The Man with the Golden Arm* about a drug addict on Division St. Saul Bellow grew up in Humboldt Park and taught at the University of Chicago. He won the 1954 National Book Award for *The Adventures of Augie March,* which is set in the city.

CHICAGO'S MONUMENTAL PUBLIC ART

Chicago has a standard-setting public policy that made it an international center for public art: in 1978, the city council approved an ordinance stipulating that more than 1% of costs for constructing or renovating municipal buildings be set aside for the commission or purchase of original artworks. The result? A public art collection that's as much a part of the city's character as is its groundbreaking architecture.

The most prominent public artworks go well beyond the staring eyes of the Picasso (p55) at Daley Plaza or Millennium Park's Cloud Gate (p46), aka 'the Bean'. Sculptor Alexander Calder has a couple of major works in the city, both completed in 1974. The most visible is the arching red Flamingo (p55) at Federal Plaza, while *Flying Dragon* floats in the Art Institute's North Stanley McCormick Memorial Garden. Joan Miró's Chicago (p55) sculpture – originally titled *The Sun, The Moon and One Star* – is also conveniently in the Loop, as is Jean Dubuffet's Monument with Standing Beast (p55) sculpture and an expansive mosaic by Marc Chagall titled Four Seasons (p55).

Pilsen is known for its extensive collection of murals (p192). Logan Square is also big in the street art scene (p165).

To find more free public artwork locations all around town, visit www.cityofchicago.org/publicart.

Sandra Cisneros likewise grew up in Humboldt Park. *The House on Mango Street,* her 1984 novel about a young immigrant girl, takes place on the northwest side. Richard Wright's 1940 novel *Native Son* depicts a young man dealing with poverty and racism on Chicago's South Side. Wright lived in Bronzeville for a time. More recently, Pulitzer Prize–winning local David Mamet wrote 2018's *Chicago* about a mysterious murder in the city during the Capone era.

The city is also home to the nation's gold standard of poetic journals, *Poetry.* Long a bellwether for the academic establishment, the journal got a financial boost in 2003 when pharmaceutical heiress and philanthropist Ruth Lilly bequeathed almost $200 million to its publisher, renamed the Poetry Foundation (p74). The group sponsors big-name readings and events around town. It's a very different scene from the verse that gets spoken at the long-running Uptown Poetry Slam (p127).

For author readings and other literary events around the city, browse the *Chicago Reader* (www.chicagoreader.com), or turn up for the Printers Row Lit Fest (p22) in June or the **Chicago Humanities Festival** (312-605-8444; www.chicagohumanities.org) in October/November.

Theater & Comedy

Chicago's theater scene draws international acclaim. Many plays that premiere here export to Broadway. Steppenwolf Theatre (p107) has been cultivating stunning talent and groundbreaking programming since 1976. Hollywood heavyweights Joan Allen, John Malkovich, Tracy Letts and Gary Sinise are Steppenwolf members, and they exemplify Chicago's bare-knuckled, physical style of acting. Goodman Theatre (p64) and Lookingglass Theatre Company (p93) are award-winning drama houses with big, shiny theaters downtown. Many smaller theater companies are transient, setting up DIY productions in whatever space they can get their hands on – and their sheer volume of makeshift productions defies every convention.

Along with Wonder Bread, spray paint and house music, add improvised ('improv') comedy to the heap of Chicago's wide-reaching cultural contributions. Were it not for Chicago's Second City comedy troupe – which evolved from intentionally unstructured skits by the Compass Players, a mid-1950s group of University of Chicago undergrads – the proverbial chicken might still be crossing the road of American comedy.

The Compass Players' original gag of incorporating audience suggestions into quick-witted comedy became standard fare after 1959 at Second City (p107) theater. Its tongue-in-cheek name adopted from *New Yorker* articles mocking Chicago, Second City has produced some of the country's most capable funny-bone ticklers including John Belushi, Bill Murray, Stephen Colbert, Tina Fey and Steve Carell.

Dance

Like many of the city's other expressive hallmarks, jazz dance is an art form based on jarring contradictions. At its core, it relies on controlled yet fluidly expressive motion, a style whose invention is credited to legendary Chicago dance teacher Gus Giordano. Exhilarating performances by his namesake company, **Giordano Dance Chicago** (☑312-922-1332; www.giordanodance.org), are these days overseen by his daughter Nan.

Chicago's cultural landscape is crowded with A-list dance companies. At the forefront is the Joffrey Ballet (p65), which relocated here from NYC in 1995. The renowned Hubbard Street Dance Chicago (p64) keeps the attention of the international community with its modern moves.

In the Loop, Columbia College supplies dancers and choreographers to innovative fledgling companies that set up shop in performance spaces around the city. The *Chicago Reader* (www.chicagoreader.com) and See Chicago Dance (www.seechicagodance.com) cover the scene and list events.

Cinema & Television

Cinespace (www.chicagofilmstudios.com), a short distance west of Pilsen in Douglas Park, is where the action is. It's the largest soundstage in the US outside of Hollywood and a prime filming location. TV shows including *Empire, Chicago Fire, Chicago PD* and *Chicago Med* shoot there, as do big-budget movies such as *Widows* when they come to town.

Chicago serves as the backdrop to numerous TV series. Top picks include *Shameless* (2011–), about a raucous, working-class, Irish American family living in South Side, and *The Chi* (2018–), which follows interconnected characters in an African American neighborhood in South Side.

Survival Guide

Transportation

ARRIVING IN CHICAGO

Most visitors arrive by air. The city has two airports: O'Hare International Airport and Midway International Airport. O'Hare is larger and handles most of the international flights, as well as domestic flights. It is one of the world's busiest airports, with delays galore should the weather go awry. Midway handles domestic services plus some flights to Canada and Mexico, and is a bit closer to the Loop. Both airports have easy L train links into the city. Bus services are a popular means of getting to Chicago from nearby cities such as Minneapolis, Indianapolis and Detroit. Tickets are cheap, the routes are direct to the city center, and the buses usually have free wi-fi and power outlets. It's also easy to reach Chicago by train from major cities across the country. Union Station is a hub for regional and national Amtrak services.

Flights, cars and tours can be booked online at lonelyplanet.com/bookings.

O'Hare International Airport

Seventeen miles northwest of the Loop, **O'Hare International Airport** (ORD; ☎800-832-6352; www.fly chicago.com/ohare; 10000 W O'Hare Ave) is the headquarters for United Airlines and a hub for American Airlines. Most non-US airlines and international flights use Terminal 5. The domestic terminals are 1, 2 and 3. ATMs and currency exchanges are available throughout. Wi-fi is free, but slow.

Transport Options

TRAIN

The airport has its own L train station on the Blue Line operated by the **Chicago Transit Authority** (www. transitchicago.com). Trains run 24/7 and cost $5. The station is a long walk from the flight terminals. Follow the signs to baggage claim, then ones that are variously marked as 'Trains to City' and 'CTA.' Trains depart every 10 minutes or so and reach downtown in 40 minutes. Unless you are staying right in the Loop, you will likely have to transfer (or hail a taxi) to complete your journey.

SHUTTLE VAN

The **GO Airport Express** (www.airportexpress.com) shared-van service goes downtown for $35 per person. Vans run between 4am and 11:30pm, departing every 15 minutes. It takes an hour or more, depending on traffic and where your hotel is in the drop-off order. Look for ticket counters by baggage claim.

TAXI

Rides to the center take 30 minutes and cost around $50. Taxi queues can be lengthy, and the ride can take longer than the train, depending on traffic. Taxi stands are outside baggage claim at each terminal.

Midway International Airport

Eleven miles southwest of the Loop, **Midway International Airport** (MDW; ☎773-838-0600; www.flychicago. com/midway; 5700 S Cicero Ave, Clearing) has three concourses: A, B and C. Southwest Airlines uses B; most other airlines go out of A. There's a currency exchange in A and ATMs throughout. Wi-fi is free, but slow.

Transport Options

TRAIN

The airport has its own L train station on the Orange Line operated by the Chicago Transit Authority. Trains run between 4am and 1am and cost $3. They depart every 10 minutes or so and reach downtown in 30 minutes. The station is a fairly long haul from the concourses; follow the signs for 'Trains to City' and 'CTA.'

SHUTTLE VAN

The GO Airport Express door-to-door shuttle goes downtown for $28. Vans run

CLIMATE CHANGE & TRAVEL

Every form of transport that relies on carbon-based fuel generates CO_2, the main cause of human-induced climate change. Modern travel is dependent on airplanes, which might use less fuel per mile per person than most cars but travel much greater distances. The altitude at which aircraft emit gases (including CO_2) and particles also contributes to their climate change impact. Many websites offer 'carbon calculators' that allow people to estimate the carbon emissions generated by their journey and, for those who wish to do so, to offset the impact of the greenhouse gases emitted with contributions to portfolios of climate-friendly initiatives throughout the world. Lonely Planet offsets the carbon footprint of all staff and author travel.

between 4am and 10:30pm. The journey takes approximately 50 minutes. Look for ticket counters by baggage claim.

TAXI

Rides to the center take 20 minutes or longer (depending on traffic) and cost $35 to $40. Taxis queue outside the main entrance.

Train

Grand, Doric-columned **Union Station** (www.chicago unionstation.com; 225 S Canal St; Ⓜ Blue LIne to Clinton) is the city's rail hub, located at the Loop's western edge. **Amtrak** (www.amtrak.com) has more connections here than anywhere else in the country.

For public transportation onward, the Blue Line Clinton stop is a few blocks south (though not a good option at night). The Brown, Orange, Purple and Pink Line station at Quincy is about a half-mile east.

Taxis queue along Canal St outside the station entrance.

Bus

Megabus (Off Map 298; ☑877-462-6342; www.mega bus.com/us; W Polk St, btwn S Canal & S Clinton Sts; ☏; Ⓜ Blue Line to Clinton) Travels to and from major Midwestern cities. Prices are often less, and quality and efficiency

better, than Greyhound on these routes. All tickets must be purchased online in advance (you cannot buy a ticket from the driver). The bus stop is outdoors by a parking lot, on a forlorn stretch of Polk St. It's only a few blocks from the L, but it's a spooky walk at night. **Greyhound** (☑312-408-5821; www.greyhound.com; 630 W Harrison St) Travels nationwide. The main station is two blocks southwest of the CTA Blue Line Clinton stop. The station is open 24 hours, but it's pretty desolate late at night. It's not an ideal walk to the L at night.

Car & Motorcycle

The main highways into Chicago are I-90 and I-94; I-90 becomes a toll road at the city's far northern and southern edges. Both roads are multi-lane behemoths with lots of traffic, lots of construction and lots of jams.

GETTING AROUND

The L (a system of elevated and subway trains) is the main way to get around. Buses are also useful. Buy a day pass for $10 at L stations. The Chicago Transit Authority runs the transport system.

Bicycle Abundant rental shops and the Divvy bike-share program make cycling doable.

Boat Water taxis travel along the river and lakefront and offer a fun way to reach the Museum Campus or Chinatown. **Bus** Buses cover areas that the L misses. Most run at least from early morning until 10pm; some go later. Some don't run on weekends.

Taxi Easy to find downtown, north to Andersonville and west to Wicker Park/Bucktown. Costly.

Train L trains are fast, frequent and ubiquitous. Red and Blue Lines operate 24/7, others between roughly 4am and 1am.

Bicycle

Chicago is a cycling-savvy city with a well-used bike-share program. Riders can take bikes free of charge onto L trains, except during rush hour (7am to 9am and 4pm to 6pm Monday to Friday). Most buses are equipped with a bike rack on the front that accommodates two bikes at a time.

Divvy (www.divvybikes. com) has some 5800 sky-blue bikes at 580 stations around Chicago and neighboring suburbs. The $15 day pass allows unlimited rides in a 24-hour period, up to three hours each. Or opt for a $3 single-ride pass for 30 minutes. Both are available for purchase at station kiosks or via the Divvy app. Rates rise fast if you don't dock the bike in your allotted time.

Having the Divvy app makes life much easier for finding docks, checking availability and paying.

Bike rentals for longer rides (with accoutrements such as helmets and locks) start at around $8 per hour. Try the following:

Bike & Roll (Map p298; 312-729-1000; www.bike chicago.com; 239 E Randolph St; tours adult/child from $45/35; 9am-7pm; Brown, Orange, Green, Purple, Pink Line to Washington/Wabash) Near Millennium Park

Bobby's Bike Hike (Map p304; 312-245-9300; www. bobbysbikehike.com; 540 N Lake Shore Dr, Streeterville; per hr/day from $8/27, tours $38-70; 8:30am-8pm Mon-Fri, 8am-8pm Sat & Sun Jun-Aug, 9am-7pm Mar-May & Sep-Nov; Red Line to Grand).

They also rent children's bikes, and offer discounts if you book online.

Boat

Water taxis, operated by two separate companies, offer an interesting alternative to walking or busing between major sights.

Shoreline Water Taxi (312-222-9328; www.shore linesightseeing.com) operates three different lines from late May to early September. The Lake Taxi transports you from Navy Pier (at the south-western corner) to the South Loop's Shedd Aquarium. The River Taxi connects Polk Bros Park (just west of Navy Pier) to Willis Tower (via the Adams St Bridge's southeast side). Prices depend on the day of travel, but a one-way adult ticket is $8 to $10 (child $4 to $5). Weekends are peak travel times.

There's also a Commuter Taxi that runs from the Michigan Ave Bridge (north-east side, near the Tribune

Tower) to Willis Tower/ Union Station.

Chicago Water Taxi (312-337-1446; www.chicago watertaxi.com) is aimed primarily at commuters, and runs from March to October. It plies the river from the Michigan Ave Bridge (northwest side, by the Wrigley Building) to Madison St (near the Metra Ogilvie Transportation Center), stopping at LaSalle St en route. In summer it continues on to Chinatown. A one-way ride is $5 on weekdays, $6 on weekends. An all-day pass is $9 on weekdays, $10 on weekends.

Bus

City buses operate from early morning until late evening. The fare is $2.25 ($2.50 if you want a transfer). You can use a Ventra Card (a rechargeable fare card that you buy at L stations) or pay the driver with exact change. Buses are particularly useful for reaching the Museum Campus, Hyde Park and Lincoln Park's zoo.

Car & Motorcycle

Driving in Chicago is no fun. Traffic snarls not only at rush hours, but also just about every hour in between. Especially for short trips in town, use public transportation to spare yourself the headache.

Parking

➡ Meter spots and on-street parking are plentiful in outlying areas, but the Loop, Near North, Lincoln Park and Lake View neighborhoods can require serious circling before you find a spot.

➡ Note that 'meter' is a bit of a misnomer – you actually feed coins or a credit card into a pay box that serves the entire block. Decide how much time you want, type in your license plate

number, and you're good to go. Per-hour costs range from $2 in outlying areas to $6.50 in the Loop. In many areas, you do not have to pay between 10pm and 8am. Check the pay box's instructions.

➡ Downtown garages cost about $40 per day, but will save you time and traffic tickets. **Millennium Park Garages** (www.millenniumgarages.com) are some of the cheapest.

➡ Some meter-free neighborhoods require resident parking passes, some don't. Read signs carefully.

➡ Never park in a spot or red-curbed area marked 'Tow-Away.' Your car *will* be towed.

Road Rules

➡ The speed limit is 30mph unless posted otherwise.

➡ You must wear your seat belt and restrain kids under eight years in child-safety seats.

➡ Driving while using a hand-held cell phone is illegal.

➡ Be aware that many intersections have cameras that snap a photo if you go through a red light or speed. A $100 ticket arrives in your mailbox not long thereafter.

Auto Associations

For emergency road service and towing, members can call the **American Automobile Association** (www.aaa.com). It has reciprocal membership agreements with several international auto clubs.

Car-Share Services

The car-share service **Zipcar** (www.zipcar.com) is popular in Chicago. Hourly/daily rates are $8.50/74 weekdays and $9.25/79 on weekends. That includes gas and insurance and good parking spaces around town. You need to become a member first ($70 annually plus a $25 application fee).

Rental

All major car-rental agencies are in Chicago. Rates fluctuate radically. In general, it's more expensive to rent at the airport than downtown. To rent a car you typically need to be at least 25 years old, hold a valid driver's license and have a major credit card. Unless stated otherwise, these companies have outlets at both Chicago airports and downtown.

Alamo (www.alamo.com)

Avis (www.avis.com)

Budget (www.budget.com)

Dollar (www.dollar.com) At the airports only.

Enterprise (www.enterprise. com)

Hertz (www.hertz.com)

National (www.nationalcar. com)

Thrifty (www.thrifty.com)

Pedway

Come wintertime, when the going gets tough and icy sleet knifes your face, head down to the Pedway. Chicago has a 40-block labyrinth of underground walkways, built in conjunction with the subway trains. The system isn't entirely connected (ie it would be difficult to walk from one end of the Loop to the other underground), and you'll find that you rise to the surface in the oddest places – say, an apartment building, a hotel lobby or Macy's.

The walkways are also hit-or-miss for amenities: some have coffee shops and fast-food outlets tucked along the way, some have urine smells, but they're an interesting place to soak up local life. The city posts 'Pedway' signs above ground at points of entry. **Chicago Detours** (📋312-350-1131; www. chicagodetours.com; tours from $28) provides a free map to download from its website for DIY jaunts. The company also offers guided excursions that include the passageways.

Taxi & Rideshare

Taxis are plentiful in the Loop, north to Andersonville and northwest to Wicker Park/Bucktown. Hail them with a wave of the hand. Fares are meter-based and start at $3.25 when you get into the cab, then it's $2.25 per mile. The first extra passenger costs $1; extra passengers after that are 50¢ apiece. Add 10% to 15% for a tip. All major companies accept credit cards.

Reliable companies include:

Checker Taxi (312-243-2537; www.checkertaxichicago. com)

Flash Cab (773-561-4444; www.flashcab.com)

The ridesharing companies **Uber** (www.uber.com), **Lyft** (www.lyft.com) and **Via** (www. ridewithvia.com) are also popular in Chicago. They can be a bit cheaper than taxis.

Train

Elevated/subway trains are part of the city's public transportation system. Metra commuter trains venture out into the suburbs.

L Train

The L (a system of elevated and subway trains) is fast, frequent and will get you to most sights and neighborhoods.

Two of the eight color-coded lines – the Red Line, and the Blue Line to O'Hare airport – operate 24 hours a day. The other lines run from roughly 4am to 1am daily, departing every 10 minutes or so.

The standard fare is $3 (except from O'Hare airport, where it costs $5) and includes two transfers. Enter the turnstile using a Ventra Ticket, which is sold from vending machines at train stations.

You can also buy a Ventra Card, aka a rechargeable fare card, at stations. It has a one-time $5 fee that gets refunded once you register the card. It knocks around 75¢ off the cost of each ride.

Unlimited ride passes (one-/three-/seven-day $10/20/28) are another handy option. Get them at train stations and drugstores.

For maps and route planning, check the website of the Chicago Transit Authority (www.transit chicago.com). The 'Trackers' section tells you when the next train or bus is due to arrive at your station.

Metra

Metra (www.metrarail.com) commuter trains traverse 12 routes serving the suburbs from four terminals ringing the Loop: LaSalle St Station; **Millennium Station** (151 N Michigan Ave; ⓜBrown, Orange, Green, Purple, Pink Line to Washington/Wabash), which is below street level – look for the stairs down; **Union Station** (www. chicagounionstation.com; 225 S Canal St; ⓜBlue Line to

---

BUSES & TRAINS

The **Chicago Transit Authority** (www.transitchicago. com) has L and bus schedules on its website, as well as a useful trip-planning feature (which basically harnesses Google). Or click 'Trackers' to find out when the next train or bus is due to arrive.

Clinton); and **Richard B Ogilvie Transportation Center** (OTC, Ogilvie Station; 500 W Madison St; [M]Green, Pink Line to Clinton), a few blocks north of Union Station. Some train lines run daily, while others operate only during weekday rush hours. Buy tickets from agents and machines at major stations.

TOURS

Chicago offers loads of tours. Jaunts by boat, foot or bus are popular. They provide a fine introduction to the city, particularly if you're short on time. Bicycle rental companies such as Bike & Roll (p66) and Bobby's Bike Hike (p80) also run worthy excursions. Outdoor-oriented tours usually operate from April to November only. Many companies offer discounts if you book online.

Bus Tours

A couple of quirky bus tours get you to unusual and hard-to-reach sights:

Untouchable Gangster Tours (Map p304; [J]773-881-1195; www.gangstertour.com;

BOAT TOURS

Boat tours are the most popular way to see the city. Most run April to November, several times daily. The Chicago Architecture Center does the best job, but several other companies offer similar tours from the docks at Michigan Ave. They cruise the river and lakefront for around 90 minutes; costs are $40/19 per adult/child on average. Check online to see what works for your schedule and budget.

Shoreline Sightseeing (p80)

Mercury Cruises (Map p298; [J]312-332-1353; www. mercurycruises.com; tours adult/child from $35/14; ⊙late Apr-early Oct; [M]Brown, Orange, Green, Purple, Pink Line to State/Lake)

Wendella Boats (Map p304; [J]312-337-1446; www. wendellaboats.com; 400 N Michigan Ave, River North; 90min tours adult/child $39/18; ⊙Mar-Oct; [M]Red Line to Grand)

Other fun boat tours depart from Navy Pier, such as **Seadog Speedboats** (Map p303; [J]888-636-7737; www. seadogcruises.com; 600 E Grand Ave; tours $28-35; ⊙Mar-Oct; 🚌65), where you'll likely get splashed, and Windy (p80), a kid-favorite four-masted schooner.

---

600 N Clark St, River North; 2hr tours $35; [M]Red Line to Grand)

Weird Chicago Tours (Map p304; [J]217-791-7859; www. weirdchicago.com; 600 N Clark St, River North; 3hr tours $40; [M]Red Line to Grand)

Walking Tours

Walking tours are a great way to explore off-the-beaten-path neighborhoods or delve into a particular topic of interest (eg art deco buildings, historic pubs, jazz shrines etc). Recommended walking tours include:

Chicago Architecture Center Tours (CAC; [J]312-922-3432; www.architecture. org; 111 E Wacker Dr; tours $20-55)

Chicago by Foot ([J]312-612-0826; www.freetoursby foot.com/chicago-tours)

Chicago Detours ([J]312-350-1131; www.chicagodetours. com; tours from $28)

InstaGreeter (Map p298; www.chicagogreeter.com/ instagreeter; 77 E Randolph St; ⊙10am-3pm Fri & Sat, 11am-2pm Sun; [M]Brown, Orange, Green, Purple, Pink Line to Washington/Wabash) FREE

Chicago History Museum Tours ([J]312-642-4600; www.chicago history.org; tours $25-55)

Chicago Greeter (www. chicagogreeter.com) FREE

Directory A–Z

Accessible Travel

Most museums and major sights are wheelchair accessible, as are most large hotels and restaurants.

All city buses are wheelchair accessible, but about one-third of L stations are not. Resources include:

Easy Access Chicago (www.easyaccesschicago.org) A free resource that lists museums, tours, restaurants and lodgings, and provides mobility, vision and hearing accessibility information for each place.

Mayor's Office for People with Disabilities (www.cityofchicago.org/ disabilities) Can answer questions about the availability of services in the city.

Customs Regulations

For a complete list of US customs regulations, go online to US Customs and Border Protection (www. cbp.gov).

Duty-free allowance per person is as follows:

➜ 1L of liquor (provided you are at least 21 years old)

➜ 100 cigars and 200 cigarettes (if you are at least 18 years old)

➜ $200 worth of gifts and purchases ($800 if a returning US citizen)

If you arrive with $10,000 or more in US or foreign currency, it must be declared. There are heavy penalties for attempting to import illegal drugs. Note that fruit, vegetables and other food must be declared (whereupon you'll undergo a time-consuming search) or left in the bins in the arrival area.

Discount Cards

All of the below let you skip the regular queues at sights:

Go Chicago Card (www. smartdestinations.com/ chicago) Allows you to visit an unlimited number of attractions for a flat fee. It's good for one, two, three or five consecutive days. The company also offers a three-, four- or five-choice Explorer Pass where you pick among 29 options for sights. It's valid for 30 days. Architecture cruises, the Navy Pier Ferris wheel and all major museums are among the choices.

CityPass (www.citypass. com/chicago) Gives access to five of the city's top draws, including the Art Institute, Shedd Aquarium and Willis Tower, over nine consecutive days. It's less flexible than Go Chicago's pass, but cheaper for those wanting a more leisurely sightseeing pace.

PRACTICALITIES

➜ **Newspapers** The *Chicago Tribune* (www.chicago tribune.com) is the conservative daily newspaper. The *Chicago Sun-Times* (www.suntimes.com) is its tabloid-style competitor. The *Chicago Reader* (www. chicagoreader.com) is a free alternative weekly, great for politics and entertainment coverage.

➜ **TV** The main channels are Channel 2 (CBS), Channel 5 (NBC), Channel 7 (ABC), Channel 9 (WGN) and Channel 32 (FOX).

➜ **Radio** National Public Radio (NPR) can be found on WBEZ-FM 91.5.

➜ **Smoking** Chicago is entirely smoke-free in restaurants, bars and workplaces, and within 15ft of the entrances of these establishments.

Electricity

120V/60Hz

120V/60Hz

Emergency

Nonemergency police matters	311
Police, fire, ambulance	911

Internet Access

➜ Wi-fi is common in lodgings across the price spectrum. Lower-speed internet typically is free, but you sometimes have to pay for premium-speed service. Many properties also have an internet-connected computer for public use.

➜ Many bars, cafes and museums – including the **Chicago Cultural Center** (Map p298; 312-744-6630; www.chicagoculturalcenter.org; 78 E Washington St; 10am-7pm Mon-Fri, to 5pm Sat & Sun; M Brown, Orange, Green, Purple, Pink Line to Washington/Wabash) FREE – offer free wi-fi.

➜ Outlets of the **Chicago Public Library** (www.chipublib.org) offer free wi-fi. There are no passwords required or time limits. Libraries also offer free computer terminals for one hour; get a 'day pass' at the counter.

➜ For a list of wi-fi hot spots, visit **Wi-Fi Free Spot** (www.wififreespot.com).

Legal Matters

➜ The blood alcohol limit is 0.8%. Driving under the influence of alcohol or drugs is a serious offense, subject to stiff fines and even imprisonment.

➜ Possession of illicit drugs, including cocaine, ecstasy, LSD, heroin, hashish or more than an ounce of pot, is a felony potentially punishable by lengthy jail sentences.

➜ The state has decriminalized possession of small amounts of marijuana. However, if you're caught with 10g or less of pot, you can be ticketed for $100 to $200.

➜ It's against the law to have an open container of any alcoholic beverage in public. However, this is overlooked during most concerts at Millennium Park, as well as at Navy Pier if you buy from one of the vendors on-site.

➜ If you are arrested, you are allowed to remain silent, though never walk away from an officer; you are entitled to have access to an attorney. The legal system presumes you're innocent until proven guilty. All arrested persons have the right to make one phone call. If you don't have a lawyer or family member to help you, call your embassy or consulate. The police will give you the number on request.

Medical Services

The cost of health care in the United States can be prohibitively expensive. It is essential to buy health insurance before you travel if your home policy doesn't cover you for medical expenses abroad.

Chicago has no unexpected health dangers and excellent medical facilities, including the following:

Advocate Illinois Masonic Medical Center (773-975-1600; www.advocatehealth.com/immc; 836 W Wellington Ave, Lake View; M Brown, Purple Line to Wellington) Big hospital located in Lake View.

Lurie Children's Hospital (312-227-4000; www.luriechildrens.org; 225 E Chicago Ave, Streeterville; 24hr; M Red Line to Chicago) The city's best for kids.

Northwestern Memorial Hospital (312-926-5188; www.nmh.org; 251 E Erie St, Streeterville; 24hr; M Red Line to Chicago) Well-respected downtown hospital.

Stroger Cook County Hospital (312-864-6000; www.cookcountyhhs.org; 1969 W Ogden Ave, Medical District;

⊘24hr; Ⓜ Blue Line to Illinois Medical District) Public hospital serving low-income patients; 2.5 miles west of the Loop.

Pharmacies

Walgreens pharmacies are located all around the city. CVS is another local chain with branches throughout town.

There's a convenient **Walgreens** (☑312-346-5727; www.walgreens.com; 79 W Monroe St; ⊘6:30am-8pm Mon-Fri, 9am-5pm Sat; Ⓜ Red, Blue Line to Monroe) in the Loop that has a health clinic inside, staffed by a nurse practitioner to treat minor infections, allergies and injuries; no appointment needed.

Money

The US dollar ($) is the currency.

ATMs

➡ ATMs are widely available 24/7 at banks, airports and convenience stores.

➡ Most ATMs link into worldwide networks (Plus, Cirrus, Exchange etc).

➡ ATMs typically charge a service fee of $3 or more per transaction, and your home bank may impose additional charges.

Credit Cards

Major credit cards are almost universally accepted. In fact, it's next to impossible to rent a car or make hotel or ticket reservations without one. Visa and MasterCard are the most widely accepted.

Money Changers

Although the airports have exchange bureaus, better rates can usually be obtained in the city.

Tipping

Tipping isn't optional. Only withhold tips in cases of outrageously bad service.

Airport & hotel porters $2 per bag, minimum per cart $5

Bartenders 15% to 20% per round, minimum $1/2 per drink for standard drinks/specialty cocktails

Housekeeping staff $2 to $5 daily

Restaurant servers 18% to 20% (unless gratuity already on bill)

Taxi drivers 10% to 15% (round up to next dollar)

Parking valets $2 to $5 when handed back the keys

Opening Hours

Typical normal opening times are as follows:

Banks & businesses 9am to 5pm Monday to Friday

Bars 5pm to 2am (to 3am on Saturday); some licensed until 4am (to 5am on Saturday)

Nightclubs 10pm to 4am; often closed Monday through Wednesday

Restaurants Breakfast 7am or 8am to 11am, lunch 11am or 11:30am to 2:30pm, dinner 5pm or 6pm to 10pm Sunday to Thursday, to 11pm or midnight Friday and Saturday

Shops 11am to 7pm Monday to Saturday, noon to 6pm Sunday

Post

The **US Postal Service** (www.usps.com) is reliable and inexpensive. The postal rates for 1st-class mail within the USA are 55¢ for letters up to 1oz (15¢ for each additional ounce) and 35¢ for standard-size postcards.

International airmail rates are $1.15 for a 1oz letter or postcard.

Public Holidays

Banks, schools, offices and most shops close on these days:

New Year's Day January 1

Martin Luther King Jr Day Third Monday in January

Presidents' Day Third Monday in February

Pulaski Day First Monday in March (observed mostly by city offices)

Memorial Day Last Monday in May

Independence Day July 4

Labor Day First Monday in September

Columbus Day Second Monday in October

Veteran's Day November 11

Thanksgiving Day Fourth Thursday in November

Christmas Day December 25

Safe Travel

➡ You've probably heard about Chicago's high murder rate, but this is mostly concentrated in a handful of far west and far south neighborhoods.

➡ Overall, serious crime in Chicago has been dropping in recent years, and major tourist areas are all reasonably safe.

➡ That doesn't mean you shouldn't take normal, big-city precautions, especially if solo at night. Many crimes involve cell phone theft, so be subtle when using yours.

Taxes

A tax is levied on most goods and services. In Chicago it is 17.4% for lodgings, 10.5% to 11.5% in restaurants and bars (it's higher the closer you are to downtown), and 10.25% for other items. The tax is typically not included in the price, but added afterward when you pay.

Telephone

Phone numbers within the US consist of a three-digit area code followed by a seven-digit local number. In Chicago, you will always dial 11 numbers: ☑1 + the three-digit area code + the seven-digit number.

Cell Phones

If buying a US SIM card, you'll want to go with either AT&T or T-Mobile (or companies using their networks) as these carriers run on the GSM network, the standard used in most other countries. You may be able to preorder a card at home, or you can simply purchase one from the relevant carrier's store in Chicago.

If purchasing a cheap US phone, you can also look into Verizon and Sprint, which use the CDMA network. Phones can be bought in telecom stores, drugstores, grocery stores and big retailers like Target.

If you plan on traveling outside Chicago, make sure you are using AT&T or Verizon – these two carriers have the best coverage in more rural areas.

Phone Codes

US country code ☑1
Chicago area codes ☑312, 773, 872

Making international calls ☑011 + country code + area code + local number

Calling other US area codes or Canada ☑1 + three-digit area code + seven-digit local number

Calling within Chicago ☑1 + three-digit area code + seven-digit local number

Directory assistance nationwide ☑411
Toll-free numbers ☑1+ 800 (or 888, 877, 866) + seven-digit number. Some toll-free numbers only work within the US.

Phonecards

Private prepaid phonecards are available from convenience stores, supermarkets and pharmacies. AT&T sells a reliable card that is widely available.

Time

Chicago is in the Central Standard Time (CST) zone, six hours behind Greenwich Mean Time (London) and two hours ahead of Pacific Standard Time (Los Angeles). Chicago, like almost all of the USA, observes daylight saving time: clocks go forward one hour from the second Sunday in March to the first Sunday in November, when the clocks are turned back one hour.

Toilets

Public toilets are few and far between. There are some at **Millennium Park** (Map p298; ☑312-742-1168; www.millenniumpark.org; 201 E Randolph St; �l6am-11pm; ☒; Ⓜ Brown, Orange, Green, Purple, Pink Line to Washington/Wabash) near Pritzker Pavilion and at **Maggie Daley Park** (Map p298; www.maggiedaleypark. com; 337 E Randolph St; �l6am-11pm; ☒; Ⓜ Brown, Orange, Green, Purple, Pink Line to Washington/Wabash) at the field house, but they aren't always open.

There are limited facilities at the **Chicago Cultural Center** (Map p298; ☑312-744-6630; www.chicagoculturalcenter.org; 78 E Washington St;

�l10am-7pm Mon-Fri, to 5pm Sat & Sun; Ⓜ Brown, Orange, Green, Purple, Pink Line to Washington/Wabash) FREE, by the Landmark Gallery. The Loop's **Target** (Map p298; www.target.com; 1 S State St; �l7am-10pm Mon-Fri, from 8am Sat & Sun; ☏; Ⓜ Brown, Orange, Green, Purple, Pink Line to Madison) store is another option.

Tourist Information

Choose Chicago (www.choosechicago.com) is the city's official tourism site, with loads of information online.

Visas

➡ The Visa Waiver Program (VWP) allows nationals from some 38 countries (including most EU countries, Japan, Australia and New Zealand) to enter the US without a visa for up to 90 days.

➡ VWP visitors require an e-passport (with electronic chip) and approval under the Electronic System For Travel Authorization at least three days before arrival. There is a $14 fee for processing and authorization (payable online). Once approved, the registration is valid for two years.

➡ Those who need a visa – ie anyone staying longer than 90 days, or from a non-VWP country – should apply at the US consulate in their home country.

➡ Check with the **US Department of State** (www.travel.state.gov) for updates and details on entry requirements.

Behind the Scenes

SEND US YOUR FEEDBACK

We love to hear from travelers – your comments keep us on our toes and help make our books better. Our well-traveled team reads every word on what you loved or loathed about this book. Although we cannot reply individually to your submissions, we always guarantee that your feedback goes straight to the appropriate authors, in time for the next edition. Each person who sends us information is thanked in the next edition – the most useful submissions are rewarded with a selection of digital PDF chapters.

Visit **lonelyplanet.com/contact** to submit your updates and suggestions or to ask for help. Our award-winning website also features inspirational travel stories, news and discussions.

Note: We may edit, reproduce and incorporate your comments in Lonely Planet products such as guidebooks, websites and digital products, so let us know if you don't want your comments reproduced or your name acknowledged. For a copy of our privacy policy visit lonelyplanet.com/privacy.

WRITERS' THANKS

Ali Lemer

My thanks to Jo Wright, Zina Alam and Igor Enin for looking after my furchildren; to Karla Zimmerman, Cate Hugelet, Trisha Ping and Krystyn Wells for Chi-town inspiration and socializing; and to Laura and Karla Ruiz for their hospitality and local recommendations — and especially to their dog Bruno, who's a very good boy indeed.

Karla Zimmerman

Deep appreciation to all of the locals who spilled the beans on their favorite places. Special thanks to Kari Lydersen, Ali Lemer, Lisa Dunford and Chris and Kevin Kohl. Thanks most to Eric Markowitz, the world's best partner-for-life, who kindly indulges my beer and doughnut fixations. You top my Best List.

ACKNOWLEDGEMENTS

Cover photograph: Chicago skyline and Lake Michigan, Susanne Kremer/4Corners Images ©

THIS BOOK

This 9th edition of Lonely Planet's *Chicago* guidebook was curated by Ali Lemer and researched and written by Ali, Mark Baker, Kevin Raub and Karla Zimmerman. The 8th edition was researched, written and curated by Karla, and the 7th edition was researched and written by Karla and Sara Benson. This guidebook was produced by the following:

Destination Editor Trisha Ping
Senior Product Editors Elizabeth Jones, Martine Power
Regional Senior Cartographers Corey Hutchison, Alison Lyall
Product Editor Amanda Williamson
Book Designer Wibowo Rusli
Assisting Editors Michelle Bennett, Jennifer Hattam, Anne Mulvaney, Charlotte Orr
Cover Researcher Meri Blazevski
Thanks to Imogen Bannister, Jess Boland, Evan Godt, Victoria Harrison, Karen Henderson, Cate Huguelet, Kate Kiely, Max Magura

Index

See also separate subindexes for:

✗ EATING P289

🍷 DRINKING & NIGHTLIFE P291

☆ ENTERTAINMENT P291

🛍 SHOPPING P292

🏃 SPORTS & ACTIVITIES P293

🛏 SLEEPING P293

Chicago Maps

Sights
- Beach
- Bird Sanctuary
- Buddhist
- Castle/Palace
- Christian
- Confucian
- Hindu
- Islamic
- Jain
- Jewish
- Monument
- Museum/Gallery/Historic Building
- Ruin
- Shinto
- Sikh
- Taoist
- Winery/Vineyard
- Zoo/Wildlife Sanctuary
- Other Sight

Activities, Courses & Tours
- Bodysurfing
- Diving
- Canoeing/Kayaking
- Course/Tour
- Sento Hot Baths/Onsen
- Skiing
- Snorkeling
- Surfing
- Swimming/Pool
- Walking
- Windsurfing
- Other Activity

Sleeping
- Sleeping
- Camping
- Hut/Shelter

Eating
- Eating

Drinking & Nightlife
- Drinking & Nightlife
- Cafe

Entertainment
- Entertainment

Shopping
- Shopping

Information
- Bank
- Embassy/Consulate
- Hospital/Medical
- Internet
- Police
- Post Office
- Telephone
- Toilet
- Tourist Information
- Other Information

Geographic
- Beach
- Gate
- Hut/Shelter
- Lighthouse
- Lookout
- Mountain/Volcano
- Oasis
- Park
- Pass
- Picnic Area
- Waterfall

Population
- Capital (National)
- Capital (State/Province)
- City/Large Town
- Town/Village

Transport
- Airport
- BART station
- Border crossing
- Boston T station
- Bus
- Cable car/Funicular
- Cycling
- Ferry
- Metro/Muni station
- Monorail
- Parking
- Petrol station
- Subway/SkyTrain station
- Taxi
- Train station/Railway
- Tram
- Underground station
- Other Transport

Routes
- Tollway
- Freeway
- Primary
- Secondary
- Tertiary
- Lane
- Unsealed road
- Road under construction
- Plaza/Mall
- Steps
- Tunnel
- Pedestrian overpass
- Walking Tour
- Walking Tour detour
- Path/Walking Trail

Boundaries
- International
- State/Province
- Disputed
- Regional/Suburb
- Marine Park
- Cliff
- Wall

Hydrography
- River, Creek
- Intermittent River
- Canal
- Water
- Dry/Salt/Intermittent Lake
- Reef

Areas
- Airport/Runway
- Beach/Desert
- Cemetery (Christian)
- Cemetery (Other)
- Glacier
- Mudflat
- Park/Forest
- Sight (Building)
- Sportsground
- Swamp/Mangrove

Note: Not all symbols displayed above appear on the maps in this book

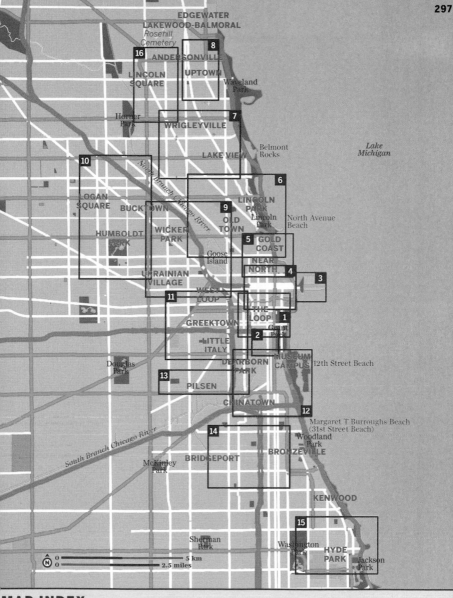

MAP INDEX

THE LOOP

Key on p300

A B C D

See map
p304

W Kinzie St

N Clinton St
N West Water St
North Branch Chicago River
N Orleans St
N Wells St
N LaSalle Dr
N Dearborn St

Merchandise
Mart

Chicago Water Taxi,
LaSalle St

W Wacker Dr

W Fulton St

Clinton

West Loop
(0.4mi)

N Canal St

N Wacker Dr

50

W Lake St
W Franklin St

56

Clark/Lake

30

64
41

N Riverside Plaza

W Randolph St

82
59

Washington/
Wells

W Washington St

County
Building
& Chicago
City Hall

Richard
J Daley
Center

14 32

Washington

27

49

42 Chicago-Ogilvie
Transportation
Center (Metra)

68

Chicago Water Taxi,
Ogilvie/Union

THE
LOOP

S Riverside Plaza

S Wacker Dr

W Madison St

See map
p324

W Monroe St

18

W Marble
Pl

S LaSalle St

S Clark St

S Dearborn St

48 25

Greektown
(0.4mi)

40

Shoreline Water Taxi,
Willis Tower/
Union Station

W Adams St

36

79

44

17

Chicago-Union
Station (Metra)

Willis
Tower 3

Quincy

W Quincy St

W Jackson Blvd

29

22

South Branch Chicago River

9

28

S Clinton St

S Canal St

W Van Buren St

S Franklin St

S Wells St

S Financial Pl

LaSalle/
Van Buren

77

S LaSalle St

S Clark St

S Federal St

Clinton

W Congress Pkwy

LaSalle

Chicago-
LaSalle St
Station (Metra)

W Harrison St

W Harrison St

S Wells St

S Financial Pl

S LaSalle St

S Clark St

Megabus
(0.1mi)

See map
p302

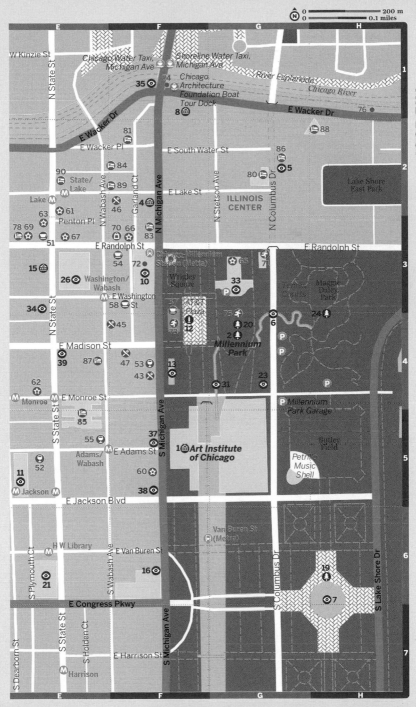

THE LOOP *Map on p298*

Top Sights (p46)
1 Art Institute of Chicago............................F5
2 Millennium Park G4
3 Willis Tower C5

Sights (p52)
4 American Writers Museum F2
5 Aqua Tower G2
6 BP Bridge...G4
7 Buckingham Fountain...............................H6
8 Chicago Architecture Center...................F1
9 Chicago Board of Trade...........................D6
10 Chicago Cultural Center F3
11 Chicago Federal Center E5
12 Cloud Gate...F4
13 Crown Fountain...F4
14 Daley Plaza..D3
15 Design Museum of Chicago.....................E3
16 Fine Arts Building.......................................F6
17 Flamingo D5
18 Four Seasons..D4
19 Grant Park...H6
20 Great Lawn G4
21 Harold Washington Library Center E6
22 Kluczynski Federal Building D5
23 Lurie Garden...G4
24 Maggie Daley Park.....................................H4
25 Marquette Building....................................D5
26 Marshall Field Building.............................E3
27 Miró's Chicago D3

28 Monadnock Building D6
29 Money Museum..C5
30 Monument with Standing Beast.............D3
31 Nichols Bridgeway G4
32 Picasso's Untitled.....................................D3
33 Pritzker Pavilion..G3
34 Reliance Building.......................................E3
35 Riverwalk F1
36 Rookery..D5
37 Route 66 Sign...F5
38 Santa Fe Building F5
39 Sullivan Center E4
40 Union Station A5

Eating (p58)
41 Do-Rite Donuts D3
42 French Market A4
43 Gage F4
44 Native Foods Cafe.....................................D5
45 Oasis F4
46 Pastoral...F2
47 Pizano's F4
48 Revival Food Hall D5
49 Trattoria No 10...D4
50 Veggie Grill C2

Drinking & Nightlife (p60)
51 Argo Tea E3
52 Berghoff...E5
53 Cindy's F4

SOUTH LOOP

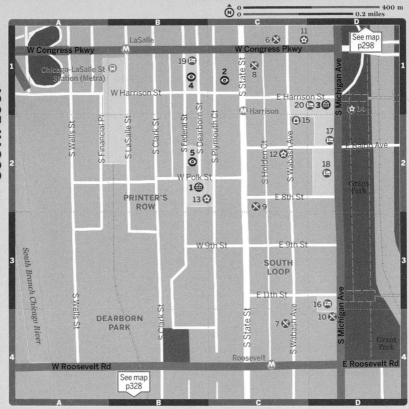

N 0 _____ 400 m
0 _____ 0.2 miles

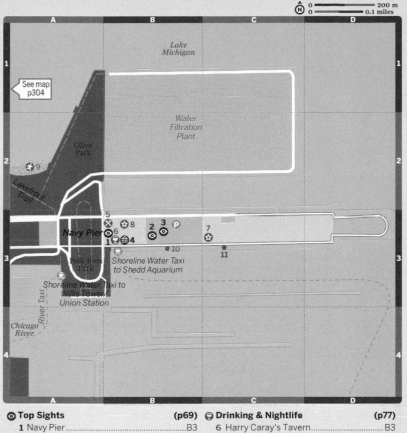

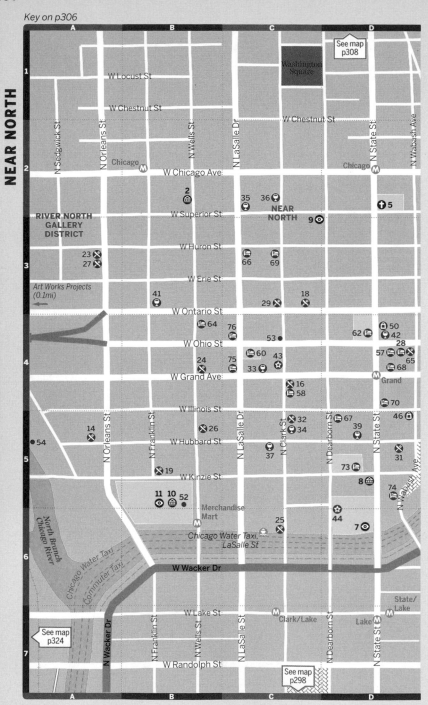

Key on p306

See map p308

W Locust St

W Chestnut St

W Chestnut St

N Sedgwick St

N Orleans St

N Wells St

N LaSalle Dr

N State St

N Wabash Ave

Chicago

Chicago

W Chicago Ave

2

35 **36**

**NEAR
NORTH**

5

W Superior St

9

**RIVER NORTH
GALLERY
DISTRICT**

W Huron St

66 **69**

23
27

W Erie St

Art Works Projects
(0.1mi)

41

18

29

W Ontario St

64

76

50
42

62

53

W Ohio St

28

24

75

60

43

57 **65**

33

68

W Grand Ave

70

16
58

W Illinois St

14

32
34

67
39

46

26

W Hubbard St

37

31

N Orleans St

N Franklin St

N LaSalle Dr

N Clark St

N Dearborn St

N State St

19

W Kinzie St

73

8

54

11 **10** **52**

Merchandise
Mart

74

N Wabash Ave

25

44

7

Chicago Water Taxi,
LaSalle St

North Branch
Chicago River

Chicago Water Taxi

Commuter Taxi

W Wacker Dr

State/
Lake

W Lake St

Clark/Lake

Lake

See map
p324

N Wacker Dr

N Franklin St

N Wells St

N LaSalle St

N Dearborn St

N State St

W Randolph St

See map
p298

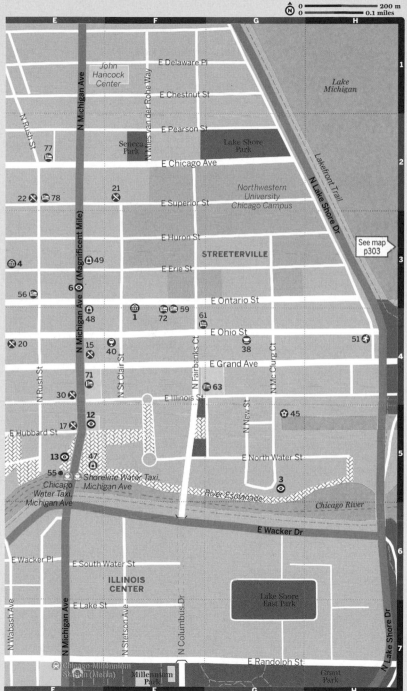

NEAR NORTH *Map on p304*

GOLD COAST

Key on p307

GOLD COAST

W North Ave

Sedgwick Ⓜ

N Orleans St
N North Park Ave
N Wieland St
N Wells St
N LaSalle Dr
N Clark St
N Dearborn St
N State Pkwy

W Blackhawk St

N Hudson Ave
N Sedgwick St

W Burton Pl

Lincoln Park

3 ⊙

W Schiller St

10 ⊙

W Evergreen Ave

24 🍴

26 🍴

W Goethe St

37 🛏

W Goethe St

W Scott St

30 ✪

N Clybourn Ave

Clark/Division Ⓜ

W Division St

27 🍴
34 🔒
28 🛏

N Clark St
N Dearborn St

W Elm St

43 🛏
23 🍴

Seward Park

W Elm St

W Hill St

W Maple St

19 🍴

W Oak St

15 🍴

W Oak St

8 ⊙

W Walton St

12 🌲

N Orleans St
N Franklin St
N Wells St
N LaSalle Dr

W Locust St

20 🍴
22 🍴

39 🛏

25 🍴

N Hudson Ave
N Sedgwick St

W Chestnut St

W Chestnut St

N State St

W Institute Pl

Chicago Ⓜ

W Chicago Ave

Chicago Ⓜ

See map p304

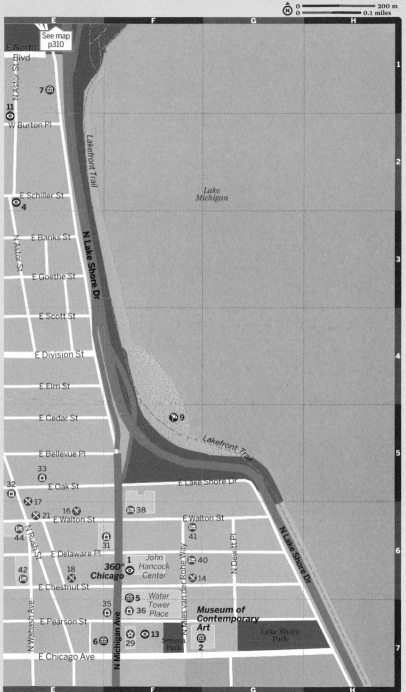

0 200 m
0 0.1 miles

See map
p310

E North
Blvd

N Astor St

7

11
W Burton Pl

Lakefront Trail

E Schiller St
4

E Banks St

N Lake Shore Dr

N Astor St

E Goethe St

E Scott St

E Division St

E Elm St

E Cedar St

9

E Bellevue Pl

Lakefront Trail

E Lake Shore Dr

33

32
E Oak St

17
16
21   E Walton St

38

E Walton St
41

N Rush St

44

31

E Delaware Pl

N Miles van der Rohe Way

40

N Dewitt Pl

N Lake Shore Dr

42

18

360°
Chicago
1

John
Hancock
Center

14

E Chestnut St

N Wabash Ave

35

5   Water
Tower
Place

Museum of
Contemporary
Art

36

Lake Shore
Park

E Pearson St

N Michigan Ave

6

29   13

Seneca
Park

2

E Chicago Ave

Lake
Michigan

Key on p312

LINCOLN PARK & OLD TOWN

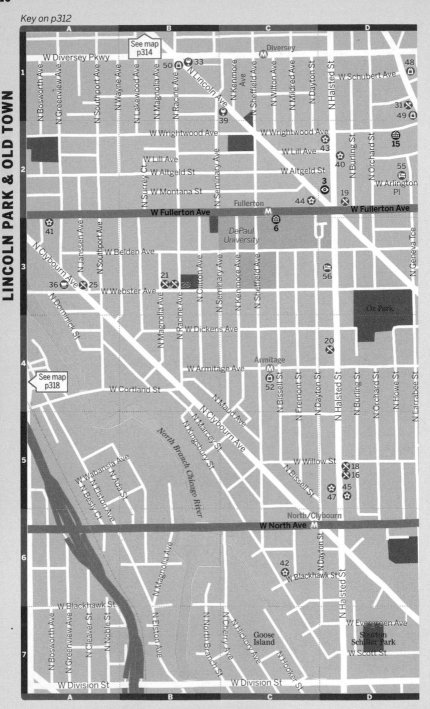

See map
p314

See map
p318

LINCOLN PARK & OLD TOWN *Map on p310*

LAKE VIEW & WRIGLEYVILLE *Map on p314*

LAKE VIEW & WRIGLEYVILLE

Key on p313

LAKE VIEW & WRIGLEYVILLE

Lincoln Square
(0.4mi)

See map
p334

A **B** **C** **D**

W Belle Plaine Ave

W Belle Plaine Ave

W Cuyler Ave
Irving Park Ⓜ

1

W Irving Park Rd

W Irving Park Rd

W Byron St

Ⓠ 36

W Byron St

N Lincoln Ave

N Ravenswood Ave

Ⓧ 43

48
✪

2

W Grace St

W Grace St

Ⓧ 17

N Hoyne Ave

N Damen Ave

N Hermitage Ave

N Paulina St

N Marshfield Ave

N Ashland Ave

N Southport Ave

✪ 45

W Waveland Ave

W Waveland Ave

3

Addison Ⓜ

W Addison St

W Addison St

🔒 56

W Cornelia Ave

W Cornelia Ave

N Lincoln Ave

4

16
Ⓧ

🍴
28

Paulina

Southport Ⓜ

W Roscoe St

Ⓧ 18

W Roscoe St

W Henderson St

Ⓠ 35

N Southport Ave

W School St

W School St

5

W Melrose St

W Melrose St

39 ✪

W Belmont Ave

W Belmont Ave

✪ 47

Hungry Brain (0.3mi);
Constellation (0.4mi);
Chicago River Canoe
& Kayak (0.8mi)

W Fletcher St

W Fletcher St

N Ravenswood Ave

N Paulina St

N Ashland Ave

N Hoyne Ave

N Damen Ave

W Barry Ave

W Barry Ave

6

W Nelson St

W Wellington Ave

N Clybourn Ave

N Lincoln Ave

W Oakdale Ave

✪
41

W George St

7

W Wolfram St

W Diversey Ave

A **B** **C** **D**

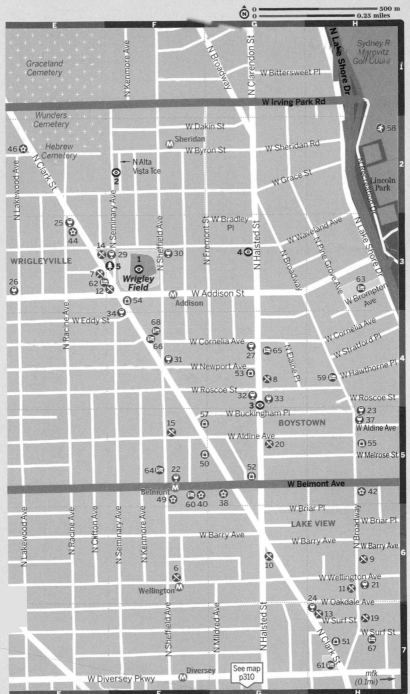

LAKE VIEW & WRIGLEYVILLE

0 500 m
0 0.25 miles

Graceland Cemetery

N Kenmore Ave

N Broadway

N Clarendon St

W Bittersweet Pl

N Lake Shore Dr

Sydney R Marovitz Golf Course

W Irving Park Rd

Wunders Cemetery

Hebrew Cemetery

46

N Lakewood Ave

N Clark St

W Dakin St

Sheridan

W Byron St

W Sheridan Rd

W Grace St

N Lake Shore Dr

Lincoln Park

N Recreation Dr

58

N Alta Vista Tce

2

N Seminary Ave

N Sheffield Ave

25

44

14

29

5

7

62

12

WRIGLEYVILLE

26

N Racine Ave

W Bradley Pl

N Fremont St

W Waveland Ave

N Pine Grove Ave

N Halsted St

N Broadway

30

4

1

Wrigley Field

54

W Addison St

Addison

34

W Eddy St

68

66

31

W Cornelia Ave

W Newport Ave

53

W Roscoe St

32

57

W Buckingham Pl

15

W Cornelia Ave

W Stratford Pl

W Hawthorne Pl

63

W Brompton Ave

27

65

N Elaine Pl

8

59

W Roscoe St

33

3

23

37

W Aldine Ave

BOYSTOWN

W Aldine Ave

20

55

W Melrose St

50

52

64

22

W Belmont Ave

Belmont

49

60 40

38

42

W Briar Pl

N Broadway

W Briar Pl

LAKE VIEW

W Barry Ave

W Barry Ave

N Clifton Ave

N Seminary Ave

N Kenmore Ave

W Barry Ave

10

9

6

Wellington

N Sheffield Ave

N Mildred Ave

N Halsted St

W Wellington Ave

11

21

24

W Oakdale Ave

13

19

W Surf St

N Clark St

51

67

W Surf St

61

W Diversey Pkwy

Diversey

See map p310

mfk (0.1mi) →

N Lakewood Ave

N Racine Ave

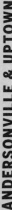

0 — 200 m
0 — 0.1 miles

W Bryn Mawr Ave

↑ House 5863
(0.3mi)

↑ Leather Archives
& Museum (1.2mi)

**LAKEWOOD-
BALMORAL**

Ⓜ Bryn Mawr

W Catalpa Ave

N Ashland Ave

N Clark St

W Rascher Ave

N Glenwood Ave

N Wayne Ave

N Lakewood Ave

N Magnolia Ave

N Broadway

N Winthrop Ave

N Kenmore Ave

N Sheridan Rd

Lincoln
Park

14
20
22   7
6
W Balmoral Ave

W Summerdale Ave

12

W Berwyn Ave

Ⓜ Berwyn

4
29   30
34
33   W Farragut Ave
23   3
31   11   **ANDERSONVILLE**

W Foster Ave   W Foster Ave

28   21
16   9

W Winona St

W Carmen Ave

N Glenwood Ave

W Carmen Ave

W Winona St

26

W Winnemac Ave

W Winnemac Ave

W Carmen
Ave

13 19
5   18

1 Argyle
Ⓜ
15   8

10
24

W Argyle St

W Ainslie St

W Ainslie St

35

St Boniface
Cemetery

N Ashland Ave

N Clark St

N Broadway

N Winthrop Ave

N Kenmore Ave

N Sheridan Rd

32
27

W Lawrence Ave   Ⓜ   W Lawrence Ave
Lawrence

Chase
Park

UPTOWN

W Leland Ave

N Racine Ave

N Sheridan Rd

17

W Wilson Ave

Ⓜ Wilson

W Wilson Ave

N Broadway

25

N Ashland Ave

N Clark St

N Dover St

N Beacon St

N Malden St

N Magnolia Ave

Kayak Chicago (1mi);
Montrose Beach (1mi)

Hutchinson Street
District (0.3mi)

W Montrose Ave
2

ANDERSONVILLE & UPTOWN

WICKER PARK, BUCKTOWN & UKRAINIAN VILLAGE

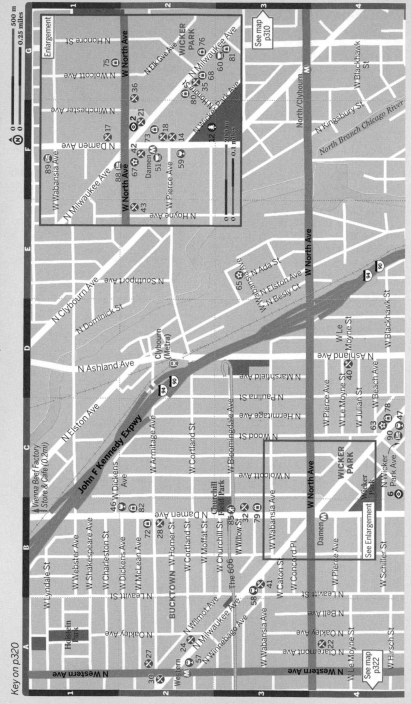

Key on p320

See map p310

See Enlargement

See map p322

See map p324

WICKER PARK, BUCKTOWN & UKRAINIAN VILLAGE

WICKER PARK, BUCKTOWN & UKRAINIAN VILLAGE Map on p318

WICKER PARK, BUCKTOWN & UKRAINIAN VILLAGE

LOGAN SQUARE & HUMBOLDT PARK

WEST LOOP & NEAR WEST SIDE

See map
p318

W Hubbard St
W Kinzie St
W Carroll Ave
48
40
37
W Fulton St
W Walnut Ave
N Damen Ave
W Lake St
N Ashland Ave
N Justine St
N Ogden Ave
W Lake St
30
N Ada St
N Elizabeth St
S Wood St
S Paulina St
N Wolcott Ave
Union Park
43
W Washington Blvd
52
W Warren Blvd
39
W Madison St
W Madison St
45
S Damen Ave
S Honore St
W Monroe St
W Monroe St
S Laflin St
S Loomis St
S Throop St
W Adams St
W Adams St
S Ashland Ave
W Jackson Blvd
W Jackson Blvd
44
W Van Buren St
W Van Buren St
Dwight D Eisenhower Expwy
290
Illinois
Medical
District
W Harrison St
W Ogden Ave
S Hermitage Ave
S Paulina St
S Laflin St
Arrigo Park
W Polk St
Illinois
Medical
District
Polk
W Polk St
W Cabrini St
Lagunitas Brewing
Company (1.4mi)
S Wood St
S Paulina St
S Ashland Ave
27
W Taylor St
W Taylor St
31 29
S Loomis St
W Roosevelt Rd
S Damen Ave
W Washburne Ave
W 13th St

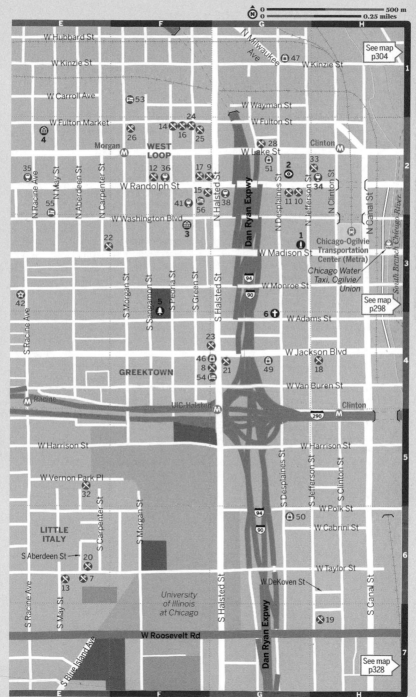

WEST LOOP & NEAR WEST SIDE *Map on p324*

NEAR SOUTH SIDE

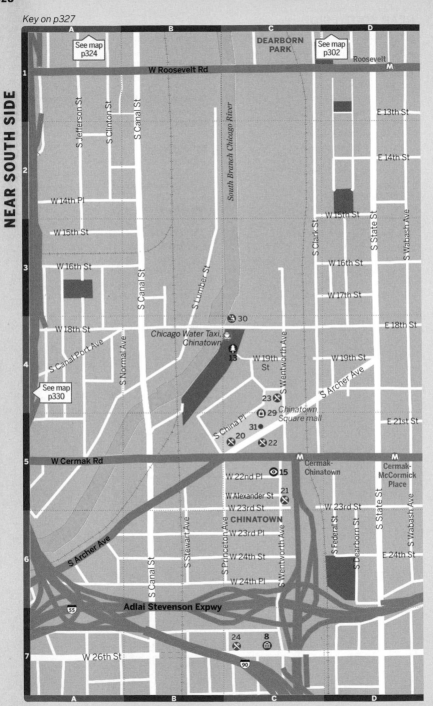

NEAR SOUTH SIDE

See map p324

DEARBORN PARK

See map p302

Roosevelt

W Roosevelt Rd

S Jefferson St

S Clinton St

S Canal St

South Branch Chicago River

E 13th St

E 14th St

W 14th Pl

W 15th St

S Clark St

W 15th St

S State St

S Wabash Ave

W 16th St

S Canal St

W 16th St

S Lumber St

W 17th St

W 18th St

E 18th St

30

S Canal Port Ave

Chicago Water Taxi, Chinatown

S Normal Ave

13

W 19th St

S Wentworth Ave

W 19th St

S Archer Ave

23

S China Pl

29

Chinatown Square mall

E 21st St

20

31

22

W Cermak Rd

15

Cermak-Chinatown

Cermak-McCormick Place

W 22nd Pl

W Alexander St

21

W 23rd St

W 23rd St

S State St

S Wabash Ave

CHINATOWN

S Stewart Ave

S Princeton Ave

W 23rd Pl

S Archer Ave

S Canal St

W 24th St

S Wentworth Ave

S Federal St

S Dearborn St

E 24th St

W 24th Pl

Adlai Stevenson Expwy

55

24

8

90

W 26th St

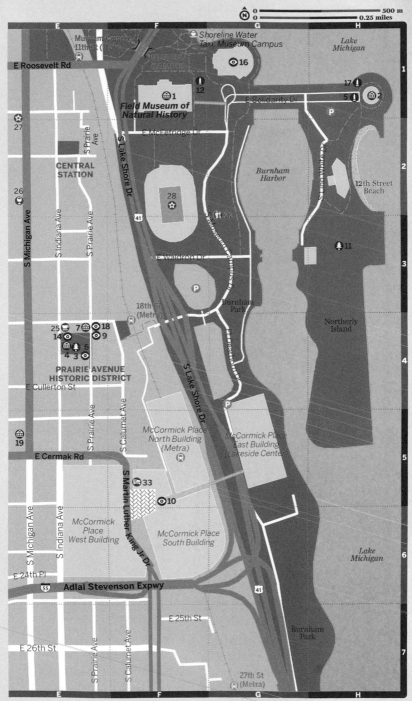

500 m
0.25 miles

Shoreline Water Taxi, Museum Campus

Lake Michigan

E Roosevelt Rd

Museum Campus/ 11th St

MUSEUM CAMPUS

16

12

17
5
2

1
Field Museum of Natural History

E Solidarity Dr

P

E McFetridge Dr

27

S Prairie Ave

S Lake Shore Dr

CENTRAL STATION

Burnham Harbor

12th Street Beach

26

S Michigan Ave

S Indiana Ave

S Prairie Ave

41

28

11

22

Northerly Island

E Waldron Dr

Burnham Park

P

18th St (Metra)

25
14
7
4 3
18
9
5

S Lake Shore Dr

PRAIRIE AVENUE HISTORIC DISTRICT

E Cullerton St

S Prairie Ave

S Calumet Ave

P

19

E Cermak Rd

McCormick Place North Building (Metra)

McCormick Place East Building (Lakeside Center)

S Michigan Ave

S Indiana Ave

S Martin Luther King Jr Dr

33

10

Lake Michigan

McCormick Place West Building

McCormick Place South Building

E 24th Pl

55

Adlai Stevenson Expwy

41

E 25th St

E 26th St

S Prairie Ave

S Calumet Ave

Burnham Park

27th St (Metra)

PILSEN

Pilsen

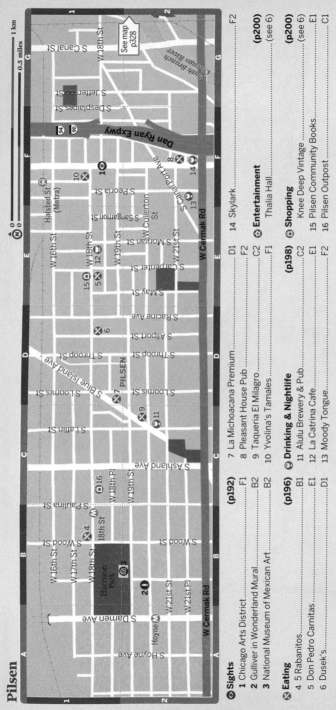

See map p328

0 0.5 miles
0 1 km

BRIDGEPORT & BRONZEVILLE

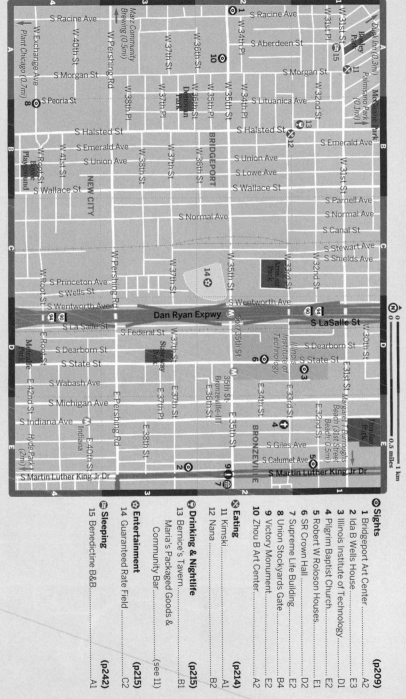

HYDE PARK & SOUTH SIDE

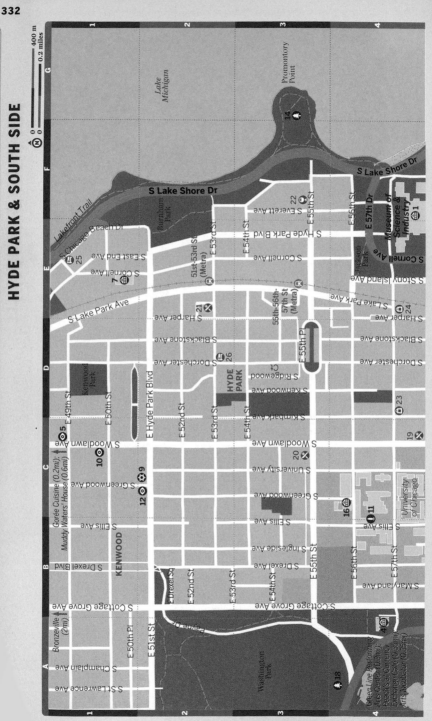

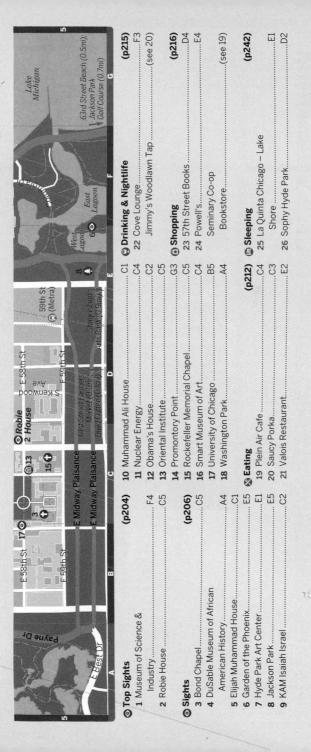

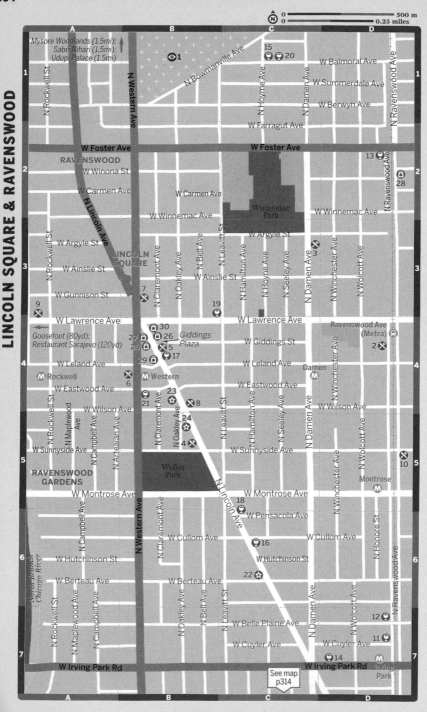

0   500 m
0   0.25 miles

Mysore Woodlands (1.5mi);
Sabri Nihari (1.5mi);
Udupi Palace (1.5mi)

◉1

15 ⊙⊙ 20

W Balmoral Ave

W Summerdale Ave

W Berwyn Ave

N Western Ave

N Bowmanville Ave

N Hoyne Ave

N Damen Ave

N Ravenswood Ave

W Farragut Ave

W Foster Ave

W Foster Ave

RAVENSWOOD

W Winona St

13 ⊙

N Ravenswood Ave

🔒 28

W Carmen Ave

W Carmen Ave

N Lincoln Ave

W Winnemac Ave

Winnemac
Park

W Winnemac Ave

N Rockwell St

W Argyle St

W Argyle St

LINCOLN
SQUARE

N Claremont Ave

N Oakley Ave

N Bell Ave

N Leavitt St

N Hamilton Ave

N Hoyne Ave

N Seeley Ave

N Damen Ave

N Winchester Ave

N Wolcott Ave

W Ainslie St

W Ainslie St

3 ⊗ 3

W Gunnison St

7 ⊗

9 ⊗

19 ⊙

W Lawrence Ave

W Lawrence Ave

Ravenswood Ave
(Metra) ⊙

Goosefoot (80yd);
Restaurant Sarajevo (120yd)

27 🔒 30
🔒 26
25 🔒 5
29 🔒

Giddings
Plaza

17

W Giddings St

2 ⊗

W Leland Ave

W Leland Ave

Damen
Ⓜ

Ⓜ Rockwell

W Eastwood Ave

6 ⊗

Ⓜ Western

W Eastwood Ave

21 ⊙

23 ⊗

W Wilson Ave

W Wilson Ave

N Campbell Ave

N Artesian Ave

N Oakley Ave

8 ⊗

24

N Hamilton Ave

N Seeley Ave

N Damen Ave

N Winchester Ave

N Wolcott Ave

W Sunnyside Ave

4 ⊗

W Sunnyside Ave

10 ⊗

RAVENSWOOD
GARDENS

Welles
Park

Montrose
Ⓜ

W Montrose Ave

W Montrose Ave

N Western Ave

N Claremont Ave

N Lincoln Ave

18

W Pensacola Ave

N Honore St

N Ravenswood Ave

W Cullom Ave

16 ⊙

W Cullom Ave

North Branch Chicago River

W Hutchinson St

W Hutchinson St

W Berteau Ave

W Berteau Ave

22 ✪

N Rockwell St

N Maplewood Ave

N Campbell Ave

N Oakley Ave

N Bell Ave

N Leavitt St

W Belle Plaine Ave

12 ⊙

W Cuyler Ave

W Cuyler Ave

11 ⊙

14 ⊙

Ⓜ
Irving
Park

W Irving Park Rd

W Irving Park Rd

See map
p314

LINCOLN SQUARE & RAVENSWOOD

LINCOLN SQUARE & RAVENSWOOD

Our Story

A beat-up old car, a few dollars in the pocket and a sense of adventure. In 1972 that's all Tony and Maureen Wheeler needed for the trip of a lifetime – across Europe and Asia overland to Australia. It took several months, and at the end – broke but inspired – they sat at their kitchen table writing and stapling together their first travel guide, *Across Asia on the Cheap*. Within a week they'd sold 1500 copies. Lonely Planet was born.

Today, Lonely Planet has offices in Franklin, London, Melbourne, Oakland, Dublin, Beijing and Delhi, with more than 600 staff and writers. We share Tony's belief that 'a great guidebook should do three things: inform, educate and amuse'.

Our Writers

Ali Lemer

Andersonville & Uptown; Gold Coast; Lincoln Park & Old Town; The Loop; Wicker Park, Bucktown & Ukrainian Village Ali has been a Lonely Planet writer and editor since 2007, and has written guidebooks and travel articles on Russia, Germany, New York City, Chicago, Los Angeles, Melbourne, Bali, Hawaii, Japan and Scotland. A native New Yorker, Ali has also lived in Melbourne, Chicago, Prague and England, and has traveled extensively around Europe, North America, Oceania and Asia. Follow her on Instagram (instagram.com/alilemer).

Karla Zimmerman

Hyde Park & South Side; Lake View & Wrigleyville; Lincoln Square & Ravenswood; Logan Square & Humboldt Park; Near North & Navy Pier; Pilsen & Near South Side; West Loop & Near West Side; Saugatuck & Douglas Karla lives in Chicago, where she eats doughnuts, yells at the Cubs and writes stuff for books, magazines and websites when she's not doing the first two things. She has contributed to 70-plus Lonely Planet guidebooks and travel anthologies covering destinations in Europe, Asia, Africa, North America and the Caribbean. To learn more, follow her on Instagram (instagram.com/karlazimmerman) and Twitter (@karlazimmerman). Karla also wrote the Plan, Understand and Survival Guide sections.

Contributing Writers: Mark Baker (Milwaukee) and Kevin Raub (Galena, Indiana Dunes, Oak Park) contributed to the Day Trips from Chicago chapter.

Published by Lonely Planet Global Ltd
CRN 554153
9th edition – Jan 2020
ISBN 978 1 78701 347 6
© Lonely Planet 2020   Photographs © as indicated 2020
10 9 8 7 6 5 4 3 2 1
Printed in China